Dresdner Beiträge zur Hethitologie

Herausgegeben von
Johann Tischler

Band 37

2011
Harrassowitz Verlag · Wiesbaden

Susanne Zeilfelder

Hittite Exercise Book

Second, revised edition

2011
Harrassowitz Verlag · Wiesbaden

The illustration on the cover page 4 shows a drawing of the Hieroglyphic Luwian seal ZN 1769 stored in the Skulpturensammlung of the Staatliche Kunstsammlungen Dresden.

Bibliografische Information Der Deutschen Bibliothek:
Die Deutsche Bibliothek verzeichnet diese Publikation in der Deutschen Nationalbibliografie; detaillierte bibliografische Daten sind im Internet über http://dnb.ddb.de abrufbar.

Bibliographic information published by Die Deutsche Bibliothek:
Die Deutsche Bibliothek lists this publication in the Deutsche Nationalbibliografie; detailed bibliographic data is available in the internet at http://dnb.ddb.de.e-mail: cip@dbf.ddb.de

For further information about our publishing program have a look at our website http://www.harrassowitz.de/verlag

Printed on permanent/durable paper.
Typesetting and Layout: Susanne Zeilfelder
Printing and binding: AZ Druck und Datentechnik GmbH, Kempten
Printed in Germany

ISSN 1619-0874
ISBN 978-3-447-06268-8

Preface to the second edition

The present „Hittite exercise book“ arose from academic practice and is first and foremost designed to serve didactic purposes. On the one hand, critics of the first edition have not accepted these aims and reviewed the book from a purely scientific point of view[1]. However, this is like expecting a „Lingua Latina for lower classes“ to be suitable for teaching the complete course of Latin linguistics in an adequate way – of course it is not. On the other hand, the book was sold out and a second edition was possible, and so I still believe that there is a need for an exercise book of this type. I will try to make my intentions with it clearer.

First of all, the situation for historical linguistics is, at least in central Europe, more than critical. In the German-speaking countries we have an average loss of one academic chair every year, and this tendency is certainly going to continue. If we are willing to be realistic we will have to admit that we cannot survive with the traditional 5-7 inscribed students and an average of 3 participants in our lectures. Nevertheless, this might be a problem but it could be a chance as well. Indo-Europeanists always believed in the dogma that every student would or should aim to become a professor of Indo-European Studies in the end. This thesis is not only wrong and unrealistic[2], it is simply dangerous because it is a sort of self-fulfilling prophecy. Consequently, it has lead to a situation where the whole course of study has become extremely inaccessible, impossible to be studied as a minor. And this is a crucial point: there are good reasons why historical linguistics is not attractive enought as to be studied as a main subject, but there is absolutely no sound reason why it should not be a perfect subsidiary subject for half a philosophical department. So why shouldn't we at least start teaching *every* student who is interested instead of concentrating on the training of prospective scholars in a science that will disappear anyway, as long as we continue our tradition of strategic suicide?

---

1 With the exception of Gary Beckman in JAOS 129: 376 f., whose remarks were very helpful.

2 A teacher who really believes in this can logically and statistically not have more than one disciple in his whole life, namely his own successor.

And this means: Start at the beginning and take note of reality. Hardly any bachelor course in Indo-European or Oriental Studies contains more than one modul of Hittite, that means: two seminars. As we need one of them for the historical phonology, there is one left for learning the Hittite language and philology. How much information can you pack into it without chasing away half your auditory? Is it realistic to expect students to be able not only to translate Hittite, but to have mastered cuneiform writing, text chronology, cultural history of Anatolia and of course historical reconstruction of Proto-Anatolian in only half a year? More importantly, is it necessary? There are actually only two possibilities: Some of the students will continue their studies, and then they will learn all that sooner or later. Others will turn to something completely different after the exam, and then it actually does *not* matter if they can list all features of Late Old Hittite in detail or if they can only remember having heard that there *is* such a thing like Old Hittite. And this is a chance: We need fans and we need them urgently.

The second topic of criticism I would like to dwell on is the practical point of view. I was very astonished to learn from a review that a student working with my book would not read a single complete text in the whole course. It actually never occured to me that a teacher could use this little exercise book as an *exclusive* teaching aid, simply because this would result in the most boring class I could imagine. So of course the student has to read complete texts as well, but why on earth shouldn't we simply take one of those many volumes of StBoT or TdH for that purpose? All that this exercise book can do is to help students memorise morphological forms and show them some of the many strange grammatical features of Hittite. It goes without saying that for further teaching it has to be combined with other material.

The third point is the harshly critised synchronic approach of the book. I fully agree with collegues that find the chronological mix-up of the examples problematic. However, I have to repeat that the time we have for teaching is extremely restricted and that we have to stop teaching highly enthousiastic hardcore linguists exclusively. At the moment we are struggling against decreasing possibilities to teach Hittite altogether. Therefore, discussions about how to teach the complicated details for prospective experts is clearly a *cura posterior*. And, by the way, I find that the differences between Old Hittite and later stages should not be exaggerated.

Fourthly, the problem of broad transcription: I capitulate on this point because everybody seems to know better than I do how to transcribe Hittite phonetically, but unfortunately everbody knows it differently. As a result, I could not solve this problem with pure obedience and that is why I have left that experiment out of this edition because, as my dear collegue Christian Zinko put it: "If you try a broad transcription, you're the idiot no matter what"[3]. Students should realise that the phonetics of Hittite are highly debated, that some scholars believe in a Hittite /o/ and some do not[4] and that there is a very promising research project at the Leiden University on Hittite stress and accent[5]. Therefore, I delegate this problem to the teachers.

Apart from that, there is not much change in the concept of this book[6] because I still believe that in the practice of lecturing there will always be the need for compromises. On the one hand, it is not possible in a Hittite exercise book - unlike its counterparts in Latin or Greek - to fall back upon pedagogically useful examples not attested in the corpus because it would simply not prepare the student for the actual research on Hittite. On the other hand, it is neither useful to force upon the beginner all the philological and hermeneutical problems that every single original Hittite text presents. In this exercise book, we have compromised on chosing examples that are all attested, but, for the sake of legibility, parentheses and editorial diacritica have been left out. Therefore, only well-preserved examples or those with minor and reliable additions have been selected. The translated examples can be found on pp. 132 ff. To facilitate their handling they have been numbered throughout. Another practical problem was the necessary thematical limitation of an exercise book which should be possible to be mastered in one or two semesters. Hence, I have concentrated on those parts of grammar which have proved to be the most problematic for the translation of texts while I had to leave out grammatical features that are more important and interesting from a diachronic point of view.

3 Of course he said: "Wannst broad transcription machst, bist eh der Depp", which I find absolutely charming.

4 I don't, as long as the clear counter-examples listed in Riecken 2005: 543 ff. are put aside by ad-hoc-explanations like „analogy", „unspecific nature of the anaptyctic vowel" or „purely graphical".

5 Cf. http://www.hum.leidenuniv.nl/indo-europees/onderzoek/over/kloekhorst-stressing-the-facts.html.

6 As I learned from Beckman's review cited in note 1, we have driven our principle of literal rather than elegant translations too far in the first edition. Now the English text has been revised by a native speaker - special thanks to Christopher Prilop. And I added some more context information here and there to make the examples better understandable.

Each chapter concentrates on one area of grammar, which can be practised in the following exercises. This means that, in the course of translation, some grammatical features have to be dealt with that are described only in subsequent paragraphs. To make the handling of the exercise book easier, there is a tabular summary at the beginning of each chapter for quick reference. Additionally, all word forms are specified in the glossary. At the end of each paragraph there are examples for further practice of the topic just covered.

The chapters are not based on each other. Thus, the book can be worked through in any order, and the single paragraphs can be abridged, supplemented or left out in the lectures. The exercise book has been structured in the traditional text book order noun-verb-pronoun-syntax, while the endings are covered first, followed by the stem formation. The latter is presented only in very short form as it is a subject of further lectures and cannot be explained adequately in a synchronic framework. However, a small collection of reference material is offered.

The bibliographies to the individual chapters are only intended to be a first introduction to the topic and do not raise any claim to completeness - in fact completeness is totally unnecessary since we have the marvellous „Grammar of the Hittite Language“ by Harry A. Hoffner and H. Craig Melchert (Winona Lake 2008), which contains lots of information.

Contents

1. Introduction

1.1. Hittite: An Indo-European language in Near Eastern context

At first sight, it does not seem very obvious that Hittite is an Indo-European language. The vocabulary is to a considerable extent of foreign origin, and the grammar differs in many regards from that which is commonly considered typically Indo-European. The Indo-European character of Hittite only reveals itself in the study of its linguistic structure. As this will not be the focus of the following exercises, the beginner should be made aware of some standard works of Hittitology: For the language history, see H. Craig Melchert, Anatolian Historical Phonology[1], Amsterdam/Atlanta 1994; about the history and cultural history of the Hittites, cf. two standard books of Trevor Bryce, Life and Society in the Hittite world, Oxford 2001, and The Kingdom of the Hittites, Oxford 2005; about the linguistic context cf. Michael Streck (ed.), Sprachen des Alten Orients, Darmstadt 2007[3].

1.2. Cuneiforms

1.2.1. The Hittite cuneiform is based on a North Babylonian writing system, that was transmitted to the Hittites, presumably through Hurrite mediation. Viewed objectively, a syllabary is not really suitable for the representation of an Indo-European language. For example, it makes it impossible to render a consonantal cluster in initial position, a problem that causes scribes to resort to the notation of additional vowels. However, this notation confronts the scholar with the problem whether the additional vowels were actual substitute spellings or really spoken.

For instance, given the Indo-European verbal root **spend-* „vow, swear", the Hittite spelling *is-pa-an-d°* at first makes it impossible to discern whether the intital *i-* was either only graphical or really part of the word. This problem is only solved by the fact that there also is the alternative spelling *si-pa-an-d°*. The rendering of vowel quantities constitutes further difficulties. Meanwhile, there is a consensus of opinion in favour of the

1 Everybody should at least read the introduction, p. 1-45.

assumption that the so-called plene spellings of vowels, e.g. initial *a-aš°* instead of *aš-*, or *hu-u-da-ak* instead of *hu-da-ak*, represents the graphical representation of a long vowel. However, as scribes were not very consistent in their writing and could obviously simply omit the plene vowel, it is often hard to decide, in cases of rarely attested words, whether the vowel is long or short and a Leiden project (cf. note 4) might show that the plene-writing is actually polyfunctional[2].

1.2.2. As there is a distinction between voiced and unvoiced consonants in Semitic languages, hence, the sign inventary transmitted to the Hittites has different signs for the tenues and mediae series at its disposal. However, the Hittites did not use the distinct signs to differentiate the phonetic opposition inherited from Indo-European but in many cases the tenues signs represent mediae as well and vice versa. This may account for the assumption that the Hittites did not borrow the writing system directly from the Babylonians but rather through Hurrite mediation, for in Hurrite there is only differentiation between explosives and implosives.

At least in word medial position, the problem is solved through the „Sturtevant's spelling rule", where tenues sounds are represented by double writing of the consonant while mediae sounds are rendered by simple writing. Accordingly, the sign sequence *a-pa-a-aš* „this" stands for media */abās/*, while *a-ap-pa* „back" would be read */āpa/*. Still, this spelling rule is optional. However, a lexicographical convention for the representation of Hittite words has now been established, which does not always correspond to the actual phonetic form. Thus, one will cite „*apā-* „this" and „*appa* „back" as customary in the dictionaries. In the alphabet, there is no differentiation between mediae and tenues sounds, but words with initial *b*, *d*, *g* will be registered under *p*, *t*, *k*. For practical reasons, our glossary follows that tradition.

1.2.3. There is no general consensus in Hittite research as to the phonetic values of the *s*-signs because the question whether the signs have to be rendered *š* as in Babylonian or *s* as expected from the Indo-European point of view cannot be answered with certainty. However, it should be noted that the hitherto undisputed reading of the Hitt. *z*-series as affricates rather in-

2 In a lecture at the Copenhagen conference on „The sound of Indo-European" in April 2009 Alvin Kloekhorst showed in a very convincing way that at least in some instances the plene writing actually means a glide in an *hiatus*.

dicates the phonetic value *s*; otherwise words like *šiwaz* „day" from the dental stem *šiwat-* + nominative-*s* would have to be explained with a sound law „*s* > *š* except after dental"[3]. The phonetic value of Hitt. *h* presents another problem. In his „Elementarbuch" (32 f.), Friedrich pointed out that while *h* alternates with *k* in some words (*tetkiššar* „thunderstorm" beside more frequent *tetheššar*) it completely disappears in others (*eššar* „blood" beside more common *ešhar*). This may point to two different phonemes, but could also represent two different dialects within Hittite.

1.2.4. One peculiarity of the Hittite writing system is the use of Sumerian and Akkadian words within the regular Hittite text, in the same manner as modern texts employ digits that were derived from Arabic signs. That this is a purely graphical issue and does not mean the use of loanwords can be told by the phonetic complements which indicate the ending of the word. For instance, the scribe writes the Sumerian sign for „king", LUGAL[4], but cannot give a case ending to the indeclinable Sumerian word. Therefore, he signals the intended nominative by adding the ending of the underlying Hittite word *haššuš* and writes LUGAL-*uš*. From this it can be inferred that a native Hittite reader would have read the sign LUGAL automatically as *haššuš* in the same way as a European reader of latin script would read the sign „5" as *fünf*, *cinque*, *fem* or *five*. The consequence of this spelling is that the Hittite reading of a number of attested words is not known. It also takes practise to get used to the mixture of akkadographic and sumerographic spellings and the coding of grammatical structures. While the genitive attribute precedes its regens in Hittite, it takes second place in Sumerian; and so a Sumerian EN SISKUR „Lord of the ritual" is to be read as Hitt. *maltešnaš išhaš* „the ritual's master". Futhermore, we often find in Hittite texts that the case of Sumerian words is indicated by Akkadian prepositions, i.e. *ša* for the genitive, *ana* for the dative. This results in the astonishing possibility for the scribe to choose between simple case forms like *haššauwaš* „the king's" and *haššui* „to the king", and the more complicated *ŠA* LUGAL-*wa-aš* and *A-NA* LUGAL-*i*. Even more sportive are Akkadian phonetic complements of sumerograms, which still represent Hittite words: a spelling DINGIR^{LUM}

3 A lecture of Ilya Yakubovich at the Copenhagen conference on „The sound of Indo-European" in April 2009 showed that the s-reading is more plausible even from a semitistic point of view. We are looking forward to the publication.

4 In transliterations, the sumerograms are rendered by capitals and dots between syllables while akkadograms are rendered by italic capitals and hyphens between syllables.

„deity“ at first indicates the reading of Akkadian *ilum* „deity“, but has to be understood as Hitt. *šiunaš* „god“. Incidentally, the incorrect use of the Akkadian case forms leads to the emergence of hybrid spellings, e.g. DINGIR^{LIM}*-i,* a sumerogram with Akkadian genitive and Hittite dative complement.

Another peculiarity of the Hittite writing system is the use of sumerographic determinatives. These interpretation signs represent purely graphical indications of certain semantic groups of words. For instance, terms for any kind of vessel are accompanied by the Sumerian sign for „vessel“ (DUG), words for wooden objects are supplied with the sumerogram GIŠ „wood“, while female personal names show MUNUS „woman“ etc. Furthermore, there are the grammatical determinatives HI.A, MEŠ and DIDLI to indicate plural forms. In transliteration, the determinatives appear superior.

1.2.5. For practical reasons, the transliteration in this exercise book essentially complies with the conventional American transliteration, where the semivowels are rendered as *y* und *w* instead of *i̯* und *u̯*. In the *s*-series, the diacriticon *š* has been retained because at least akkadograms and names show signs of the *s*-series with voiced *s*. On the other hand, against common use the diacritic sign *ḫ* is dispensable because Hittite only has one *h*-series at its disposal. The rendering of ambiguous phonetic signs presents another problem. A number of signs can render both *e*- and *i*- vocalism (e.g. *di* or *de*, *gi* or *ge* etc.), while with other signs the vocalism is preordained (*ti* versus *te*, *ši* versus *še* etc.). There are cases where the intended vowel is indicated by the following sign: the spelling *a-pí/é-e-da-ni* points to */abedani/* in actual speech and suggest that co-occuring *a-pí/é-da-ni* will have to be read with *e*-vocalism, too. On the other hand, an actual sound change *e* > *i* cannot be ruled out from the beginning. In order not to prejudge, one would have to examine the chronological evidence in the sources for every single case. Hence, the „neutral“ reading with *i*- has been chosen throughout this exercise book. Also, the consonantism is not always laid down unambiguously: *ip* or *ib*, *ig* or *ik* etc. In these cases, the reading is adjusted to the following sign, thus *ad-da-aš* and *at-ta-aš* for the ambiguous sign *ad/t* before varying signs *da* und *ta*. Both forms are given in „Sturtevant’s spelling rule“ for the tenues sounds, and therefore any misunderstanding of the intended phonetic form is excluded. In word final position, the tenues are always given as the neutral reading. From all this it becomes clear, that the cuneiform can render Hittite only in an approximate way. – The sumerograms are rendered in accordance with the guidelines of the „Hethitisches Zeichenlexikon“ by C. Rüster and E. Neu.

1.3.1. The texts

Most Hittite texts were written on clay tablets, but some findings also testify the use of metal tablets. Before being inscribed, the tablets were smoothed over and organized by lines which divided the tablet into columns, and the columns into paragraphs. Occasionally, the scribe miscalculated the space and was forced to write on the edge of the tablet. After the obverse side was inscribed, the tablet was turned around. This was not done like the turning of pages in modern books, but rather upside down over the bottom edge. This explains why in damaged tablets, for instance, the end of the obverse side and the beginning of the reverse side page can be broken. Tablet sides with two or three columns are the most common; they are cited by the modern publishers as obverse and reverse (obv. and rev.) plus numbering by Roman numerals. However, as the numbering of the columns is continuous, the citation of the obverse and reverse side is not necessary and can be omitted. Also the census of lines and the occasional paragraph numbering goes back to the modern editors. When a text is broken at the beginning, and it cannot be inferred how many lines are missing, the numbering of the first preserved line starts with „x+1“, and all further line numbers are given with an apostrophe. Tablets at first receive archeological survey numbers, like Bo (for Boğazköi) 4951, which are later replaced in the editions by a siglum. The most important edition series are the now completed „Keilschrifturkunden aus Boğazköi“ = KUB and the continuing „Keilschrifttexte aus Boğazköi“ = KBo, but there are also other important texts published in IBoT („Istanbul Boğazköi textlerindı“), ABoT („Ankara Boğazköi textlerindı“) etc.. Also, the interesting letters from the site Maşat (abbreviated „Mşt.“) published by Sedat Alp have been taken into account in this work.

In the course of 3500 years, clay tablets are likely to have been considerably damaged. Hence, it is a very important and work intensive research task to join together broken clay tablets or to restore damaged parts of texts with the help of duplicates. Luckily, the Hittites had a qualified administrative machinery that had important texts copied repeatedly, in some cases over centuries. This provides the advantage that many gaps in the texts can be completed, but on the other hand there is the disadvantage that, in many cases, the actual age of a text is very hard to discern. First, it has to be determined whether one is dealing with an original text or a later copy. This is aided by the fact that the whole writing ductus has considerably changed after the Old Hittite period, and that single signs undergo changes in the course of the text history which can be dated quite precisely. However, there are still disagreements about the dating of texts.

While there are drawings of the tablets and parts of tablets in the editions, in many cases this still does not give the actual text. It was the achievement of Émanuel Laroche to compile and order the published texts in his „Catalogue des textes hittites" (CTH). In this work, which cannot be praised enough, all texts that belong together are united under one CTH number, and are as far as possible grouped thematically. However, fourty years on a revision of the CTH is overdue.

1.3.2. The corpus

The examples come from a corpus of about 150 well preserved and revised texts of varied text sorts: historical and legal texts, rituals and prayers, letters, omina, oracle records. There are also a few examples that I happened to stumble upon in other texts. Some forms of the inflectional paradigms were so rarely attested in the corpus that the number of examples was not sufficient for grammatical analyses. It is likely that a few more examples could be found in other texts. However, it should be noted as quite conspicuous that only two examples for the 1st pl. pret. med. can be found in all those texts.

The forms have not been ordered chronologically, and I am aware that this decision could be challenged. However, this avoids the restriction to „old" and „young" forms which in many cases is still disputed. Also, the interest of Indo-European scholars mainly focusses on Old Hittite, while the main corpus of existing texts emerged from later periods. It seems to me quite difficult to decide whether students should be prepared for everyday reading of texts or should gain insights about Anatolian linguistic history. However, considering the present state of Hittite research, a synchronous approach seems more tenable and reasonable for the time being.

1.4. Scientific aids

Apart from the introductory works mentioned above and the literature that will be cited in the respective chapters, the following titles are indispensable for the study of Hittite:

Grammar and phonology:

Harry J. Hoffner & H. Craig Melchert, A Grammar of the Hittite language, Winona Lake 2008

Johannes Friedrich, Hethitisches Elementarbuch, Heidelberg 1960[2]

H. Craig Melchert, Anatolian historical phonology, Amsterdam 1994

Dictionaries:

Johannes Friedrich, Kurzgefaßtes hethitisches Wörterbuch, Heidelberg 1991 (repr.), with three supplementary issues

Hans Gustav Güterbock / Harry Hoffner, The Hittite Dictionary of the Oriental Institute of the University of Chicago, Chicago 1988 ff.

Annelies Kammenhuber, Hethitisches Wörterbuch, 1.-12. Lieferung, Heidelberg 1975-1994

Jaan, Puhvel, Hittite etymological dictionary, Berlin 1984-

Johann Tischler, Hethitisches eytmologisches Glossar, Innsbruck 1983 ff.

Johann Tischler, Hethitisches Handwörterbuch, Innsbruck 2001

Sign list:

Christel Rüster / Erich Neu, Hethitisches Zeichenlexikon, Wiesbaden 1989

Catalogue of texts:

Émmanuel Laroche, Catalogue des textes hittites, Paris 1971.

2. Exercises

2.1. The Noun

2.1.1. Nominal inflection

Hittite shows the two genera commune and neuter, which differ in their inflection only in the nominative and accusative. The genus is only partly assigned to certain stem classes: *s*-stems and heteroclitics are always neutral, *a*- and *-nt-* stems always commune. Some declension classes inflect nouns of both genera.

There is singular and plural in Hittite, while possible remnants of the dual are assigned to the plural. Regarding the declension, it has to be noted that there are several formants for the plural formation of the neuters (*-a*, *-i* and the lengthened grade in the suffix in heteroclitics) while syntactically, neutral plurals are construed with the verb in the singular. The functions of the eight cases by and large correspond with the common concepts of Indo-European cases. The nominative marks the subject but has the vocative as a second function. The accusative indicates the direct object but also serves to express extension or direction. The genitive usually indicates possession, but there is also genitivus obiectivus and partitivus. Dative and locative are formally identical. The dative marks the indirect object while the locative expresses location and aim. Means or tools stand in the instrumental while a comitativus as in other Indo-European languages cannot be established. The ablative functions as separativus and marks the starting point of an action. There is a secondary blending of the functions of the instrumental and ablative. Old Hittite additionally has the directive at its disposal to mark the aim, in later times the case is only kept in certain phrases and is otherwise replaced by the locative. Finally, the vocative indicates an addressed person. Originally, the vocative has the form of the plain stem form but is later often substituted by the nominative, while the *u- stems* have their own vocative formant *-i* (originally probably *e*).

The forms of the instrumental, ablative and directive are indifferent regarding the numerus. Plural meaning ensues from the context, but is still occasionally indicated in the script by the use of the plural determinative together with the phonetic complement of the word ending.

The exact phonetic forms of both ablative and instrumental are not certain. The spellings *-az/-za* and *-it/-ta* could be substitute spellings with silent vowel which are only supposed to render the consonants */z/* and */t/*. Otherwise one would have to assume different forms of anaptyxis. For the phonetic form of the nominative it has to be taken into consideration that in dental stems the sound sequence */ts/* can be rendered by the *z-* series. As */ts/* produces a cluster in word final position which cannot be represented in a syllabary, the texts show the signs *-za* or *-az*, e.g. *ha-an-da-a-an-za* „every, each“ for */handant-s/*, or *kar-tim-mi-ya-az* „rage“ for */kartimmiyat-s/*.

In akkadographical spelling, the dative is covered up by Akk. *ana*, the genetive by *ša*, the instrumental by *ištu* and the locative by *ina* (rarely also *ana*). Further, it should be noted that the case endings of names can often not be rendered in the script.

Lit.: Friedrich 1960: 42 ff., 119 ff.; Starke 1977; Neu 1979; Eichner 1985; Harðarson 1994; Zeilfelder 2001: 21-99, 141-151; Hoffner/Melchert 2008: 64 ff.

	singular		plural	
	com.	neutr.	com.	neutr.
nom.	*-š*	-Ø	*-eš*, *-iš*	*-a*, *-i*, length. gr.
acc.	*-n*	-Ø	*-uš*	*-a*, *-i*, length. gr.
gen.	*-aš*		*-aš*, *-an*	
dat.-loc.	*-i*		*-aš*	
instr.	*-it*, *-ta*		–	
abl.	*-az*, *-za*		–	
dir.	*-a*		–	
voc.	-Ø, *-i*, *-š*	–	*-eš*	–

1.a. nom.sg.com: *-š*

1. KUB XVII 10 I 5 (Myth of Telipinu)
^{GIŠ}*lu-ut-ta-a-uš* ***kam-ma-ra-aš*** *IṢ-BAT*[1] É-*ir* ***túh-hu-iš*** *IṢ-BAT*

2. KBo III 1+ II 28 (Proclamation of Telipinu)
nu-uš ***pa-an-ku-uš*** *pa-ra-a hi-in-ga-ni har-ta*

3. KUB XVII 10 I 19 (Myth of Telipinu)
GAL-*iš-za* **^{D}UTU-*uš*** EZEN$_4$ *i-e-it*

4. KUB I 1+ IV 1 f. (Apology of Hattušili III)
nu-uš-ši GIM-*an ki-e* INIM^{MEŠ} *wa-tar-na-ah-hu-un* / *e-hu-wa*[2]
a-pa-a-aš*-ma-kán* ^{URU}*Ma-ra-aš-ša-an-ti-ya-za ar-ha pár-aš-ta*

5. KUB XIII 4 II 82 (Instructions for the priests and temple officials)
nu ***ne-ku-uz*** *me-e-hu-u-ni hu-u-da-a-ak* GAM *pa-it-tin*

1.b. nom.sg.n.: -Ø

6. KBo III 8 III 61 (Rituals of Ayatarša, Wattiti, & Šušmanniga)
ki-i-ma ***ut-tar*** *na-ak-ki-i*[3]

7. KUB I 1+ I 70 (Apology of Hattušili III)
ka-ni-iš-šu-u-wa-ar*-ma-mu ŠA* ^{D}*IŠTAR-pát* GAŠAN-*YA e-eš-ta*

8. KUB XVII 10 II 35 f. (Myth of Telipinu)
nu-za ha-ra-na-aš^{MUŠEN} ***pár-ta-u-wa-ar*** / *an-da-an ar-nu-ut*[4]

9. KBo XV 10+ II 5 f. (Purification ritual for Tuthaliya and Nikalmati)
ki-i ^{NA4}***pí-e-ru*** *ma-a-ah-ha-an* ***uk-tu-u-ri***[5] *BE-LU Ù* DAM-*ZU* /
DUMU^{MEŠ}-*ŠU QA-TAM-MA uk-tu-u-ri-eš a-ša-an-du*

---

1 Lit. „grasped“ , here: „covered“ or „filled“.
2 Verb + particle *-wa* is direct speech.
3 Nominal sentence, add „is“ in the translation.
4 Object drop, add „him“ in the translation.
5 Nominal senctence, add „is“ in the translation.

10. KBo IV 1 22 f. (Ritual before a campaigne against the Gaška)
na-at A-NA DINGIR^{MEŠ} / *me-ik-ki kat-ta-wa-tar e-eš-du*

2. gen.sg. both genera: *-aš*

11. KBo II 1+ II 7 (Proclamation of Telipinu)
nu-za-kán ^{m}***Ti-it-ti-ya-aš*** *ha-aš-ša-tar QA-DU* DUMU^{MEŠ}*-ŠU ku-en-ta*

12. KBo IV 10+ obv. 38' (Treaty with Ulmitešub)
ki-e-ma ṬUP-PA$^{HI.A}$ ***iš-hi-ú-ul-la-aš*** *ka-ru-ú a-ni-ya-an e-eš-ta*

13. KUB XXIX 1 II 8 (Foundation ritual)
nu **LUGAL-*wa-aš*** MU.KAM$^{HI.A}$*-uš ma-al-ki-ya-an-zi*[6]

14. KBo XV 10+ I 1 f. (Purification ritual for Tuthaliya and Nikalmati)
ma-a-an ***iš-ha-na-a-aš*** ^{D}UTU*-un* ^{D}IM*-na* EGIR*-pa li-la-a-an-zi*[7] / *nu ki-i*[8] *da-an-zi*

15. KBo III 22 rev. 51 (Proclamation of Anitta)
na-an[9] ***ne-pí-ša-aš*** ^{D}IM*-aš ha-az-zi-e-it-tu*

3. dat./loc.sg. both genera: *-i*

16. KBo III 1+ IV 33 f. (Proclamation of Telipinu)
nu ú-iz-zi[10] / ***a-pí-e-da-ni*** **UN-*ši*****-pát i-da-la-u-e-eš-zi*

17. KBo III 1+ II 34 (Proclamation of Telipinu)
nu ^{m}*Te-li-pí-nu-uš*[11] ^{URU}***Ha-at-tu-ši*** *tu-li-ya-an hal-zi-ih-hu-un*

6 Subjects are the „deities of the underworld“.
7 The plural is impersonal: „when they reconcile“ simply means „somebody“.
8 Kataphorical, a list of material follows in the text.
9 = *nu* + *-an* „and him“.
10 Periphrastical: „it will come, that …, it is going to happen, that …“, but in Hittite we have a main clause.
11 The verb is 1.sg., so the name has to be treated as an apposition in the translation: „I, Telipinu...“

18. KBo III 1+ II 18 f. (Proclamation of Telipinu)
ÉRIN^{MEŠ}*-za-mi-iš-ša* ^{URU}***Zi-iz-zi-li-ip-pí*** *e-eš-ta* / *nu* ^{URU}***Zi-iz-zi-li-ip-pí***
hu-ul-la-an-za-iš ki-ša-at

19. KBo III 22 obv. 48 (Proclamation of Anitta)
pí-e-di-iš*-ši-ma* ZÀ.AH.LI*-an a-ni-e-nu-un*

20. KUB XVII 6 I 14 f. (Myth of Illuyanka)
nu-za-an ^{D}*I-na-ra-aš* ^{NA4}***pí-ru-ni*** *še-ir* / É*-ir ú-e-te-it*

4.a. acc.sg.com.: *-n*

21. KUB XXVI 29+ obv. 13 (Treaty of Arnuwanda I with the people of Ura)
nu ***tu-uz-zi-in*** **SIG$_5$*-an*** **KASKAL*-an*** *ú-i-da-at-tin*

22. KUB XXVI 71 IV 16 (Ammuna chronicle)
hal-ki-in **GEŠTIN*-an*** *ú-te-eš-kir*

23. KBo III 1+ I 68 (Proclamation of Telipinu)
nu-kán ^{m}***Zi-dan-ta-an ad-da-aš-ša-an***[12] *ku-en-ta*

24. KUB XIV 10+ I 16 ff. (Plague prayer of Muršili II)
am-mu-uk-ma-az ŠÀ*-az* ***la-ah-la-ah-hi-ma-an*** / *Ú-UL tar-ah-mi*
NÍ.TE*-az-ma-za* / ***pít-tu-li-ya-an*** *nam-ma Ú-UL tar-ah-mi*

25. KUB I 1+ III 9 f. (Apology of Hattušili III)
nu pa-a-un nu ^{URU}***Ha-wa-ar-ki-na-an*** ^{URU}***Di-el-mu-na-an-na*** /
ú-e-da-ah-hu-un

4.b. acc.sg.n: -Ø

26. KUB I 1+ I 5 (Apology of Hattušili III)
ŠA ^{D}*IŠTAR* ***pa-ra-a ha-an-da-an-da-tar*** *me-ma-ah-hi*

12 = *attan-šan*

27. KBo III 1+ II 15 (Proclamation of Telipinu)
nu tar-ši-ki-mi[13] *a-pí-e-wa-mu* ***i-da-lu*** *i-e-ir ú-ga-wa-ru-uš* **HUL-*lu*** *Ú-UL i-ya-mi*

28. KUB I 1+ III 3 (Apology of Hattušili III)
nu-un-na-aš DINGIR^{LUM} *ŠA* ^{LÚ}*MU-DU* DAM ***a-aš-ši-ya-tar*** *pí-eš-ta*

29. KUB I 1+ I 30 f. (Apology of Hattušili III)
GIM-*an* UN^{MEŠ}-*an-na-an-za* / *ŠA* ^{D}*IŠTAR* GAŠAN-*YA*
ka-ni-iš-šu-u-wa-ar *ŠA* ŠEŠ-*YA-ya* / ***a-aš-šu-la-an*** *a-ú-e-ir*[14] *nu-mu ar-ša-ni-i-e-ir*

30. KBo VI 2+ IV 52 (Laws, first tablet)
ták-ku LÚ-*aš* *EL-LUM* **É-*ir*** *lu-uk-ki-iz-zi* **É-*ir*** EGIR-*pa ú-e-te-iz-zi*

31. KUB XXXIII 96 I 7' (Myth of Ullikummi)
nu ^{D}U-*ni* IGI-*an-da* ***i-da-la-wa-tar*** *ša-an-hi-iš-ki-iz-zi*

5. instr.sg.n: *-it*, *-ta*

32. KBo V 1 IV 4 (Papanikri's ritual)
nu SILA$_4$ ***ú-e-te-ni-it*** *kat-ta a-an-ša-an-zi*

33. KBo XXXII 14 II 43 f. (Epos of liberation)
la-a-hu-ša-an[15] *ti-iš-ša-a-it na-an* ***šu-up-pí-iš-du-wa-ri-it*** / *da-iš*

34. KBo XIX 128+ II 16 f. (AN.TAH.ŠUM festival)
EGIR-*an-da-ma* ^{UZU}NÍG.GIG$^{HI.A}$ **IZI-*it*** / *za-nu-an-da ú-da-an-zi*

35. KUB XVII 5 I 15 ff. (Myth of Illuyanka)
^{m}*Hu-u-pa-ši-ya-aš-ša ú-it* / *nu* ^{MUŠ}*Il-lu-ya-an-ka-an* ***iš-hi-ma-an-ta*** / *ka-li-e-li-e-it*

36. KBo XXII 2 obv. 2 f. (Tale of Zalpa, A)
tup-pu-uš ***ša-kán-da*** *šu-un-na-aš*[16] / *nu* DUMU^{MEŠ}-*ŠU an-da-an zi-ki-e-it*

13 The following is direct speech.
14 *Constructio ad sensum* with formally singular subject.
15 Covered subject; a smith is meant, and the object is a cup.

37. KBo XXV 1 2 (Oracle)
LÚ-*aš a-aš-šu* ***ki-iš-šar-ta*** *e-ip-zi*

6. abl.sg. both genera: *-za*, *-az*

38. KBo III 22 obv. 5 (Proclamation of Anitta)
LUGAL ^{URU}*Ku-uš-ša-ra* **URU-*az*** *kat-ta pa-an-ga-ri-it ú-wa-it*

39. KUB XXIX 4 III 43 ff. (Ritual for the transfer of the Black Goddess)
nu DINGIR^{LAM} ^{URU}***A-ag-ga-ta-az*** ^{URU}**KÁ.DINGIR.RA-*az*** / ^{URU}***Šu-u-ša-az*** ^{URU}***E-lam-ta-az*** ^{URU}**HUR.SAG.KALAM.MÁ-*az*** / *I-NA* URU^{LIM} *ŠA TA-RA-AM-MI* **HUR.SAG-*az*** **ÍD-*az*** / ***a-ru-na-az ha-a-ri-ya-az ú-e-el-lu-wa-az uš-ša-ru-un-ta-az*** / ***ne-pí-ša-az ták-na-az*** *IŠ-TU* 7 KASKAL^{MEŠ} *Ù IŠ-TU* 7 KA.GÌR-*ya* / *hu-it-ti-ya-an-zi*

40. KUB XVII 6 I 25 f. (Myth of Illuyanka)
ma-a-an ^{D}*I-na-ra-aš-ša* ***gi-im-ra-az*** EGIR-*pa* / *ú-it a-pa-a-ša ú-e-eš-ga-un da-a-iš*

41. KUB XIII 8 obv. 6 (Instruction of Queen Ašmunikal)
na-at-kán ***ša-ah-ha-na-za lu-zi-ya-za*** *a-ra-u-e-eš a-ša-an-du*

42. KUB XXIX 4 IV 24 ff. (Ritual for the transfer of the Black Goddess)
É DINGIR^{LIM} *ku-ut-ta-an* ***ku-e-iz ú-i-te-na-za*** *ar-ra-an-zi* / *nu-uš-ši a-pa-a-at ka-ru-ú-i-li* ^{GIŠ}*tal-la-ya-aš* Ì.DÙG.GA / *an-da i-mi-ya-an-zi*

7. dir.sg. both genera: *-a*

43. KBo III 34 I 12 (Palace chronicle)
ku-it ú-e-mi-iz-zi a-pa-aš-ša ***pár-na-a****š-ša pí-it-ta-iz-zi*

44. KUB XLIII 50+ obv. 8 f. (Muršili's speech loss)
nu-mu-kán za-az-hi-i an-da ŠU DINGIR^{LIM} *a-ar-aš*[17] KAxU-*iš-ša-mu-kán* / ***ta-pu-ú-ša*** *pa-it*

---

16 Subject is the Queen of Zalpa. The beginning of the myth is similar to the story of the child Moses who was set adrift on the Nile river, or to the story of the Egyptian Horus.

17 King Mursili had a stroke and this is his description of what happened in that fatal night.

45. KBo III 41 rev. 16' (Chronicle of Puhanu)
ÉRIN^MEŠ[18] *Hur-ri* ***ut-ni-ya*** *ú-iz-zi*

46. KUB XVII 6 I 27 (Myth of Illuyanka)
a-ap-pa-wa-mu **É-*na*** *tar-na*

47. KUB XXXI 4+ obv. 3 (Chronicle of Puhanu)
nu ***ú-wa-a-ar-ra***[19] *hal-za-iš*

8. voc.sg.com.: -Ø, *-š*, *-i*

48. KUB XXXIII 106+ III 30 f. (Myth of Ullikummi)
Ú-UL-wa ša-ak-ti / ^D***Ú-pí-el-lu-ri*** *me-mi-ya-an-na-wa-at-ta Ú-UL ku-iš-ki ú-da-aš*[20]

49. KUB XII 60 I 9 (Myth of Telipinu)
e-hu ^D***Te-li-pí-nu***

50. KUB IX 25+ I 42 f. (Ambazzi's ritual)
^D***Tar-pa-at-ta-aš-ši-iš*** / *ku-u-un*[21]*-za zi-ik da-a*

51. KUB XXXVI 35 I 15 (El, Ašertum, and the stormgod)
nu a-pád-da ú-wa-nu-un am-me-el ***at-ta-aš-mi-eš***

52. KUB XXX 10 rev. 11 f. (Kantuzzili's prayer)
ši-i-ú-ni*-mi* / *zi-ik-mu i-ya-aš zi-ik-mu ša-am-na-a-eš*

53. KUB XXXII 137 II 2 (Foundation ritual)
pí-e-ta-an-ti *e-it-za nu-za du-uš-ki-iš-ki*

9.a. nom.pl.com.: *-eš*, *-iš*

---

18 „Army" is usually singular in Hittite, in spite of the plural marker MEŠ in the sumerogram.
19 The word is direct speech.
20 Yes-no question.
21 Meaning the mouse which is sacrificed to Tarpattassi in the course of the ritual.

54. KUB VII 1+ II 8 f. (Rituals of Ayataršа, Wattiti, & Šušmanniga)
ka-ra-a-du-uš-wa-za ***ka-ra-a-ti-iš*** / *tar-ru-uh-ha-an-zi*

55. KBo III 1+ I 42 (Proclamation of Telipinu)
na-pa ^{m}*Mur-ši-i-li-ya-aš e-eš-har* **DINGIR**^{MEŠ}***-iš*** *ša-an-hi-ir*[22]

56. KUB XVII 10 I 15 (Myth of Telipinu)
ar-ma-u-wa-an-te-ša ku-i-eš[23] *nu-za a-pí-ya Ú-UL ha-aš-ša-an-zi*

57. KBo V 3+ I 6 f. (Treaty with Hukkanā of Hayasa)
nu-ut-ta KUR ^{URU}*Ha-at-ti hu-u-ma-an-za* KUR ^{URU}*Ha-ya-ša*
KUR.KUR^{MEŠ}*-ya* / ***hu-u-ma-an-te-eš a-ra-ah-zé-ni-eš an-tu-u-ri-e-eš***
ar-ha iš-ta-ma-aš-šir

58. KUB XIII 8 obv. 5 f. (Instruction of Queen Ašmunikal)
$^{\text{LÚ.MEŠ}}$***hi-lam-mi-e-eš-ša*** *ku-i-e-eš ka-ru-ú* / *A-NA* É.NA$_4$ *pí-ya-an-te-eš*
na-at-kán[24]*ša-ah-ha-na-za lu-zi-ya-za a-ra-u-e-eš a-ša-an-du*

9.b. nom.pl.n.: *-a*, *-i*, lengthened grade

59. KUB VII 1+ I 17 (Rituals of Ayatarša, Wattiti, & Šušmanniga)
nu ***šu-up-pa*** *PA-NI* DINGIR$^{\textit{LIM}}$ *še-eš-zi*[25]

60. KBo X 2 I 25 (Apology of Hattušili I)
nu-mu[26] **KUR.KUR**^{MEŠ} ***hu-u-ma-an-da*** *me-na-ah-ha-an-da*
ku-ru-ri-ah-hi-ir

61. KBo V 8 II 10 f. (Extensive annals of Muršili II)
EGIR-*az-ma* ^{URU}*Ga-aš-ga-az* / ***ku-u-ru-ri***$^{\text{HI.A}}$ *me-ik-ki ni-ni-ik-ta-at*

62. KUB XL 1 rev. 15 f. (Letter)
^{D}UTU$^{\textit{ŠI}}$*-ma* EN-*YA ku-it-ma-an ki-e-iz-za* ZAG-*za nu-un-tar-aš a-wa-an*
ar-ha / *pa-a-i pár-za-aš-ša da-a-ya-al-la* ***me-hur-ri***$^{\text{HI.A}}$ *ar-ta-ri-i*

---

22 Idiomatic, „search somebody's blood" means „demand retaliation for somebody's blood".
23 Nominal sentence, add „are" in the translation.
24 Here, the form of the neuter correlates with the pl.com. of the relative clause.
25 As noted above a neuter pl. with a singular verb is possible in Hittite.
26 The pronoun belongs to *menahhanda*.

63. KBo XI 14 II 24 f. (Hantitaššu's ritual)
na-at-ta am-me-el ***ud-da-a-ar*** / ^{D}UTU-*aš* ^{D}*Kam-ru-ši-pa-aš-ša* ***ud-da-a-ar***[27]

64. KBo XVII 1+ IV 19 f. (Ritual for the royal couple)
hal-ki-aš ***har-ša-a-ar*** *iš-hi-ya-an-da*[28] / ZÍZ$^{HI.A}$-*aš-ša* ***har-ša-a-ar*** *iš-hi-ya-an-da*

10.a. gen.pl. both genera: *-aš*

65. KUB XVII 7+ I 6 (Myth of Ullikummi)
^{D}*Ku-mar-bi-iš* **DINGIR^{MEŠ}*-aš*** *ad-da-aš e-eš-zi*

66. IBoT I 36 II 22 f. (Instructions for the royal body guard)
nu ^{GIŠ}*hu-lu-ga-an-ni-ya pí-ra-an* / GAL $^{LÚ.MEŠ}$***ša-a-la-aš-ha-aš*** *hu-ya-an-za* ^{GIŠ}GIDRU-*ya har-zi*

67. Mşt. 75/17 obv. 3 ff. (Letter)
ma-an-za ÉRIN^{MEŠ} EGIR-*an* / *ka-ru-ú pa-ah-ha-aš-nu-ut* / ***an-tu-uh-ša-****ša-kán ut-tar* /*ki-iš-ša-ri-i an-da* / *ka-ru-ú da-iš*[29]

68. KUB XXX 19+ IV 9 (Funerary ritual)
ma-ah-ha-an-ma **GÌR^{MEŠ}*-aš***[30] *kar-ap-ta-ri nu šum-ma-an-za-na-an ú-da-an-zi*

69. KUB XIII 4 II 29 (Instructions for the priests and temple officials)
DINGIR^{MEŠ}*-aš*-*ma* ZI-*an-za da-aš-šu-uš*[31]

10.b. Old Hitt. gen.pl. c.: *-an*

70. KBo III 22 obv. 24 ff. (Proclamation of Anitta)
^{URU}*Ne-e-ša-aš* / *ku-ru-ur e-eš-tu nu a-pa-aš* ***ut-ni-an-da-an hu-u-ma-an-da-an*** / *ku-ru-ur e-eš-tu*

---

27 Rhetorical interrogative clause.
28 Nominal sentence, add „are“ in the translation.
29 „The deity“ probably has to be added as the subject.
30 So called „suspended genitive“ : „ (that) of the feet“ = „the matter of the feet“.
31 Nominal sentence, add „is“ in the translation.

71. KBo III 1+ I 5 f. (Proclamation of Telipinu)
ku-wa-at-ta-aš la-ah-ha-ma pa-iz-zi / nu ^{LÚ}**KÚR-*an*** *ut-ne-e ku-ut-ta-ni-it tar-ah-ha-an har-ta*

72. KBo XVII 1+ I 11' (Ritual for the royal couple)
ka-a-ša-ta-aš-ma-aš-kán ***ut-ni-ya-an-da-an*** *la-a-lu-uš da-a-ah-hu-un*[32]

73. KBo VI 2+ III 63 ff. (Laws, first tablet)
ták-ku GU_4-*un* ANŠE.KUR.RA ANŠE.GÌR.NUN.NA-*an ku-iš-ki ú-e-mi-ya-zi / na-an* **LUGAL-*an*** *a-aš-ka / u-un-na-i*

74. KUB LVII 63 II 8 ff. (Ritual to the sun goddess of Arinna)
a-aš-šu-ma / KÙ.BABBAR GUŠKIN *an-da* ^{URU}*Ha-at-tu-ši /* ^{URU}*A-ri-in-na* ***ši-ú-na-an*** URU-*aš / píd-da-a-an-du*

11. dat./loc.pl. both genera: *-aš*

75. KBo III 1+ I 62 (Proclamation of Telipinu)
nu-uš-ša-an ***ha-ah-hal-la-aš*** *pár-hi-ir*[33]

76. KUB IV 1+ I 11 f. (Incantation at the enemy border)
^{D}*Zi-it-ha-ri-ya-aš* **DINGIR**^{MEŠ}***-na-aš hu-u-ma-an-ta-aš*** */ ar-ú-i-iš-ki-iz-zi*

77. KBo V 1 II 7 (Papanikri's ritual)
na-aš-ta 1 UDU ***ad-da-aš*** **DINGIR**^{MEŠ}***-aš*** *ši-pa-an-da-an-zi*

78. KUB XXXIII 120+ I 8 (Myth of Kummarbi)
ka-ru-ú-i-li-ya-aš **MU**$^{\text{HI.A}}$***-aš*** ^{D}*A-la-lu-uš* AN-*ši* LUGAL-*uš e-eš-ta*

79. KUB VI 45+ III 53 (Muwatalli's prayer)
nu-wa-ra-an-kán aš-ša-nu-ut nu-wa-ra-an-kán ***me-e-hu-na-aš*** *ar-nu-ut*

12.a. acc.pl.com.: *-uš*

32 Here: „took away" or the like.
33 Object is „the enemies".

80. KBo III 42 rev. 5’ (Chronicle of Puhanu)
nu-uk-kán ***hu-u-ma-an-du-uš***[34] *ú-e-en-ta*

81. KBo III 1+ III 43 (Proclamation of Telipinu)
nu-kán ***hal-ki-uš*** EGIR-*an ma-ak-nu-nu-un*

82. KBo II 3 I 42 f. (Maštigga’s ritual)
i-da-la-u-e-eš-wa-kán[35] ***hur-da-a-uš*** *pa-ra-a al-la-pa-ah-tin / nu te-kán píd-da-an-zi*[36]

83. KUB I 1+ II 28 (Apology of Hattušili III)
$^{\text{LÚ.MEŠ}}$***pí-ra-an hu-u-i-ya-tal-lu-uš***-*ma e-ip-pu-un*

84. KUB VII 1+ II 5 f. (Rituals of Ayatarša, Wattiti, & Šušmanniga)
Ù ŠA UDU ***ka-ra-a-du-uš*** / *IŠ-TU ha-ap-pí-ni-it za-nu-uš-kán-zi*

13.b. acc.pl.n.: *-a*, *-i*, lengthened grade

85. KUB I 1+ III 21 ff. (Apology of Hattušili III)
KUR.KUR$^{\text{ME.EŠ}}$ ^{URU}*Hat-ti-ma-wa-kán* / ***hu-u-ma-an-da*** ^{D}*IŠTAR A-NA* ^{m}*Ha-at-tu-ši-li an-da-an / ne-ih-hu-un*

86. KBo IV 10+ obv. 42’ (Treaty with Ulmitešub)
nu-za ŠA DINGIR^{LIM} ***ša-ah-ha-na*** *IŠ-TU* KUR^{TI}-*ŠÚ Ú-UL tar-ah-ta*

87. KUB VI 45+ I 26 f. (Muwatalli’s prayer)
EN^{MEŠ} GEŠTU-*an pa-ra-a e-ip-tin nu-mu ki-e* ***ar-ku-wa-ar-ri***$^{\text{HI.A}}$ / *iš-ta-ma-aš-tin*

88. KUB V 6 II 34 f. (KUŠ oracle)
nu ^{m}*An-ta-ra-wa-aš pí-en-ni-iš-ta na-aš ka-ru-ú* / ***za-an-ki-la-tar-ri***$^{\text{HI.A}}$ SUM-*eš-ta*

89. KUB I 16+ III 46 (Political testament of Hattušili I)
šu-me-eš-ma la-ba-ar-na-aš LUGAL.GAL ***ud-da-a-ar***-*me-it pa-ah-ha-aš-nu-ut-te-en*

---

34 Add „people“ or the like.
35 Nominative for accusative.
36 Lit. „they run“, here rather „they fall“.

90. KBo XVII 1+ I 22 f. (Ritual for the royal couple)
har-kán-zi-ma-an / ^{D}*Ha-an-ta-še-pí-eš an-du-uh-ša-aš* ***har-ša-a-ar**-ra*
^{GIŠ}ŠUKUR$^{\mathrm{HI.A}}$*-ya*

EXERCISES

91. KBo III 22 rev. 55 (Proclamation of Anitta)
nu ^{URU}*Ne-e-ši* URU^{DIDLI} *ú-e-te-nu-un*[37]

92. KUB VII 53+ I 41 f. (Tunnawi's ritual)
nu ku-wa-pí har-ša-u-wa-ar ma-ni-in-ku-wa-an NU.GÁL / ^{GIŠ}APIN *UL a-ra-an-za nu* ^{GIŠ}ZA.LAM.GAR *a-pí-ya i-ya-an-za*[38]

93. KUB XXXI 113, 3' (Fragment of an instruction)
ša-ra-a-kán ku-it wa-a-tar[39] *na-at li-e ú-da-at-tin*[40]

94. KBo III 22 obv. 41 f. (Proclamation of Anitta)
ap-pí-iz-zi-ya-na ^{m}*A-ni-it-ta-aš*[41] LUGAL.GAL ^{D}*Ši-ú-šum-mi-in*[42] /
^{URU}*Za-a-al-pu-wa-az a-ap-pa* ^{URU}*Ne-e-ša pí-e-tah-hu-un*

95. KBo III 22 obv. 39 f. (Proclamation of Anitta)
ka-ru-ú ^{m}*U-uh-na-aš* LUGAL ^{URU}*Za-a-al-pu-wa* ^{D}*Ši-u-šum-mi-in* /
^{URU}*Ne-e-ša-az* ^{URU}*Za-a-al-pu-wa pí-e-da-aš*

96. KUB XVII 5 I 5 f. (Myth of Illuyanka)
na-aš-ta ^{MUŠ}*Il-lu-ya-an-ka-an*[43] / *ha-an-te-eš-na-az ša-ra-a kal-li-iš-ta*

97. KBo III 7 I 11 (Myth of Illuyanka)
nu-za ^{MUŠ}*Il-lu-ya-an-ka-aš* ^{D}IM*-an tar-ah-ta*

98. KUB VII 53+ II 25 (Tunnawi's ritual)
EGIR-*ŠU-ma-za-kán ú-e-te-ni-it a-ar-ri*[44]

---

37 Here: „rebuild, reinforced" or the like.
38 Nominal sentence, add „is" in the translation.
39 Nominal sentence, add „is" in the translation.
40 The imperative after the prohibitive particle *lē* is irregular!
41 The verb is 1.sg., so this is apposition.
42 Meaning the statue of the god.
43 A mythical dragon.

2.1.2. Nominal stem formation

The nominal stem formation is too complex a matter to be presented here in detail. However, some stems with inflectional peculiarities will be examined in the following, namely the *i*- and *u*-stems, diphthongal stems with ablaut in the suffix, and the so-called heteroclitics, where the nom.-acc. (casus rectus) comes from a different stem than the rest of the cases (casus obliqui). For the details cf. Hoffner/Melchert 2008: 52 ff.

2.1.2.1. i- stems

i-stems are divided into two different classes, one with and one without ablaut, which differ in the gen., dat.-loc., abl. sg. and in the acc., gen. and dat.-loc. pl. The class with ablaut mostly contains adjectives, the class without ablaut shows both adjectives and nouns. Similar classes hold for the *u*-stems (see next chapter). The endings, however, do not differ from the vocalic classes.

Lit.: Friedrich 1960: 47 ff.; Neu 1985; Rieken 1994, 1999; Hoffner/Melchert 2008: 85 ff.

	singular		plural	
	no ablaut	ablaut	no ablaut	ablaut
nom.c.	*-iš*		*-eš*	
acc.c.	*-in*		*-iuš*	*-auš*
nom.-acc.n.	*-i*		*-a*	
gen.	*-iyaš*	*-ayaš*	*-iyaš*	*-ayaš*
dat.-loc.	*-iya*	*-ai*	*-iyaš*	*-ayaš*
instr.	*-it, -ta*		–	
abl.	*-iyaz*	*-ayaz*	–	

44 Subject is a priestess.

99. KUB XVII 10 IV 21 (Myth of Telipinu)
^{GIŠ}*lu-ut-ta-i kam-ma-ra-aš tar-na-aš* É-*ir* ***túh-hu-iš*** *tar-na-aš*

100. KBo XII 126+ II 23’ ff. (Malli’s ritual)
nu al-wa-an-za-ta i-da-la-u-e-eš te-eš-hu-uš[45] / *tar-ma-a-an-te-eš a-ša-an-du na-at-kán nam-ma ša-ra-a li-e ú-iz-zi* / *na-at* ***da-an-ku-i-iš*** *da-ga-an-zi-pa-aš har-du*

101. KBo XXXII 14 II 42 (Epos of liberation)
te-eš-šum-mi-in ^{LÚ}SIMUG *wa-al-li-ya-an-ni la-a-hu-uš*

102. KBo XI 14 III 26 f. (Hantitaššu’s ritual)
nu ***da-an-ku-in-n****a-pa ta-ga-an-zi-pa-an*[46] / *i-it zi-ik* EGIR-*pa ha-a-aš*

103. KBo III 22 obv. 34 (Proclamation of Anitta)
UR-RA-AM ŠE-RA-AM ki-i ***tup-pí*** *li-e ku-iš-ki hu-ul-li-e-iz-zi*[47]

104. KUB LVII 63 I 11 ff. (Ritual to the sun goddess of Arinna)
ma-a-an lu-uk-kat-ta-ma ka-ru-ú-wa-ri-wa-ar / *na-aš-ta* ARAD-*YA kat-ta pa-iz-zi* / *na-aš-ta IŠ-TU* ^{DUG}*KU-KU-BI wa-a-tar* ***pár-ku-i*** / *ša-ra-a ú-da-a-i*

105. KUB XXXIII 106+ II 3 f. (Myth of Ullikummi)
I-NA GÌR^{MEŠ}-*ŠÚ-ma-za* ^{KUŠ}E.SIR$^{\text{HI.A}}$-*uš li-li-wa-an-du-uš* / *šar-ku-it na-aš-kán pár-ga-u-wa-aš* ***a-ú-ri-ya-aš*** *ša-ra-a pa-it*

106. KBo X 26 I 28 ff. (KI.LAM festival)
GAL *ME-ŠE-DI za-a-u* KÙ.BABBAR / *ŠA* ^{LÚ}SANGA ***šu-up-pa-ya-aš*** / *ŠA* ^{URU}*Zi-ip-pa-la-an-da* / *ú-da-i*

107. KUB XXIX 4 I 67 f. (Ritual for the transfer of the Black Goddess)
a-pí-e-da-ni UD-*ti hu-it-ti-ya-an-zi na-an*[48]*-kán* ***ka-ru-ú-i-li-aš*** / *A-NA* É DINGIR^{LIM} *an-da hu-it-ti-ya-an-zi*

108. KUB XXVIII 99, 5’ f. (Festival for the stormgod of Nerik)
ma-a-an LUGAL-*uš* $^{\text{NA4}}$***hu-u-wa-ši-ya*** *ha-an-ta-iz-zi* / GAL $^{\text{LÚ.MEŠ}}$SAGI.A

45 Accusative for nominative.
46 The accusative syntactically belongs to *hās*.
47 The form is indicative but used as an imperative.
48 Namely a ritual shield.

^{DUG}*KU-KU-UB* GEŠTIN *da-a-i* LUGAL-*i pa-a-i*

109. KUB I 1+ IV 64 ff. (Apology of Hattušili III)
nu-mu ^{D}*IŠTAR* GAŠAN-*ma ma-ši-wa-an / da-at-ta nu-mu* ***šal-la-i*** *pí-di*
A-NA KUR ^{URU}*Hat-ti* LUGAL-*iz-na-ni / ti-it-ta-nu-ut*

110. KBo XVII 74+ I 28 f. (Ritual of storm and thunder)
ma-a-an ^{D}IM-*aš ti-it-ha* LUGAL-*uš* ^{GIŠ}***hu-lu-ga-an-ni-az*** *kat-ta ú-iz-zi / ta a-ru-wa-a-iz-zi ta ši-pa-an-ti ta nam-ma a-ru-wa-a-iz-zi*

111. KBo XVII 74+ II 35 (Ritual of storm and thunder)
LÚ ^{GIŠ}BANŠUR ***šu-up-pa-az*** ^{GIŠ}BANŠUR-*az* 2 *tu-ni-in-ga-aš* ^{NINDA}*har-ša-uš da-a-i*

112. KBo X 25 I 32 ff. (KI.LAM festival)
LÚ ^{GIŠ}BANŠUR / ***šu-up-pa-ya-az***[49] ^{GIŠ}BANŠUR-*az* / 1 NINDA.GUR$_4$.RA KU$_7$ *da-a-i* LUGAL-*i* / *pa-a-i*

113. KUB XXXVI 90 obv. 5 ff. (Prayer to the stormgod of Nerik)
nu-kán ^{D}U ^{URU}*Ne-ri-ik* / ***ša-ni-iz-zi-ya-az*** *te-eš-ha-az ša-ra-a / ar-nu-ud-du*

114. KBo XIX 128+ I 3 ff. (AN.TAH.ŠUM festival)
na-aš-šu ^{GIŠ}GIGIR-*it na-aš-ma* / ^{GIŠ}***hu-lu-ga-an-ni-it*** *I-NA* É^{TIM}.GAL / *pa-iz-zi*

115. KUB XXXIII 120+ I 31 ff. (Myth of Kummarbi)
a-aš-ma-at-ta ar-ma-ah-hu-un[50] ^{D}IM-*ni-it* ***na-ak-ki-it*** / *da-an-ma-at-ta ar-ma-ah-hu-un* ^{ÍD}*A-ra-an-za-hi-it ú-ul-la-az-zu-wa-aš* / 3-*an-na-at-ta ar-ma-ah-hu-un* ***na-ak-ki-it*** ^{D}*Ta-aš-mi-šu-ut*

116. Mşt. 75/13 rev. 15 ff. (Letter)
nu-uš-ša-an ma-a-an / ***hal-ki-e-eš*** *a-ra-an-te-eš*[51] / *na-aš*[52]*-kán ar-ha wa-ar-aš-tin* / *na-aš*[53]*-kán A-NA* KISLAH *pa-ra-a / ar-nu-ut-tin*

---

49 *suppi-* means „clean" or „pure" in a ritual sense; maybe we could even translate it as „holy".

50 In the myth Kummarbi bites off and swallows the genitals of his father Anu and becomes pregnant thereof; in the quote Anu is speaking.

51 Nominal sentence, add „is" in the translation.

52 Nominative for accusative.

53 Nominative for accusative.

117. KUB XIII 4 I 14 (Instructions for the priests and temple officials)
nam-ma NINDA.GUR$_4$.RA UD^{MI} *ku-i-e-eš e-eš-ša-an-zi na-at*[54] ***pár-ku-wa-iš*** *a-ša-an-du*

118. KUB XLIII 38 rev. 29 f. (Second military oath)
ma-a-an-wa ki-i-ma NI-IŠ DINGIR^{LIM} *pa-ah-ha-aš-te-ni nu-wa-aš-ma-aš* / ***uk-tu-u-ri-eš***[55] *šu-me-eš-ša-wa-az QA-TAM-MA* ***uk-tu-u-ri-eš*** *e-eš-te-ni*

119. Mşt. 75/74 obv. 3 ff. (Letter)
ud-da-a-ar-mu ku-e ha-at-ra-a-eš[56] / ^{LÚ}KÚR *ma-ah-ha-an* ***hal-ki-uš*** / *dam-me-iš-hi-iš-ki-iz-zi* / ^{URU}*Kap-pu-ši-ya ma-ah-ha-an* / *ŠA* É MUNUS.LUGAL[57] *wa-al-ah-ta* / *nu ŠA* É MUNUS.LUGAL 1 GU$_4$ *ha-ap-pu-ut-ri da-a-ir* / *ŠA* $^{LÚ.MEŠ}$MÁŠDA-*ya* / 30 GU$_4^{HI.A}$ 10 LÚ^{MEŠ}-*ya pí-hu-te-ir* / *na-at AŠ-ME*

120. KUB XXXVI 89 rev. 56 f. (Ritual for the stormgod of Nerik)
^{D}*Te-ši-mi-wa-kán a-aš-ši-ya-an-ti* / *gi-nu-wa* ***ša-ni-iz-zi-uš*** *ti-eš-hu-uš šu-up-pa-ri-ya-an-za e-eš-ta*

121. KBo V 5 III 11 f. (Deeds of Šuppiluliuma)
tu-uk-ma-wa DUMU^{MEŠ}-*KA* ***me-ig-ga-uš***[58] / *me-mi-iš-kán-zi*

122. KUB VII 1+ I 9 f. (Rituals of Ayataršа, Wattiti, & Šušmanniga)
nu-kán ^{UDU}*i-ya-an-ta-an ar-kán-zi na-aš-ta* ^{UZU}*hu-i-šu* / ***šu-up-pa*** *da-an-zi*

123. KUB XIII 4 I 15 f. (Instructions for the priests and temple officials)
iš-hi-e-ni-uš-ma-aš-kán[59] / UMBIN^{MEŠ}-*ya da-a-an e-eš-du* ***pár-ku-wa-ya*** TÚG$^{HI.A}$ *wa-aš-ša-an har-kán-du*

124. Mşt. 75/63 rev. 34 f. (Letter)
zi-ga ^{mD}IM-*BE-LÍ-iš* ^{GIŠ}***zu-up-pa-ri-ya-aš*** / *ŠA* Ú$^{HI.A}$-*ya ut-tar ša-a-ak-ti*

---

54 Neuter as correlate of the pl. com. in the relative clause.
55 Nominal sentence, add „are" in the translation.
56 Formula in the letters which makes the syntax somewhat difficult to translate, but it can be helpful to insert a „namely" after the formula „what you have written to me". The main clause is the resuming *na-at AŠ-ME* „I heard it".
57 „Suspended genitive":„this of the palace" = „the property of the palace".
58 Nominal, possessive: add „have" in the translation.
59 Accusative for nominative.

125. KUB XVII 7+ IV 15’ f. (Myth of Ullikummi)
ku-iš-wa-ra-an nam-ma uš-ki-iz-zi[60] ***šal-la-ya-aš*** DINGIR^{MEŠ}-*aš* /
da-aš-ša-u-uš za-ah-ha-a-uš

126. KUB XXXIII 106+ III 51’ (Myth of Ullikummi)
nu ***ka-ru-ú-i-li-ya-aš*** *ad-da-aš* $^{\text{NA4}}$KIŠIB *ú-da-an-du*

127. KBo IV 1 rev. 5 f. (Foundation ritual)
A-NA 4 ***hal-hal-du-um-ma-ri-ya-aš-ša*** *QA-TAM-MA ku-wa-pí-ya*
1-*e-da-ni hal-hal-du-um-ma-ri* / 4 *wa-al-lu-uš da-a-i*

128. KUB XXXIII 106+ III 48’ (Myth of Ullikummi)
^{D}*É-A-aš* ***ka-ru-ú-i-li-ya-aš*** DINGIR^{MEŠ}-*aš* EGIR-*pa me-mi-iš-ki-u-an*
da-a-iš

129. KUB X 21 III 12 ff. (AN.TAH.ŠUM Festival)
na-an-kán a-ap-pa / ***šu-up-pa-ya-aš*** ^{GIŠ}BANŠUR$^{\text{HI.A}}$-*aš* / *ŠA* LUGAL
MUNUS.LUGAL *ti-an-zi*

2.1.2.2. u- stems

Similar to the *i*-stems, there are two different classes within the *u*-stems which differ in the the gen., dat.-loc., abl. and instr. sg.and pl. Accordingly, the class with ablaut shows for the most part adjectives, while the class without ablaut contains adjectives and nouns.

Lit.: Friedrich 1960: 50 ff.; Weitenberg 1984; Neu 1985; Hoffner/ Melchert 2008: 97 ff.

---

60 As Hittite is principally a verb-last-language the word order here is somewhat poetic; but a postponed object demands a kataphoric pronoun in the Wackernagel position, therefore we have *kuiš=war=an* at the beginning.

	singular		plural	
	no ablaut	ablaut	no ablaut	ablaut
nom.c.	*-uš*		*-eš*	*-a(u)weš*
acc.c.	*-un*		*-uš*	*-amuš*
nom.-acc.n.	*-u*		*-uwa*	*-a(u)wa*
gen.	*-uwaš*	*-a(u)waš*	*-uwaš*	*-a(u)waš*
dat.-loc.	*-ui*	*-a(u)wi*	*-uwaš*	*-a(u)waš*
instr.	*-uit*	*-a(u)wit*	–	
abl.	*-uwaz*	*-a(u)waz*	–	

130. KUB IX 27+ I 44 f. (Paškuwatti's ritual against sexual impotence)
nu-ut-ták-kán hu-u-wa-an-te-eš$_{17}$ ***hé-e-u-uš*** IGI$^{HI.A}$*-wa li-e* /
wa-al-ha-an-ni-ya-an-zi

131. KUB XXIV 2 I 3 (Muršili's prayer to Telipinu)
^{D}*Te-li-pí-nu-uš* ***šar-ku-uš*** *na-ak-ki-iš* DINGIR^{LIM}*-iš zi-ik*[61]

132. KUB VII 53+ II 38 f. (Tunnawi's ritual)
ŠA DUMU.LÚ.U$_{19}$.LU*-ma-aš-ši-kán* / *pa-an-ga-u-wa-aš* ***i-da-lu-un***
EME*-un*[62] *da-aš-ki-mi*

133. KBo III 34 I 15 f. (Palace chronicle)
^{m}***Šar-ma-aš-šu-un*** ^{m}***Nu-un-nu-un-na*** / $^{HUR.SAG}$*Ta-ha-ya-i pí-hu-te-ir*

134. KBo XVII 62+ IV 17' f. (Birth ritual)
ka-a-ša ŠA DUMU.MUNUS ***a-aš-šu-u*** *ú-da-ah-hu-un pa-ra-a-ma-wa* /
MU*-an-ni ŠA* DUMU.NITA ***a-aš-šu-u*** *ú-da-al-lu*

135. KUB IX 25+ II 20 (Ambazzi's ritual)
ar-ha-ši-kán ***i-da-a-lu*** *hu-it-ti-eš-šar hu-it-ti-ya*

---

61 Nominal sentence, add „are" in the translation.
62 „Evil tongue" means „defamation, slander".

136. KBo XVII 74+ I 9 f. (Ritual of storm and thunder)
DUMU.É.GAL *ŠA* LUGAL DUMU.É.GAL MUNUS.LUGAL *pa-a-an-zi ta* LUGAL-*aš* MUNUS.LUGAL-*aš-ša* / ***gi-nu-wa-aš*** GADA$^{\mathrm{HI.A}}$ *pa-ta-a-an-na* ^{GIŠ}GÌR.GUB *da-a-an-zi*

137. KUB VII 53+ III 39 ff. (Tunnawi's ritual)
ki-e-da-ni-ya-kán A-NA EN SISKUR *i-da-lu* / *pa-ap-ra-tar al-wa-za-tar a-aš-ta-ya-ra-tar* / DINGIR^{MEŠ}-*aš kar-pí-in NI-IŠ* DINGIR^{LIM} ***pa-an-ga-u-wa-aš*** EME-*an* / *ma-ni-in-ku-u-wa-an-da-an* MU-*an ar-ha QA-TAM-MA hu-it-ti-ya*

138. KUB XXXVI 89 rev. 4 (Ritual for the stormgod of Nerik)
a-ru-na-aš-ša-aš 9-*aš* ***wa-ap-pu-ú-i*** GAM-*an pa-a-it*

139. KUB VIII 1, 6 (Lunar omen)
nu ma-a-an ^{D}XXX-*aš a-ki*[63] *za-ah-hi-ya-kán* ***pa-an-ga-u-i*** ÉRIN^{MEŠ} *ma-uš-zi*

140. KUB XV 34+ I 1 ff. (Evocatio)
ma-a-an $^{\mathrm{LÚ.MEŠ}}$AZU DINGIR^{MEŠ} *IŠ-TU* 8 KASKAL^{MEŠ} ***ú-el-lu-u-wa-az*** HUR.SAG^{MEŠ} ÍD^{MEŠ} / *a-ru-na-az* PÚ^{MEŠ}-*az pa-ah-hu-e-na-az ne-pí-ša-az ták-na-a-az* / *hu-it-ti-ya-an-zi nu ki-i da-an-zi*

141. KUB I 1+ II 21 (Apology of Hattušili III)
ÉRIN^{MEŠ}-*ma-mu* ANŠE.KUR.RA^{MEŠ} ***te-pa-u-wa-az*** *pa-iš*

142. KUB XXXVI 89 obv. 27 f. (Ritual for the stormgod of Nerik)
DUMU ^{D}*Šu-li-kat-ti na-na-ku-uš-ši-ya-an-ta-za* 4 *hal-hal-tu-ma-ra-za* / ***hal-lu-u-wa-za*** *hu-u-un-hu-e-eš-na-za* UGU *e-hu* EGIR-*pa-wa-za* ^{URU}*Ne-ri-ik-ki an-da-an ne-i-ya*

143. VBoT 121 II 14 (Muršili's prayer to the sun goddess of Arinna)
KUR ^{URU}*Ha-at-ti-ma-aš-ta an-da* ***aš-ša-u-it*** IGI$^{\mathrm{HI.A}}$-*it a-uš-te-en*

144. KBo IV 10+ obv. 48' f. (Treaty with Ulmitešub)
ki-e-da-ni-ma me-mi-ni ^{D}U HI.HI-*aš-ši-iš* ^{D}UTU ^{URU}PÚ-*na* ^{D}U ^{URU}*Ha-at-ti* ^{D}U ^{URU}*Ne-ri-ik* ^{D}*IŠTAR* ^{URU}*Ša-mu-ha* ^{D}*IŠTAR*

---

63 „The moon dies" refers to a lunar eclipse.

^{URU}*La-wa-za-an-ti-ya LI-IM* DINGIR^{MEŠ} / *ŠA* KUR ^{URU}*Ha-at-ti*
ku-ut-ru-e-eš *a-ša-an-du*

145. KUB VII 1+ II 32 ff. (Rituals of Ayatarša, Wattiti, & Šušmanniga)
hu-i-ša-aš-wa pa-an-za-ki-it-ti-iš GIM-*an* / *ú-e-ha-at-ta* DUMU-*li-ya*
i-da-a-la-u-eš *ka-ra-a-te-eš* / *kat-ta-an ar-ha a-pí-ni-eš-ša-an*
wa-ha-an-du

146. KUB XXVIII 4 III 6 ff. (Story of the moon that fell from heaven)
EGIR-*ŠU-ma te-it-hi-im-mu-uš* / *hu-wa-an-te-mu-uš al-pu-ú-uš* ***hé-e-uš*** /
ŠA ^{D}U GUB-*aš* 3-*ŠU e-ku-zi*[64]

147. KBo XV 10+ II 12 (Purification ritual for Tuthaliya and Nikalmati)
QA-DU ku-úr-da-a-li ***i-da-a-la-mu-uš*** EME$^{HI.A}$ *ar-ha šu-uh-ha-ir*

148. KBo II 3 III 42 ff. (Maštigga's ritual)
kat-ta-wa-ra-aš-ma-aš-kán / *wa-ar-ša-an e-eš-tu* ***i-da-a-la-u-wa***
ud-da-a-ar / KAxU-*aš* EME-*aš*

149. KUB II 5 II 59 f. (AN.TAH.ŠUM festival)
DUMU^{MEŠ}.É.GAL-*kán* ***gi-nu-wa-aš*** GADA$^{HI.A}$ / *ti-an-zi*

150. KUB I 1+ IV 50 f. (Apology of Hattušili III)
nu-mu LUGAL$^{ME.EŠ}$ *MAH-RU-YA* ***a-aš-ša-u-wa-aš*** *me-mi-ya-na-aš*
ku-i-e-eš e-šir / *na-at-mu* ***a-aš-ša-u-wa-aš****-pát me-mi-ya-na-aš*
ki-ša-an-ta-at

151. KBo VI 34+ II 39 ff. (First military oath)
LÍL-*ma-aš-ši* A.ŠÀ *har-ša-ú-na-aš* / ***ú-el-lu-wa-aš*** *an-da ú-el-ku-wa-an*
li-e / *hu-wa-a-i* $GU_4$$^{HI.A}$-*ŠU* UDU$^{HI.A}$-*ŠÚ* AMAR $SILA_4$ *li-e ha-a-ši*

152. KUB IX 25+ I 38 ff. (Ambazzi's ritual)
ar-ha-wa-aš-ma-aš-kán da-ah-hu-un / *i-da-a-lu nu-wa-ra-at-kán A-NA*
PÉŠ.TUR *ne-ih-hu-un* / *nu-wa-ra-at ka-a-aš* PÉŠ.TUR ***pár-ga-u-wa-aš***
HUR.SAG$^{HI.A}$-*aš* / ***hal-lu-u-wa-aš*** *ha-a-ri-ya-aš* ***da-a-lu-ga-u-wa-aš***
KASKAL$^{HI.A}$-*aš pí-e-da-a-ú*

64 „to drink a god" = „to drink a cup in honour of the god".

2.1.2.3. Diphthongal stems

Diphthongal stems in *-āi-* show the ablaut.

Lit.: Friedrich 1960: 48 f.

	singular	plural
nom.c.	*-aiš*	*-a(y)eš*
acc.c.	*-ain*	*-auš*
nom.-acc.n.	*-ai*	*-ai*
gen.	*-iyaš*	*-iyaš*
dat.-loc.	*-iya*	*-iyaš*
instr.	*-it*	–
abl.	*-iyaz*	–

153. KBo XIII 34 III 11' ff. (Birth omen)

ták-ku MUNUS-*za ha-a-ši nu-uš-ši*[65] / SAG.DU-*ZU ŠA* MUŠ *ki-ša* / *ŠA* ^D^GIŠ."GIM".MAŠ ***ša-ga-iš***[66]

154. KUB VI 41 II 24 f. (Treaty with Kupanta-^D^KAL, D version)

nu ka-a-aš-ma PA-NI NI-IŠ DINGIR^MEŠ^ / ***wa-aš-ta-i-iš***[67] *nu-kán NI-EŠ* DINGIR^*LIM*^ *šar-ra-at-ti*

155. KUB XVII 1 II 4 ff. (Tale of Kešši)

4-*an-na-za-kán* ***za-aš-ha-in*** *a-uš-ta nu-kán da-aš-šu-uš* ^NA4^*ku-un-ku-nu-uz-zi-iš* / *ne-pí-ša-az kat-ta ma-uš-ta-at nu-kán* SAG.GÉME.ARAD^MEŠ^ DINGIR-*aš-ša* LÚ-*ya* / *kat-ta ta-ma-aš-ta*

156. KUB XXX 10 obv. 12 (Kantuzzili's prayer)

nu A-NA DINGIR-*YA Ú-UL ku-uš-ša-an-ka li-in-ku-un* ***li-in-ga-in-na****-aš-ta Ú-UL ku-uš-ša-an-ka šar-ra-ah-ha-at*

---

65 The dative refers to the newborn child.

66 Nominal sentence, add „this is" in the translation.

67 Nominal sentence, add „this is" in the translation.

157. KBo XI 14 II 27 (Hantitaššu's ritual)
nu ku-u-un ***hu-u-uk-ma-in*** *7-ŠÚ hu-u-uk-zi*

158. KUB XIII 4 III 36 ff. (Instructions for the priests and temple officials)
mar-ri iš-hal-túh-me-ya-an-za ŠÀ É DINGIR^{LIM} *na-aš-ma ta-me-e-da-ni* / ^{É}*ka-ri-im-me ku-iš-ki ni-ik-zi na-aš-kán ma-a-an* ŠÀ É DINGIR^{LIM} / *ni-ni-ik-ta-ri nu* ***hal-lu-u-wa-a-in*** *i-ya-zi*

159. KBo II 3 II 37 f. (Maštigga's ritual)
EGIR-*an-da-ma* ^{DUG}***hu-pu-wa-i*** *da-a-i na-at-kán* GEŠTIN-*it* / Ì.GIŠ *SE*$_{20}$*-IR-TUM* LÀL-*it šu-un-na-i*

160. KUB XXIX 4 III 24 f. (Ritual for the transfer of the Black Goddess)
nu-uš-ša-an Ì.DÙG.GA ^{GIŠ}***tal-la-i*** / *la-a-hu-u-wa-an-zi*

161. KBo V 3+ left edge (Treaty with Hukkanā of Haysa)
DUB.2.KAM *ŠA* ^{m}*Hu-uq-qa-na-a* ***li-in-ki-ya-aš***[68]

162. KBo XVII 62+ I 13' (Birth ritual)
nu ***hu-uk-mi-ya-aš*** DUB$^{HI.A}$-*TIM ar-ha-ya-an*[69]

163. KBo X 2 I 33 (Apology of Hattušili I)
EGIR-*an-da-ma I-NA* KUR ^{URU}*Ul-ma* ***za-ah-hi-ya*** *pa-a-un*

164. KBo XVI 47 obv. 15' f. (Treaty)
an-da-ma-kán UDU-*un ku-wa-a-pí ku-e-u-e-en nu* ***li-in-ki-ya*** / *kat-ta-an ki-iš-ša-an da-i-ú-en*

165. KBo XVI 47 obv. 13' f. (Treaty)
ma-a-na-an[70] *Ú-UL-ma za-ah-hi-ya-ši nu-kán ka-a-aš-ma NI-IŠ* DINGIR^{LIM} / *zi-ik šar-ra-at-ta* ^{URU}*Ha-at-tu-ša-ša* ***li-in-ki-ya-az*** *pár-ku-iš*[71] *e-eš-tu*

166. KUB XIII 4 III 43 (Instructions for the priests and temple officials)
nu-za ***hal-lu-wa-ya-za*** *me-ik-ki na-ah-ha-an-te-eš e-eš-tin*[72]

---

68 This is part of the colophon, so it's not a complete sentence.
69 Nominal sentence, add „are" in the translation.
70 The pronoun refers to an enemy.
71 Lit. „clean", here: „free"; the normal adjective for „free", *arāwa-*, is not used here because an oath is and remains a religious obligation even if it is sworn in a political treaty.
72 Arguments in a ritual building are supposed to be dangerous: They could offend the

167. KBo II 3 I 58 ff. (Maštigga's ritual)
nu-wa ka-a-aš GIM-*an Ú-UL ne-pí-iš a-uš-zi* / EGIR-*pa-ma-wa-za-kán* ŠAH.TUR$^{\text{HI.A}}$ *Ú-UL a-uš-zi* / *nu ku-u-uš* EN^{MEŠ} SISKUR *i-da-a-la-u-e-eš* ***hur-da-a-e-eš*** / *QA-TAM-MA li-e ú-wa-an-zi*

168. IBoT I 36 III 42 ff. (Instructions for the royal body guard)
nu ma-a-an ^{GIŠ}ŠUKUR *ku-iš* / *Ú-UL har-zi nu-za* ^{GIŠ}GIDRU$^{\text{HI.A}}$ *ku-it ta-an-zi na-at-kán ŠA* ^{GIŠ}*kal-mu-ša-aš* / DUMU.É.GAL *Ú-UL ha-an-da-a-an-ta-ri pa-ra-a* ***da-ma-a-e-eš*** 2 DUMU.É.GAL / *ti-en-zi*

169. KUB VII 53+ I 43 ff. (Tunnawi's ritual)
nu ^{MUNUS}ŠU.GI *wa-ap-pu-wa-aš* IM-*an ša-ku-ni-ya-aš-ša* IM-*an a-pí-ya pí-e-da-i* / 2 *še-na-aš* IM 12 EME IM EGIR-*an ha-lu-pa-an-te-eš* 2 GU$_4$ IM 2 *wa-wa-ar-ki-ma-aš* IM / SÍG *an-da-ra-aš te-pu* SÍG *mi-i-ti-iš te-pu nu šu-um-ma-an-za* SÍG *mi-i-ti-iš-ša* / *an-da ta-ru-up-pa-an-za* Á^{MUŠEN}-*aš pát-tar* ***ha-aš-ta-i*** *te-pu wa-al-li-in te-pu*

170. KBo VI 34+ II 21 ff. (First military oath)
ki-i-wa BAPPIR GIM-*an IŠ-TU* $^{\text{NA4}}$ARA$_5$ *mal-la-an-zi* / *na-at ú-e-te-ni-it i-mi-ya-an-zi na-at za-nu-an-zi* / *na-at har-ra-nu-uš-kán-zi ku-i-ša-kán ki-e NI-IŠ* DINGIR^{MEŠ} / *šar-ra-ad-da nu-uš-ša-an A-NA* LUGAL MUNUS.LUGAL / *A-NA* DUMU^{MEŠ}.LUGAL *A-NA* KUR ^{URU}*Hat-ti* HUL-*lu ták-ki-iz-zi* / *na-an ki-e NI-EŠ* DINGIR^{LIM} *ap-pa-an-du nu* ***ha-aš-ta-i****-ši-it* / *QA-TAM-MA ma-al-la-an-du na-an QA-TAM-MA i-nu-uš-ki-du*

171. KUB IX 27+ IV 6 ff. (Paškuwatti's ritual against sexual impotence)
nu-za-kán ***za-aš-hi-mu-uš*** *ku-i-e-eš uš-ki-iz-zi* / *na-aš me-mi-iš-ki-iz-zi ma-a-an-ši* DINGIR^{LUM} / IGI$^{\text{HI.A}}$-*wa pa-ra-a te-ik-ku-uš-ki-iz-zi*[73]

172. KBo VI 34+ III 39 ff. (First military oath)
ku-iš-wa-kán ki-e / ***li-in-ga-uš*** *šar-ri-iz-zi nu-uš-ši* ^{D}IM-*aš* / ^{GIŠ}APIN *ar-ha du-wa-ar-na-a-ú*

---

gods, and they could distract the officials from their duties.

73 All verb forms are iteratives. Obviously it takes a while to cure his impotence.

173. KUB XXX 15+ obv. 1 f. (Funerary ritual)
ma-a-an I-NA UD.2.KAM *lu-uk-kat-ta nu* MUNUS^{MEŠ} *uk-tu-u-ri-ya* ***ha-aš-ti-aš*** *li-eš-šu-u-wa-an-zi / pa-a-an-zi*

174. KUB XIX 49+ I 35 f. (Treaty with Manapa-Datta)
nu-mu[74] ^{m}*Uh-ha*-LÚ-*iš ku-it NI-EŠ* DINGIR^{MEŠ} *šar-ri-it / na-an* ***li-in-ki-aš*** DINGIR^{MEŠ} *e-ip-pir*

175. KBo XVII 74+ I 26 (Ritual of storm and thunder)
^{NINDA}*har-ši-in pár-ši-ya ta* ***lu-ut-ti-ya-aš*** *da-a-i*

176. KUB XXX 15+ obv. 50 (Funerary ritual)
3 GÍN *IŠ-TU* Ì.DÙG.GA ***ha-aš-ti-ya-aš*** *pí-ra-an ti-ya-an-zi*

2.1.2.4. r-/n-Heteroclitics

r-/n-heteroclitics are neuters, which go back to a *r*-stem in the *casus rectus* (nom.-acc.) and to *n*-stem in the *casus obliqui*. Productive abstract nouns ending with *-(ā)tar* and the *rei actae* nouns ending with *-eššar*, and also some fossilized forms like *pahhur* „fire“ and *wātar* „water“, which are inherited from Indo-European, belong to this class.

Lit.: Friedrich 1960: 55 ff.; Oettinger 1986: 11 ff.; Rieken 1999: 290 ff.; Hoffner/Melchert 2008: 92 ff., 101 ff.

	singular	plural
nom.-acc.	*-r*	*-ār*
gen.	*-naš*	*-naš*
dat.-loc.	*-ni*	*-naš*
instr.	*-nit*	–
abl.	*-naz*	–
dir.	*-na*	–

74 Dativus incommodi.

177. KBo XII 126+ III 27’ f. (Malli’s ritual)
ma-a-an zi-in-ni-iz-zi nu-uš-ša-an ***wa-a-tar*** / *I-NA* 5 GAL.GIR$_4$ *la-a-hu-wa-i*

178. KUB LV 43 I 3 f. (Ritual for a protective god)
ma-a-an I-NA MU.9.KAM *ma-a-na-aš ku-wa-pí ku-wa-pí ne-wa-ah-ha-an-zi* / ***me-hur*** *Ú-UL du-uq-qa-a-ri*

179. KBo XV 10+ I 22 (Purification ritual for Tuthaliya and Nikalmati)
šu-ma-aš qa-a-ša ***iš-ha-na-aš*** ^{D}UTU-*an* ^{D}IM-*an-na* EGIR-*pa li-la-a-ri-iš-ki-wa-ni*

180. KBo XIX 128+ I 9 (AN.TAH.ŠUM festival)
LUGAL-*uš* ^{É}***hi-lam-na-aš*** KÁ-*aš a-ri*

181. KBo VI 2+ II 54 (Laws, first tablet)
ták-ku LÚ-*an* ***pa-ah-hu-e-ni*** *ku-iš-ki pí-eš-ši-iz-zi na-aš a-ki nu-uš* EGIR-*pa* DUMU.NITA-*an pa-a-i*[75]

182. KUB I 1+ III 61 f. (Apology of Hattušili III)
nu ŠA ŠEŠ-*YA* / ***na-ak-ki-ya-an-ni*** *ha-an-da-aš Ú-UL ma-an-qa* DÙ-*nu-un*

183. KUB I 1+ II 78 f. (Apology of Hattušili III)
^{URU}*Ša-mu-ha-an-na* URU^{LUM} DINGIR^{LIM} ***al-wa-an-zi-eš-na-za*** / *še-ir šu-un-ni-iš-ta*

184. KUB XXV 37+ III 20’ f. (Lallupiya tablet)
nu ma-ah-ha-an ša-wa-tar ša-ra-a da-an-zi / *na-at-kán* ***ú-e-te-na-az*** *ar-ha ša-an-ha-an-zi*

185. KUB VII 53+ II 25 (Tunnawi’s ritual)
EGIR-*ŠU-ma-za-kán* ***ú-e-te-ni-it*** *a-ar-ri*

186. KBo XVI 47 obv. 4’ (Treaty)
nu-uš-kán ^{m}*Hu-u-ha-za-al-ma-na* ***ha-an-ne-eš-ni-it*** *ta-ru-uh-hu-un*

187. KBo XI 14 III 8 ff. (Hantitaššu’s ritual)
nu 1 ŠAH.TUR *da-a-i* / *na-an-kán* ***ha-at-te-eš-na*** GAM-*an-ta ha-at-ta-ri* / *e-eš-har-še-it kat-ta-an-ta tar-na-i*

---

75 As a substitute for the lost worker.

188. KBo X 23 I 6’ ff. (KI.LAM festival)
LUGAL-*uš* ***tu-un-na-ki-iš-na*** / *pa-iz-zi nu-za* KIN$^{\text{HI.A}}$-*ta* / *da-a-i*

189. KUB I 16 II 11 f. (Political testament of Hattušili I)
nu-uš-ši ŠEŠ^{MEŠ}-*uš* NIN^{MEŠ}-*uš*[76] ***ud-da-a-ar*** *e-ku-na*[77] *pí-e-da-eš-kir nu a-pí-en-za-an* / ***ud-da-a-ar*** *iš-ta-ma-aš-ki-it*

190. KBo X 24 I 11 ff. (KI.LAM festival)
ki-e / ***hu-u-i-ta-a-ar*** *ša-ra-az-zi-ya-az* / ^{É}*ka-aš-ga-aš-ti-pa-az* / KÁ.GAL-*az kat-ta a-ri*

191. KUB XVII 10 II 23 f. (Myth of Telipinu)
DIM$_4$ BAPPIR ZI-*it ma-ah-ha-an ták-ša-an-ta Ù ŠA* ^{D}*Te-li-pí-nu* / ZI-*KA ŠA* DUMU.LÚ.U$_{19}$.LU^{MEŠ} ***ud-da-na-a-aš*** *QA-TAM-MA ták-ša-an-za e-eš-du*

192. KUB XXX 29 I 4 f. (Birth ritual)
1$^{EN\ \text{KUŠ}}$*šar-pa-aš-ši-ša-kán* ^{GIŠ}***ku-up-pí-iš-na-aš*** *iš-tar-na* / *ta-ga-a-an iš-pa-ra-an-zi*

193. KBo XII 126+ II 37’ (Malli’s ritual)
1 NINDA.SIG KASKAL-*aš* ***ha-at-ta-ri-eš-na-aš*** *pár-ši-ya* KASKAL-*ši* GÙB-*za da-a-i*

194. KBo IV 9 V 48 ff. (AN.TAH.ŠUM festival)
LÚ ^{GIŠ}GIDRU *A-NA* $^{\text{LÚ.MEŠ}}$*Ú-BA-RUM* EN ^{GIŠ}*za-hur-ti-aš* / ***tu-un-na-ak-ki-eš-na-aš*** $^{\text{LÚ.MEŠ}}$DUGUD / *pí-ra-an hu-u-wa-i tu-uš a-ša-a-ši*

EXERCISES

195. KUB XXXVI 89 rev. 5 (Ritual for the stormgod of Nerik)
na-ak-ki-ya-ša-aš ÍD-*aš wa-ap-pu-wa-aš kat-ta-an pa-a-it*

196. KUB IX 27+ I 41 ff. (Paškuwatti’s ritual against sexual impotence)
nu-za ma-a-an ú-e-el-lu-ú-i nu-za ma-a-an ha-a-ri-ya / *ku-wa-pí-it-za kat-ta-an aš-šu-li e-hu* / *an-tu-uh-ši kat-ta-an aš-šu-li e-hu*

---

76 Accusative for Nominative.
77 Lit. „cold“, here: „heartless, cruel“.

197. KUB XIII 4 III 44 (Instructions for the priests and temple officials)
an-da-ma-za pa-ah-hu-u-e-na-aš-ša ud-da-ni-i me-ik-ki na-ah-ha-an-te-eš e-eš-tin

198. KBo X 33+ III 7' f. (KI.LAM festival)
LUGAL-*uš šu-up-pa-ya-aš* ^{GIŠ}NÁ-*aš* / *pa-iz-zi*

199. KUB XVII 27 III 7 (Ritual for Hannahanna)
nu pa-ah-hur ú-e-te-ni-it ki-iš-ta-nu-zi

200. KUB XVII 10 I 26 (Myth of Telipinu)
ha-a-ri-i-uš-kán hal-lu-wa-mu-uš ša-a-ah hu-wa-an-hu-eš-šar-kán ku-wa-a-li-ú ša-a-ah

201. KUB XXIV 3+ II 55 f. (Muršili's prayer to the sun goddess of Arinna)
na-aš-ta li-e / *a-aš-ša-u-e-eš i-da-a-la-u-wa-aš an-da*[78] *har-kán-zi*

202. KUB VII 53+ I 27(Tunnawi's ritual)
na-aš ma-ah-ha-an wa-ap-pu-i a-ri nu 1 NINDA.SIG *wa-ap-pu-wa-aš* ^{D}MAH *pár-ši-ya*

78 Here: „together with".

2.1.3. Nominal word formation

2.1.3.1. Secondary nouns

Hittite has a number of productive suffixes at its disposal which, combined with other words, can form nouns.

Lit.: Friedrich 1960: 38 ff.; Oettinger 1986, 1987.

-āi	*nomina actionis*
-al(l)a	expressions of affiliation, *nomina agentis*
-alli	expressions of affiliation, *nomina instrumenti*
-an	abstract nouns
-att	abstract nouns
-ašti	abstract nouns
-ātar	abstract nouns
-ēl	abstract nouns, *nomina actionis/instrumenti*
-eššar	*nomina rei actae, nomina actionis*
-ima	abstract nouns
-šha	abstract nouns
-tara	*nomina agentis*
-talla	*nomina agentis*
-ul	abstract nouns, *nomina instrumenti*
-ur	abstract nouns
-uzzi	*nomina instrumenti*
-zēl	*nomina actionis*

203. KUB XXXIII 120+ I 12 f. (Myth of Kummarbi)
10-*ti-ma* MU-*ti* / ^{D}*A-la-lu-u-i* ^{D}*A-nu-uš me-na-ah-ha-an-da* ***za-ah-ha-in***
pa-iš tar-ah-ta-an-za-an ^{D}*A-la-lu-un*

204. KBo III 22 rev. 64 (Proclamation of Anitta)
ú-e-it-ta-an-da-an-ni-eš-ši-ma ^{URU}*Ša-la-ti-wa-ra* ***za-ah-hi-ya*** *pa-a-un*

205. KUB XIV 10+ III 41' ff. (Plague prayer of Muršili II)
nu-kán ki-e-uš[79] *ku-i-e-eš* LÚ^{MEŠ} NÍG.SI.SÁ /
$^{\mathrm{LÚ.MEŠ}}$***iš-pa-an-tu-uz-zi-ya-li-e-eš*** *te-e-pa-u-e-eš* / *a-aš-ša-an-te-eš*
na-at-mu li-e ak-kán-zi

206. KUB XIII 9+ III 6 f. (Instruction of Tuthaliya)
^{LÚ}AGRIG-*ma* $^{\mathrm{LÚ.MEŠ}}$***ha-at-tal-wa-la-aš*** / ^{LÚ}APIN.LÁ-*aš* LUGAL-*wa-aš*
ÉSAG-*an PA-NI* ZI-*ŠU li-e ku-iš-ki ki-nu-uz-zi*[80]

207. KBo IV 9 V 18 f. (AN.TAH.ŠUM festival)
^{É}*hi-i-li-ma-kán* ***zé-ri-ya-al-li*** / GADA-*it wa-aš-ša-an-ta ka-ru-ú ar-ta*

208. KUB I 13+ I 43 ff. (Kikkuli's hippological texts)
ma-ah-ha-an-ma-aš[81] EGIR-*pa u-un-na-i na-aš ar-ha* / *la-a-an-zi*
na-aš-kán aš-nu-zi nu-uš-ma-aš ***pu-ri-ya-al-li*** / *da-a-i na-aš A-NA* ^{GIŠ}GAG
ša-ra-a hu-it-ti-ya-zi

209. Mşt. 75/16 rev. 18 ff. (Letter)
ka-a-ša-wa / $^{\mathrm{LÚ.MEŠ}}$***ša-pa-ša-al-li-e-eš*** / *AŠ-PUR nu-wa* ^{URU}*Ma-la-az-zi-an*
/ ^{URU}*Tág-ga-aš-ta-an-na* / *ša-ú-ši-ya-ar*

210. KUB XIII 3 III 18 ff. (Instructions for the palace servants)
ták-ku ša-a-na-at-te-e-ni-ma[82] *ap-pí-iz-zi-ya-an-ma-at* / *iš-tu-wa-a-ri*
nu-uš-ma-aš QA-DU DAM^{MEŠ}-*KU-NU* / DUMU^{MEŠ}-*KU-NU i-da-a-lu*
hi-in-kán *pí-ya-an-zi*

79 Accusative for nominative.

80 As the negation *lē* is prohibitive, the verb form should be translated as modal: „may" or „are allowed to open".

81 Here and in the following three instances of *na-aš* the nominative is used for the accusative. The pronouns refer to horses.

82 Refers to a ritual infringement in the palace.

211. KUB XV 17+ III 41 (Vow of Puduhepa)
ki-i É^{TUM} ***hi-in-ga-na-za*** *ta-ma-aš-ša-an*

212. KUB XVII 10 IV 6 f. (Myth of Telipinu)
nam-ma-ya am-me-el ŠA LÚ.U$_{19}$.LU *ut-ta-na-an-te-eš* ^{D}*Te-li-pí-nu-i* /
kar-pí-in ***kar-di-mi-ya-at-ta-an*** *ša-a-u-ar QA-TAM-MA a-ra-an-du*

213. KBo XVII 74+ II 28 (Ritual of storm and thunder)
LUGAL-*uš-za* ***a-ni-ya-at-ta*** *da-a-i ta-aš-ta pa-ra-a pa-iz-zi*

214. KUB XXXVIII 1 IV 10 (Description of a cult inventory)
pár-qa-aš-ti *ŠA* 1 SIG.KÙŠ[83]

215. KUB XXXIII 106+ I 21 (Myth of Ullikummi)
pal-ha-aš-ti-iš*-ma-aš-ši*[84] 9 *LI-IM* DANNA[85]

216. KBo III 1+ IV 31 f. (Proclamation of Telipinu)
ku-iš-za ha-aš-ša-an-na-an iš-tar-na ***al-wa-an-za-tar*** *ša-ak-ki*
šu-me-e-ša-an / ha-aš-ša-an-na-an-za e-ip-tin na-an A-NA KÁ É.GAL
ú-wa-te-it-tin

217. KUB I 1+ IV 23 f. (Apology of Hattušili III)
nu-za ŠA ^{D}*IŠTAR* ***pa-ra-a ha-an-da-an-da-tar*** *a-pí-ya / me-ik-ki*
u-uh-hu-un[86]

218. KBo XIII 109 II 11' ff. (Ambazzi's ritual)
HUL-*u-wa-aš-ša* UN^{MEŠ}-*aš AN-ZI-EL-LU* /
hur-ki-la-za *pa-ap-ra-an-na-za / mu-la-at-na-za* / NÍ.TE LUGAL
QA-TAM-MA pár-ku-eš-du

219. KUB XII 34+ I 22 f. (Maštigga's ritual)
na-at[87]*-ša-ma-aš-kán* ^{MUNUS}ŠU.GI *ar-ha da-a-i / nu-uš-ma-aš-kán* ***šu-ú-il***
ar-ha túh-ša-ri

220. KUB I 1+ IV 52 f. (Apology of Hattušili III)
$^{LÚ.MEŠ}$*TE-ME-ya-mu u-i-iš-ki-u-wa-an ti-i-e-ir* ***up-pí-eš-šar***$^{HI.A}$*-ma-mu* /

---

83 Nominal sentence, add „is" in the translation.
84 Possessive dativ.
85 Nominal sentence, add „is" in the translation.
86 „saw" means „experienced" here.
87 „it" is the ritual material.

up-pí-iš-ki-u-wa-an ti-i-e-ir

221. KUB XV 17+ I 31 (Vow of Puduhepa)
ŠA MU.2.KAM ***ma-al-te-eš-šar*** *A-NA* ^{D}*Li-el-wa-ni*[88]

222. KBo III 23 I 5 ff. (Pimpira fragment)
ma-a-na-an / ha-an-da-iš wa-la-ah-zi[89] *zi-ga-an* ***e-ku-ni-mi*** *da-i /*
ták-ku-wa-an[90] ***e-ku-ni-ma-aš*** *wa-la-ah-zi na-an ha-an-da-ši / da-i*

223. KUB XXXIII 118, 12 f. (Myth of the pregnancy of mount Wašitta)
$^{HUR.SAG}$*Wa*$_a$*-a-ši-it-ta-aš túh-ha-a-it* ***túh-hi-ma-an****-ma /* URU-*ri*
^{D}*Ku-mar-bi-iš iš-ta-ma-aš-ta*

224. KUB IV 1+ II 7 ff. (Incantation at the enemy border)
ŠA KUR ^{URU}*Ha-at-ti-kán* DINGIR^{MEŠ} *šu-ma-aš / A-NA* DINGIR^{MEŠ} *ŠA*
KUR ^{URU}*Ga-aš-ga ar-ha Ú-UL / ku-it-ki har-kán-zi*
dam-mi-iš-ha-an*-na-aš-ma-aš / Ú-UL ku-it-ki har-kán-zi*

225. KUB XLIII 50+ rev. 33 ff. (Muršili's speech loss)
na-at GIM-*an a-pí-ya-ya / a-ra-an-zi nu ta-ma-in* GU$_4$ *pu-u-hu-ga-ri-in*
a-pí-e-iz-za / ***ú-nu-wa-aš-ha-za*** *ú-nu-wa-an-da-an na-an-na-an-zi nu*
ta-ma-i-in SUM-*an-zi / nu a-pu-u-uš* ***ú-nu-wa-aš-hu-uš*** *a-pí-e-da-ni IT-TI*
GU$_4$ *pu-u-hu-ga-ri / wa-ar-nu-wa-an-zi*

226. KUB XXX 10 rev. 1 (Kantuzzili's prayer)
^{D}UTU-*uš hu-u-ma-an-da-aš an-tu-uh-ša-aš* ***ú-e-eš-ta-ra-aš*** *zi-ik*[91]

227. KUB I 1+ I 58 ff. (Apology of Hattušili III)
^{LÚ}KÚR^{MEŠ}*-mu-kán /* $^{LÚ.MEŠ}$***ar-ša-na-tal-lu-uš*** ^{D}*IŠTAR* GAŠAN-*YA* ŠU-*i*
da-a-iš / na-aš-za kat-ta-an ar-ha zi-en-na-ah-hu-un

228. KUB XIII 4 III 7 ff. (Instructions for the priests and temple officials)
nam-ma-kán GE$_6$*-az* $^{LÚ.MEŠ}$***ú-e-hi-eš-kat-tal-li-iš*** *da-an-te-eš a-ša-an-du /*
nu GE$_6$*-an hu-u-ma-an-da-an ú-e-hi-eš-kán-du / nu a-ra-ah-za ha-a-li*
$^{LÚ.MEŠ}$***ha-li-ya-at-tal-li-iš*** *uš-kán-du*

---

88 Colophon, not a complete sentence.
89 „beats" means „pesters, plagues" here.
90 = *takku* + *-an* with gliding sound *-w-*.
91 Nominal sentence, add „are" in the translation.

229. KUB XXIV 1 III 2 (Muršili's prayer to Telipinu)
Ù A-NA KUR ^{URU}*Ha-at-ti an-da* ***aš-šu-li*** *ne-iš-hu-ut*

230. KUB XIV 11+ III 30' f. (Plague prayer of Muršili II)
ŠA A-BU-ŠU-kán ***wa-aš-túl*** *A-NA* DUMU-*ŠU a-ri* / *nu-kán am-mu-uq-qa*
ŠA A-BI-YA ***wa-aš-túl*** *a-ar-aš*

231. KUB XIII 3 III 21 ff. (Instructions for the palace servants)
an-da-ma-aš-ma-aš šu-me-eš ku-i-e-eš $^{\text{LÚ.MEŠ}}$A.ÍL.LÁ[92] / *nu-uš-ma-aš*
ú-wi-te-na-aš na-ah-ha-an-te-eš e-eš-tin / *nu ú-wi-ta-ar* ^{GIŠ}***še-ša-ru-li-it***
še-ša-ri-iš-ki-tin

232. KUB XXIX 4 I 6 f. (Ritual for the transfer of the Black Goddess)
$^{\text{LÚ.MEŠ}}$SIMUG-*ma* DINGIR^{LAM} GUŠKIN *i-en-zi A-NA* DINGIR^{LIM}-*ma* /
a-ni-u-ur*-še-it ma-ah-ha-an*[93] *na-an a-ni-ya-u-wa-an-zi*

233. KUB XXIV 3+ II 32 ff. (Muršili's prayer to the sun goddess of Arinna)
nu-uš-ša-an hi-in-kán ***ku-ru-ur*** *ga-aš-ta-an i-da-a-lu-un* / *ta-pa-aš-ša-an*
A-NA KUR ^{URU}*Mi-it-ta-an-ni Ù A-NA* KUR ^{URU}*Ar-za-u-wa* / *tar-na-at-tin*

234. KBo XV 10+ III 62' (Purification ritual for Tuthaliya and Nikalmati)
EGIR-*pa-ma* 3 *pí-e-da-an* ***la-ah-hu-ur-nu-zi*** *da-iš*

235. KUB XXXIII 121 II 7 (Tale of Kešši)
nu-za nam-ma ^{m}*Ki-eš-ši-iš* DINGIR^{MEŠ}-*uš* ^{NINDA}*har-ši-it* ***iš-pa-an-du-uz-zi***
Ú-UL kap-pu-iz-zi

236. KUB XIII 9+ II 16 f. (Instruction of Tuthaliya)
ták-ku EL-LAM-ma ku-iš-ki da-i-ya-zi / *nu da-i-ya-zi-la-aš*
šar-ni-ik-zi-el[94]

237. KBo VI 2+ II 29 f. (Laws, first tablet)
ták-ku MUNUS-*an ku-iš-ki pít-te-nu-uz-zi* EGIR-*an-da-ma-aš-ma-aš*
šar-di-ya-aš pa-iz-zi / *ták-ku* 2 LÚ^{MEŠ} *na-aš-ma* 3 LÚ^{MEŠ} *ak-kán-zi*
šar-ni-ik-zi-il NU.GÁL

92 Nominal sentence, add „are" in the translation.
93 Nominal sentence, add „is" or „is prescribed".
94 Nominal sentence, add „shall follow" or the like.

2.1.3.2. Adjectives

Hittite adjectives inflect like nouns and have no comparative degree. They are used as attributes, predicates and adverbials, the latter being formed from the neutral. Secondary adjectives can be formed with productive suffixes.

Lit.: Friedrich 1960: 40 ff., 127 ff.; Oettinger 1986: 20 ff.; Weitenberg 1984: 77 ff., 381 ff.; Hoffner/Melchert 2008: 51 ff.

-ala	expressions of affiliation
-alli	expressions of affiliation
-ant	expressions of individualisation
-ili	„in the way of, kind of"
-umna	ethnica
-want	„provided with, supplied with"

238. KUB XXXIII 106+ 50' f. (Myth of Ullikummi)
EGIR-*pa-at hi-e-eš-tin* ***an-na-al-la at-ta-al-la hu-u-ha-da-al-la*** / É.^{NA4}KIŠIB$^{HI.A}$

239. KUB XXX 13 I 39 f. (Muršili's prayer to the sun goddess of Arinna)
zi-ik-pát-za ^{D}UTU ^{URU}*A-ri-in-na* ***gi-in-zu-wa-la-aš*** DINGIR^{LUM} *zi-ik / nu gi-in-zu zi-ik-pát da-aš-ki-ši*

240. KUB XXIV 7 II 18 (Hymn to Ištar)
ANŠE-*aš-ma-za* GIM-*an* ***pu-un-tar-ri-ya-li-iš*** *zi-ik*

241. Bo 86/299 I 25 (Bronze tablet, treaty of Tuthaliya IV)
ki-nu-na-aš-ši ^{D}UTU^{ŠI} ***an-na-al-li-in*** ZAG EGIR-*pa te-ih-hu-un*

242. KUB VII 1+ I 1 ff. (Rituals of Ayatarša, Wattiti, & Šušmanniga)
ma-a-an DUMU-*la-aš* / ***al-pa-an-za***[95] *na-aš-ma-aš-ši-kán ga-ra-a-ti-eš a-da-an-te-eš / nu-uš-ši i-na-na-aš* ^{D}UTU-*un ki-iš-ša-an ši-pa-an-ta-ah-hi*

95 Nominal sentence, add „is" and „are" in the following clause after *adanteš*.

243. KBo XIII 34 IV 14’ ff. (Birth omen)
ták-ku MUNUS-*za ha-a-ši nu-uš-ši*[96] ZAG-*an* / GEŠTU-*ŠU* *pár-še-nu-šu-uš* / *ma-an-ni-in-ku-wa-an ki-it-ta-ri* / *I-NA* É LÚ-*kán an-da* / ***mar-la-an-da-an*** / *ha-aš-ša-an-zi*

244. KUB LVII 63 II 4 f. (Ritual to the sun goddess of Arinna)
nu-uš-ma-aš pa-ra-a ne-ya-an-ta-an / ***tar-hu-i-li-in*** ^{GIŠ}ŠUKUR *pa-iš*

245. KUB XXIV 8+ I 36 f. (Story of Appu)
MUNUS-*an-za-wa-za* **MUNUS-*ni-li-ya-az*** *zi-ik* / *nu-wa Ú-UL ku-it-ki ša-ak-ti*

246. KBo III 42 rev. 6’ (Chronicle of Puhanu)
na-at ^{URU}***Uš-šu-um-na-aš*** ^{LÚ}*ša-la-aš-hi me-mah-hu-un*

247. KBo VI 2+ I 53 ff. (Laws, first tablet)
ták-ku ARAD LÚ ^{URU}***Lu-i-um-na-aš*** *IŠ-TU* KUR ^{URU}*Lu-ú-i-ya-az ku-iš-ki ta-a-i-iz-zi* / *na-an A-NA* KUR ^{URU}*Ha-at-ti ú-wa-te-iz-zi iš-ha-aš-ši-ša-an ga-ni-eš-zi* / *nu-za* ARAD-*ZU-pát da-a-i šar-ni-ik-zi-il* NU.GÁL

248. KUB LVII 63 II 16 ff. (Ritual to the sun goddess of Arinna)
nu tu-wa-ad-du ne-pí-ša-aš / ^{D}UTU-*u-i ma-iš-za-aš-ti-iš ku-e-el* / ***mi-iš-ri-wa-an-za***[97] *ha-ap-pár-nu-wa-aš-hi-eš* / *ku-e-el* ***la-lu-uk-ki-u-wa-an-te-eš***

249. KUB XXIV 8+ I 25 f. (Story of Appu)
ša-aš-ta-aš-ša-an / ^{GIŠ}NÁ-*aš* ***šar-ku-wa-an-za*** *še-eš-ki-it*

EXERCISES

250. KUB XII 34+ II 33 f. (Maštigga’s ritual)
nu ki-iš-ša-an me-ma-a-i pa-ra-a-wa-ra-an-kán al-la-pa-ah-tin / *a-pí-e-el* UD.KAM-*aš hur-ti-ya-aš*

251. KBo III 8 III 6 ff. (Rituals of Ayataréa, Wattiti, & Šušmanniga)
pár-ti-an-za ha-a-ra-aš^{MUŠEN} / *ha-mi-ik-ta ša-ma-an-ku-úr-wa-du-uš-kán* MUŠ$^{\text{HI.A}}$-*uš* / *an-da hu-u-la-liš-ni ha-mi-ik-ta*

---

96 Possessive, refers to the newborn child.
97 Nominal sentence, add „is“ in the translation.

252. KBo XIII 109 III 6 ff. (Ambazzi's ritual)
^{GIŠ}*ha-at-tal-wa-an-za* GIM-*an* / ^{GIŠ}SAG.KUL EGIR-*pa na-an-na-a-i* / ^{GIŠ}IG-*ya* EGIR-*pa hi-eš-ki-iz-zi* / LUGAL-*i-ya* HUL-*u-wa-aš* UN^{MEŠ} *AN-ZI-EL-LU* / *hur-ki-il pa-ap-ra-tar mu-la-a-tar* / *QA-TAM-MA ar-ha a-ra-id-du*

253. KUB XXVIII 5 (+) II 14 (Story of the moon that fell from heaven)
e-ip-ta-an na-ah-ša-ra-az e-ip-ta-an ú-e-ri-te-ma-aš

254. KBo XVII 65 obv. 13 (Birth ritual)
hur-li-li-ma-kán ma-ah-ha-an an-da me-ma-i na-at ha-an-ti tup-pí[98]

255. KUB XIV 8 I 40' (Plague prayer of Muršili II)
nu-za-kán ka-a-ša A-NA PA-NI ^{D}IM *wa-aš-túl tar-na-ah-hu-un*

256. KUB XXIV 8+ I 9 ff. (Story of Appu)
nu-kán še-ir LÚ-*aš*[99] / ^{m}*Ap-pu ŠUM-an-še-it*[100] KUR-*e-kán iš-tar-na a-pa-a-aš* / *ha-ap-pí-na-an-za*[101]

257. KBo XII 126+ I 16 f. (Malli's ritual)
ma-a-na-an MUNUS-*ma i-ya-an har-zi*[102] *na-an zi-ik* ^{D}UTU-*uš ša-ak-ti*[103] / *na-at-ši* ^{TÚG}*ku-ri-eš-šar e-eš-du na-at-ša-an I-NA* SAG.DU-*ŠU ši-ya-an har-du*

98 Add „is written" or the like.
99 Nominal sentence, add „is".
100 Naming parenthesis: „Appu his name".
101 Hittite has no morphological graduation, but this *happinanza* is obviously used as a superlative.
102 Here: „has treated him with black magic". According to the Hittite laws black magic is strictly forbidden, but it is allowed to send the spell back to the person responsible.
103 *na-an zi-ik ... ša-ak-ti* is a parenthesis.

2.2. The Verb

2.2.1. The conjugation of the verb

There are two conjugations classes to inflect Hittite verbs which are called *mi-* and *hi- c*onjugations according to the endings of the 1.sg.pres.act. As the endings of the paradigms do not generally differ, they are treated together. Originally the *hi-* inflection goes back to the Indo-European perfect but, for the synchronical examination, the assignment of verbs to certain inflection classes cannot easily be inferred. Therefore, sometimes mixing of both conjugation classes occurs.

Hittite shows three persons and two *numeri*, singular and plural. There are only two *tempora*, present and preterite. The present can render the future, and concluded anteriority can also be expressed by participial constructions (see 2.2.4.2.).

The two *modi* are indicative and imperative. It should be noted that prohibitive constructions are formed with the negation *lē*, with the verb in the indicative (see 2.4.4.1.). For the expression of modal conditions there is a particle construction with *man*, that can render *irrealis* and *potentialis* (see 2.4.5.). Finally, beside the active there is a medium (mediopassive) which can be reflexive or passive. *media tantum* occur, too.

From a diachronic point of view the Hittite verb is slightly strange, because it is extremely reduced in the grammatical categories, compared with Indo-European. Especially the loss of the perfect, aorist and optative is unusual, but of course there is a lot of discussion about the possible relics of such formations.

Lit.: Friedrich 1960: 73 ff.; Neu 1968a and 1968b; Eichner 1975; Cowgill 1979; Oettinger 1992, 2002; Hoffner/Melchert 2008: 173 ff.

2.2.1.1. Present active

	mi- conjugation	*hi-* conjugation
1.sg.	*-mi*	*-hi*
2.sg.	*-ši*	*-ti*
3.sg.	*-zi*	*-i*[104]
1.pl.	*-weni*[105], *-wani*	
2.pl.	*-teni*, *-tani*	
3.pl.	*-anzi*	

1.a. 1.sg.pres.act. *mi-* conjugation: *-mi*

258. KUB I 1+ IV 14 f. (Apology of Hattušili III)
ki-nu-na-ya-wa-ra-an ***kar-ap-mi*** *nu-wa-ra-an A-NA* ^{D}UTU ^{URU}PÚ-*na* / *AŠ-ŠUM* ^{LÚ}SANGA-*UT-TIM* ***ti-it-ta-nu-mi***

259. KUB XV 17+ III 42 (Vow of Puduhepa)
na-at ***pu-nu-uš-mi*** *na-at-kán an-da* ***šar-ni-ik-mi***

260. KBo III 7 I 25 f. (Myth of Illuyanka)
ma-a-wa[106] *kat-ti-ti* ***še-eš-mi***[107] *nu-wa* ***ú-wa-mi*** / *kar-di-aš-ta-aš*[108] ***i-ya-mi***

261. KUB XXIX 1 I 20 (Foundation ritual)
ú-ga tu-e-el pár-na Ú-UL ***ú-wa-a-mi***

---

104 With *hi-* verbs ending with *–iya, -i* disappears in the 3.sg. ending, e.g. *paršiya-* „to crumble" : 3.sg.pres.act. *paršiya* (< **paršiyai*).

105 Beside /*u*/, /*w*/ is dissimilated to /*m*/. This is why verbs ending with °-*u*- show the 1.pl. -*meni*, e.g. *arnu-* „ to bring" : 1.pl.pres.act. *arnumeni.*

106 Assimilation of *mān* + *-wa*.

107 „sleep" means „have sexual intercourse" here, with the same euphemism as we have in modern languages.

108 So called „supended genitive": „that of your heart" = „your wish".

262. KUB XXXI 4+ obv. 8 f. (Chronicle of Puhanu)
*ta **za-ah-hi-iš-ki-mi** / ta-a ut-ne-e **har-ni-ik-mi***

1.b. 1.sg.pres.act. *hi- c*onjugation: *-hi*

263. KUB XIV 8 II 34' ff. (Plague prayer of Muršili II)
*na-aš-ma-kán ma-a-an / am-mu-uk-ma ku-it-ki šar-ni-ik-zi-el ha-an-ti iš-hi-ya-at-te-e-ni / na-at-mu te-eš-ha-az me-mi-eš-tin nu-uš-ma-ša-at **pí-ih-hi***

264. KBo V 3+ I 33 (Treaty with Hukkanā of Hayasa)
nu-ut-ta ^{D}UTU^{ŠI}*-ya aš-šu-li **pa-ah-ha-aš-hi***

265. KUB XIII 35+ II 5 (Law court records)
ANŠE.GÌR.NUN.NA$^{HI.A}$ É.GAL^{LIM}*-ma-wa-za am-mu-uk* EGIR*-pa* ***da-ah-hi***

266. KUB XIII 3 III 16 f. (Instructions for the palace servants)
LUGAL*-ša-at* ^{LÚ}*a-ra-a-ah-ze-e-ni-ma **up-pa-ah-hi** / na-aš-ma-at A-NA* ARAD ***pí-ih-hi***

267. KUB VII 1+ I 4 f. (Rituals of Ayataršа, Wattiti, & Šušmanniga)
ha-an-te-iz-zi-kán UD*-ti* ^{UDU}*i-ya-an-ta-an i-na-na-aš* ^{D}UTU*-i* / ***ši-pa-an-ta-ah-hi***

2.a. 2.sg.pres.act. *mi- c*onjugation: *-ši*

268. KUB XVII 4+ 5' (Song of Silver)
*nu-wa-na-aš-kán ku-wa-at **ku-wa-aš-ki-ši***

269. KUB XXIII 1+ II 29 f. (Treaty with Šaušgamuwa)
nu zi-iq-qa ku-at-qa / ŠA ^{m}*Ma-aš-tu-ri i-wa-ar **i-ya-ši***

270. Mşt. 75/25 rev. 16 f. (Letter)
*ki-nu-na-mu nam-ma / Ú-UL ku-it-ki **ha-at-ra-a-ši***

271. KUB XXIII 1+ II 6 (Treaty with Šaušgamuwa)
ta-ma-i-za EN-*UT-TA* *li-e* ***i-la-li-ya-ši***

272. KBo III 7 III 10 ff. (Myth of Illuyanka)
ma-a-an-wa A-NA É DAM-*KA* ***pa-a-i-ši*** / *nu-wa-aš-ma-aš-ta* ^{UZU}ŠÀ *ša-ku-wa-ya* / *ú-e-ik*[109]

2.b. 2.sg.pres.act. *hi-* conjugation: *-ti*

273. KBo VI 34+ III 36 (First military oath)
nu-uš-ma-aš IM.ŠU.NÍG.RIN.NA *pí-ra-an kat-ta* ***da-it-ti***

274. KBo III 1+ II 45 (Proclamation of Telipinu)
ha-aš-ša-an-na-ša-an-za-kán li-e ku-in-ki ***ku-en-ti*** *Ú-UL* SIG_5-*in*[110]

275. KUB I 16+ III 52 f. (Political testament of Hattušili I)
ma-a-an-ga-an / *pa-ra-a* ***na-it-ti*** *i-da-a-lu-ma-an ka-ru-ú-i-li-iš*[111]

276. KUB XXIII 1+ IV 15 f. (Treaty with Šaušgamuwa)
a-pí-el-ma-kán ^{LÚ}DAM.GÀR / ŠÀ KUR-*KA* *li-e* ***tar-na-at-ti***

277. KBo V 3+ III 23 f. (Treaty with Hukkanā of Hayasa)
zi-ga-aš-ma-ša-at ma-a-an ***pa-it-ti*** **EGIR-*pa*** ***me-ma-at-ti***[112] / *ne-it-ta* *ŠA-PAL NI-IŠ* DINGIR^{LIM} GAR-*ru*

3.a. 3.sg.pres.act. *mi-* conjugation: *-zi*

278. KBo III 1+ I 8 f. (Proclamation of Telipinu)
ma-a-na-aš la-ah-ha-az-ma EGIR-*pa* ***ú-iz-zi*** / *nu* DUMU^{MEŠ}-*ŠU* *ku-iš-ša ku-wa-at-ta ut-ne-e* ***pa-iz-zi***

109 The sun god has lost his heart and eyes in a fight with the dragon Illuyanka and wants both back.
110 Nominal sentence, but in this case one could translate a laconic „not good!“.
111 Nominal sentence in the irrealis, as the particle *man* indicates, add „would be“.
112 The first verb could be periphrastic: „go and tell“, or final „go to tell“.

279. KBo III 1+ II 34 f. (Proclamation of Telipinu)
ki-it pa-da-la-az URU*Ha-at-tu-ši* / *ha-aš-ša-an-na-aš*[113] DUMU-*an i-da-lu li-e ku-iš-ki* ***i-ya-zi*** *nu-uš-ši-ša-an* GÍR-*an* ***ták-ki-eš-zi***

280. KUB XV 17+ I 46 (Vow of Puduhepa)
2 ANŠE.KUR.RA TUR m*Na-na-ta-al-li nu-u-wa* EGIR-*pa* ***har-zi***

281. KUB XIII 4 III 17 f. (Instructions for the priests and temple officials)
nu-uš-ma-aš te-eš-ha-aš / *li-e* ***e-eš-zi***

282. KBo VI 2+ II 25 f. (Laws, first tablet)
ták-ku MUNUS-*an EL-LUM* LÚAGRIG *na-aš-ma* LÚSIPA ***pít-te-nu-zi*** / *ku-u-ša-ta-aš-ši Ú-UL* ***píd-da-a-iz-zi*** *na-aš I-NA* MU.3.KAM **GÉME-*aš-ša-ri-eš-zi***

3.b. 3.sg.pres.act. *hi*- conjugation: *-i*

283. KUB I 1+ II 30 (Apology of Hattušili III)
D*IŠTAR-mu-kán* GAŠAN-*YA* IGI-*zi pal-ši ŠUM*^{UM} *ki-e-da-ni* KASKAL-*ši* ***hal-za-a-i***

284. KBo VI 2+ I 33 (Laws, first tablet)
ták-ku LÚ.U$_{19}$.LU-*an EL-LAM* KIR$_4$-*še-it ku-iš-ki* ***wa-a-ki*** 1 MA.NA KÙ.BABBAR ***pa-a-i***

285. KUB IX 22 II 25 ff. (Birth ritual)
Ì.DÙG.GA-*ya-aš-ši-iš-ša-an* / SAG.DU-*ŠU* ***la-hu-i*** *A-NA QA-TI-ŠU-ya-aš-ši-iš-ša-an* / SÍG SA$_5$ ***ha-ma-an-ki***

286. KUB LVII 63 I 10 (Ritual to the sun goddess of Arinna)
nu-wa ***me-ma-a-i*** *li-e ku-iš-ki ku-it-ki*

287. KBo III 1+ II 14 f. (Proclamation of Telipinu)
i-da-a-lu-ma-aš-ma-aš-kán li-e ku-iš-ki / ***tág-ga-aš-ši***

4. 1.pl.pres.act. both conjugations: *-weni, -wani*

113 This refers to the royal clan in the capital.

288. KUB XVII 10 I 30 (Myth of Telipinu)
ki-iš-ta-an-ti-it ***har-ku-e-ni***

289. KUB XVII 10 I 29 (Myth of Telipinu)
^{D}IM-*aš* ^{D}NIN.TU-*ni te-e-it ma-ah-ha-an*[114] ***i-ya-u-e-ni***

290. KUB XIII 35+ IV 3 ff. (Law court records)
GIM-*an-ma-wa-ra-at* ***zi-in-nu-um-me-e-ni*** / *nu-wa-ra-at* EGIR-*pa* ***ú-du-um-me-e-ni*** / *nu-wa-ra-at-kán A-NA MI-NU-TI an-da* ***ti-ya-u-e-ni***

291. KUB XVII 21 I 4 f. (Prayer of Arnuwanda and Ašmunikal)
šu-ma-a-aš DINGIR^{MEŠ}-*aš na-ah-ša-ra-at-ta-an* ^{URU}*Ha-at-tu-ša-aš-pát* / KUR-*ya* ***zi-ik-ki-u-wa-ni***

292. KUB XVII 21 II 6 f. (Prayer of Arnuwanda and Ašmunikal)
nu-uš-ma-aš-ša-an / *DI-NAM* ***ar-nu-uš-ki-u-wa-ni***[115]

293. KUB XVII 21 IV 11 f. (Prayer of Arnuwanda and Ašmunikal)
LÚ^{MEŠ} ^{URU}*Ga-aš-ga-ma* ***hal-zi-wa-ni*** *nu-uš-ma-aš* NÍG.BA$^{\text{HI.A}}$ / ***pí-ú-e-ni*** *nam-ma-aš* ***li-in-ga-nu-ma-ni***

5. 2.pl.pres.act. both conjugations: *-tani, -teni*

294. Mşt. 75/66 lower edge 29 f. (Letter)
$^{\text{LÚ.MEŠ}}$*TE-MI-YA-mu ku-wa-at Ú-UL* / ***u-i-eš-ki-it-ta-ni***[116]

295. VBoT 58 I 18 (Myth of the disappearing stormgod)
ki-i ***az-zi-ik-ki-ta-ni ak-ku-uš-ki-it-ta-ni***

296. KUB XVII 21 II 13 (Prayer of Arnuwanda and Ašmunikal)
nu šu-me-eš-pát DINGIR^{MEŠ}-*aš iš-ta-an-za-ni-it* ***še-ik-te-ni***

297. KUB XV 34+ II 34 ff. (Evocatio)
nu ma-a-an 1-*ŠU Ú-UL* ***iš-ta-ma-aš-ta-ni*** / *nu* 2-*ŠU-ma iš-ta-ma-aš-tin nu ma-a-an* 2-*ŠU-ma Ú-UL* ***iš-ta-ma-aš-ta-ni*** / *nu* 3-*ŠU* 4-*ŠU* 5-*ŠU* 6-*ŠU* 7-*ŠU iš-ta-ma-aš-tin*

114 Lit. „how", in English rather: „what".
115 Iterative form: „again and again..."
116 Iterative form: „every time, regularly...", the same in the following example.

298. KUB XIII 4 II 77 (Instructions for the priests and temple officials)
nu NINDA-*an* ***e-iz-za-at-te-ni*** *wa-a-tar-ma* ***e-ku-ut-te-ni***

299. KUB XIII 3 III 13 (Instructions for the palace servants)
ta-ma-a-i-ma li-e ***da-at-te-ni***

6. 3.pl.pres.act. both conjugations: *-anzi*

300. KUB IV 1+ I 8 f. (Incantation at the enemy border)
1 UDU-*ma-kán A-NA* ^{D}*Zi-it-ha-ri-ya* / ***ši-ip-pa-an-da-an-zi***

301. KUB IV 1+ III 7 (Incantation at the enemy border)
nu ^{UZU}Ì NINDA-*an ar-ha* ***a-da-an-zi***

302. KUB IV 1+ III 13 (Incantation at the enemy border)
na-at EGIR-*pa tu-uz-zi-ya* ***ú-wa-an-zi***

303. KBo XV 2 I 5' f. (Substitution ritual for the king)
ar-ha-ya-an-ma a-pí-ya-pát ma-an-ni-in-ku-wa-an ^{É}*kip-pa-an* / ***i-ya-an-zi***

304. KBo IV 10+ obv. 10' f. (Treaty with Ulmitešub)
É^{TUM}*-ma-aš-ši-kán* / KUR^{TUM}*-ya li-e* ***da-an-zi*** *na-at da-me-e-el*
NUMUN-*aš li-e* ***pí-ya-an-zi***

EXERCISES

305. KBo V 3+ II 37 (Treaty with Hukkanā of Hayaša)
nu-wa Ú-UL ku-it-ki me-ma-ah-hi i-ya-mi-ya-wa Ú-UL ku-it-ki

306. KBo V 3+ I 35 f. (Treaty with Hukkanā of Hayaša)
nu ma-a-an SIG$_5$*-in ku-wa-pí iš-ša-at-ti nu* ^{D}UTU^{ŠI} *aš-šu-li pa-ah-ha-aš-ti*
/ *nu-ut-ta* ^{D}UTU^{ŠI} *kat-ta-ya A-NA* DUMU^{MEŠ}*-KA* SILIM.BI *i-ya-mi*

307. KUB XVII 5 I 18 ff. (Myth of Illuyanka)
ma-a-wa[117] *gi-im-ra* / *pa-i-mi zi-ig-ga-wa-ra-aš-ta* ^{GIŠ}*lu-ut-ta-an-za* /
ar-ha li-e a-ut-ti

---

117 = *mān=wa.*

308. KBo VI 2+ I 6 f. (Laws, first tablet)
ták-ku LÚ-*an na-aš-ma* MUNUS-*an EL-LAM wa-al-ah-zi ku-iš-ki na-aš a-ki ki-eš-šar-ši-iš / wa-aš-ta-i*[118] *a-pu-u-un ar-nu-zi*

309. KBo VI 2+ I 10 (Laws, first tablet)
ták-ku ^{LÚ}DAM.GÀR ^{URU}*Ha-at-ti ku-iš-ki ku-en-zi* 1 *ME* MA.NA KÙ.BABBAR *pa-a-i*[119]

310. KUB XXXI 4+ obv. 14 (Chronicle of Puhanu)
a-ru-na-an tar-ma-a-mi nu a-ap-pa na-at-ta la-a-hu-i

311. KBo XVI 47 obv. 16' ff. (Treaty)
ku-it-ma-an-wa ha-an-ne-eš-šar / ar-ha na-a-ú-i a-ri-ya-u-e-ni nu-wa ^{D}UTU$^{\textit{ŠI}}$ *tu-el* KUR-*i / Ú-UL pár-ah-zi*

312. KUB XIII 9+ III 9 f. (Instruction of Tuthaliya)
ma-a-an Ú-UL-ma / ú-wa-da-te-e-ni nu ÉSAG-*an* LÚ^{MEŠ} URU$^{\textit{LIM}}$ *šar-ni-in-kán-zi*

2.2.1.2. Present medium

The medium (or mediopassive) is a *diathesis* which is used to render all events where the *agens* is not known or mentioned, or where the subject is the affected *patiens*. These can be both passive expressions in the strict sense (*Peter is being beaten*) or the so-called anti-causative where the *agens* is simply not mentioned (*the door opens*), and also events where the subject is less *agens* but rather a *patiens* affected by the verbal action (*the glass breaks*).

Lit.: Friedrich 1960: 135 ff.; Neu 1968a, 1968b; Eichner 1975; Oettinger 1976; Yoshida 1990; Hoffner/Melchert 2008: 230 ff.

---

118 Add another „if" in the translation. The „sin of the hand" means an accident in contrast to a planed murder.

119 Modal: „must give".

	mi- conjugation	*hi-* conjugation
1.sg.	*-ha, -hari*	
2.sg.	*-ta, -tati, -tari*	
3.sg.	*-ta, -tari*	*-a, -ari*
1.pl.	*-wašta, -waštati*[120]	
2.pl.	*-duma, -dumari*[121]	
3.pl.	*-anta, -antari*	

1. 1.sg.pres.med. both conjugations: *-ha, -hari*

313. KUB XXXVI 75 III 14 f. (Kantuzzili's prayer)
du-ud-du-wa-ra-an-za-kán LÚ-*aš ma-ah-ha-an pít-te-ya-u-wa-ar*
pí-eš-ši-ya-nu-un nu-uš-ša-an nam-ma da-an-ku-wa-i ta-ka-an-zi-pí[122]
ka-ru-ú-i-li-ya-at-ta Ú-UL / ***ú-e-ha-ah-ha***

314. KBo XXII 2 rev. 15' (Tale of Zalpa, A)
ú-uk-wa LUGAL-*uš-mi-iš* ***ki-iš-ha***

315. KBo III 1+ I 35 (Proclamation of Telipinu)
nu-wa-kán ***pa-ah-ha-aš-ha***[123]

316. KBo XI 11 I 4 (Uruwanda's ritual)
na-aš-ta ^{UZU}SA *A-NA* GI *an-da* ***hu-it-tah-ha-ri***

317. KBo XVI 98 II 11 ff. (Oracle)
nu-kán GIM-*an* ^{D}UTU$^{\check{S}I}$ *IŠ-TU* KUR ^{URU}*Kum-ma-an-ni* UGU *a-ar-hi* /

120 In the table of verbal endings in Oettinger 2002: 521, the forms *-wasta* and *-wastari* are given for the 1.pl.med.; however, after the list of Yoshida 1990: 181 ff., the expected *-wastari* is not attested. Accordingly, the only attested variant to *-wasta* is the secondary form *-wastati*.

121 This form is rarely attested and thus only two suitable example could be found.

122 „dark earth" is a traditional epitheton.

123 Interrogative clause.

nu-za-kán LUGAL-*iz-na-an-ni* ***e-eš-ha-ha-ri***[124] *nam-ma-za* EZEN$_4^{\text{MEŠ}}$ / DÙ-*mi*

318. KUB V 1 III 54 f. (Hattušili's III oracle questions about the campaign in Gaška areal)
ki-nu-na-ya QA-TAM-MA ki-e-da-ni-za-kán LÍL-*ri* / *ku-wa-tin im-ma ku-wa-tin* ***ne-ya-ah-ha-ri*** *nu-mu pí-an hu-u-i-ya-ši*

2. 2.sg.pres.med. both conjugations: *-ta, -tati, -tari*

319. KUB XXXIII 120+ I 28 f. (Myth of Kummarbi)
A-NA PA-NI ŠÀ-*KA-wa-az* / ***du-uš-ki-iš-ki-it-ta*** LÚ-*na-tar-mi-it-wa ku-it pa-aš-ta*[125]

320. KUB XXIX 1 I 11 f. (Foundation ritual)
LÚ^{MEŠ}-*aš-mi-iš* / *li-e* ***ki-iš-ta*** *ga-a-i-na-aš-mi-iš li-e* ***ki-iš-ta***

321. KBo V 9 I 32 f. (Treaty of Muršili II with Duppi-Tešub of Amurru)
nu-za-kán da-me-e-da-ni IGI$^{\text{HI.A}}$-*wa li-e* / ***ne-ya-at-ta-ti***

322. KBo X 13 (+) II 21 f. (Treaty with Aziru of Amurru)
nu ma-a-an zi-ik ^{m}*A-zi-ra-aš IŠ-TU* ÉRIN^{MEŠ} ANŠE.KUR.RA^{MEŠ} *ša-ku-wa-aš-ša-ri-it* ZI-*ni-it Ú-UL* ***ne-ni-ik-ta-ti*** [...][126] / *nu-kán ka-a-aš-ma MA-ME-TUM šar-ra-at-ti*

323. KUB XXXII 130 obv. 29 f. (Muršili's prayer)
I-NA KUR ^{LÚ}KÚR-*ya ku-wa-pí pa-i-mi* / *nu-mu kat-ti-mi aš-šu-li* ***ar-ta-ri***

324. KUB XXXII 130 obv. 27 f. (Muršili's prayer)
A-NA ^{D}UTU$^{\check{S}I}$-*kán an-da aš-šu-li* / ***na-iš-ta-ri*** *kat-ti-mi aš-šu-li* ***ar-ta-ri***

3.a. 3.sg.pres.med. *mi-* conjugation: *-ta, -tari*

124 „sit down to kingdom" means „be enthroned".
125 In the myth Kummarbi bites off and swallows the genitals of his father Anu and becomes pregnant thereof; in the quote Anu is speaking. Cf. example 115.
126 Abridged example.

325. KUB XVII 10 IV 27 f. (Myth of Telipinu)
^{D}*Te-li-pí-nu-wa-aš pí-ra-an* / ^{GIŠ}*e-ya* ***ar-ta***

326. KUB XXX 19+ I 1 f. (Funerary ritual)
ma-a-an I-NA UD.12.KAM ***lu-uk-kat-ta*** ALAM-*kán nu-u-wa* É-*ri an-da* /
nu-kán A-NA ALAM 1 GU$_4$.NIGA 7 UDU$^{\text{HI.A}}$-*ya ši-pa-an-da-an-zi*

327. KBo XI 14 IV 8 (Hantitaššu's ritual)
UD.9.KAM ***túh-hu-uš-ta***

328. KUB XIII 8 obv. 8 (Instruction of Queen Ašmunikal)
Ì-*an-ma-kán* ***la-hu-wa-ta-ri*** *a-pu-uš*[127]*-ma-kán pa-ra-a li-e ú-wa-an-zi*

329. KUB XV 17+ III 39 (Vow of Puduhepa)
A-NA ^{GIŠ}TUKUL-*ma-aš-ši* ^{LÚ}NINDA.DÙ.DÙ ***ar-ta-ri***

330. Bo 86/299 II 89 (Bronze tablet, treaty of Tuthaliya IV)
nu a-pa-a-aš me-mi-ya-aš Ú-UL ***da-at-ta-ri***

3.b. 3.sg.pres.med. *hi* -conjugation: *-a, -ari*

331. KBo VI 2+ IV 21 (Laws, first tablet)
ták-ku-an Ú-UL-ma pa-a-i na-aš ^{LÚ}NÍ.ZU-*aš* ***ki-i-ša***

332. KUB X 88 VI 5 f. (Ritual for the stormgod of Nerik)
LUGAL-*uš* ^{É}*ha-li-in-tu-wa-az* / *ú-iz-zi* ^{GIŠ}*hu-u-lu-ga-an-ni* ***e-ša***

333. KUB XXV 36 II 17' f. (Festival ritual for a prince)
^{LÚ}SAGI-*aš ka-an-gur* GEŠTIN / *ú-da-i še-e-ra-aš-ša-an* GAL.GIR$_4$
ki-it-ta

334. KBo III 22 rev. 78 f. (Proclamation of Anitta)
ma-a-an tu-un-na-ki-iš-na-ma pa-iz-zi a-pa-a-ša / *pí-e-ra-am-mi-it*
ku-un-na-az ***e-ša-ri***

335. KUB XXXI 113 14' f. (Fragment of an instruction)
GIM-*an ne-ku-uz-za me-hur* ***ki-ša-ri*** / *nu-kán ša-ša-an-na-aš da-a-i*

---

127 Accusative for nominative.

336. KUB XXV 22 III 12 (Festival ritual of Tuthaliya IV)
hal-zi-ya-ri[128] GAL$^{HI.A}$*-kán aš-ša-nu-wa-an-zi*

4. 1.pl.pres.med. both conjugations: *-wašta, -waštati*

337. KUB XXXI 143 II 36 (Invocatio)
pa-i-wa-ni-wa ***e-šu-wa-aš-ta***

338. KUB XVII 21 IV 5 (Prayer of Arnuwanda and Ašmunikal)
nu DINGIR^{MEŠ}*-aš A-NA* EZEN$_4^{HI.A}$ EGIR*-an-da-pát* ***ar-wa-aš-ta***

339. KUB XII 66 IV 9 f. (Myth of Illuyanka)
ma-a-an-wa A-NA ^{URU}*Ne-ri-iq-qa pa-i-u-wa-ni / nu-wa-aš-ša-an ku-wa-pí* ***e-šu-wa-aš-ta***

340. KUB XXXIII 106+ II 13 (Myth of Ullikummi)
ku-wa-pí-kán an-da-an I-NA $^{HUR.SAG}$*Kán-dur-na še-ir* ***e-šu-wa-aš-ta-ti***

341. KUB XXIV 8+ IV 19 f. (Story of Appu)
nu DINGIR^{MEŠ} GIM*-an ar-ha-ya-an a-ša-an-zi / ú-e-ša-za QA-TAM-MA ar-ha-ya-an* ***e-šu-wa-aš-ta-ti***

342. KBo III 4+ II 13 (Annals of Muršili II)
ki-nu-na-wa e-hu nu-wa ***za-ah-hi-ya-u-wa-aš-ta-ti***

5. 2.pl.pres.med. both conjugations: *-duma, -dumari*

343. KUB I 16+ III 48 f. (Political testament of Hattušili I)
ma-a-an / Ú-UL-ma ***pa-ah-ha-aš-du-ma***[129] KUR*-e-še-me-it ta-me-u-ma-an ki-i-ša-ri*

344. KBo VIII 35 II 14 f. (Treaty with the Gaška)
nu ma-a-an ku-u-uš li-in-ga-a-uš ***pa-ah-ha-aš-du-ma*** */ šu-ma-a-ša* DINGIR^{MEŠ}*-eš pa-ah-ša-an-da-ru*

---

128 Ritual calls are part of many ceremonies, but the text sometimes leave out *what* has been called.

129 *uttar* „word“ has to be added as an object.

345. KUB I 16+ II 49 (Political testament of Hattušili I)
li-e-ma ***šar-ka-li-ya-tu-ma-ri***

346. KBo XXII 2 obv. 19 (Tale of Zalpa, A)
nu li-e ***ša-li-ik-tu-ma-ri***

6. 3.pl.pres.med. both conjugations: *-anta, -antari*

347. KBo XVII 74+ IV 41’ (Ritual of storm and thunder)
LUGAL *Ù* MUNUS.LUGAL ***e-ša-an-da***

348. KBo XII 126+ III 18’ (Malli’s ritual)
na-at ka-a-ša pí-ra-an-ti ***a-ra-an-ta***

349. KBo XVII 1+ I 24’ f. (Ritual for the royal couple)
ú-e-eš-ša-an-da[130]*-ma* / *iš-har-wa-an-tu-uš* TÚG$^{\text{HI.A}}$*-uš*

350. KBo XIX 128+ I 6 ff. (AN.TAH.ŠUM festival)
ma-ah-ha-an-ma LUGAL*-uš I-NA* É^{TIM}.GAL / a-*ri ha-an-te-iz-z i-az-ma* $^{\text{LÚ.MEŠ}}$ALAM.ZU$_9$ / *ka-ru-ú* ***a-ra-an-ta-ri***

351. KBo XIX 128+ IV 12’ f. (AN.TAH.ŠUM festival)
nu DUMU^{MEŠ}.LUGAL ***e-ša-an-da-ri*** / *nu* $^{\text{LÚ.MEŠ}}$MUHALDIM ÚTUL$^{\text{HI.A}}$ *ti-an-zi*

352. KUB LV 43 I 18 f. (Ritual for a protective god)
ma-ah-ha-an-ma-kán EZEN$_4^{\text{HI.A}}$ ***kar-pa-an-ta-ri*** / *na-aš-ta* 2 ^{KUŠ}*kur-šu-uš* SUMUN^{TIM} *pa-ra-a QA-TAM-MA ne-an-zi*

EXERCISES

353. KUB XXXIII 120+ I 9 f. (Myth of Kummarbi)
da-aš-šu-ša-aš-ši ^{D}*A-nu-uš* DINGIR^{MEŠ}*-aš ha-an-te-iz-zi-ya-aš-me-iš pí-ra-an-še-it* / *ar-ta*

354. KUB XXIV 8+ I 15 ff. (Story of Appu)
nu-uš-ši-pa Ú-UL ku-it-ki wa-aq-qa-ri / *nu-uš-ši-pa-an ut-tar wa-aq-qa-ri*

130 Verb first position is highly marked in Hittite.

DUMU.NITA-*ši* DUMU.MUNUS-*iš* / NU.GÁL

355. KUB XXIV 8+ IV 5 f. (Story of Appu)
ú-e-ša-wa-za šar-ra-u-e-ni[131] *nu-wa-an-na-aš ar-ha-ya-an* /
e-šu-wa-aš-ta-ti

356. KUB XXIX 4 II 14 f. (Ritual for the transfer of the Black Goddess)
I-NA UD.3.KAM-*ma ma-a-an lu-uk-kat-ta nu* EN SÍSKUR
ka-ru-ú-a-ri-wa-ar / *hu-u-da-ak I-NA* É DINGIR^{LIM} *ú-iz-zi* MUL$^{HI.A}$
nu-u-a a-ra-an-da

357. KUB XXIX 4 III 48 (Ritual for the transfer of the Black Goddess)
EN SÍSKUR EGIR-*an i-ya-at-ta-ri*

358. KBo V 1 I 28 f. (Papanikri's ritual)
ma-ah-ha-an-ma ^{UZU}Ì / *zé-e-a-ri nu zé-e-ya-an-te-it*[132] *ši-pa-an-ti*

359. KUB XXX 16+ I 6 f. (Funerary ritual)
DINGIR^{LIM}-*iš-ma-aš ku-e-da-ni* UD-*ti ki-ša-ri*[133] *nu a-pí-e-da-ni* / UD-*ti*
kiš-an i-ya-an-zi

360. KUB I 16+ III 64 f. (Political testament of Hattušili I)
LUGAL.GAL *la-ba-ar-na-aš A-NA* ^{f}*Ha-aš-ta-ya-ar me-mi-iš-ki-iz-zi* /
li-e-ma-mu-uš-ša-an[134] *pa-aš-ku-i-it-ta*

131 As object, „the inheritance“ or something similar has to be added.
132 Add „fat“.
133 „become a god“, said of the king, means „die“.
134 Direct speach, although the particle *-wa(r)* is missing.

2.2.1.3. Preterite active

	mi- conjugation	*hi-* conjugation
1.sg.	*-un*	*-hun*
2.sg.	*-š, -t, -ta*	*-š, -ta, -šta*
3.sg.	*-t, -ta*	*-š, -ta, -šta*
1.pl.	*-wen*	
2.pl.	*-ten*	
3.pl.	*-er*	

1.a. 1.sg.pret.act. *mi-* conjugation: *-un*

361. KBo X 2 I 9 f. (Apology of Hattušili I)
EGIR-*an-da-ma I-NA* ^{URU}*Za-al-pa* ***pa-a-un*** / *na-an* ***har-ni-in-ku-un***

362. KBo XV 10+ II 32 f. (Purification ritual for Tuthaliya and Nikalmati)
iš-ha-na-aš ^{D}UTU-*uš* ^{D}IM-*aš* DINGIR.LÚ^{MEŠ}-*ya qa-a-ša-aš-ma-aš* *aš-šu-la-aš* NINDA.GUR$_4$.RA$^{\text{HI.A}}$ / ***pár-ši-ya-nu-un***

363. KBo III 22 rev. 76 f. (Proclamation of Anitta)
ma-a-an a-ap-pa-ma ^{URU}*Ne-e-ša* ***ú-wa-nu-un*** / *nu* LÚ ^{URU}*Pu-ru-uš-ha-an-da kat-ti-mi* ***pí-e-hu-te-nu-un***

364. KUB XIII 9+ I 2 ff. (Instruction of Tuthaliya)
ma-a-an ^{URU}*A-aš-šu-wa* ***har-ni-in-ku-un*** / *a-ap-pa-ma* ^{URU}*Ha-at-tu-ši* ***ú-wa-nu-un*** / *nu-kán* DINGIR^{MEŠ} ***aš-ša-nu-nu-un***

365. KBo X 2 II 47 f. (Apology of Hattušili I)
LUGAL.GAL-*ma-an-kán* SAG.DU-*ZU* / ***ku-e-ir-šu-un***

1.b. 1.sg.pret.act. *hi-* conjugation: *-hun*

366. KBo III 1+ II 26 (Proclamation of Telipinu)
LUGAL-*uš Ú-UL* ***ša-qa-ah-hu-u-un***[135]

367. KBo III 22 rev. 59 (Proclamation of Anitta)
nu ***ma-a-al-tah-hu-un*** *nu* ***hu-u-wa-ar-tah-hu-un***

368. KBo III 1+ II 30 (Proclamation of Telipinu)
^{GIŠ}TUKUL$^{HI.A}$-*uš-šu-uš-ta* ZAG.UDU-*za* ***da-ah-hu-un*** *nu-uš-ma-aš maš-du-uš* ***pí-ih-hu-un***

369. KBo X 2 II 45 (Apology of Hattušili I)
nu-za KUR ^{URU}*Ha-aš-šu-wa I-NA* MU.1.KAM ***tar-ah-hu-un***

370. KBo X 2 I 19 ff. (Apology of Hattušili I)
a-aš-šu-ma-aš-ši / ša-ra-a ***da-ah-hu-un*** *nu* É-*ir-mi-it a-aš-ša-u-i-it / ša-ra-a* ***šu-un-na-ah-hu-un***

371. KUB XIII 35+ II 33 (Law court records)
GIM-*an-ma-wa-ra-at* ***u-uh-hu-un*** *nu-wa-za-kán še-ir* ***na-a-hu-un***

2.a. 2.sg.pret.act. *mi-* conjugation: *-š*, *-t*, *-ta*

372. KUB XXX 10 obv. 6 (Kantuzzili's prayer)
am-me-el DINGIR-*YA ku-it-mu-za* AMA-*YA ha-a-aš-ta nu-mu am-me-el* DINGIR-*YA* ***ša-al-la-nu-uš***

373. KUB I 1+ III 74 f. (Apology of Hattušili III)
an-ni-ša-an-wa-ra-an LUGAL-*iz-na-an-ni ku-wa-at /* ***ti-it-ta-nu-ut***

374. KUB XXIV 8+ I 33 f. (Story of Appu)
Ú-UL-wa ku-uš-ša-an-qa kat-ta ***e-ip-ta***[136] */ nu-wa ki-nu-un kat-ta* ***e-ip-ta***

375. Mşt. 75/51 obv. 4 ff. (Letter)
ki-i ku-it[137] ***i-ya-aš*** */ na-aš-ta ka-a-ša* ÉRIN$^{MEŠ.HI.A}$ */ pa-ra-a tu-uk-pát / e-eš-zi*[138]

135 Object drop, a pronoun „it" has to be added in the translation.
136 „embrace" meant in a sexual sense.
137 Idiomatic topicalizing cleft sentence: „what (is it), what …" means „this is, what...".
138 Verbs in the singular occur frequently with formally plural ÉRIN^{MEŠ} „troups, soldiers"

376. KUB I 1+ III 68 (Apology of Hattušili III)
šu-ul-li-ya-at-*wa-mu-kán*

377. KUB XXII 70 obv. 55 (Oracle concerning the intrigues at the Hittite court)
nu DINGIR$^{\textit{LIM}}$-*ma* ^{TÚG}*te-ir-ma-az ku-it-ki* ***ša-an-ah-ta***[139]

2.b. 2.sg.pret.act. *hi-* conjugation: *-š*, *-ta*, *-šta*

378. KBo XI 14 I 24 (Hantitaššu's ritual)
nu-za da-pí-uš DINGIR^{MEŠ}-*uš* ***hal-za-a-iš***[140] / *nu-za hu-u-ma-an-da-an* DUMU.LÚ.U$_{19}$.LU-*an* ***hal-za-a-iš***

379. Mşt. 75/66 obv. 16 f. (Letter)
nu a-pí-e NUMUN$^{\text{HI.A}}$ *ku-wa-pí* / ***pa-iš***

380. KBo V 3+ III 56 (Treaty with Hukkanā of Hayaša)
zi-ik-wa-kán a-pu-u-un[141] *an-da ku-wa-at* ***a-uš-ta***

381. KUB XXIV 7 II 5 (Hymn to Ištar)
nu-za LÚ^{MEŠ} *hu-el-pí* GA.RAŠ^{SAR} *i-wa-ar ar-ha* ***ka-ri-ip-ta***

382. KUB XXI 27+ I 4 ff. (Puduhepa's prayer to the sun goddess of Arinna)
nu-za-kán I-NA KUR ^{URU}*Ha-at-ti* ^{D}UTU ^{URU}PÚ-*na ŠUM-an* ***da-iš-ta*** / *nam-ma-ma-za ku-it* KUR-*e* ^{GIŠ}ERIN-*aš i-ya-at* / *nu-za-kán* ^{D}*Hé-pát* *ŠUM-an* ***da-iš-ta***[142]

383. KUB XIII 35+ III 9 f. (Law court records)
1-*NU-TUM* ANŠE.GÌR.NUN.NA$^{\text{HI.A}}$-*wa* / *A-NA* ^{m}*Hi-el-la-ri-iz-zi* ***pí-eš-ta***

384. KUB XV 5 III 11 11 f. (Dream of the queen)
ku-e ^{GIŠ}*hu-hu-pa-a-la* $^{\text{NA4}}$ZA.GÌN-*ya* ***me-mi-iš-ta*** / *ku-wa-at-wa-ra-at-si Ú-UL pí-eš-ta*

3.a. 3.sg.pret.act. *mi-* conjugation: *-t*, *-ta*

139 Interrogative clause.
140 Ritual call.
141 Meaning a female servant of the palace.
142 The sun goddess of Arinna is supposed to be equivalent to the Hurrian Hepat.

385. KUB XXVI 71 IV 9 (Ammuna chronicle)
LUGAL-*uš-ša* EGIR-*pa* ^{URU}*Ha-at-tu-ši* ^{URU}PÚ-*na* ***ú-it***

386. KBo III 7 I 12 f. (Myth of Illuyanka)
^{D}IM-*aš-ta-aš-ša* DINGIR^{MEŠ}-*na-aš hu-u-ma-an-da-aš* / ***mu-ú-ga-it***

387. KBo XV 10+ III 63' (Purification ritual for Tuthaliya and Nikalmati)
nu li-in-ki-ya-aš ^{D}IM *Ù* DINGIR.LÚ^{MEŠ}-*ŠU* 3 NINDA.GUR$_4$.RA
pár-ši-at

388. KBo III 22 obv. 2 (Proclamation of Anitta)
ne-pí-iš-za-aš-ta ^{D}IM-*un-ni a-aš-šu-uš* ***e-eš-ta***

389. KBo III 22 obv. 7 f. (Proclamation of Anitta)
DUMU^{MEŠ} ^{URU}*Ne-e-ša-aš* / *i-da-a-lu na-at-ta ku-e-da-ni-ik-ki* ***ták-ki-iš-ta***

390. KBo III 1+ I 65 (Proclamation of Telipinu)
ha-an-te-iz-zi-uš-ša ARAD^{MEŠ}-*ŠU* ***ku-en-ta***

3.b. 3.sg.pret.act. *hi-* conjugation: *-š*, *-ta*, *-šta*

391. KUB I 1+ III 57 f. (Apology of Hattušili III)
KUR.KUR^{MEŠ}-*ya ku-e dan-na-at-ta am-mu-uk* EGIR-*pa* /
a-še-ša-nu-nu-un *nu-mu-kán a-pí-e-ya hu-u-ma-an-da ar-ha* ***da-a-aš***

392. KBo XXXII 14 II 17 f. (Epos of liberation)
Ú-UL-ma a-li-ya-na-aš[143] *nu*[144] *an-tu-wa-ah-ha-aš* / *a-pa-a-aš* LÚ-*aš*
a-pí-el-kán URU-*az ku-iš ar-ha* ***hu-wa-iš***

393. KBo XXII 2 obv. 1 (Tale of Zalpa, A)
MUNUS.LUGAL ^{URU}*Ka-ni-iš* 30 DUMU^{MEŠ} 1^{EN} MU-*an-ti* ***ha-a-aš-ta***

394. KBo XXXII 13 II 26 f. (Epos of liberation: Festival for Allāni)
ka-ru-ú-li-uš-ma-za DINGIR^{MEŠ}-*uš* / ^{D}IM-*aš* ZAG-*az* ***a-ša-aš-ta***

395. KBo III 38 obv. 27' (Tale of Zalpa, B)
nu-uš-ma-aš ***me-mi-iš-ta*** *ki-i-mu*[145] LUGAL-*uš* ***pa-iš-ta***

143 Nominal sentence, add „is“ in the translation.
144 Here adversative „but“.

396. KBo XXXII 14 II 11 (Epos of liberation)
nu HUR.SAG-*aš a-li-ya-na-an a-ap-pa* ***hu-wa-ar-za-aš-ta***

4. 1.pl.pret.act. both conjugations: *-wen*

397. KBo XXII 2 obv. 14 (Tale of Zalpa, A)
UM-MA-NI-ša-an ***ú-e-mi-ya-u-en***

398. KBo V 3+ I 39 f. (Treaty with Hukkanā of Hayaša)
nu ka-a-ša ki-e-da-ni ud-da-ni-i LI-IM DINGIR^{LIM} / *tu-li-ya* ***hal-zi-ú-en***

399. KUB I 1+ III 4 (Apology of Hattušili III)
nu-un-na-aš DUMU.NITA^{MEŠ} DUMU.MUNUS^{MEŠ} ***i-ya-u-en***

400. KUB XIII 35+ III 25 f. (Law court records)
nu-wa-ra-an-kán dam-mi-eš-ha / *Ú-UL* ***ku-in-nu-um-mi-en***

401. KBo XII 126+ I 25 (Malli's ritual)
na-an-wa ***da-a-ri-ya-u-en*** *nu-wa i-na-an* ***a-ni-ya-u-e-en***

5. 2.pl.pret.act. both conjugations: *-ten*

402. KUB XXXI 4+ obv. 7 (Chronicle of Puhanu)
ku-wa-at ša-ra-am-mu ki-iš-ša-an ***i-ya-at-te-en***

403. KUB IV 1+ II 11 (Incantation at the enemy border)
šu-me-ša DINGIR^{MEŠ} *ŠA* KUR ^{URU}*Ga-aš-ga* ***šu-ul-li-it-te-en***

404. KBo XXII 2 obv. 9 (Tale of Zalpa, A)
ka-a-ni-wa tu-un-na-ak-ki-iš-šar ***i-nu-ut-te-en***

405. KUB XXXI 4+ obv. 10 (Chronicle of Puhanu)
^{URU}*A-ri-in-na*^{KI} *ku-in* ***pí-e-hu-te-it-te-en*** *u-ni hu-ur-ta-li-im-ma-an*[146]

406. KUB XXIX 39 obv. 11' f. (Protocol of a market)
ka-ru-ú ŠA 1 ^{TÚG}*a-tu-up-li* 3 GÍN KÙ.BABBAR *ŠI-IM-ŠU* / ***i-ya-at-te-en***

---

145 Direct speech, although the particle *-wa(r)* is missing.
146 Rhetorical interrogative clause and answer.

407. KUB XXXI 101 obv. 15’ (Letter)
šu-me-ša Á^{MUŠEN} *ku-wa-at Ú-UL* ***hu-u-uš-ki-it-tin***[147]

6. 3.pl.pret.act. both conjugations: *-er*

408. KBo XXII 2 obv. 4 f. (Tale of Zalpa, A)
DINGIR^{DIDLI}*-ša* DUMU^{MEŠ}*-uš* A.AB.BA*-az* / *ša-ra-a* ***da-a-ir*** *šu-uš* ***ša-al-la-nu-uš-kir***

409. KBo XXII 2 obv. 15 f. (Tale of Zalpa, A)
ma-a-an ^{URU}*Ne-e-ša* ***pa-a-ir*** / *nu-uš-ma-aš* DINGIR^{DIDLI}*-eš ta-ma-i-in ka-ra-a-ta-an* ***da-i-ir***

410. KBo III 1+ I 33 (Proclamation of Telipinu)
nu HUL*-lu ut-tar* ***i-e-ir*** *nu-kán* ^{m}*Mur-ši-li-in* ***ku-en-nir***

411. KUB I 1+ IV 27 f. (Apology of Hattušili III)
$^{LÚ.MEŠ}$*Ga-aš-ga*$^{HI.A}$ *ku-i-e-eš ku-u-ru-ur* ***e-še-ir*** / *na-at-mu* EGIR*-an* ***ti-i-e-ir***

412. KUB XVII 5 I 9 f. (Myth of Illuyanka)
na-aš-ta ^{MUŠ}*Il-lu-ya-an-ka-aš QA-DU* DUMU^{MEŠ}*-ŠU* / *ša-ra-a* ***ú-e-ir*** *nu-za* ***e-te-ir e-ku-ir***

EXERCISES

413. KUB I 1+ II 23 f. (Apology of Hattušili III)
nu-kán ^{LÚ}KÚR *I-NA* ^{URU}*Ha-ah-ha da-ma-aš-šu-un* / *na-an za-ah-hi-ya-nu-un*

414. KBo X 2 I 24 (Apology of Hattušili I)
EGIR*-az-ya-za-ma-mu-kán* ^{LÚ}KÚR *ŠA* ^{URU}*Hur-ri* KUR*-e an-da ú-it*

415. KUB I 1+ IV 68 f. (Apology of Hattušili III)
an-na-al-la-an ku-it e-eš-ta a-pa-a-at-ši[148] *pa-ra-a pí-ih-hu-un* / *am-mu-uq-qa ku-it har-ku-un a-pád-da-ya pa-ra-a pí-ih-hu-un*

---

147 Concerning a flight of oracle birds .
148 Meaning Ištar.

416. KUB I 1+ II 26 f. (Apology of Hattušili III)
^{URU}*Ha-at-tu-ša-an-ma ku-in pí-e har-ta na-an-kán ar-ha / da-ah-hu-un na-an hu-u-ma-an-da-an* EGIR-*pa a-še-ša-nu-nu-un*

417. KBo X 2 I 4 f. (Apology of Hattušili I)
I-NA ^{URU}*Ša-na-u-i-it-ta pa-it*[149] *ša-an na-at-ta / har-ni-ik-ta*

418. KUB I 16+ III 10 (Political testament of Hattušili I)
ku-wa-at-mu ki-i te-pu pa-it-ta

419. KUB XXXIII 106+ III 42' f. (Myth of Ullikummi)
ú-e-ir-ma[150] AN-*iš ku-wa-pí te-kán-na* ^{URUDU}*ku-ru-uz-zi-it ar-ha ku-e-ri-ir / nu a-pád-da-ya Ú-UL ša-aq-qa-ah-hu-un*[151]

420. KUB I 1+ II 65 (Apology of Hattušili III)
nu-za ^{LÚ}KÚR^{MEŠ} *ku-i-e-eš*[152] *tar-ah-hu-un ku-i-e-eš-ma-mu ták-šu-la-a-ir*

149 Military context, so it means „marched in".
150 Verb first position is highly marked in Hittite.
151 Ubelluri is speaking, a sort of stone monster with reduced faculty of perception.
152 *kuiš … kuiš* „the one … the other".

2.2.1.4. Preterite medium

	mi- conjugation	*hi-* conjugation
1.sg.	*-h(a)hat, -hati*	
2.sg.	*-tat*[153]	
3.sg.	*-ta, -tat, -tati*	*-at, -ati*
1.pl.	*-waštat*	
2.pl.	*-dumat*	
3.pl.	*-antat, -antati*	

1. 1.sg.pret.med. both conjugations: *-h(a)hat, -hati*

421. KUB I 1+ III 12 (Apology of Hattušili III)
nu-za am-mu-uk LUGAL KUR ^{URU}*Ha-ak-piš* ***ki-iš-ha-ha-at***

422. KBo III 1+ II 16 f. (Proclamation of Telipinu)
ma-a-an-ša-an ^{m}*Te-li-pí-nu-uš I-NA* ^{GIŠ}GU.ZA *A-BI-YA* ***e-eš-ha-at*** */ nu* ^{URU}*Ha-aš-šu-wa la-ah-ha pa-a-un*

423. KUB I 1+ II 79 ff. (Apology of Hattušili III)
GIM-*an-ma IŠ-TU* KUR *Mi-iz-ri-i* / EGIR-*pa* ***i-ya-ah-ha-ha-at*** *nu I-NA* ^{URU}*La-wa-za-an-ti-ya / A-NA* DINGIR^{LIM} BAL-*u-wa-an-zi*
i-ya-ah-ha-ha-at

424. KBo III 29 I 18’ (Palace chronicle)
ki-iš-ši-ri-mi GAL-*ri-ya*[154] ***ar-ha-ti***

---

153 Generally, another form *-tati* is assumed here which can only be attested with difficulty in the corpus. The examples in question could also be interpreted as present. – Unusual is the ending *-at* in CTH 291.I.a, II 30 (Laws, table I: *zi-ik-wa* UR.BAR.RA ***ki-ša-at*** „You have become a wolf“).

154 Syntactically difficult, but it must be „*with* a cup“.

425. KUB XXX 10 obv. 11 (Kantuzzili's prayer)
ku-i-ta im-ma ***mi-eš-ha-ti*** *nu-za-ta ŠA* DINGIR-*YA du-ud-du-mar ha-at-ta-ta hu-u-ma-an-ta ša-ki-nu-un*

426. KUB XXXI 64 (+) III 6 (Campaign of Muršili I)
nu-za I-NA ^{GIŠ}GIGIR^{MEŠ}-*ŠU ka-ru-ú* ***e-eš-ha-ti***

2. 2.sg.pret.med. both conjugations: *-tat*

427. KUB XIV 1 rev. 90 (Madduwatta indictment)
a-pí-e-da-aš[155]*-za an-da ku-wa-at* ***ha-an-da-a-it-ta-at***

428. KBo V 9 I 14 f. (Treaty of Muršili II with Duppi-Tešub of Amurru)
tu-uk[156]*-ma / iš-tar-ak-ki-it nu* ***ir-ma-al-li-ya-at-ta-at***

429. Mşt. 75/111 obv. 12 ff. (Letter)
nu-mu-uš-ša-an im-ma ku-it / ***pár-ki-ya-at-ta-at*** *nu-za* $^{\text{LÚ.MEŠ}}$*TE-MI-ŠU-NU / ku-it Ú-UL ú-e-mi-ya-at*[157]

430. KBo XVII 65 rev. 57 (Birth ritual)
zi-ik-wa-az A-NA ^{D}*Hé-pát* GÉME ***ki-iš-ta-at***

3.a. 3.sg.pret.med. *mi-* conjugation: *-ta*, *-tat*, *-tati*

431. KBo XXXII 13 II 11 f. (Epos of liberation: Festival for Allāni)
nu-za-an an-da iš-hu-zi-ya-it ták-na-a-aš ^{D}UTU-*uš / na-aš A-NA* ^{D}IM *pí-ra-an* ***ú-e-ha-at-ta***

432. KUB XXXIII 120+ I 26 f. (Myth of Kummarbi)
ma-a-an ***ú-li-iš-ta****-ma-a-an* ^{D}*Ku-mar-bi-iš ŠA* ^{D}*A-nu* LÚ-*na-tar kat-ta* ***pa-aš-ta*** */ na-aš-za* ***du-uš-kat-ta*** *na-aš-za* ***ha-ah-har-aš-ta***

433. KUB XXIV 8+ I 31 (Story of Appu)
^{m}*Ap-pu-uš* Ù-*az* ***pár-ki-i-ya-ta-at***

155 Namely the enemies.
156 Accusative for nominative.
157 Interrogative clause.

434. KBo X 13 (+) I 23 ff. (Treaty with Aziru of Amurru)
na-aš / *IŠ-TU* KÁ *ŠA* KUR ^{URU}*Mi-iz-ri ú-it na-aš A-NA ŠA-PAL* GÌR^{MEŠ} ^{D}UTU^{ŠI} *kat-ta-an* / ***ha-li-ya-at-ta-at***

435. KBo III 1+ I 35 (Proclamation of Telipinu)
nu ^{m}*Ha-an-ti-li-iš* ***na-ah-ša-ri-ya-ta-ti***

436. KBo III 1+ II 33 (Proclamation of Telipinu)
ka-a-ša-wa ^{URU}*Ha-at-tu-ši e-eš-har*[158] ***pa-an-ga-ri-ya-at-ta-ti***

3.b. 3.sg.pret.med. *hi-* conjugation: *-at*, *-ati*

437. KUB XXX 10 rev. 14 (Kantuzzili's prayer)
nu-mu É-*YA i-na-ni pí-ra-an pít-tu-li-ya-aš* É-*ir* ***ki-ša-at***

438. KBo XXXII 14 II 9 f. (Epos of liberation)
HUR.SAG-*aš-ša*[159] *ma-ah-ha-an iš-ta-ma-aš-ta* / *nu-uš-ši-kán* ŠÀ-*ŠU an-da* ***iš-tar-ak-ki-at***

439. KBo III 1+ IV 23/15' (Proclamation of Telipinu)
ne a-pád-da ***ši-ú-ni-ya-ah-ha-ti***[160]

440. KBo III 1+ II 11 f. (Proclamation of Telipinu)
ma-a-nu-uš-kán[161] ^{m}*Hu-uz-zi-ya-aš ku-en-ta nu ut-tar* ***iš-du-wa-a-ti*** / *nu-uš* ^{m}*Te-li-pí-nu-uš ar-ha pár-ah-ta*

441. KBo XII 3 III 4' (Fragment)
a-pa-a-aš-ša nam-ma ***e-ša-ti***

4. 1.pl.pret.med. both conjugations: *-waštat*

442. KBo XVI 59 obv. 13' f. (Protocol)
I-NA ^{URU}*Zi-ik-pa-ra-ya-aš-ša-an A-NA* ^{NA4}*hur-wa-ši* ^{m}*Šar-ru-up-še-en-na-aš* / *am-mu-ug-ga* ***ar-wa-aš-ta-at***

158 Here: „bloodshed“.
159 The text is a myth, so a mountain *can* be offended by a roebuck running him down.
160 Lit. „to have to do with a god“, but it actually means „to be struck with illness“.
161 *man* in the particle of the irrealis here, not the conditional conjunction.

443. KUB XVII 21 II 11 ff. (Prayer of Arnuwanda and Ašmunikal)
ki-nu-un-pát ú-e-eš ^{m}*Ar-nu-wa-an-ta* LUGAL.GAL / *Ù* ^{f}*Aš-mu-ni-kal* MUNUS.LUGAL.GAL *šu-ma-a-aš* DINGIR^{MEŠ}*-pát* / EGIR*-an* ***ar-wa-aš-ta-at***

5. 2.pl.pret.med. both conjugations: *-dumat*

444. KUB XXIX 1 I 28 (Foundation ritual)
ne-pí-ša-aš kat-ta-an[162] ***ú-li-li-iš-ki-id-du-ma-at***

445. KUB XXIII 103 rev. 4' (Letter of Tuthaliya IV to Baba-ah-iddinammi)
ŠA 1^{EN} *A-BI* AMA ***kiš-du-um-ma-at***

446. KUB XXXVI 44 IV 14 (Myth of the disappearing stormgod)
wa-al-lu-uš-ki-id-du-ma-at*-wa-za*

447. KBo III 7 IV 9 ff. (Myth of Illuyanka)
ma-a-wa[163]*-aš-ša-an* $^{\text{NA4}}$ŠU.U ŠÚ.A ***e-eš-tum-ma-at*** / *nu-za* ^{LÚ}GUDU$_{12}$ *ma-a-an pu-u-ul ti-an-zi* / ^{LÚ}GUDU$_{12}$ ^{D}*Za-li-nu-un ku-iš har-zi* / *nu wa-tar-wa še-ir* $^{\text{NA4}}$ŠU.U ŠÚ.A *ki-it-ta* / *na-aš-ša-an a-pí-i-a e-ša-a-ri*

448. KBo II 3 I 32 ff. (Maštigga's ritual)
a-pí-da-ni-wa-aš-ma-aš-kán / UD*-ti ku-it* ***ha-aš-ši-ik-du-ma-at*** *ki-nu-na-wa-aš-ma-aš-kán* / *ka-a-ša a-pí-da-aš* UD*-aš* EME$^{\text{HI.A}}$ ^{D}*A-an-da-a-li-ya-aš* / *IŠ-TU* GÍR *kar-aš-ta*

6. 3.pl.pret.med. both conjugations: *-antat*, *-antati*

449. KUB XXXIX 14 I 14 f. (Funerary ritual)
nu SAG.DU^{MEŠ} ANŠE.KUR.RA^{MEŠ} SAG.DU GU$_4$$^{\text{HI.A}}$ *ku-wa-pí* ***wa-ra-an-da-at*** / *nu-uš a-pí-ya iš-hu-u-wa-i*[164]

---

162 A tree is addressed.
163 = *mān=wa.*
164 As object, „ashes" has to be supplemented.

450. KBo III 4+ II 52 f. (Annals of Muršili II)
nu-kán ^m*U-uh-ha*-LÚ-*iš a-ru-ni an-da* BA.ÚŠ DUMU^MEŠ-*ŠU-NU-ma-za ar-ha* / ***šar-ra-an-da-at***

451. KBo II 2 I 21 f. (Oracle)
ki-i ku-it[165] *ku-u-uš* MUŠEN *HUR-RI kal-la-ra-an-ni* / *ar-ha* ***ap-pa-an-ta-at***

452. KUB XVII 10 I 6 f. (Myth of Telipinu)
I-NA GUNNI-*ma kal-mi-i-ša-ni-iš* ***ú-i-šu-u-ri-ya-an-ta-ti*** *iš-ta-na-na-aš an-da* / DINGIR^MEŠ ***ú-i-šu-u-ri-ya-an-ta-ti***

453. KUB XXXVI 19 l.Kol. 11' f. (Song of Silver)
^DUTU-*uš* ^D*SÎN-aš-ša kat-ta-an ka-ni-ni-e-ir na-at* KÙ.BABBAR-*i* / ***hi-in-kán-ta-ti***

EXERCISES

454. KUB XXX 16+ I 10 f. (Funerary ritual)
zi-ik-wa-za GIM-*an ki-iš-ta-at* / *ka-a-ša-wa-az QA-TAM-MA ki-ša-ru*

455. KUB XXXIII 120+ I 15 (Myth of Kummarbi)
^GIŠŠÚ.A-*ki-ma-aš-ša-an* ^D*A-nu-uš e-ša-at*

456. KUB I 1+ IV 48 (Apology of Hattušili III)
nu-za LUGAL.GAL *ki-iš-ha-ha-at*

457. KUB XXXIII 120+ I 37 f. (Myth of Kummarbi)
ma-a-an ^D*A-nu-uš me-mi-ya-u-wa-an-zi zi-in-ni-it na-aš-ša-an ša-ra-a* AN-*ši pa-it* / *na-aš-za mu-un-na-it-ta-at*

458. KUB XXX 10 obv. 18 f. (Kantuzzili's prayer)
ma-a-am-ma-an[166] *in-na-ra-ah-ha-at-ma nu tu-el* / *ši-ú-na-aš ud-da-an-ta Ú-UL in-na-ra-ah-ha-at*[167]

459. KBo IV 6 obv. 26' f. (Gaššuliyawiya's prayer)
nu DINGIR^MEŠ-*az a-ri-ya-ir na-at* DINGIR^MEŠ-*az-zi-ya* / *ha-an-da-it-ta-at*

---

165 Idiomatic: „concerning this".
166 = *mān* + *man*.
167 Rhetorical interrogative clause.

460. KBo VI 34+ III 16 f. (First military oath)
na-an li-in-ka-an-te-eš / e-ip-pir na-aš-ša-an ŠÀ-*ŠU šu-ut-ta-ti*

461. KUB XXXIII 121 II 66 (Tale of Kešši)
^{m}*Ki-eš-ši-iš* ITU.3.KAM-*aš* HUR.SAG^{MEŠ}-*aš an-da ú-e-ha-at-ta*

2.2.1.5. Imperative active

As Hittite has an imperative for the 1.sg., the grammars also show a 1.pl., though this is formally identical with the indicative. As there is no criterion for how to distinguish a 1.pl.imp. from a 1.pl.ind. in modal use, and because there is also no special form for the 1.pl.imp.med., we do not give a form for the 1.pl. contrary to common custom.

Lit.: Hoffner/Melchert 2008: 182 ff., 313 f.

	mi- conjugation	*hi-* conjugation
1.sg.	*-(a)llu*[168]	
2.sg.	-Ø, *-i*	
3.sg.	*-du*	*-u*
2.pl.	*-ten*	
3.pl.	*-andu*	

1.a. 1.sg.imp.act. both conjugations: *-(a)llu*

462. KBo XVII 62+ IV 14' f. (Birth ritual)
ka-a-ša-wa ki-nu-un ŠA DUMU.NITA *a-aš-šu-u ú-da-ah-hu-un /*
pa-ra-a-ma-wa MU-*an-ni ŠA* DUMU.MUNUS *a-aš-šu-u* ***ú-da-al-lu***

168 For the copula, there are also the forms *ešlit, -lut* beside more frequent *ašallu*.

463. KUB VI 45+ III 73 f. (Muwatalli's prayer)
nu ha-an-da-an / ú-uk ki-iš-ša-an ***me-ma-al-lu***

464. KUB VI 45+ III 64 ff. (Muwatalli's prayer)
nu NINDA.GUR$_4$.RA *iš-pa-an-du-uz-zi-ya / ku-in A-NA* ^{D}U *pí-ha-aš-ša-aš-ši* EN-*YA pí-eš-ki-mi / na-an-ši du-uš-ga-ra-u-wa-an-za* ***pí-iš-ki-el-lu***

465. KUB XIV 11+ III 19' f. (Plague prayer of Muršili II)
nu SISKUR *ŠA* ^{ÍD}*Ma-a-la* ***i-ya-al-lu*** */ na-at-kán* ***a-aš-ša-nu-ul-lu*** *i-ya-mi-ya-at-za*

466. KBo XV 34 (+) II 5' ff. (Ritual for the stormgod of Kuliwišna)
nu-kán ma-ah-ha-an ^{GIŠ}*wa-ar-aš-ma-an kar-aš-mi / A-NA* ^{D}IM ^{URU}*Ku-li-ú-iš-na-ya kar-pí-in* ***kar-ša-al-lu*** */ kar-di-mi-ya-at-ta-an* ***kar-ša-al-lu*** *wa-aš-du-ul* ***kar-ša-al-lu*** */ ša-a-u-wa-ar* ***kar-ša-al-lu*** *kar-di-mi-at-ta-aš* IGI$^{HI.A}$*-wa / kar-pí-wa-a-la ha-an-ta* ***kar-ša-al-lu***

2. 2.sg.imp.act. both conjugations: -Ø, *-i*

467. KUB XIX 6+ IV 45 (Treaty with Alakšandu of Wiluša)
nu-kán A-NA ^{D}UTU^{ŠI} ŠU*-i an-da a-aš-šu lu-ú-lu* ***a-ú***

468. KUB I 16+ II 14 (Political testament of Hattušili I)
da-a-la *Ú-UL* DUMU-*YA a-pa-a-aš*

469. KBo V 3+ I 8 (Treaty with Hukkanā of Hayaša)
nu-za zi-ik ^{m}*Hu-uq-qa-na-a-aš* ^{D}UTU^{ŠI}*-pát AŠ-ŠUM BE-LU-TIM* ***ša-a-ak***

470. KUB I 16+ II 62 f. (Political testament of Hattušili I)
DUMU-*la-ma-aš-ša-an tu-el / ku-it kar-di nu-za a-pa-a-at* ***e-iš-ši***

471. KUB XXIII 1+ II 9 f. (Treaty with Šaušgamuwa)
nu ^{D}UTU^{ŠI} *AŠ-ŠUM* EN-*UT-TI* ***pa-ah-ši*** *kat-ta-ya* DUMU^{MEŠ} DUMU.DUMU^{MEŠ} / NUMUN *ŠA* ^{D}UTU^{ŠI} *AŠ-ŠUM* EN-*UT-TI* ***pa-ah-ši***

3.a. 3.sg.imp.act. *mi-* conjugation: *-du*

472. KBo III 22 obv. 35 (Proclamation of Anitta)
ku-i-ša-at[169] *hu-ul-li-iz-zi* ^{URU}*Ne-e-ša-aš* ^{LÚ}KÚR-*ŠU* ***e-eš-tu***

473. KUB I 16+ II 33 (Political testament of Hattušili I)
nu ***az-zi-ik-ki-id-du ak-ku-uš-ki-id-du***

474. KBo III 1+ IV 28/20' f. (Proclamation of Telipinu)
ták-ku te-iz-zi[170]*-ma* / ***šar-ni-ik-du***[171]*-wa nu* ***šar-ni-ik-du***

475. KBo IV 10+ obv. 11' (Treaty with Ulmitešub)
ŠA ^{m}*Ul-mi-*^{D}U*-up-pát* NUMUN*-aš* ***da-ad-du***[172]

476. KBo XI 14 I 21 f. (Hantitaššu's ritual)
MUN GIM*-an* UDU$^{\mathrm{HI.A}}$ *li-li-pa-an-ti nu* ***ú-id-du*** *ku-u-uš* / *hu-u-uk-ma-uš* ^{D}UTU*-uš QA-TAM-MA* ***li-li-pa-iš-ki-id-du***

3.b. 3.sg.imp.act. *hi-* conjugation: *-u*

477. KBo VI 34+ I 45 (First military oath)
nu i-da-a-lu hi-in-kán ***pí-e-da-ú***

478. KUB XVII 5 I 8 (Myth of Illuyanka)
nu-wa a-da-an-na a-ku-wa-an-na ***e-hu***

479. KUB I 1+ IV 79 f. (Apology of Hattušili III)
É*-ir-ma ku-it A-NA* DINGIR^{LIM} *AD-DIN* / *nu hu-u-ma-an-za*[173] *A-NA* DINGIR^{LIM} *kar-na-an ma-ar-na-an* ***e-eš-ša-ú***

480. KUB XIII 2+ II 42 f. (Instructions for the Bēl-Madgalti)
nam-ma ŠA DINGIR^{LIM} *Ú-NU-TUM a-ú-wa-ri-ya-aš* EN*-aš* GUL*-aš-du* / *na-at*[174] *MA-HAR* ^{D}UTU^{ŠI} ***up-pa-ú***

481. KUB XXIV 3+ II 19 ff. (Muršili's prayer to the sun goddess of Arinna)
nu DINGIR^{MEŠ} *ku-it wa-aš-du-ul uš-ka-at-te-ni* / *nu na-aš-šu*

169 Meaning *tuppi* „clay tablet".
170 Meaning „the king".
171 Meaning „the delinquent".
172 Here: „to take her as a wife".
173 Meaning „everybody in the house".
174 Namely the list.

DINGIR^{MEŠ}*-ni-ya-an-za* ***ú-id-du*** *na-at* ***me-e-ma-a-ú*** / *na-aš-ma-at* $^{\text{MUNUS.MEŠ}}$ŠU.GI $^{\text{LÚ.MEŠ}}$AZU $^{\text{LÚ.MEŠ}}$MUŠEN.DÙ SIxSÁ*-an-du*

4. 2.pl.imp.act. both conjugations: *-ten*

482. KUB XIII 9+ III 8 f. (Instruction of Tuthaliya)
ku-iš ki-nu-uz-zi[175]*-ma šu-me-eš-ša-an* LÚ^{MEŠ} URU^{LIM} ***e-ip-tin*** / *na-an* LUGAL*-wa-aš a-aš-ki* ***ú-wa-te-it-tin***

483. KUB XIII 4 I 38 (Instructions for the priests and temple officials)
nu-za A-NA INIM DINGIR^{LIM} *me-ik-ki mar-ri na-ah-ha-an-te-eš* ***e-eš-tin***

484. KUB XIII 4 III 17 (Instructions for the priests and temple officials)
nu É^{MEŠ} DINGIR^{MEŠ} *me-ik-ki mar-ri* ***pa-ah-ha-aš-tin***

485. KUB IV 1+ II 3 f. (Incantation at the enemy border)
nu ***ú-wa-at-te-en*** / *nu* ***iz-za-at-te-en e-ku-ut-te-en***

486. KBo VI 2+ III 22 f. (Laws, first tablet)
i-it-te-en *ma-ah-ha-an a-ri-eš-me-eš šu-me-eš* / *a-pí-e-ni-iš-ša-an* ***e-eš-te-en***

5. 3.pl.imp.act. both conjugations: *-andu*

487. KBo III 1+ II 13 f. (Proclamation of Telipinu)
pa-a-an-du*-wa-az* ***a-ša-an-du*** / *nu-wa-za* ***az-zi-ik-kán-du ak-ku-uš-kán-du***

488. KUB I 16+ III 56 f. (Political testament of Hattušili I)
nu ki-i / *tup-pí* ITU*-mi* ITU*-mi pí-ra-an-ti-it* ***hal-zi-eš-ša-an-du***

489. KBo III 1+ III 48 (Proclamation of Telipinu)
ku-i-ša-at i-ya-zi nu-uš-ši HUL*-lu hi-in-kán* ***pí-an-du***

490. KBo IV 10+ obv. 50' f. (Treaty with Ulmitešub)
nu ka-a-ša a-pí-e-da-ni me-mi-ni LI-IM DINGIR^{MEŠ} *tu-li-ya hal-zi-ya-an-te-eš* / *nu* ***uš-kán-du iš-ta-ma-aš-kán-du****-ya na-at ku-ut-ru-e-eš* ***a-ša-an-du***

175 „Granary" has to be added as object.

491. KUB XIII 8 obv. 11 (Instruction of Queen Ašmunikal)
na-at-kán hu-u-ma-an-ta-za a-ra-u-e-eš ***a-ša-an-du***

492. KBo IV 10+ obv. 13' (Treaty with Ulmitešub)
nu NUMUN *ŠA* DUMU.MUNUS *ŠA* ᵐ*Ul-mi-*ᴰU*-up-pát* EGIR-*an* ***ša-an-ha-an-du***

2.2.1.6. Imperative medium

	mi-conjugation	*hi*-conjugation
1.sg.	*-haharu*	
2.sg.	*-hut*	
3.sg.	*-taru*	*-aru*
1.pl.	–	
2.pl.	*-dumat, -dumati*	
3.pl.	*-antaru*	

1. 1.sg.imp.med. both conjugations: *-haharu*

493. VBoT 120+ II 20 (Allaiturahi's ritual)
nu-uš-ma-aš še-ir NÍ.TE-*iš-ši* ***ar-ha-ha-ru***

494. KUB XIV 14+ rev. 42 (Plague prayer of Muršili II)
nu-uš-ma-aš-kán ***ú-wa-ah-ha-ru***

495. KBo IV 14 III 6 (Treaty)
nu-wa ki-e-da-aš A-NA MA-MIT GAM-*an ar-ha* ***ar-ha-ha-ru***

496. KUB XXVI 35, 7 (Fragment of a treaty)
ú-ga ᴸᵁ́KÚR-*KA me-e-na-ah-ha-an-da* ***za-ah-hi-ya-ah-ha-ru***

2. 2.sg.imp.med. both conjugations: *-hut*

497. KBo V 3+ III 49 f. (Treaty with Hukkanā of Hayaša)
ŠA É.GAL^{LIM} *ku-wa-pí* MUNUS *ú-iz-zi* / *na-aš-ta* KASKAL-*az ar-ha me-ik-ki* ***wa-at-ka-ah-hu-ut***

498. KUB XIX 6+ IV 46 (Treaty with Alakšandu of Wiluša)
nu-kán A-NA ^{D}UTU^{ŠI} ŠU-*i an-da* ***mi-ya-hu-wa-an-ta-ah-hu-ut***

499. KBo V 9 II 18 (Treaty of Muršili II with Duppi-Tešub of Amurru)
wa-ar-ri lam-mar ***ar-hu-ut***

500. KBo IV 6 obv. 16' (Gaššuliyawiya's prayer)
A-NA DUMU.MUNUS.GAL-*ma-kán an-da aš-šu-li nam-ma* ***ne-eš-hu-ut***

501. KBo V 3+ III 44 (Treaty with Hukkanā of Hayaša)
ŠA É.GAL^{LIM}-*ya-za* MUNUS^{TUM} *me-ik-ki* ***uš-ga-ah-hu-ut***

3.a. 3.sg.imp.med. *mi-* conjugation: *-taru*

502. KBo III 1+ II 36 (Proclamation of Telipinu)
LUGAL-*uš-ša-an ha-an-te-iz-zi-ya-aš-pát* DUMU.LUGAL DUMU^{MEŠ} ***ki-ik-ki-iš-ta-ru***

503. KBo IV 6 obv. 15' (Gaššuliyawiya's prayer)
nu PA-NI DINGIR^{LIM} EN-*YA ka-a-aš* MUNUS-*aš* ***ú-e-ha-at-ta-ru***

504. KBo VI 34+ II 2 (First military oath)
na-aš DUH.LÀL-*aš i-wa-ar* ***šal-li-it-ta-ru***

505. KBo VI 34+ I 44 (First military oath)
na-aš-kán i-na-na-aš še-ir ar-ha ***pár-ši-ya-ad-da-ru***

506. KUB XIII 8 obv. 9 (Instruction of Queen Ašmunikal)
nu-uš-ma-aš-kán pí-an ^{GIŠ}*e-ya-an* ***ar-ta-ru***

3.b. 3.sg.imp.med. *hi-* conjugation: *-aru*

507. KBo III 1+ II 36 ff. (Proclamation of Telipinu)
ták-ku DUMU.LUGAL / *ha-an-te-iz-zi-iš* NU.GÁL *nu ku-iš ta-a-an pí-e-da-aš* DUMU^{RU} *nu* LUGAL-*uš a-pa-a-aš* / ***ki-ša-ru***

508. KUB IX 25+ II 7 f. (Ambazzi's ritual)
ma-ah-ha-an-kán ki-i ki-iš-ta-nu-nu-un i-da-a-lu-ya-kán / *A-NA* EN^{MEŠ}-*TIM še-ir QA-TAM-MA* ***ki-iš-ta-ru***

509. KUB XIX 6+ II 44 (Treaty with Alakšandu of Wiluša)
nu 1-*aš* 1-*an* ***pa-ah-ša-ru***

510. KUB XIII 4 III 71 f. (Instructions for the priests and temple officials)
na-aš-kán lu-uk-kat-ti DINGIR^{MEŠ}-*aš* / *a-da-an-na-aš me-e-hu-u-ni hu-u-da-a-ak* ***a-ru***

511. KUB XII 34+ I 26 f. (Maštigga's ritual)
túh-ša-ru *a-pí-el* UD-*aš* EME$^{HI.A}$ ***túh-ša-ru*** *a-pí-el* UD-*aš* / *ud-da-a-ar*

4. 2.pl.imp.med. both conjugations: *-dumat*, *-dumati*

512. KUB I 16+ III 33 f. (Political testament of Hattušili I)
nu LUGAL-*aš ud-da-a-ar-mi-it* / ***pa-ah-ha-aš-du-ma-at***

513. KUB XIII 20 I 7 f. (Instruction of Tuthaliya)
ma-a-an KIN-*ma ku-it-ki* / *na-aš-ma ú-e-tum-mar na-aš-ma ku-iš im-ma* KIN-*az nu-uš-ša-an an-da* ***ar-du-ma-at***

514. KUB XXVI 29+ obv. 15 (Treaty of Arnuwanda I with the people of Ura)
ÉRIN^{MEŠ}-*it-ma pa-an-ga-ri-it* ***ni-ni-ik-tum-ma-at***

515. KUB XLI 8 IV 11 (Ritual for netherworld deities)
nu-za ú-wa-at-tin iz-za-at-tin e-ku-ut-tin nu-mu-uš-ša-an ***har-ap-du-ma-ti***

516. KUB XXXIII 106+ II 24 (Myth of Ullikummi)
ku-wa-at-qa ***wa-aš-du-ma-ti***[176]

517. KBo V 3+ IV 5 ff. (Treaty with Hukkanā of Hayaša)
nu-mu ma-a-an aš-šu-li / *pa-ah-ha-aš-te-ni nu-mu-uš-ša-an*

176 = **wašt-dumati*.

SAG.DU^{MEŠ}-*KU-NU A-NA* SAG.DU-*YA* / ***ki-id-du-ma-ti***

5. 3.pl.imp.med. both conjugations: *-antaru*

518. KBo XV 25 obv. 14 (Ritual for Wiššuriyanza)
ÍD$^{HI.A}$-*wa pí-ra-an* ***ar-mi-iz-zi-ya-an-da-ru***

519. KBo XXXII 14 II 59 f. (Epos of liberation)
šu-up-pí-iš-du-wa-ri-i-e-eš-ma-kan an-da / ÍD-*i* ***mu-wa-an-ta-ru***

520. Mşt. 75/112 lower edge 45 f. (Letter)
nu-ut-ta DINGIR^{MEŠ} TI-*an har-kán-du* / *nu-ut-ta aš-šu-li* ***pa-ah-ša-an-da-ru***

521. KBo III 27 obv. 11 f. (Edict of Hattušili I)
ARAD-*mi-iš li-e*[177] *kap-ru-uš-še-it* / ***ha-at-ta-an-ta-ru*** *na-an a-aš-ki-iš-ši kán-kán-du*

522. KUB XIII 4 II 47 f. (Instructions for the priests and temple officials)
uš-ša-ni-ya-zi-ma-at-za ku-wa-pí na-at hur-wa-ši pí-di li-e uš-ša-ni-ya-zi / EN^{MEŠ} ^{URU}*Ha-at-ti* ***a-ra-an-ta-ru*** *nu uš-kán-du*

EXERCISES

523. KUB XXIV 5+ obv. 16' (Substitution ritual for the king)
nu-wa ku-u-uš[178] *ak-kán-du am-mu-uk-ma-wa li-e ak-mi*[179]

524. KUB XXXIII 102+ II 15 f. (Myth of Ullikummi)
ša-ra-a ti-i-ya / *nu I-NA* É-*YA ar-ha e-hu*

525. KBo III 7 I 21 ff. (Myth of Illuyanka)
^{m}*Hu-u-pa-ši-ya ka-a-ša-wa* / *ki-i-ya ki-i-ya ut-tar i-ya-mi*[180] / *nu-wa-mu-uš-ša-an zi-iq-qa har-ap-hu-ut*

177 Nominal sentence, add „shall be".
178 Accusative for nominative.
179 Modal: „want to die".
180 Modal: „want to do".

526. KBo V 3+ I 31 f. (Treaty with Hukkanā of Hayaša)
nu zi-ik ^{m}*Hu-uq-qa-na-a-aš* ^{D}UTU$^{\check{S}I}$*-pát aš-šu-li pa-ah-ši* EGIR*-pa-an-na* / *A-NA* ^{D}UTU$^{\check{S}I}$*-pát ar-hu-ut*

527. KBo III 1+ IV 28/20' (Proclamation of Telipinu)
ták-ku te-iz-zi a-ku-wa-ra-aš na-aš a-ku

528. KUB XIII 4 I 60 (Instructions for the priests and temple officials)
IŠ-TU NINDA KAŠ GEŠTIN *I-NA* É DINGIR^{LIM} *hu-u-ma-an*[181] *ša-ra-a pí-e har-tin*

529. KUB XVII 27 III 11 ff. (Ritual for Hannahanna)
na-aš-kán še-ir al-la-pa-ah-hu-un na-at an-da / GÌR$^{ME\check{S}}$*-it iš-pár-ra-ah-hu-un na-at-kán* ANŠE*-aš še-hur-ri-eš-ki-id-du* / *na-at-kán* GU$_4$*-uš kam-mar-ši-eš-ki-id-du*

530. Mşt. 75/111 left edge 1 ff. (Letter)
GI.É.DUB.BA*-mu-kán har-ak-ta* / *nu-mu* ŠEŠ.DÙG.GA-*YA* GI.É.DUB.BA / *up-pí*

2.2.2. Verbal stem formation

To go into detail about the stem formation of Hittite verbs would exceed the objective of this exercise book. As Oettinger treats this topic extensively, the reader should refer to his works for all particular questions. However, at least some examples of verbs with root ablaut will be given in the following because experience has shown that their translation often creates difficulties for beginners.

Lit.: Oettinger 2002; Hoffner/Melchert 2008: 173 ff.

2.2.2.1. Verbs with root ablaut e:a

Some verbs show synchronous *e:a*-ablaut in the present. Therefore, different types can be distinguished while sometimes also secondary analogy formations occur:

---

181 Meaning „all leftovers".

1.sg.	*epmi*	*ekumi*	*saggahhi*	*arhi*
2.sg.	*epsi*	*ekusi*	*sakti*	*arti*
3.sg.	*epzi*	*ekuzi*	*sakki*	*ari*
1.pl.	*epweni*	*akweni*	*sekkweni*	*erweni*
2.pl.	*epteni*	*ekuteni*	*sekteni*	*erteni*
3.pl.	*appanzi*	*akuwanzi*	*sekanzi*	*aranzi*

531. KUB I 16+ III 68 f. (Political testament of Hattušili I)
ki-nu-un-wa-az nu-u-wa $^{\text{MUNUS.MEŠ}}$ŠU.GI-*uš* / *pu-nu-uš-ki-iz-zi Ú-UL* ***ša-ag-ga-ah-hi***

532. KUB XXXIII 67 IV 17 (Anzili and Zukki)
ki-nu-un-za ***e-it-mi e-ku-mi***

533. KUB XIX 6+ III 68 ff. (Treaty with Alakšandu of Wiluša)
ma-a-an-kán ^{LÚ}*MU-NAB-TUM ku-iš-ki IŠ-TU* ^{LÚ}KÚR *ap-pa-an-za*[182] / *na-aš IŠ-TU* KUR ^{URU}*Ha-at-ti hu-u-wa-a-i* KUR.KUR-*KA-ma-aš-kán iš-tar-na ar-ha* / *pa-iz-zi zi-ga-an* ***e-ip-ti*** *na-an-kán pa-ra-a* / *Ú-UL ne-ya-ti na-an A-NA* ^{LÚ}KÚR EGIR-*pa pí-eš-ti* / *nu a-pád-da ŠA-PAL NI-EŠ* DINGIR^{LIM} *ki-it-ta-ru*

534. KUB XXXIII 106+ III 38' f. (Myth of Ullikummi)
nu-za ^{D}*Ú-pí-el-lu-ri-iš ku-it* GE$_6$-*ya-aš* KI-*aš* / KI.BAD-*aš nu-za a-ši nu-ut-ta-ri-ya-an* DINGIR^{LIM}-*in Ú-UL* ***ša-ak-ti***

535. KUB XXV 22 III 13 (Festival ritual of Tuthaliya IV)
IGI-*zi pal-ši* ^{D}UTU ^{URU}PÚ-*na* ^{D}*Mi-iz-zu-la-an* 3-*ŠU* ***e-ku-zi***[183]

536. KUB IX 22 III 20 ff. (Birth ritual)
na-aš-ša-an ma-ah-ha-an KASKAL-*ša-aš ha-at-ri-eš-na-aš* / *pa-ra-a* ***a-ri*** *nu* 1 UZ$_6$.TUR *A-NA* DINGIR.LÚ^{MEŠ} *ši-na-ap-ši-ya-aš* / *ši-pa-an-ti*

182 Nominal sentence, add „is“ in the translation.
183 „To drink a god“ = „to drink a cup in honour of the god“.

537. KUB XXII 70 obv. 38 (Oracle concerning the intrigues at the Hittite court)
a-pu-u-un-wa me-mi-an Ú-UL ***še-ik-ku-e-ni***

538. KBo XVII 1+ IV 6 (Ritual for the royal couple)
a-tu-e-ni a-ku-e-ni LÚ.MEŠA.ZU-*ša kat-ti-mi*[184]

539. KUB XVII 21 I 6 (Prayer of Arnuwanda and Ašmunikal)
nu šu-me-eš-pát DINGIR^{MEŠ} DINGIR^{MEŠ}-*aš iš-ta-an-za-ni-it* ***še-ik-te-ni***

540. KUB I 16+ III 34 (Political testament of Hattušili I)
nu NINDA-*an az-za-aš-te-ni wa-a-tar-ra* ***e-ku-ut-te-ni***

541. Bo 2710+ obv. 6 (Ritual from Nerik)
nu INIM$^{HI.A}$ *tal-li-ya-u-wa-aš* GIM-*an* ***še-ik-kán-zi*** *na-at-kán QA-TAM-MA an-da me-ma-an-zi*

542. KUB XXXVI 104 rev. 7' (Palace chronicle)
$^{LÚ.MEŠ}$DUGUD $^{LÚ.MEŠ}$ŠUKUR.ZABAR *pí-ra-aš-mi-it*[185] ***a-ša-an-zi***

EXERCISES

543. KUB I 13+ II 28 ff. (Kikkuli's hippological texts)
nu-uš-ma-aš 1 ^{DUG}GAL / *ŠA ME-E* MUN 1 ^{DUG}GAL *ME-E ŠA* DIM$_4$ AL.GAZ / *pa-a-i na-at ar-ha a-ku-wa-an-zi*

544. KBo III 34 III 8 f. (Palace chronicle)
na-at na-a-ú-i / e-it-mi

545. KBo XVII 65 obv. 23 (Birth ritual)
kat-ti-iš-ši-ya-aš im-ma e-eš-zi[186] *kat-ti-iš-ši-ma* MUNUS-*za Ú-UL e-iz-za-zi*

546. KUB XXXIII 96 II 21 f. (Myth of Ullikummi)
nu ma-a-an A-NA KÁ É ^{D}*É-A pí-ra-an e-ru-u-e-ni nu* ^{D}*É-A-aš* ^{GIŠ}IG-*aš* / *hi-in-ku-e-ni*

---

184 Nominal sentence, add „are" in the translation.
185 = *piran* + *-šmit*.
186 Modal: „may be".

547. KUB I 16+ III 28 f. (Political testament of Hattušili I)
ma-a-an at-ta-aš ut-tar pa-ah-ha-aš-ta / NINDA-*an e-iz-za-aš-ši wa-a-tar-ra e-ku-uš-ši*

548. KBo V 1 IV 23 f. (Papanikri's ritual)
ma-ah-ha-an-ma-at KÁ ^{É}*ši-na-ap-ši a-ra-an-zi* / *nu-za* EN SÍSKUR *e-ša-ri*

549. KUB XXX 25+ obv. 29 (Funerary ritual)
EGIR-*ŠU-ma* ^{D}U ^{URU}*Zi-ip-pa-la-an-da e-ku-zi*[187]

550. KUB XVII 1 II 17 f. (Tale of Kešši)
ki-i ma-ah-ha-an i-ya-u-e-ni / *an-da* HUR.SAG-*i pa-i-u-e-ni nu* HUR.SAG-*i ak-ku-e-ni*[188]

187 „to drink a god" = „to drink a cup in honour of the god".
188 Interrogative clauses.

2.2.2.2. Verbs with ablaut ā:e:i and the paradigm of auš- „to see“

Some rather frequent *hi-* verbs ending with *-āi* inflect with root ablaut. - Synchronically irregular is the inflection of *auš-* „to see“ where the partial retention of the *s-* element makes the paradigm unclear.

	dāi- „to set“	*pāi-* „to give“	*nāi-* „to turn“	*auš-* „to see“
1.sg.pres.act.	*tehhi*	*pihhi*	*nehhi*	*uhhi*
2.sg.pres.act.	*dāitti*	*pāitti*	*nāitti*	*autti*
3.sg.pres.act.	*dāi*	*pāi*	*nāi*	*aušzi*
1.pl.pres.act.	*tiya(u)weni*	*piya(u)weni*	*neya(u)weni*	*(a)ummeni*
2.pl.pres.act.	*tāitteni*	*pēšteni*	*nāišteni*	*autteni*
3.pl.pres.act.	*tiyanzi*	*piyanzi*	*neyanzi*	*uwanzi*
1.sg.pret.act.	*tehhun*	*pehhun*	*nehhun*	*uhhun*
3.sg.pret.act.	*dāiš*	*pāiš*	*nāiš*	*aušta*
3.pl.pret.act.	*dāir*	*piēr*	*nāir*	*auir*

551. KUB XIX 49+ I 69 f. (Treaty with Manapa-Datta)

nu A-NA ^{D}UTU^{ŠI} *ma-a-an ku-wa-pí-ik-ki* ZI-*an-za*[189] / *na-aš a-pí-ya* ***te-ih-hi***

552. KUB XIII 35+ II 1 ff. (Law court records)

MUNUS.LUGAL-*ya-wa ku-e-da-aš* UN^{MEŠ}-*aš* ANŠE.GÌR.NUN.NA$^{HI.A}$ / *ma-ni-ya-ah-zi*[190] *i-it-wa-aš-ma-aš pa-a-i am-mu-uk-ma-wa-ra-aš-kán* / *an-da wa-ah-nu-uš-ki-nu-un*[191] *nu na-aš-šu am-me-el* ***da-ah-hi***[192] / *na-aš-ma-wa ta-me-el* ***da-ah-hi*** *nu-wa-aš-ši a-pu-uš* ***pí-ih-hi***

189 Lit. „where ever my wish (was)“.

190 Add: „ with the words“, as direct speech starts here, ending with *pa-a-i*.

191 Namely the mules.

192 Object drop, add „them“ in translation, also for the next *dahhi*.

553. KBo III 34 I 23 (Palace chronicle)
pa-i-mi na-a-ú-i ***u-uh-hi***[193] *na-a-ú-i*

554. KBo VI 34+ III 46 (First military oath)
nu-uš-ma-aš KUŠ SA$_5$ ***pa-it-ti***

555. KUB XVII 6 I 21 f. (Myth of Illuyanka)
ma-a-wa-ra-aš-ta[194] *ar-ha-ma* ***a-ut-ti*** / *nu-wa-za* DAM-*KA* DUMU^{MEŠ}-*KA* ***a-ut-ti***

556. KBo VI 2+ IV 9 f. (Laws, first tablet)
ták-ku UDU-*un A-NA* UR.BAR.RA *ku-iš-ki pí-eš-ši-iz-zi iš-ha-aš-ši-iš* / ^{UZU}Ì ***da-a-i*** *a-pa-a-ša-az* KUŠ UDU ***da-a-i***

557. KBo IV 1 obv. 11 (Foundation ritual)
EN SÍSKUR-*ya-kán ŠUM-an* ***hal-za-a-i***

558. KBo V 3+ III 55 (Treaty with Hukkanā of Hayaša)
A-BI ^{D}UTU$^{\textit{ŠI}}$-*ma-kán im-ma* ^{GIŠ}AB-*az ar-ha* ***a-uš-zi***

559. KUB XXI 27+ II 3 f. (Puduhepa's prayer to the sun goddess of Arinna)
nu-un-na-aš šu-me-el ŠA DINGIR^{MEŠ} *iš-hi-ú-ul* / *QA-TAM-MA kat-ta* ***a-ú-um-me-ni***

560. KUB XXII 70 obv. 42 f. (Oracle concerning the intrigues at the Hittite court)
Ú-NU-TE^{MEŠ}-*wa-kán ku-e I-NA* É $^{\text{NA4}}$*hé-kur* ^{D}LAMMA[195] *nu-wa-ra-at A-NA* DINGIR$^{\textit{LIM}}$ ^{URU}*A-ru-uš-na ku-it* / ***pí-eš-te-ni***

561. KUB XXXI 115, 21' (Pimpira fragment)
ku-it ***a-ut-te-ni*** *na-at te-it-te-en*

562. KBo XI 14 III 18 f. (Hantitaššu's ritual)
ka-ru-ú-li-uš DINGIR^{MEŠ}-*uš* / ***hal-zi-ya-an-zi***

563. KBo III 34 II 33 (Palace chronicle)
ma-a-an LUGAL-*wa-aš pí-ra-an ši-eš-kán-zi ku-iš ha-az-zi-iz-zi nu-uš-še* GEŠTIN-*an a-ku-wa-an-na* ***pí-an-zi***

---

193 Meaning „the reason for going" or the like.

194 = *mān=war*°.

195 Nominal sentence, add „are" in the translation.

564. KBo XVII 65 obv. 42 (Birth ritual)
ma-ah-ha-an-ma-kán pa-ra-a ti-ya-az-zi na-an ***ú-wa-an-zi***

565. KBo X 2 III 6 f. (Apology of Hattušili I)
nu I-NA ^{URU}*Ha-ah-ha pa-a-un nu-kán I-NA* ^{URU}*Ha-ah-ha* / KÁ.GAL$^{\text{HI.A}}$*-aš* 3-*ŠU an-da* MÈ-*in* ***te-ih-hu-un***

566. KUB I 1+ I 20 (Apology of Hattušili III)
nu-za-kán A-NA ŠU ^{D}*IŠTAR* GAŠAN-*YA lu-ú-lu* ***u-uh-hu-un***[196]

567. KUB I 1+ I 63 f. (Apology of Hattušili III)
nu-mu EGIR-*pa da-a-aš nu-mu-kán* KARAŠ ANŠE.KUR.RA^{MEŠ} / *ŠA* KUR ^{URU}*Ha-at-ti* ŠU-*i* ***da-a-iš***

568. KUB XXIV 7 III 20 f. (Tale of the sun god and the cow)
GU$_4$-*uš-za-kán* EGIR-*pa ne-pí-ši hal-za-a-iš nu A-NA* ^{D}UTU / *ar-ha tar-ku-wa* ***a-uš-ta***

569. KBo III 7 III 13 ff. (Myth of Illuyanka)
ma-a-na-aš pa-a-i-ta nu-uš-ma-aš ^{UZU}ŠÀ / *ú-e-ik-ta na-aš-ši* ***pí-i-e-ir*** / *ap-pí-iz-zi-ya-an-na-aš-ma-aš ša-a-ku-wa* / *ú-e-ik-ta nu-uš-ši a-pí-e-ya* ***pí-i-e-ir***

570. KBo X 2 I 34 f. (Apology of Hattušili I)
nu-mu LÚ^{MEŠ} ^{URU}*Ul-ma* MÈ-*ya me-na-ah-ha-an-da* / 2-*ŠU* ***a-ú-ir*** *na-aš* 2-*ŠU-pát hu-ul-li-ya-nu-un*

EXERCISES

571. KBo XV 10+ II 36 (Purification ritual for Tuthaliya and Nikalmati)
nu la-ah-hu-ur-nu-zi ša-ra-a da-a-ir na-at PA-NI ALAM$^{\text{HI.A}}$ *da-a-ir*

572. KUB XIII 35+ III 7 f. (Law court records)
^{GIŠ}PISAN-*ya-wa-kán A-NA* ^{m}*Ib-ri*-LUGAL-*ma* / *Ú-UL ku-in-ki u-uh-hu-un*

573. KBo III 34 II 5 f. (Palace chronicle)
na-at-ta a-pu-u-un GEŠTIN-*an pí-i-e-ir* LUGAL-*uš ku-in* / *a-uš-ta*

---

196 Lit. „saw“ here: „experienced, found“.

574. KUB XXXIX 14 IV 9 (Funerary ritual)
nu UD.KAM-*aš* *NAP-TA-NU* GAL *hal-zi-an-zi*[197]

575. KBo X 2 I 11 (Apology of Hattušili I)
Ù 3 ^{GIŠ}GIGIR^{MEŠ} *MA-AD-NA-NU A-NA* ^{D}UTU ^{URU}PÚ-*na pí-ih-hu-un*

576. KUB X 88 I 5’ ff. (Ritual for the stormgod of Nerik)
^{GIŠ}BANŠUR$^{\text{HI.A}}$ DINGIR^{MEŠ}-*ya ti-an-zi* / *ŠA* LUGAL MUNUS.LUGAL DUMU^{MEŠ}.LUGAL $^{\text{LÚ.MEŠ}}$DUGUD / 18 ^{GIŠ}BANŠUR *ti-an-zi*

577. KBo X 2 II 17 f. (Apology of Hattušili I)
nu kap-pu-wa-an-da-aš UD.KAM$^{\text{HI.A}}$-*aš* ^{ÍD}*Pu-u-ru-na-an* / *zi-ih-hu-un*

578. KBo X 2 I 12 (Apology of Hattušili I)
1 GU$_4$ KÙ.BABBAR 1 GÉŠPU KÙ.BABBAR *I-NA* É ^{D}IM *pí-ih-hu-un*

2.2.3. Verbal word formation

2.2.3.1. -ahh-, -annāi-, -ēš-, -šš- and -nu-

Verbs can be produced with a number of productive suffixes. Denominal are the factitive suffix *-ahh-* and the fientive suffix *eš-*, deverbal the durative suffix *-annāi-* and the intensive suffix *šš-*; with the causative suffix *-nu-* new verbs can be formed both from verbs and nouns. All these derived verbs can produce further *-šk*-formations which will be dealt with in the following chapter.

Lit.: Friedrich 1960: 73 ff.; 171 ff.; Luraghi 1979.

factitive	*-ahh-*
durative	*-annāi-*
fientive	*-ēš-*
causative	*-nu-*[198]
intensive	*-šš-*

197 Lit. „shout, call“, here: „announce“.

198 Rarely, the nasal infix formations *ištarnink-* „make ill“ and *harnink-* „destroy, ruin“ can have causative meaning.

579. KUB LV 43 I 3 f. (Ritual for a protective god)
ma-a-an I-NA MU.9.KAM *ma-a-na-aš ku-wa-pí ku-wa-pí* **ne-wa-ah-ha-an-zi** / *me-hur Ú-UL du-uq-qa-a-ri*

580. KBo V 3+ III 15 f. (Treaty with Hukkanā of Hayaša)
a-ši-wa an-tu-wa-ah-ha-aš ku-it i-da-a-lu-uš[199] ***i-da-la-u-wa-ah-zi****-ya-mu* / *nu-wa-ra-an* ^{D}UTU^{ŠI}*-ya* **i-da-la-u-wa-ah-mi**

581. KUB I 1+ II 18 (Apology of Hattušili III)
nu KUR ^{URU}*Ga-aš-ga*$^{HI.A}$ *hu-u-ma-an-te-eš* ***ku-ru-ri-ya-ah-hi-ir***

582. KBo III 38 rev. 22' f. (Tale of Zalpa, B)
LUGAL*-uš-ša IŠ-ME ša-aš* ***i-ya-an-ni-eš*** / ^{URU}*Ha-ra-ah-šu-wa-aš a-ra-aš*

583. KUB IX 27+ II 24' ff. (Paškuwatti's ritual against sexual impotence)
NINDA.GUR$_4$.RA$^{HI.A}$*-ya* / *ku-i-uš ka-ru-ú-wa-ri-wa-ar* / ***pár-ši-ya-an-na-ah-hi*** *iš-tar-na* UD.KAM*-ti-ma* / NINDA.GUR$_4$.RA *da-ma-uš* ***pár-ši-ya-an-na-ah-hi*** / *ne-ku-uz me-hur-ra da-ma-uš* ***pár-ši-ya-an-na-ah-hi*** / *me-ma-al-la-aš-ša da-ma-a-i* / ***iš-hu-u-wa-an-na-ah-hi***

584. KUB I 1+ III 7 f. (Apology of Hattušili III)
nu-un-na-aš É*-ir pa-ra-a* / ***i-ya-an-ni-iš***[200]

585. KBo XXXII 14 II 4 (Epos of liberation)
na-aš ***wa-ar-ki-eš-ta*** *na-aš šu-u-ul-li-e-it*

586. KUB LVII 63 II 39 ff. (Ritual to the sun goddess of Arinna)
nu la-ba-ar-na-aš LUGAL*-wa-aš* / *an-tu-uš-me-it pa-ra-a* / *pa-ra-a* ***ma-ak-ki-iš-kat-ta-ru***

587. KUB XIII 4 IV 32 f. (Instructions for the priests and temple officials)
ták-ku ***pár-ku-eš-te-ni*** *šu-me-el* ^{D}LAMMA*-KU-NU*[201] / *ták-ku* ***pa-ap-ri-iš-te-ni****-ma nu-uš-ma-ša-at* SAG.DU*-aš wa-aš-túl*

588. KBo V 13+ III 1 f. (Treaty with Kupanta-^{D}KAL, C version)
ÉRIN^{MEŠ}*-wa-az* ANŠE.KUR.RA^{MEŠ} *pí-ra-an* ***hu-u-i-nu-ut*** /

---

199 Nominal sentence, add „is" in the translation.
200 Metaphorical: „made progress"; „house" means the family, not the building.
201 Add „incumbent upon him" or similar construction.

nu-wa-ra-at-mu-kán wa-ar-ri lam-mar ***ar-nu-ut***

589. KBo VI 2+ II 1 f. (Laws, first tablet)
ták-ku MUNUS-*za a-pí-ya a-ki nu* LÚ-*aš* / *a-aš-šu-še-it* ***wa-ar-nu-an-zi*** *i-wa-ru-še-ta-az* LÚ-*aš da-a-i*

590. KBo V 9 I 17 f. (Treaty of Muršili II with Duppi-Tešub of Amurru)
nu-ut-ta tu-uk / NIN-*uš* ŠEŠ^{MEŠ}-*KA* KUR ^{URU}*A-mur-ri-ya še-ir* ***li-in-ga-nu-nu-un***

591. KUB XXXVI 89 obv. 24 (Ritual for the stormgod of Nerik)
ka-a-ša-wa-ta ***hal-zi-eš-ša-i*** *hal-zi-ya-u-wa-an-zi ú-id-du-aš* ^{MUŠEN}*šu-ra-aš-šu-ra-aš*

592. Mşt. 75/57 obv. 13 f. (Letter)
A-NA $^{\text{LÚ.MEŠ}}$DUB.SAR^{MEŠ} *ša-ah-ha-an lu-uz-zi* / *a-pí-ya-ma-at ku-wa-at* ***iš-ša-i***

2.2.3.2. -šk-formations

The iterative suffix *-šk-* is used to express verbal plurality. *-šk-* formations (which can be derived from every verb) indicate that an action (habituel or actual) is repeatedly performed or aims at several objects. Inchoative meaning like in the Latin *-šk-* formations is rarely attested in Hittite.

Lit.: Friedrich 1960: 95 ff., 140 f.; Dressler 1968.

593. KUB XXXI 71 IV 2 ff. (Protocol of a dream)
nu-wa-kán za-aš-hi-ya DUMU.LUGAL *ma-a-an* / *ku-iš-ki an-da ú-it* / *nu-wa-mu* ***me-mi-eš-ki-iz-zi*** *e-hu-wa-at-ta* / *ma-ni-ya-ah-mi* ŠÀ É^{TI}-*KA-wa-ták-kán* / *ku-it ne-ya-at-ta-at*

594. KUB XVII 10 II 33 f. (Myth of Telipinu)
^{D}*Te-li-pí-nu-uš li-e-la-ni-ya-an-za ú-it ú-wa-an-ti-wa-an-ta-az* / ***ti-it-hi-iš-ki-it-ta*** *kat-ta da-an-ku-i te-e-kán* ***za-ah-hi-iš-ki-iz-zi***

595. KBo VI 2+ III 46 f. (Laws, first tablet)
ták-ku GU_4.APIN.LÁ *ku-iš-ki da-a-i-iz-zi ka-ru-ú* 15 $\text{GU}_4^{\text{HI.A}}$ ***pí-eš-kir*** *ki-nu-na* 10 $\text{GU}_4^{\text{HI.A}}$ / *pa-a-i*

596. KBo XV 10+ III 53' (Purification ritual for Tuthaliya and Nikalmati)
nu A-NA BE-LÍ QA-DU DAM-*ŠU* DUMU^{MEŠ}-*ŠU a-aš-šu nam-ma* ***me-mi-iš-ki-te-en***

597. KUB XXXI 113, 5' f. (Fragment of an instruction)
wa-a-tar ŠA DINGIR^{LIM} NINDA.GUR$_4$.RA UD^{MI} ^{GIŠ}TIR *ga-ú-ri-ya-az* / ^{GIŠ}TIR *du-un-na-ri-ya-za* ***píd-da-iš-ki-it-tin***

598. KUB I 1+ I 69 (Apology of Hattušili III)
nu-za KUR.KUR^{MEŠ} ^{LÚ}KÚR *tar-ah-hi-iš-ki-nu-un*

599. KBo XV 2 IV 27' ff. (Substitution ritual for the king)
nam-ma LUGAL-*uš ku-e-da-aš ku-e-da-aš* / *A-NA AŠ-RI*$^{\text{HI.A}}$ ***a-še-eš-kat-ta-ri*** *nu-za a-pa-a-ša a-pí-e-da-aš A-NA AŠ-RI*$^{\text{HI.A}}$ / ***a-še-eš-kat-ta-ri***

600. KUB XVII 7+ IV 23' f. (Myth of Ullikummi)
I-NA UD.1.KAM-*ya-aš* 1 *AM-MA-DU* ***pár-ki-iš-kat-ta-ri*** / *I-NA* ITU.1.KAM-*ma-aš* 1 IKU-*an* ***pár-ki-iš-kat-ta-ri***

601. KUB I 1+ IV 72 f. (Apology of Hattušili III)
na-an-kán hu-u-ma-an-ti-ya-pát EGIR-*an* $^{\text{NA4}}$ZI.KIN / ***ti-it-ta-nu-uš-kán-zi*** ^{DUG}*har-ši-ya-li-ya-kán* ***iš-hu-iš-kán-zi***

602. KBo V 1 I 38 f. (Papanikri's ritual)
nu ŠA 4 UDU$^{\text{HI.A}}$ ^{UZU}Ì NINDA$^{\text{HI.A}}$-*ya ku-e-iš* ***pár-ši-ya-an-ni-iš-ki-it*** / *na-aš A-NA* DINGIR^{LIM} EGIR-*pa hi-in-ga-zi*

603. KUB XVII 7+ IV 33' (Myth of Ullikummi)
nu-kán ^{D}UTU-*uš ne-pí-ša-az kat-ta ša-ku-wa-it nu-za* ^{D}*Ul-lu-kum-mi-in* ***ša-ku-iš-ki-iz-zi***

604. KUB XXIV 8+ I 29 f. (Story of Appu)
pa-a-i-ta-aš[202] / MUNUS-*za na-aš-za IT-TI* ^{m}*Ap-pu wa-aš-ša-an-za* ***še-eš-ki-it***

202 Topicalized verb.

EXERCISES

605. KBo II 3 I 52 f. (Maštigga's ritual)
nu UDU *ha-at-ta-an-zi nam-ma-an ar-ha ha-ap-pí-eš-na-an-zi* / *nu* GUNNI *i-ya-an-zi na-an ar-ha wa-ar-nu-wa-an-zi*

606. KUB VIII 27 edge 1b f. (Lunar omen)
ták-ku ^{D}XXX *ú-iz-zi na-aš* GE$_6$-*iš-zi* / ^{D}GAŠAN *A-NA* KUR^{TI} HUL-*lu i-ya-an-na-i*

607. KBo III 1+ III 49 f. (Proclamation of Telipinu)
UR-RA-AM ŠE-RA-AM ku-iš am-me-el EGIR-*an* LUGAL-*uš ki-ša-ri nu hal-ki-uš* / *ŠUM-aš-mi-it ši-i-e-eš-ki*

608. KUB XXI 27+ IV 30' f. (Puduhepa's prayer to the sun goddess of Arinna)
nu ^{D}IM *A-BU-KA* ^{D}UTU ^{URU}PÚ-*na* AMA-*KA* / *tu-el me-mi-an Ú-UL wa-ah-nu-wa-an-zi iš-ta-ma-aš-ša-an-zi-ta*

609. KUB I 1+ IV 39 f. (Apology of Hattušili III)
^{D}*IŠTAR-ma-mu-kán* GAŠAN-*YA i-la-ni i-la-ni* / *nam-ma ti-iš-ki-it*

610. KUB XXIX 1 IV 2 (Foundation ritual)
nu DUMU.NITA^{MEŠ} DUMU.MUNUS^{MEŠ} *ha-aš-še-eš ha-an-za-aš-še-eš ma-ak-ki-eš-ki-an-du*

611. KUB XIII 35+ I 4 (Law court records)
nu Ú-NU-TUM ku-it ku-e-da-ni pí-eš-ki-it na-at Ú-UL ši-ya-eš-ki-it

612. KUB XVII 21 I 2 f. (Prayer of Arnuwanda and Ašmunikal)
SÍSKUR$^{HI.A}$-*aš-ma-aš pár-ku-i šal-li ša-ne-iz-zi* / ^{URU}*Ha-at-tu-ša-aš-pát* KUR-*ya pí-iš-ga-u-e-ni*

2.2.4. Nominal forms of the verb

2.2.4.1. Verbal substantives and infinitives

From every verb, a verbal substantive ending in *-war* (*-mar* after *u*) can be derived. Their inflection varies: most frequently *obliquus* forms are derived from an *u*-stem (*pāwar* : gen. *pāuwas*) but there are also examples of heteroclitic (*miumar* : gen. *miumnas*) and *r*-inflection (*wekuwar* : gen. *wekuwaras*). Functionally, the genitive of the verbal noun corresponds to a Latin gerund, supplying the „necessity of something“. Further, there are two different infinitive forms: the so-called infinitive I with the ending *-uwanzi,* usually occuring with verbs without ablaut, and the so-called infinitive II with the ending auf *-anna* in verbs with ablaut. Additionally, there are numerous analogous forms. The syntax of the infinitives varies between nominal and verbal government.

Additionally, supina can be formed with *-wan* which only occurs in periphrastic expressions with *dāi-/tiya-* „begin/start to do something“ (see the following chapter).

Lit.: Friedrich 1960: 142 ff.; Ose 1944; Kammenhuber 1954; Disterheft 1984; Boley 1992; Hoffner/Melchert 2008: 330 ff.

613. KUB XXVII 68 IV 1’ f. (Revision of the god’s festivals)
3-*ŠU ṬUP-PU* EGIR-*an* ***tar-nu-wa-aš*** / *ŠA* DINGIR^{MEŠ} ^{URU}*Ne-ri-iq-qa*[203]

614. KUB XXVIII 92 I 6’ (Ritual for the stormgod of Nerik)
INIM^{MEŠ} ***an-da-an hal-zi-ya-u-aš*** *tal-li-ya-zi*[204]

615. KBo VI 2+ III 48 (Laws, first tablet)
ták-ku ANŠE.KUR.RA ***tu-u-ri-ya-u-wa-aš*** *ku-iš-ki ta-a-i-iz-zi ut-tar-še-it QA-TAM-MA-pát*[205]

616. KUB XXXVI 89 rev. 6 (Ritual for the stormgod of Nerik)
GISKIM-*ši* ^{MUŠEN}*šu-ra-aš-šu-ra-aš* ***hal-zi-ya-u-wa-an-zi*** *ú-id-du*

617. KUB XV 17+ I 52 f. (Vow of Puduhepa)
1 DUMU.NITA ^{m}*Ta-ti-li-iš* ŠEŠ ^{f}*Ti-ta-i A-NA* ^{m}*A-pal-lu-ú*
šal-la-nu-ma-an-zi / *AD-DIN*

618. KUB XXXIII 121 II 8 (Tale of Keššі)
HUR.SAG^{MEŠ}-*ša-aš nam-ma* ***hu-ur-nu-wa-an-zi*** *Ú-UL pa-iz-zi*
na-aš-ša-an pa-ra-a A-NA DAM-*ŠU-pát IŠ-ME*

619. KBo XIX 128+ VI 14’ ff. (AN.TAH.ŠUM festival)
LUGAL-*uš* GUB-*aš* / *A-NA* $^{\text{LÚ.MEŠ}}$*BE-LU-TIM* ***a-ku-wa-an-na*** /
ki-iš-ša-ri-i pa-a-i

203 Colophon, not a complete sentence.
204 Meaning a ritual call which assembles the participitants of the ritual at a special place.
205 Nominal sentence, add „is“ in the translation.

620. KBo III 1+ IV 25/17' f. (Proclamation of Telipinu)
ku-i-ta-aš-ša ***šar-ra-an-na*** KAxU-*az ú-e-ri-iz-zi* / *na-aš-ta* É-*ir-za pa-ra-a pí-eš-ši-ya-an-du*[206]

621. KUB XXX 34 IV 20 ff. (Purification ritual)
na-aš-ta an-tu-uh-šu-uš / *ku-e-iz-za* KÁ.GAL$^{\text{HI.A}}$-*za kat-ta* ***ku-na-an-na*** / *pí-e-hu-da-an-zi a-pu-u-ša-kán a-pí-e-iz kat-ta* / *pí-da-at-ti*

2.2.4.2. Participles

The participle with suffix *-ant* is passive when derived from transitive verbs and active-intransitive from intransitive verbs, while indifferent regarding the tempus in both cases. Participles occur attributively and predicatively but are not very common in this use. Very frequent is a construction of the neutral participle with *hark-*, probably expressing partly anteriority, partly result, which is still quite disputed in Hittite research. Drop of the copula is very frequent in constructions with predicative participle.

Lit.: Friedrich 1960: 144 f.; Boley 1984; Hoffner/Melchert 2008: 339 ff.

622. KBo III 22 obv. 43 f. (Proclamation of Anitta)
^{m}*Hu-uz-zi-ya-na* LUGAL ^{URU}*Za-a-al-pu-wa* ***hu-šu-wa-an-ta-an*** / ^{URU}*Ne-e-ša ú-wa-te-nu-un*

623. KBo III 34 II 27 f. (Palace chronicle)
da-i-iš-ša-an ANŠE.KUR.RA-*aš ku-i-da* $^{\text{LÚ.MEŠ}}$KUŠ$_7$ / ***a-am-mi-ya-an-tu-uš****-mu-uš nu-uš* ^{m}*Iš-pu-ta-aš-i-na-ar-aš ma-ni-ya-ah-hi-eš-ki-iz-zi*

624. KBo III 34 II 13 f. (Palace chronicle)
^{URU}*A-an-ku-wa ka-aq-qa-pí-iš* / ***ma-ak-la-an-te-eš***

625. KUB XXXIII 102+ II 10 ff. (Myth of Ullikummi)
tu-uk-wa IGI-*an-da* / ^{GIŠ}ERIN-*pí ka-ru-ú* ***du-wa-ar-na-an*** / ÚTUL$^{\text{HI.A}}$-*ya-at-ta* IGI-*an-da ka-ru-ú* ***za-nu-wa-an***

626. KUB VIII 83, 12' f. (Birth omen)
ták-ku IZ-BU GEŠTU$^{\text{HI.A}}$-*ŠU* NU.GÁL LUGAL-*wa-aš* / UD$^{\text{HI.A}}$ ***zi-in-na-an-te-eš***

---

206 Object drop, add „him" in the translation.

627. KBo III 1+ I 12 (Proclamation of Telipinu)
nu URU$^{DIDLI.HI.A}$ GAL.GAL^{TIM} ***ti-it-ti-ya-an-te-eš e-šir***

628. KUB I 1+ III 46 ff. (Apology of Hattušili III)
nu ^{URU}*Ne-ri-iq-qa-aš* / *ku-it IŠ-TU U$_4$-UM* ^{m}*Ha-an-ti-li ar-ha* ***har-ga-an-za e-eš-ta*** / *na-an* EGIR-*pa ú-e-da-ah-hu-un*

629. KUB I 1+ II 41 f. (Apology of Hattušili III)
URU$^{DIDLI.HI.A}$-*ma ku-i-e-eš ŠA* KUR ^{URU}*Ha-at-ti* / ***iš-tap-pa-an-te-eš e-šir*** *nu-kán* GUL-*hi-eš-ki-ir*

630. KUB XXXI 47 rev. 1 ff. (Letter)
$^{LÚ.MEŠ}$*SÚ-UB-RI-E-ma-ta ku-i-e-eš ŠA A-BI-YA A-BI A-BI-YA* / *kat-ta-an* EGIR-*pa* ***ú-wa-an-te-eš e-šir*** / *ú-uq-qa ku-i-e-eš kat-ta-an* EGIR-*pa* ***ú-wa-an-te-eš e-šir*** / *na-at* UGU *ti-i-e-ir QA-DU* NÍG.GA$^{HI.A}$-*ŠU-NU* / *na-at-kán A-NA* KUR-*KA pár-ra-an-ta ú-e-ir*

631. KBo V 1 I 41 ff. (Papanikri's ritual)
ma-a-an-wa AMA-*KA na-aš-ma A-BU-KA ap-pí-iš-zi-az* / *ku-it-ki* ***wa-aš-ta-nu-wa-an har-kán-zi*** *na-aš-ma-wa zi-ik* / *ka-a pa-ra-a ha-an-da-an-ni na-aš-ma za-aš-hi-it ku-it-ki* / ***wa-aš-ta-nu-wa-an har-ta*** *nu har-na-a-uš hu-u-ni-ik-ta-at* / ^{GIŠ}GAG$^{HI.A}$-*ma-wa du-wa-ar-na-ad-da-at ki-nu-na-wa* / *ka-a-ša* DINGIR^{LUM} 2-*ta-a-an šar-ni-ik-ta*

632. KUB I 1+ III 52 ff. (Apology of Hattušili III)
ku-it IŠ-TU ^{URU}*Ne-ri-ik* / *Ù IŠ-TU* ^{URU}*Ha-ak-piš-ša* ***da-ma-aš-ša-an har-kir*** *nu-za hu-u-ma-an-da-an* / ARAD-*ah-hu-un*

633. KUB XIII 9+ IV 32 f. (Instruction of Tuthaliya)
na-aš-za ku-it ku-it ***da-a-an har-zi*** / *hu-u-ma-an ta-a-an pí-eš-ki-iz-zi*

634. KUB XIII 35+ I 32 f. (Law court records)
3 ANŠE.GÌR.NUN.NA^{MEŠ} É.GAL^{LIM}-*wa* ***tu-u-ri-ya-an har-ku-un*** / *nu-wa-ra-at e-kir*

635. KUB XXIV 3+ II 7 ff. (Muršili's prayer to the sun goddess of Arinna)
nu-ut-ta ^{m}*Mur-ši*-DINGIR^{LIM}-*iš* LUGAL-*uš ud-da-a-ar* / *ku-e*

me-mi-eš-ki-iz-zi nu ᴰUTU ᵁᴿᵁ*A-ri-in-na* GEŠTU-*an* / *pa-ra-a* ***la-ga-a-an har-ak*** *na-at iš-ta-ma-aš*

2.2.5. Periphrases

A number of semantic nuances are expressed by verbal periphrases, partly by two finite verbs, partly by verbs that semantically come close to auxiliary verbs and forms of the infinitive or supinum.

Lit.: Friedrich 1960: 142 ff.; Ose 1944; Boley 1992.

dāi-/tiya- + sup.	„to start something, be about to do something“
ašnu- + inf. I	„to be finished with, to be done with something“
zinna- + inf. I	„to finish, to stop something“
tarh- + inf. I or finite verb	„to be able to do something, to be capable of sth.“
šanh- + inf. II	„try to do something“

636. KBo III 1+ I 63 ff. (Proclamation of Telipinu)
ma-a-an ᵐ*Ha-an-ti-i-li-iš-ša* ᴸᵁ́ŠU.GI *ki-ša-at na-aš* DINGIR*ᴸᴵᴹ-iš* ***ki-ik-ki-iš-šu-u-wa-an*** / ***da-a-iš***[207] *nu-kán* ᵐ*Zi-dan-ta-aš* ᵐ*Pí-še-ni-in* DUMU ᵐ*Ha-an-ti-i-li QA-DU* DUMUᴹᴱŠ*-ŠU* / *ku-en-ta*

637. KBo XXXII 14 III 9 ff. (Epos of liberation)
ᴺᴵᴺᴰᴬ*ku-gul-la-an* UR.GI$_7$-*aš* UDUN-*ni-ya pí-ra-an ar-ha pít-te-nu-ut* / *pa-ra-a-an-kán hu-it-ti-at* UDUN-*ni-ya-az na-an-kán* Ì-*i* / *an-da šu-ú-ni-at ša-ak-ni-ya-an-kán an-da* / *šu-ú-ni-at na-aš-za e-ša-at na-an* ***a-da-a-an-na da-iš***

638. Mşt. 75/67 obv. 4 ff. (Letter)
ᴳᴵŠ*ar-mi-iz-zi-wa* / *IŠ-TU* NA$_4$ ***ú-e-du-ma-an-zi*** / *ka-ru-ú* ***zi-in-na-an-da***

207 „He started to become a god“ = „he was dying“.

639. KBo XI 45+ III 22’ ff. (Festival ritual for a prince)
ma-ah-ha-an-ma e-eš-ha-ni-i[208] EGIR-*an-da* / ***ir-ha-u-wa-an-zi***
zi-in-na-an-zi / *nu-kán* UDU$^{\text{HI.A}}$ GU$_4$.MAH$^{\text{HI.A}}$-*ya ar-kán-zi*

640. KUB XXIX 4 I 3 ff. (Ritual for the transfer of the Black Goddess)
ma-a-an a-pí-e-iz IŠ-TU É DINGIR GE$_6$ *pa-ra-a ta-ma-i* É DINGIR GE$_6$ /
ú-e-te-iz-zi nam-ma-za DINGIR$^{\textit{LAM}}$ *ha-an-ti-i a-ša-ši* / *nu-kán ku-it-ma-an*
ú-e-tum-ma-an-zi *hu-u-ma-an-ta-az-zi-ya* ***aš-nu-zi***

641. KUB XXIX 4 III 49 ff. (Ritual for the transfer of the Black Goddess)
nu-kán ma-ah-ha-an DINGIR$^{\textit{LAM}}$ ***hu-it-ti-ya-u-wa-an-zi***[209] ***aš-nu-an-zi*** /
nam-ma-aš-ša-an PA-NI ÍD ^{GIŠ}ZA.LAM.GAR$^{\text{HI.A}}$ *i-ya-an* / *nu-kán*
ú-li-hi-in ^{GIŠ}ZA.LAM.GAR-*aš an-da pí-e-da-an-zi*

642. KBo XXXII 14 III 16 f. (Epos of liberation)
na-aš me-ik-ki šu-u-ul-li-it na-aš-ta nam-ma URU-*an an-da Ú-UL* /
a-uš-zi na-an-za PA-NI BE-LÍ-ŠU ***i-ši-ya-ah-hu-u-an-zi tar-hu-ir***

643. KUB XVII 10 I 32 f. (Myth of Telipinu)
I-NA URU-*ŠU* KÁ.GAL / *ú-iz-zi nu* ***Ú-UL tar-hu-uz-zi ha-a-ši***

644. KUB I 1+ III 63 (Apology of Hattušili III)
a-pa-a-aš-ma-mu ***har-kán-na*** *IŠ-TU* INIM DINGIR$^{\textit{LIM}}$ *Ù IŠ-TU* INIM LÚ
ša-an-ah-ta

645. KBo V 4 I 41 ff. (Treaty with Targašnalli of Hapalla)
ma-a-an tu-uk-ma ku-iš-ki ^{m}*Tar-ga-aš-na-al-li-in na-aš-ma* DUMU-*KA*
ku-na-an-na ša-an-ha-an-zi / *nam-ma-ma-kán ar-ha wa-at-ku-uz-zi na-aš*
^{URU}*Ha-at-tu-ši ú-iz-zi na-aš tu-uk ma-ah-ha-an* ^{LÚ}KÚR / *ŠA* ^{D}UTU$^{\textit{ŠI}}$
QA-TAM-MA ^{LÚ}KÚR

---

208 Here: „offering of blood“.
209 The „dragging“ is the ritual transfer of the deity.

EXERCISES

646. Bo 86/299 III 27 (Bronze tablet, treaty of Tuthaliya IV)
na-at har-ga-an-na te-ip-nu-um-ma-an-zi-ya li-e tar-na-i

647. KUB XXV 36 II 12’ (Festival ritual for a prince)
LUGAL-*i a-ku-wa-an-na mar-nu-an pí-an-zi*

648. KUB XV 17+ I 11 (Vow of Puduhepa)
A-NA MUNUS$^{\textit{TI}}$-kán ^{LÚ}ŠU.DAB[210] *še-ir ar-ha tar-na-an-za*

649. KUB XXXIII 121 II 12 ff. (Tale of Kešši)
DINGIR^{MEŠ}-*eš-kán* ^{m}*Ki-eš-ši-ya* / *iš-pa-an-du-uz-zi še-ir kar-tim-mi-ya-u-wa-an-te-eš nu-uš-ši hu-u-i-tar* / *hu-u-ma-an pí-ra-an ar-ha mu-un-na-a-ir*

650. KUB XXX 15+ obv. 17 f. (Funerary ritual)
nu ku-i-e-eš ku-i-e-eš ha-aš-ti-ya-aš li-eš-šu-u-wa-an-zi ú-wa-an-te-eš / *nu a-da-an-na hu-u-ma-an-ti pí-ya-an-zi*

651. KUB VII 53+ II 61 (Tunnawi’s ritual)
na-aš-ta EN SÍSKUR *wa-ar-pu-wa-an-zi pa-iz-zi*

652. KUB XXX 26 I 1 ff. (Funerary ritual)
ma-a-an UN-*an*[211] / ^{D}*Iš-ha-ra-az* GIG-*zi na-aš iš-ha-ri-iš-ha-ri nam-ma-aš a-ki* / ^{LÚ}*MU-ZA-ŠU-ma-aš-ši A-NA* NINDA KAŠ *an-da ú-e-ri-ya-an-za e-eš-ta* / *nu ak-kán-ti* EGIR-*an-da ki-iš-ša-an i-ya-mi*

653. KBo XIX 76+ I 32’ f. (Fragment of the annals of Muršili II)
nu-mu[212] ^{LÚ}KÚR *ku-iš*[213] *Ú-UL ša-ak-ta nu-za* ^{LÚ}KÚR *hal-ki-uš wa-ar-šu-u-wa-an-zi* / *ar-ha tar-na-an har-ta*

---

210 Namely as a worker.
211 Must be a woman in this case.
212 The pronoun refers syntactically to *šakta.*
213 Can be relative or causal.

2.3. The inflection of the Pronouns

2.3.1. Personal pronouns 1st and 2nd person

Clitic pronouns of the 1st and 2nd person are only used to mark special emphasis. Only the forms of the genitive to express possession are relatively frequent.

Lit.: Friedrich 1960: 62 ff.; 131; Katz 1998; Hoffner/Melchert 2008: 132 ff.

CLITICS:	Singular		plural	
	1st pers.	2nd pers.	1st pers.	2nd pers.
nom.	*uk, ammuk*	*Zik*	*wēš, anzaš*	*šumēš, šumaš*
acc.	*uk, ammuk*	*Tuk*	*anzaš*	*šumaš*
gen.	*ammēl*	*tuēl*	*anzēl*	*šumēl, šumenzan*
dat.	*uk, ammuk*	*tuk*	*anzaš*	*šumaš*
abl.	*ammedaz*	*tuedaz*	*anzedaz*	*šumedaz*

ENCLITICS:	singular		plural	
	1st pers.	2nd pers.	1st pers.	2nd pers.
Dat./acc.	*-mu*	*-ta, -tu*	*-naš*	*-šmaš*

654. KBo X 2 III 29 ff. (Apology of Hattušili I)
ÍD*Ma-a-la-an-na Ú-UL ku-iš-ki pí-ra-an za-a-iš / na-an* ***ú-uk***
LUGAL.GAL *Ta-ba-ar-na-aš* GÌR-*it / zi-ih-hu-un*

655. KBo V 3+ II 36 f. (Treaty with Hukkanā of Hayaša)
am-mu-uk*-wa-za li-in-ga-nu-wa-an-za*[214] */ nu-wa Ú-UL ku-it-ki me-ma-ah-hi*

214 Nominal sentence, add „have“ in the translation.

656. KUB XIX 6+ III 75 (Treaty with Alakšandu of Wiluša)
na-at-za-kán ***zi-ik*** ^{m}*A-la-ak-ša-an-du-uš ša-ki*

657. KUB XXIX 1 I 19 (Foundation ritual)
zi-ik ***am-me-el*** É-*na li-e ú-wa-ši*

658. KUB XXXVI 35 I 23' f. (El, Ašertum, and the stormgod)
^{D}U-*aš A-NA* ^{D}*A-še-ir-tum IQ-BI* ***tu-e-el****-wa-kán* / DUMU^{MEŠ}-*KA* 77 *ku-e-nu-un* 88 *ku-e-nu-un*

659. KUB XXXI 4+ obv. 11 (Chronicle of Puhanu)
nu ***am-mu-uk*** *pí-e-hu-te-it-te-en*

660. KUB XIX 6+ III 73 (Treaty with Alakšandu of Wiluša)
nam-ma ki-i ku-it ṬUP-PU ***tu-uk*** ^{m}*A-la-ak-ša-an-du-uš i-ya-nu-un* / *ne-it-ták-kán* MU.KAM-*ti* MU.KAM-*ti pí-ra-an* 3-*ŠÚ hal-zi-eš-ša-an-du*

661. KUB XIX 49+ I 23 (Treaty with Manapa-Datta)
nu-ut-ta ***am-me-e-da-za*** *me-mi-ya-na-az pa-ah-ha-ša-nu-ir*

662. KUB XXXVI 90 obv. 18 ff. (Prayer to the stormgod of Nerik)
nu lu-uk-kat-ti UD-*ti* / *A-NA* EZEN$_4$-*KA e-hu e-hu IŠ-TU* $^{HUR.SAG}$*Ha-ah-ru-wa* / ***tu-e-da-az*** *a-aš-ši-ya-an-ta-za* / *tu-el* NÍ.TE ZI-*KA-ya ku-e-da-ni pí-di* / *e-hu*

663. KBo XXII 2 obv. 11 f. (Tale of Zalpa, A)
ú-e-ša *ku-wa-pí-it a-ru-me-en nu* MUNUS-*za* DUMU 1^{EN} *ha-a-ši* / *nu-uz-za an-za-aš* 1-*ŠU ha-a-aš-ta*

664. KUB XXXIII 106+ II 14 f. (Myth of Ullikummi)
ták-ku-wa-kán ***an-za-a-aš*** *I-NA* $^{HUR.SAG}$*Kán-dur-na še-ir e-šu-wa-aš-ta-ti* / *da-ma-iš-ma-wa-kán I-NA* $^{HUR.SAG}$*La-la-pa-du-wa še-ir e-eš-zi*

665. KBo III 1+ II 72 f. (Proclamation of Telipinu)
šu-ma-aš-ša *pa-an-ku-uš an-da e-ip-tin* / *nu-uš-ma-ša-an* ^{UZU}KAxZU$_9$-*it ka-ri-ip-tin*

666. KUB XIII 4 II 73 f. (Instructions for the priests and temple officials)
nu-kán ***šu-ma-aš*** UN-*aš u-wa-it-ta-ri ha-ap-pár-ra-aš-ma-aš da-at-te-ni* / DINGIR^{MEŠ}-*ma-kán* ***šu-ma-aš*** *I-NA* EGIR.UD^{MI} *an-da ša-an-hi-eš-kán-zi*

667. KUB XXXI 4+ rev. 7’ ff. (Chronicle of Puhanu)
ku-it-ma-an / ^{URU}*Hal-pa-aš* ^{D}IM-*aš* ***an-zi-ta-az*** *hu-u-wa-a-i nu* ^{URU}*Hat-ti* ^{D}IM-*aš nu-un-na-aš ú-iz-zi* / *a-pa-a-aš-pát pí-ra-an hu-wa-a-i-iš-ki-wa-an da-a-i*

668. KBo X 2 I 31 f. (Apology of Hattušili I)
*nu-**mu** ma-ah-ha-an* LÚ^{MEŠ} ^{URU}*Ni-na-aš-ša me-na-ah-ha-an-da* / *a-ú-ir nu* KÁ.GAL$^{\text{HI.A}}$ EGIR-*pa hi-eš-šir*

669. KUB XXIII 1+ II 7 (Treaty with Šaušgamuwa)
*ka-a-aš-**ta** me-mi-aš ŠA-PAL NI-EŠ* DINGIR^{LIM} *ki-it-ta-ru*

670. KUB I 1+ III 71 f. (Apology of Hattušili III)
*nu-wa-a**n-na-aš*** ^{D}*IŠTAR* ^{URU}*Ša-mu-ha* ^{D}U ^{URU}*Ne-ri-iq-qa-ya* / *ha-an-ni-eš-šar ha-an-na-an-zi*

671. KBo V 3+ II 7 (Treaty with Hukkanā of Hayaša)
*nu-u**š-ma-aš** ki-i ut-tar NI-IŠ* DINGIR^{MEŠ} EGIR-*an li-e tar-na-an-zi*

EXERCISES

672. KUB XXIII 1+ II 1 (Treaty with Šaušgamuwa)
nu-ut-ta ^{D}UTU^{ŠI} LUGAL.GAL *tu-uk* ^{D}*IŠTAR*-A.A-*an* ŠU-*ta AṢ-BAT*

673. KBo V 3+ I 5 (Treaty with Hukkanā of Hayaša)
nu-ut-ta am-me-el NIN-*YA AŠ-ŠUM* DAM-*UT-TIM AD-DIN*

674. KUB I 1+ I 37 f. (Apology of Hattušili III)
DINGIR^{LIM}-*ni-wa-at-ta* / *am-mu-uk tar-na-ah-hi nu-wa li-e na-ah-ti*

675. KUB XXI 27+ I 13 ff. (Puduhepa’s prayer to the sun goddess of Arinna)
nu-un-a-aš ^{D}UTU ^{URU}PÚ-*na* GAŠAN-*YA ku-e-da-ni pí-di* / *ti-it-ta-nu-ut na-at tu-el* / *a-aš-ši-ya-an-ta-aš* DUMU-*aš ŠA* ^{D}IM ^{URU}*Ne-ri-ik AŠ-RU*

676. KUB XXXVI 35 I 13’ ff. (El, Ašertum, and the stormgod)
nu-wa-ták-kán am-mi-ta-az / *me-mi-ya-na-az kat-ta ta-ma-aš-mi am-mi-e-da-za-ma-wa-ta* / ^{GIŠ}BAL.TUR-*az ha-at-ta-ra-a-mi*

677. KBo III 38 rev. 20’ (Tale of Zalpa, B)
ú-uk-wa at-ti-mi Ú-UL a-aš-šu-uš[215]

678. KUB I 1+ III 69 f. (Apology of Hattušili III)
nu-wa-za zi-ik LUGAL.GAL *am-mu-uk-ma-wa-kán* 1^{EN} *HAL-ṢÌ*[216] *ku-in* / *da-li-ya-at*

679. KUB XVII 21 I 6 ff. (Prayer of Arnuwanda and Ašmunikal)
nu šu-me-eš-pát DINGIR^{MEŠ} DINGIR^{MEŠ}*-aš iš-ta-an-za-ni-it še-ik-te-ni* / *ka-ru-ú-za šu-me-en-za-an* É DINGIR^{MEŠ}*-KU-NU* EGIR*-an an-zi-el* / *i-wa-ar Ú-UL ku-iš-ki kap-pu-u-wa-an har-ta*

2.3.2. Enclitic personal pronouns 3rd person

For the nominative and accusative of 3rd person pronouns, there are special enclitic forms of the pronominal stem *-a-* while the dative is formed from the pronominal stem *-ši-*. The enclitics are frequently suffixed at sentence introductory particles which often leads to vowel contractions. In particular, it should be noted that the vocalism in the contractions with *nu* is partly irregular: *nu* + *-aš* > *naš* (see 2.4.2).

Lit.: Friedrich 1960: 63; Hoffner/Melchert 2008: 135 f.

	singular	plural
nom.c.	*-aš*	*-e*
acc.c.	*-an*	*-uš*
nom.-acc.n.	*-at*	*-at*
dat.	*-ši*	*-šmaš*

215 Nominal sentence, add „am“ in the translation.

216 Add either LUGAL as regens for 1^{EN} *HALṢÌ* or *harmi* „ I have“ as supplement to *ammuk*.

680. KBo VI 2+ I 59 f. (Laws, first tablet)
ták-ku ARAD-*iš hu-u-wa-i na-***aš** *A-NA* KUR ^{URU}*Lu-ú-i-ya pa-iz-zi*
*ku-i-š***a-an** *a-ap-pa / ú-wa-te-iz-zi nu-uš-še* 6 GÍN KÙ.BABBAR *pa-a-i*[217]

681. KBo VI 2+ II 3 f. (Laws, first tablet)
*ták-ku-***aš**[218] *at-ta-aš-ša-ša* É-*ri a-ki Ù* DUMU^{MEŠ}-*ŠU a-ša-an-zi /*
i-wa-ru-uš-še-it LÚ-*aš na-at-ta da-a-i*

682. KBo V 3+ III 54 (Treaty with Hukkanā of Hayaša)
Ú-UL ^{MUNUS}SUHUR.LÁ *i-ya-at-ta-at a-pa-a-š***a-an**-*kán an-da a-uš-zi*[219]

683. KBo XI 14 III 13 f. (Hantitaššu's ritual)
1 NINDA.Ì *da-a-i na-***an** *pár-ši-ya na-***an**-*kán* DINGIR^{MEŠ}-*aš*
GAM-*an-ta-an / da-a-i*

684. KUB I 1+ IV 53 ff. (Apology of Hattušili III)
up-pí-eš-šar$^{\mathrm{HI.A}}$-*ma-mu*[220] *ku-e / up-pí-iš-kán-zi na-***at** *A-NA AB-BA*$^{\mathrm{HI.A}}$ *Ù*
AB-BA AB-BA$^{\mathrm{HI.A}}$ */ Ú-UL ku-e-da-ni-ik-ki up-pí-ir*

685. KUB XXII 70 obv. 50 (Oracle concerning the intrigues at the Hittite court)
nu ku-it SIxSÁ-*ta-ri na-***at** *A-NA* DINGIR^{LIM} *pí-an-zi*

686. KUB I 1+ III 8 (Apology of Hattušili III)
*ka-ni-iš-šu-u-wa-ar-ma-***at** *ŠA* ^{D}*IŠTAR* GAŠAN-*YA e-eš-ta*

687. KBo III 1+ II 3 f. (Proclamation of Telipinu)
la-ah-ha-ma ku-wa-at-ta ÉRIN^{MEŠ}-*uš pa-iz-zi* **ne** *a-ap-pa Ú-UL* SIG$_5$-*in /*
ú-e-eš-kán-ta[221]

688. KBo XXII 2 rev. 12' f. (Tale of Zalpa, A)
*šu-***uš** *ta-me-eš-šir /* **še** *a-kir*

689. KUB XXXIX 14 I 15 f. (Funerary ritual)
GU$_4$$^{\mathrm{HI.A}}$-*ma ha-ad-da-an-zi / nu-***uš** $^{\mathrm{LÚ.MEŠ}}$MUHALDIM *da-an-zi*

---

217 Namely the owner of the dependant.
218 Meaning the wife.
219 Rhetorical interrogative clause.
220 „present" is euphemistic for „tribute".
221 The verbs seem incongruent in numerus, but in the first case the military leader is meant whereas the second verb refers to the soldiers.

690. KUB XVII 21 I 25 ff. (Prayer of Arnuwanda and Ašmunikal)
nu-za šu-me-en-za-an / ŠA DINGIR^{MEŠ} ARAD^{MEŠ}-*KU-NU* GÉME^{MEŠ}-*KU-NU da-aš-ki-ir-ra / nu-**uš**-za* ARAD-*na-ah-hi-iš-kir* GÉME-*ah-hi-iš-kir*

691. KBo XVI 47 obv. 10' ff. (Treaty)
*nu-**uš**-kán ma-a-an ku-e-mi ma-a-**nu-uš** ar-nu-mi ma-a-an-mu-kán ar-ha-ma / ku-iš-ki iš-pár-za-zi na-**aš** ku-e-da-ni* KUR-*ya pa-iz-zi na-**an** zi-ik / a-pí-iz-za za-ah-hi-ya-ah-hu-ut ú-ga-**an*** ^{D}UTU^{ŠI} *ki-e-iz-za za-ah-hi-ya-mi*

692. KUB I 1+ III 65 (Apology of Hattušili III)
*nu-uš-**ši** ku-ru-ri-ya-ah-hu-un*

693. KUB I 1+ II 33 (Apology of Hattušili III)
*ki-e-iz-za-ma-**aš-ši*** ^{URU}*Tal-ma-li-ya-aš* ZAG-*aš e-eš-ta*

694. KBo X 2 I 23 (Apology of Hattušili I)
*nu-uš-**ma-aš**-kán* GU$_4$^{MEŠ}-*un* UDU$^{\text{HI.A}}$-*un ar-ha da-ah-hu-un*

695. KUB I 1+ II 76 ff. (Apology of Hattušili III)
*nu-uš-**ma-aš**-kán Ú-UL ku-e-iz-qa ku-it ha-ap-ta-at / nu-mu-za al-wa-an-za-ah-hu-u-wa-an-zi nam-ma QA-DU* DAM-*ZU* DUMU-*ZU / e-ip-pir*

EXERCISES

696. KBo IV 10+ obv. 9' f. (Treaty with Ulmitešub)
nu-uš-ši-kán ma-a-an wa-aš-túl a-aš-zi / nu GIM-*an A-NA* LUGAL KUR ^{URU}*Hat-ti* ZI-*an-za na-an QA-TAM-MA i-ya-ad-du*[222]

697. KUB IV 1+ II 5 f. (Incantation at the enemy border)
nu-uš-ma-aš-ša-an ka-a-ša DI-NAM ku-it / ar-nu-um-me-ni na-at iš-ta-ma-aš-te-en

698. KUB I 1+ III 20 (Apology of Hattušili III)
na-an-mu DINGIR^{LUM} GAŠAN-*YA kat-te-ir-ra-ah-ta*

---

222 Here: „treat“.

699. KUB I 1+ I 73 f. (Apology of Hattušili III)
ku-it-ma-an-ma-za TUR-*aš e-šu-un nu-za* KUR.KUR ^{LÚ}KÚR *ku-e tar-ah-hi-iš-ki-nu-un* / *na-at TUP-PU ha-an-ti-i* DÙ-*mi*

700. KUB I 1+ IV 74 f. (Apology of Hattušili III)
^{D}*IŠTAR* DINGIR^{LIM}-*aš-mu nu-uš-ma-ša-an* ^{D}*IŠTAR šar-la-im-mi-in* / *ši-pa-an-za-kán-zi*

701. KUB XXXI 57 I 16' f. (Fragment of a purification ritual)
ku-e-el[223] 6 GU$_4$$^{HI.A}$-*ŠU* 2 GU$_4$$^{HI.A}$-*ŠU*[224]/ 4 GU$_4$$^{HI.A}$-*ŠU* 1 GU$_4$-*ŠU tu-uš na-an-na-i*

702. KUB XXIII 11 III 14 (Annals of a Tuthaliya)
nam-ma-a-an-za-an EGIR-*an-da-pát IṢ-BAT*

703. Mşt. 75/47 left edge 4 (Letter)
da-at-tin-ma-aš-ši-kán li-e ku-it-ma-an ku-it-ki ha-at-ra-a-mi

2.3.3. Demonstrative and relative pronouns

With the exception of the nom.-acc.sg.n. and nom.pl.c., *apa-* „that one", *ka-* „this one", *kui-* „who, which" and the indefinite pronouns *kuiški* and *kuiška* „who ever" (which normally do not form a plural) inflect similarly. – Regarding the syntax of the relative clauses see 2.4.3.2.

Lit.: Friedrich 1960: 67; Hoffner/Melchert 2008: 142 ff.

223 Possessive with lacking copula, reformulate „whoever owns" or similar in the translation and insert this to the second colon as well.

224 Add „gives, sacrifices" or similar, also in the second colon correspondingly.

singular	demonstratives		relatives	
nom.c.	*apāš*	*kāš*	*kuiš*	*kuiški*
acc.c.	*apūn*	*kūn*	*kuin*	*kuinki*
nom.-acc.n.	*apāt*	*kā*	*kuit*	*kuitki*
gen.	*apēl*	*kēl*	*kuēl*	*kuēlki*
dat.-loc.	*apedani*	*kedani*	*kuedani*	*kuedaniki*
abl.	*apez*	*kez*	*kuez*	*kuezki*
instr.	*apedanda*	*kedanda*	–	
plural	demonstratives		relatives	
Nom.c.	*apē*	*kē*	*kuieš*	
acc.c.	*apūš*	*kūš*	*kuiuš*, *kūš*	
Nom.-acc.n.	*apē*	*kī*	*kuē*	
Gen.	*apenzan*	*kenzan*	*kuenzan*	
dat.-loc.	*apedaš*	*kedaš*	*kuedaš*	

704. Mşt. 75/16 lower edge 11 ff. (Letter)
*nu **a-pa-a-aš*** ^{LÚ}KÚR / *al-wa-an-za-ah-ha-an-za im-ma* / *e-eš-ta*[225]
na-an[226] *Ú-UL* / *ša-a-ak-ta*

705. KUB XXIII 1+ II 16 f. (Treaty with Šaušgamuwa)
^{m}*Ma-aš-tu-ri-iš **ku-iš*** LUGAL KUR ^{ÍD}*Še-e-ha e-eš-ta* / *na-an*
^{m}NIR.GÁL-*iš da-a-aš*

706. KUB XIX 6+ III 20 f. (Treaty with Alakšandu of Wiluša)

225 Interrogative clause.
226 Here introduction of consecutive clause „so that“.

zi-ik-ma ***a-pu-u-un*** *me-mi-ya-an* / *A-NA* ^{D}UTU^{ŠI} *ku-it-ma-an ŠU-PUR*

707. KBo V 3+ I 32 f. (Treaty with Hukkanā of Hayaša)
nam-ma-ma-za da-ma-a-in li-e ***ku-in-ki*** / *ša-a-ak-ti*

708. KUB XXIII 1+ I 28 ff. (Treaty with Šaušgamuwa)
GIM-*an-ma* ^{m}NIR.GÁL-*iš* ŠEŠ *A-BI* ^{D}UTU^{ŠI} / LUGAL-*iz-zi-at nu-uš-ši* LÚ^{MEŠ} KUR ^{URU}*A-mur-ra* / IGI-*an-da wa-aš-te-ir nu-uš-ši* ***a-pa-a-at*** / *wa-a-tar-na-ah-hi-ir*

709. KBo III 1+ IV 27/19' f. (Proclamation of Telipinu)
ku-iš e-eš-har[227] *i-e-iz-zi nu*[228] ***ku-it*** *e-eš-ha-na-aš-pát* / *iš-ha-a-aš te-iz-zi*

710. KBo III 1+ I 19 f. (Proclamation of Telipinu)
a-pí-e-el-la ŠU-*i* / URU$^{DIDLI.HI.A}$ GAL.GAL^{TIM} *ti-it-ti-ya-an-te-eš e-še-ir*

711. KUB XXXI 4+ obv. 6 (Chronicle of Puhanu)
ARAD^{MEŠ}-*na-aš-ta* GÉME-*ša-an na-at-ta* ***ku-el-ka*** *da-ah-hu-un*

712. KBo V 3+ III 57 (Treaty with Hukkanā of Hayaša)
na-aš ***a-pí-e-da-ni*** *ud-da-ni-i še-ir* BA.ÚŠ

713. KBo XXXII 14 II 6 f. (Epos of liberation)
ú-e-ši-ya-ah-ha-ri[229] ***ku-e-da-ni*** HUR.SAG-*i ma-a-na-an*[230] / *pa-ah-hu-e-na-an-za ar-ha wa-ar-nu-zi*

714. KBo XVII 65 obv. 34 (Birth ritual)
ma-a-an-na DUMU.MUNUS-*ma mi-i-ya-ri na-aš-ta* ***a-pí-e-iz*** ITU-*az ar-ha kap-pu-uš-kán-zi*

715. KUB XXIV 3+ II 25 f. (Muršili's prayer to the sun goddess of Arinna)
ki-e-iz-za*-at hi-in-ga-na-an-za ta-ma-a-aš-ta* ***ki-e-iz-za****-at* / *ku-ru-ra-an-za ta-ma-aš-ta*

716. KBo III 22 rev. 58 (Proclamation of Anitta)
KASKAL-*za ku-it a-aš-šu ú-tah-hu-un* ***a-pí-e-da-an-da*** *ha-liš-ši-ya-nu-un*[231]

---

227 Here: „bloodshed".
228 Add: „it will happen to that one" or similar.
229 Topicalized verb.
230 Conjunction indicating a curse, like „if only...!" or similar.

717. KBo VI 34+ I 45 f. (First military oath)
a-pí-e*-ma* / *da-ra-an-zi a-pa-a-at e-eš-du*

718. KUB XXIII 1+ II 11 ff. (Treaty with Šaušgamuwa)
ku-i-e-eš *ša-ku-wa-šar-ru-uš* DUMU$^{MEŠ\ MUNUS.MEŠ}$*I-ŠAR-TI-ya* ***ku-i-e-eš*** / *ŠA A-BI* ^{D}UTU^{ŠI} *nam-ma-ya ku-it ta-ma-i* NUMUN LUGAL-*UT-TI* / $^{LÚ.MEŠ}$*pa-ah-hur-ši-iš-ta* ***ku-i-e-eš*** *nu-za a-pí-ya* / *AŠ-ŠUM* EN-*UT-TI li-e ku-in-ki i-la-li-ya-ši*

719. Mşt. 75/47 obv. 18 ff. (Letter)
NÍ.ZU$^{HI.A}$-*ya-wa ku-i-e-eš* ^{URU}*Ma-ri-eš-ta* / *ma-an-ni-in-ku-wa-a-e-eš* ***a-pu-u-uš-ša*** / *wa-al-hu-u-wa-ni*

720. KUB XXX 24a+ 23' (Funerary ritual)
^{GIŠ}AL ^{GIŠ}MAR ***a-pí-e****-pát ŠA* GIŠ *da-an-zi*

721. KUB XXXIII 106+ II 17 f. (Myth of Ullikummi)
^{D}U EN-*YA ud-da-a-ar-mu* / *iš-ta-ma-aš ud-da-a-ar-ta* ***ku-e*** *me-mi-iš-ki-mi*

722. KUB IV 1+ I 17 f. (Incantation at the enemy border)
nu-za ***a-pí-en-za-an*** GÉŠPU *ha-aš-ta-i* / *wa-al-li-iš-kán-zi*

723. KBo X 2 II 3 f. (Apology of Hattušili I)
^{URU}*Pár-ma-an-na-aš-ma-kán* ***a-pí-e-da-aš*** *A-NA* LUGAL^{MEŠ} / SAG.DU-*aš e-eš-ta*

724. KUB XVII 4+ 9' f. (Song of Silver)
pí-ra-an a-aš-ki-za DUMU^{MEŠ} ***ku-e-da-aš*** / *kat-ta-an ha-az-zi-ik-ki-nu-un nu-mu te-ri-iš-kán-zi*

EXERCISES

725. KBo V 3+ IV 32 f. (Treaty with Hukkanā of Hayaša)
nu ku-iš a-pa-a-at ut-tar i-ya-az-zi na-an-kán ki-e / *NI-IŠ* DINGIR^{MEŠ} *QA-DU* DAM^{MEŠ}-*KU-NU* DUMU^{MEŠ}-*KU-NU* É^{MEŠ}-*KU-NU* KUR-*KU-NU har-ni-in-kán-du*

---

231 Object drop, insert „them" in the translation.

726. KUB XIII 35+ IV 1 (Law court records)
Ú-UL ku-it-ki wa-ah-nu-um-me-e-ni-wa-kán

727. KUB XIII 2+ III 29 f. (Instructions for the Bēl-Madgalti)
ku-e-da-ni-ma-aš-ša-an URU-*ri* EGIR-*pa a-ar-ti nu* LÚ^{MEŠ} URU$^{\textit{LIM}}$ / *hu-u-ma-an-du-uš pa-ra-a hal-za-a-i*

728. KUB I 1+ II 70 ff. (Apology of Hattušili III)
nu-za KUR.KUR^{MEŠ} *ku-e ki-e* EGIR-*pa a-še-ša-nu-un nu* KARAŠ ANŠE.KUR.RA^{MEŠ} / *ki-e-el ŠA* KUR$^{\textit{TI}}$ *A-NA* ŠEŠ-*YA la-ah-hi I-NA* KUR *Mi-iz-ri-i* / GAM-*an pí-e-hu-te-nu-un*

729. KUB XXXIII 106+ III 52' f. (Myth of Ullikummi)
nu-kán ka-ru-ú-i-li-ya ^{URUDU}*ar-da-a-la* / *pa-ra-a ti-ya-an-du ne-pí-iš te-kán-na ku-e-iz ar-ha ku-e-ri-ir*

730. KUB I 1+ II 54 f. (Apology of Hattušili III)
^{URU}*Dur-mi-it-ta-ma-aš* ^{URU}*Ku-ru-uš-ta-ma Ú-UL pa-it* / *na-aš-ta ki-e-da-aš A-NA* KUR.KUR^{MEŠ} *am-mu-uk an-da da-a-li-ya-at*

731. KUB XXII 70 obv. 24 (Oracle concerning the intrigues at the Hittite court)
A-NA Ú-NU-UT DINGIR$^{\textit{LIM}}$-*wa ku-it ku-it kat-ta-an* GAR-*ri nu-wa-ra-at A-NA* DINGIR$^{\textit{LIM}}$ *pí-ya-an-zi-pát Ú-UL-wa-ra-at* EGIR-*pa wa-ah-nu-wa-an-zi*

732. KUB XLIII 38 rev. 14 (Second military oath)
ki-i-wa Ú-UL GEŠTIN *šu-me-en-za-an-wa e-eš-har*

2.3.4. Possessive pronouns

The genitives of the personal pronouns are used as clitic forms. In addition, there are enclitic forms, though they are not very common in the corpus. This is partly due to the fact the possessivity is often expressed by dative or genitive constructions, but also because pronouns are often covered up by akkadographical spelling. Some case forms which are only isolated examples are omitted here.

Lit.: Friedrich 1960: 64 ff.; Hoffner/Melchert 2008: 237 ff.

singular	1.pers.sg.	2.pers.sg.	3.pers.sg.
nom. C.	*-miš*	*-tiš*	*-šiš*
acc. c.	*-min, -man*	*-tin*	*-šin, -šan*
nom./acc.n.	*-mit*	*-tit*	*-šit*
gen.	*-maš*	*-taš*	*-šaš*
dat.-loc.	*-mi*	*-ti*	*-ši*
instr.		*-tit*	*-šet*

singular	1.pers.pl	2.pers.pl.	3.pers.pl.
nom. C.	*-šummiš*	*-šmiš*	*-šmeš*
acc. c.	*-šummin*		*-šman*
nom./acc.n.		*-šmet*	*-šmet*
gen.	*-šummiš*		
dat.-loc.		*-šmi*	*-šmi*
instr.			*-šmit*
Plural	1.pers.sg.	2.pers.sg.	3.pers.sg.
nom.c.	*-maš*	*-tiš*	*-šeš*
acc.c.	*-muš*	*-tuš*	*-šuš*
nom.-acc.n.	*-mit*		*-šet*
dat.-loc.		*-taš*	

Plural	1.pers.pl.	2.pers.pl.	3.pers.pl.
nom.c.		*-šmeš*	
acc.c.	*-šummuš*		*-šmuš*
nom.-acc.n.		*-šmet*	
dat.-loc.			*-šmaš*

The corresponding non-inflecting akkadograms are:

	1.person	2.person	3.person
Singular	*-YA*	*-KA*	*-ŠU, -ZU*[232]
Plural	*-NI*	*-KU-NU*	*-ŠU-NU, -ZU-NU*

733. KUB XXIX 1 I 35 (Foundation ritual)
Ú-UL-wa LUGAL-*wa-aš a-ra-aš-**mi-iš** zi-ik*[233]

734. KBo III 22 obv. 11 f. (Proclamation of Anitta)
nu ^{m}*Pí-it-ha-a-na-aš at-ta-aš-**ma-aš** a-ap-pa-an ša-ni-ya ú-it-ti* / *hu-ul-la-an-za-an hu-ul-la-nu-un*

735. KUB I 16+ II 3 f. (Political testament of Hattušili I)
LUGAL-*ša-an-za* / DUMU-*la-**ma-an***[234] *hal-zi-ih-hu-un*

736. Mşt. 75/60 rev. 29 f. (Letter)
ARAD-***YA**-wa-mu* / *Ú-UL ha-an-na-at-te-ni*

232 The z-forms are allophones after dental – unfortunately dentals in the *accadic* equivalent of an intended Hittite word, even if it is written as a sumerogram.

233 Rhetorical interrogative clause. with missing copula.

234 Probably assimilated from DUMU-*lan-man*.

737. Mşt. 73/79 rev. 3’ f. (Letter)
^{m}*Ha-aš-ša* É-***ti****-ya-kán kat-ta-an / hu-u-ma-an* SIG$_5$-*in*

738. KUB XXIV 8+ I 43 ff. (Story of Appu)
*na-aš-ši-pa an-da i-ya-an-ni-iš / na-an pu-nu-uš-ki-wa-an da-a-iš / ku-it-wa wa-aš-túl-****ti-it***

739. KUB I 16+ II 70 f. (Political testament of Hattušili I)
*at-ta-aš-****ta-aš****-wa* / ^{GIŠ}ŠÚ.A-*ši* DUMU.NITA NU.GÁL

740. KUB XXIV 1 I 11 (Muršili’s prayer to Telipinu)
na-aš-ta EGIR-*pa* ^{É}*ka-ri-im-ni-****it-ti*** *an-da e-hu*

741. KBo IV 10+ obv. 9’ (Treaty with Ulmitešub)
ma-a-an DUMU-***KA*** DUMU.DUMU-***KA*** *kat-ta wa-aš-ta-i ku-iš-ki na-an* LUGAL KUR ^{URU}*Hat-ti pu-nu-uš-du*

742. KUB I 16+ II 20 (Political testament of Hattušili I)
*an-na-aš-****ši-iš*** MUŠ-*aš*

743. KUB I 16+ II 9 f. (Testament of Hattušili I)
LUGAL-*aš ut-tar / Ú-UL da-a-aš nu an-na-aš-****ša-aš*** MUŠ-*aš ku-it ut-tar nu a-pa-a-at da-a-aš*

744. KUB I 16+ II 34 ff. (Political testament of Hattušili I)
ma-a-an-ma-aš pu-ug-ga-an-za / ti-i-e-iz-zi na-aš-ma ku-uš-du-wa-a-ta ku-it-ki na-aš-ma har-nam-ma ku-it-ki / na-aš-kán ša-ra-a li-e ú-iš-ki-it-ta na-aš É-*ri-****iš-ši*** *e-eš-du*

745. KBo VI 2+ II 50 (Laws, first tablet)
DUMU-***ŠU*** A.ŠÀ-***ŠU*** ^{GIŠ}KIRI$_6$.GEŠTIN-***ŠU*** *li-e ku-iš-ki wa-a-ši*

746. KUB XIII 9+ I 6 f. (Instruction of Tuthaliya)
^{D}UTU^{ŠI}-*wa an-zi-el BE-LÍ-****NI*** ^{LÚ}*la-ah-hi-ya-la-aš / zi-ik*

747. KUB XXIX 1 I 43 (Foundation ritual)
ku-it-ma-aš-kán[235] *kar-di-****eš-mi*** *an-da na-at uš-ši-it-tin*

748. KUB I 16+ III 17 (Political testament of Hattušili I)
na-aš[236] *A-NA* DUMU^{MEŠ} ^{URU}*Ha-at-ti e-eš-har-****ši-mi-it*** *e-ku-ut-ta*

---

235 Probably instead of *kuit-šmaš-kan*.

749. KUB XXI 27+ IV 6' f. (Puduhepa's prayer to the sun goddess of Arinna)
A-NA ^{m}*Ha-at-tu-ši-li* ARAD-*KA* TI-*tar* MU$^{HI.A}$ GÍD.DA-*ya* / *pa-ra-a ar-nu-ut nu-uš-**ma-ša**-at-kán* KAxU-*az ú-id-du*

750. KUB XVII 21 III 8 (Prayer of Arnuwanda and Ašmunikal)
GU$_4^{HI.A}$-***KU-NU**-ya* UDU$^{HI.A}$-***KU-NU*** *ar-ha šar-ri-ir*

751. KUB XXIX 1 II 47 f. (Foundation ritual)
nu ^{D}UTU-*uš* ^{D}IM-*aš-ša* LUGAL-*wa-aš ták-šu-li-ši-it* / *da-an-du nu ut-tar-**ša-me-it*** 1^{EN}[237] *ki-ša-ru*

752. KUB XXXI 4+ obv. 23 (Chronicle of Puhanu)
^{URU}*Za-al-pa ú-it-te-en ut-ni-iš-**me-it** wa-al-ah-te-en*

753. KBo II 3 IV 4 ff. (Maštigga's ritual)
nu-za-kán 2 EN SISKUR *wa-a-tar I-NA* SAG.DU^{MEŠ}-***ŠU-NU*** / *ša-ra-a la-ah-hu-wa-an-zi QA-TI-TE*^{MEŠ}-***ŠU-NU**-ya-za-kán* / IGI$^{HI.A}$-***ŠU-NU*** *ar-ra-an-zi*

EXERCISES

754. KUB I 16+ III 56 (Political testament of Hattušili I)
ud-da-a-ar-me-it-ta pí-ih-hu-un

755. KBo XXXII 14 II 1 f. (Epos of liberation)
a-li-ya-na-an-za a-pí-el tu-e-ig-ga-az-še-it / HUR.SAG-*aš a-wa-an ar-ha šu-ú-e-it*

756. KUB I 1+ III 20 f. (Apology of Hattušili III)
ŠEŠ-*YA-ya-an-mu* / *QA-DU* É-*ZU*[238] DAM-*ŠU* DUMU-*ZU pí-ra-an na-a-iš*

757. KBo XV 10+ II 1 (Purification ritual for Tuthaliya and Nikalmati)
nu ALAM$^{HI.A}$ *pí-di-iš-mi-pát pí-e-du-me-en*

758. KUB XXX 19+ IV 3 (Funerary ritual)
nu-u-wa-za-kán A-NA DUMU^{MEŠ}-*KA an-da-an a-aš-šu-uš e-eš*

---

236 Namely „the daughter of the king".
237 Here: „in agreement".
238 The allophonic form –*ZU* of the possessive is due to the dental of akkadic *bīt* „house".

759. KBo III 1+ I 60 f. (Proclamation of Telipinu)
na-pa ha-aš-ša-tar-še-it / an-da ta-ru-up-pí-ir

760. KUB I 16+ II 31 (Political testament of Hattušili I)
DUMU-*mi la-ba-ar-ni* É-*ir pí-ih-hu-un*

761. KBo XXII 2 obv. 13 f. (Tale of Zalpa, A)
nu-uz-za DUMU.NITA^{MEŠ} *kar-ti-iš-mi / pí-ra-an me-e-mi-ir ku-in-wa ša-an-hi-iš-ki-u-e-ni*

2.4. Syntax

2.4.1. Sentence and word particles

In Hittite, we find a number of particles which are traditionally called sentence particles in literature although at least some of them have a word scope while the scope of others cannot be determined with certainty. Particles usually take the Wackernagel position, i.e. after the first clitic word in a phrase. In Hittite, this is mostly the sentence connector *nu*, but it also occurs after enclitic pronouns which stand in this Wackernagel position. They probably have modifying meaning, but their exact meaning and function are still disputed, in spite of intensive research. As these questions cannot be solved within the framework of this exercise book, the following examples refer to the general problems:

1. *-apa*: When it has sentence scope, *-apa* means „then, so", with word scope it seems to have an emphasising function.[239]

2. *-ašta*: a particle of unclear function. As *-ašta* can alternate with *-kán* (see below) in some cases, it probably refers to the verb rather than to the sentence as a whole. It should be noted that the fusion of *-ašta* with *nu* shows *a-* vocalism which probably happens in analogy to the OldHitt. sentence introductory particle *ta*.

3. *-kan*: The particle *-kan* has been referred to in older literature as „particle of local relation (Ortsbezug)" which has not proved worthwhile. In the end, every sentence in a natural language shows a (literal or figurative) local relation, so that nothing can be inferred from the use of the particle in this regard. A better approach seems to be to combine the opinion of Josephson, who defines *-kan* as a „perfectivizing" particle, with the proposal of Eich-

239 For further details see Rieken 2004.

ner[240] that *-kan* resumes Indoeuropean **kom-* and therefore intensifies as a scattered preverb the meaning of the verb: accordingly, *-kan* … *kuen-* would mean something like „*beat up (with lethal consequence) " > „kill".

4. *-pat*: *-pat* is a word particle which emphasises and, therefore, only occurs at the end of a nominal phrase and not in the beginning of a sentence. The meaning is either „especially that one, just this" or „only, exlusively that one".

5. *-šan*: This particle is like *-kan* considered a particle of „local relation" which is not particularly helpful for the interpretation of the texts.

6. *-wa(r)*: particle of direct speech.

7. *-za*: *-za* seems to correspond functionally to a dative (*commodi*, sometimes also *ethicus*). Frequently it occurs in sentences with mediopassive predicates, but the natural assumption that the particle intensified the medial verb meaning to start with and then secondarily replaced it as a kind of analytical medium can be refuted on the basis of the examples.

Lit.: Friedrich 1960: 147 ff.; Carruba 1969; Josephsson 1972; Boley 1989, 1993; Hoffner/Melchert 2008: 354 ff.

762. KBo III 1+ II 51 f. (Proclamation of Telipinu)
*ma-a-n**a-pa*** *ut-tar-še-it pa-iz-zi / nu* SAG.DU*-na-az šar-ni-ik-du*

763. KUB I 16+ II 24 f. (Political testament of Hattušili I)
*nu-š**a-pa*** *ú-iz-zi zi-in-na-i nu e-eš-har*$^{\text{HI.A}}$ */ i-iš-šu-wa-an da-a-i*

764. KBo III 7 III 29 f. (Myth of Illuyanka)
*am-mu-ug-ga-z**a-pa*** *an-da e-ip / li-e-mu gi-en-zu-wa-i-ši*

765. KUB XXIV 8+ I 24 f. (Story of Appu)
*a-ra-i-š**a-pa***[241] ^{m}*Ap-pu-uš na-aš-za pár-na-aš-ša / i-ya-an-ni-iš*

766. KUB XXX 10 obv. 20 (Kantuzzili's prayer)
*hu-iš-wa-tar-m**a-pa*** *an-da hi-in-ga-ni ha-mi-in-kán hi-in-ga-na-m**a-pa***
an-da hu-iš-wa-an-ni-ya ha-mi-in-kán

767. KUB XXIII 11 III 25 (Annals of a Tuthaliya)
*na-**aš-ta*** KUR ^{URU}*Ga-aš-ga hu-u-ma-an ku-e-nu-un*

240 Paper at the colloquium „Berthold Delbrück y la sintaxis Indoeuropea hoy", Madrid 1994, unfortuntely unpublished.

241 Topicalized verb.

768. KBo XIII 58 II 24’ f. (Instructions of Arnuwanda)
*na-**aš-ta*** ^{NA4}KIŠIB / *A-NA* KÁ.GAL *ták-ša-an kat-ta ú-wa-an-du*

769. KUB XXIV 4+ II 14 (Muršili’s prayer to the sun goddess of Arinna)
KUR ^{URU}*Ha-at-ti-ma-**aš-ta** an-da a-aš-ša-a-u-it* IGI$^{HI.A}$*-it a-uš-te-en*

770. KUB XXXI 86 II 15 (Instructions for the Bēl-Madgalti)
*na-**aš-ta** ar-ha li-e ku-it-ki har-ak-zi*

771. KBo X 2 I 26 (Apology of Hattušili I)
*na-**aš-ta*** ^{URU}*Ha-at-tu-ša-aš-pát* URU*-ri-aš* 1*-aš a-aš-ta*

772. KUB XIV 8 I 22’ ff. (Plague prayer of Muršili II)
nu-uš-ma-aš ma-ah-ha-an A-BU-YA a-pí-el DUMU*-ŠU pí-e-eš-ta na-an ma-ah-ha-an pí-e-hu-te-ir* / *na-an-**kán** ku-e-en-ni-ir A-BU-YA-ma kap-pí-la-az-za-at-ta na-aš I-NA* KUR *Mi-iz-ri* / *pa-it nu* KUR ^{URU}*Mi-iz-ri wa-al-ah-ta* ÉRIN^{MEŠ}*-ya-**kán*** ANŠE.KUR.RA^{MEŠ} *ŠA* KUR *Mi-iz-ri ku-en-ta*

773. KUB XIII 2+ II 22 f. (Instructions for the Bēl-Madgalti)
*ku-i-ša-**kán*** / *ú-e-te-na-za*[242] *ša-ha-a-ri na-an-**kán** ša-ra-a ša-an-ha-an-du*

774. KUB XXIII 1+ I 33 f. (Treaty with Šaušgamuwa)
*na-at-**kán** A-NA* LUGAL KUR ^{URU}*Mi-iz-za-ri-i* EGIR*-pa-an-da* / *ti-i-e-ir*

775. KUB XXIII 1+ III 16 f. (Treaty with Šaušgamuwa)
*nu-**kán*** INIM*-an A-NA* ^{D}UTU^{ŠI} *li-e* / *ša-an-na-at-ti A-NA* ^{D}UTU^{ŠI}*-an me-mi*

776. KBo X 2 I 7 f. (Apology of Hattušili I)
nu ku-e ku-e a-ša-u-wa-ar e-eš-ta / *na-at-**kán** A-NA* ÉRIN^{MEŠ} *a-ša-an-du-li pí-ih-hu-un*

777. KBo III 38 obv. 14’ (Tale of Zalpa, B)
*hu-ul-la-an-za-an-ni-**pát*** BA.ÚŠ

778. KBo X 2 II 49 f. (Apology of Hattušili I)
nu-kán ^{URU}*Zi-ip-pa-aš-na-an* GE$_6$*-az-**pát*** / *ša-ra-a pa-a-un*

242 Ablative for instrumental.

779. KUB XXXIII 121 II 5 f. (Tale of Kešši)
MUNUS-*aš ŠUM-še-it* ^{f}*Ši-in-ta-li-me-ni mi-iš-ri-wa-an-za*
hu-u-ma-an-da-az-za / aš-ša-nu-wa-an-za nu-uš-ša-an ^{m}*Ki-eš-ši-iš*
pa-ra-a A-NA DAM-*ŠU*-***pát*** *IŠ-ME*

780. KBo VI 2+ I 23 f. (Laws, first tablet)
ki-nu-na LUGAL-*uš ŠA* É.GAL^{LIM}[243] *pí-eš-ši-it nu-za*
hu-u-ni-in-kán-za-***pát*** / 3 GÍN KÙ.BABBAR *da-a-i*

781. KUB XXII II 1+ II 29 (Treaty with Šaušgamuwa)
^{LÚ}*pa-ah-hur-ši-in*-***pát*** *pa-ah-ha-aš-hi*[244]

782. KUB XIII 2+ III 25 f. (Instructions for the Bēl-Madgalti)
A-NA BE-LÍ-ma-at-***ša-an*** *li-e i-e-iz-zi A-NA* ŠEŠ-*ya-at*-***za-an*** / 26 NIN-*ŠU*
^{LÚ}*a-ri-ši-ya li-e i-ya-zi*

783. KBo III 1+ II 38 (Proclamation of Telipinu)
ma-a-an DUMU.LUGAL-*ma* DUMU.NITA NU.GÁL *nu ku-iš*
DUMU.MUNUS *ha-an-te-iz-zi-iš / nu-uš-ši-iš*-***ša-an*** ^{LÚ}*an-ti-ya-an-ta-an*
ap-pa-a-an-du nu LUGAL-*uš a-pa-a-aš ki-ša-ru*

784. KUB XXVI 24 II 9 f. (Instructions for the chiefs of the garrisons)
nu-un-na-aš-***ša-an*** *i-da-a-lu-un me-mi-an / ku-in-ki ha-at-ra-a-iz-zi*

785. KBo V 3+ II 22 (Treaty with Hukkanā of Hayaša)
nu-mu-uš-***ša-an*** *hu-u-ma-an-da-az pa-ah-ši*

786. KBo III 4+ II 43 f. (Annals of Muršili II)
ku-in NAM.RA^{MEŠ} *ú-wa-te-it nu-uš*-***ša-an*** *kap-pu-u-wa-u-wa-ar /*
NU.GÁL *e-eš-ta*

787. KBo III 1+ II 43 f. (Proclamation of Telipinu)
ki-iš-ša-an-na li-e te-e-ši ar-ha-wa pár-ku-nu-um-mi[245] /
pár-ku-nu-ši-ma-***za*** *Ú-UL ku-it-ki nu*-***za*** *an-da im-ma ha-at-ki-iš-nu-ši*

788. KBo III 34 II 19 f. (Palace chronicle)
ša-aš ^{m}*A-aš-ki-li-pát ti-e-it / mar-ša-an-za*-***wa*** *zi-ik*

243 „Suspended genitive“: „that of the palace“ = „the contribution to the palace“.
244 Interrogative clause.
245 As object „the matter“ or similar should be added.

789. KBo XIX 128+ IV 15’ ff. (AN.TAH.ŠUM festival)
^{LÚ}SAGI.A-*aš* / *A-NA* LUGAL *da-a-i*[246] LUGAL-*i me-ma-i* / GIŠ ^{D}INANNA$^{\text{HI.A}}$ *pa-ra-a kar-pa-an-ti*[247] / LUGAL-*uš-ša te-iz-zi pa-ra-a-**wa** kar-pa-an-du*

790. KBo V 13+ III 4 f. (Treaty with Kupanta-^{D}KAL, C version)
ma-a-an tu-uk-ma 1-*e-da-ni ha-at-ra-a-mi zi-ik-**wa*** / 1-*aš u-un-ni nu zi-ik* 1-*aš u-un-ni*

791. KUB XIII 4 I 64 ff. (Instructions for the priests and temple officials)
nam-ma-aš-ma-aš PA-NI DINGIR^{LIM} *me-mi-an* / *me-mi-eš-tin ku-i-iš-**wa**-kán tu-e-el* DINGIR^{LIM}-*az* ^{NINDA}*har-ši-ya-az* / ^{DUG}*iš-pa-an-du-uz-zi-az da-a-aš nu-**wa-r**a-an-kán* DINGIR^{LIM} EN-*YA* EGIR-*an* / *har-ni-ik-du nu-**wa**-za-kán a-pí-e-el* É-*ir kat-ta-an ša-ra-a e-ip-du*

792. KUB XXIII 1+ I 32 (Treaty with Šaušgamuwa)
*ki-nu-un-ma-wa-tu-**za** Ú-UL* ARAD^{MEŠ}[248]

793. KBo III 1+ I 31 f. (Proclamation of Telipinu)
^{m}*Ha-an-ti-li-iš-ša* ^{LÚ}SAGI.A-*aš e-eš-ta nu-**za*** ^{f}*Ha-ra-ap-še-ki-in* / NIN ^{m}*Mur-ši-i-li* DAM-*an-ni har-ta*

794. KUB XV 17+ III 58 (Vow of Puduhepa)
*e-ša-ri-ma-at-**za***[249] *I-NA* ^{URU}MUL-*ra*

795. KUB XXIII 1+ I 37 f. (Treaty with Šaušgamuwa)
KUR ^{URU}*A-mur-ri-ya IŠ-TU* ^{GIŠ}TUKUL / *ar-ha har-ga-nu-ut na-at-**za*** ARAD-*na-ah-ta*

796. KUB XXIV 8+ I 19 ff. (Story of Appu)
*nu-**za** ku-iš-ša*[250] DUMU.NITA-*li* NINDA-*an* ^{UZU}Ì-*ya pa-a-i* / *ku-iš-ma-**za*** DUMU.NITA-*li a-ku-wa-an-na pa-a-i* / ^{m}*Ap-pu-uš-ma* NINDA-*an Ú-UL ku-i-ta-ni-ik-ki pa-a-i*

---

246 Object drop, add „it“ in the translation.
247 Interrogative clause and probably despite missing particle direct speech.
248 Add „we are“.
249 Topicalized verb.
250 Coresponds to the following *kuiš*, „this one...the other“.

2.4.2. Connectives

nu, *ta* and *su* function as connectives of coordinated clauses, as introductory particles of main clauses and main clause correlates in hypotactic constructions. *ta* and *su* belong to the older language stratum of Hittite and later usually disappear being replaced by *nu*.

Lit.: Friedrich 1960: 155 ff.; Weitenberg 1992; Hoffner/Melchert 2008: 390 ff.

797. KUB XXX 19+ I 7 f. (Funerary ritual)
EGIR-*an-ma* / $^{\text{MUNUS.MEŠ}}$*tap-da-ra-aš i-ya-at-ta-ri* ***nu*** *ú-e-eš-kán-zi*

798. KBo VI 2+ I 56 f. (Laws, first tablet)
ták-ku ARAD-*aš hu-u-wa-i* ***na****-an* EGIR-*pa ku-iš-ki ú-wa-te-iz-zi ták-ku ma-an-ni-in-ku-an*[251] / *e-ip-zi* ***nu-uš****-ši* ^{KUŠ}E.SIR-*uš pa-a-i*[252]

799. KBo XII 126+ IV 11 (Malli's ritual)
nu *a-ra-ah-za ku-e-eš e-še-šir* ***nu****-uš-ma-aš* ŠExNAGA-*an-zi*

800. KUB XIII 8 obv. 7 (Instruction of Queen Ašmunikal)
UR.GI$_7$-*aš wa-ap-pí-ya-zi a-pí-ya-ma-aš a-ri* ***na****-aš ka-ru-uš-ši-ya-zi*

801. KUB I 1+ IV 35 (Apology of Hattušili III)
GIM-*an me-mi-an AŠ-ME* ***na****-an e-ip-pu-u-un*

802. KBo XXXII 19 III 45' ff. (Epos of liberation: Ebla)
ma-a-an-wa-ra-at Ú-UL-ma i-ya-at-te-ni / pa-ra-a tar-nu-mar ^{URU}*E-eb-la-i* ^{GIŠ}ŠÚ.A-*aš* URU-*ri* / ***nu****-wa nam-ma* UD.7.KAM-*az* ***nu****-wa-aš-ša-an am-mu-uk / šu-ma-a-aš tu-e-ig-ga-ša-ma-aš ú-wa-mi*

803. KBo III 22 rev. 45 ff. (Proclamation of Anitta)
ma-a-na-aš / ap-pí-iz-zi-ya-na ki-iš-ta-an-zi-at-ta-at[253] ***ša****-an* ^{D}*Hal-ma-šu-it-ti* / ^{D}*Ši-i-uš-mi-iš pa-ra-a pa-iš*

804. KBo XXII 2 obv. 3 f. (Tale of Zalpa, A)
nu DUMU^{MEŠ}-*ŠU an-da-an*[254] *zi-ke-e-it* ***šu****-uš* ÍD-*a tar-na-aš* ÍD-*ša* / *A-NA* A.AB.BA KUR ^{URU}*Za-al-pu-wa pí-e-da-aš*

251 Nominal sentence, add „is“ in the translation.
252 Namely the owner.
253 Subject is „the town“.
254 Namely into a basket.

805. KBo III 38 rev. 23' f. (Tale of Zalpa, B)
Ù ÉRIN^{MEŠ} ^{URU}*Za-al-pa me-na-ah-ha-an-da ú-it* / ***ša-an*** LUGAL-*uš hu-ul-li-iš*

806. KBo III 38 rev. 25' f. (Tale of Zalpa, B)
^{m}*Dam-na-aš-šu-un-na hu-i-iš-wa-an-da-an IṢ-BA-TU* / ***ša-an*** ^{URU}*Ha-at-tu-ša* EGIR-*pa pí-e-hu-te-it*

807. KBo III 38 rev. 29' (Tale of Zalpa, B)
nu-uš dam-mi-iš-šar ***še-a*** *e-ki-ir*

808. KBo XXII 2 obv. 6 f. (Tale of Zalpa, A)
ma-a-an MU$^{\text{HI.A}}$ *iš-tar-na pa-a-ir nu* MUNUS.LUGAL *nam-ma* 30 DUMU.MUNUS *ha-a-aš-ta* / ***šu****-uš a-pa-ši-la ša-al-la-nu-uš-kat*

809. KBo III 34 II 24 (Palace chronicle)
ta *wa-aš-ta-uš ú-e-mi-ir*

810. KBo III 28 II 20' f. (Fragment of a palace chronicle)
ki-nu-na LUGAL-*uš i-da-lu me-ik-ki u-uh-hu-un* ***ta*** LUGAL-*wa-aš ud-da-a-ar-ra-me-it* / *li-e šar-ra-at-tu-ma*

811. KBo VI 2+ II 62 f. (Laws, first tablet)
ták-ku i-wa-ru-wa-aš iš-ha-a-aš A.ŠÀ$^{\text{HI.A}}$ *ku-li-i a-ar-ki na-aš-ma* LÚ^{MEŠ} URU^{LIM} / A.ŠÀ$^{\text{HI.A}}$-*an pí-an-zi* ***ta*** *lu-uz-zi kar-pí-iz-zi*

812. KBo XVII 1+ III 3 (Ritual for the royal couple)
ta *nam-ma* ^{MUŠEN}*ha-a-ra-na-an ne-e-pí-ša tar-na-ah-hi*

813. KBo XVII 1+ III 8 f. (Ritual for the royal couple)
ú-i-il-na-aš ÉRIN^{MEŠ}-*an te-eš-šu-um-mi-uš-ša ta-ak-na-a* / *ha-ri-e-mi* ***tu-uš*** *tar-ma-e-mi* ***ta*** *ki-iš-ša-an te-e-mi*

814. KBo XVII 1+ IV 9 (Ritual for the royal couple)
ku-iš ša-ga-i-iš ki-i-ša-ri ***ta*** LUGAL-*i* MUNUS.LUGAL-*ya ta-ru-e-ni*

EXERCISES

815. KBo VI 2+ I 75 f. (Laws, first tablet)
ták-ku LÚ-*aš* DAM-*ŠU da-a-i na-an A-NA* É-*ŠU pí-e-hu-te-iz-zi* /

i-wa-ru-uš-še-it-az an-da pí-e-da-a-i

816. KUB XXXI 4+ obv. 9 (Chronicle of Puhanu)
ta-a ut-ne-e har-ni-ik-mi ki-i-da-an-da na-ti-i-da ta-an kar-da-aš-ma ša-li-ik-ti

817. KBo III 22 rev. 47 f. (Proclamation of Anitta)
ša-an[255] *iš-pa-an-di / na-ak-ki-it da-a-ah-hu-un*

818. KUB XIII 4 II 76 f. (Instructions for the priests and temple officials)
na-aš-ta DINGIR^{MEŠ}*-aš-pát* ZI*-ni / i-ya-at-tin*

819. KBo III 38 rev. 21' (Tale of Zalpa, B)
šu-wa ^{URU}*Ha-at-tu-ši hi-in-ga-ni pa-a-un Ù* DUMU^{MEŠ} ^{URU}*Za-al-pa kat-te-mi*

820. KUB XXX 19+ IV 13 f. (Funerary ritual)
ma-a-an-wa-kán Ú.SAL*-wa pa-a-i-ši na-aš-ta šum-ma-an-za-na-an li-e / hu-it-ti-ya-ši*

821. KBo V 1 III 41 (Papanikri's ritual)
nu ^{DUG}ÁBxA *ti-an-zi na-an IŠ-TU* MUŠEN *iš-har-nu-ma-an-zi*

822. KUB XXX 25+ rev. 11 f. (Funerary ritual)
GIM*-an-ma* UD.KAM*-az* SIG_5*-ri na-aš-ta ša-an-ha-an-zi / nu ha-la-an-tu-wa hal-zi-ya*

2.4.3. Subordinate clauses

2.4.3.1. Attributive clauses

Hittite does not have exclusive expressions for all the common Indo-European subordinate clauses at its disposal. For instance, it lacks special conjunctions to express definite concessivity, finality and consecutivity. Most conjunctions are polyfunctional and receive their actual meaning only from the context.

Lit.: Friedrich 1960: 163 ff.; Sternemann 1967; Lühr 1998; Zeilfelder 2001a, 2002; Hoffner/Melchert 2008: 414 ff.

---

255 Namely „the town".

kuit	„because, as, although"
kuitman	„as soon as, while, until"
kuitman … nawi	„before"
kuwapi	„when, if, as, because"
mahhan	„like, when, if, as, because"
mān	„when, if, as, whether, although"
takku	„if"

823. KUB XXII 70 rev. 21 f. (Oracle concerning the intrigues at the Hittite court)
Ú-UL-wa ki-ša-ri zi-la-aš-wa ***ku-it*** *hur-ti-ya-aš / na-a-wi*$_4$ *zi-in-na-at-ta-ri*

824. Mşt. 75/49 obv. 12 ff. (Letter)
nu tu-el ***ku-it*** ŠEŠ-*KA / ú-it na-an I-NA* É.GAL^{LIM} */ Ú-UL am-mu-uk tar-kum-mi-ya-nu-un*

825. KUB I 1+ III 22 f. 22 ff. (Apology of Hattušili III)
nu-mu ŠEŠ-*YA* ***ku-it*** / ^{m}*Ar-ma-*^{D}IM-*an* DI-*eš-na-az ša-ra-a-az-zi-ya-ah-ta / nu-uš-ši-kán i-da-la-a-wa-an-ni* EGIR-an *Ú-UL nam-ma ma-uš-ha-ha-at*

826. KBo VI 2+ IV 7 f. (Laws, first tablet)
ku-it-ma-na-*aš-ta* MUL^{MEŠ} *ú-wa-an-zi / na-aš* EGIR-*pa iš-hi-iš-ši pí-en-na-i*[256]

827. KUB XXXIX 6 III 18 ff. (Funerary ritual)
nu ***ku-it-ma-an*** ALAM *a-aš-ša-an I-NA* UD.4.KAM */ e-eš-zi nu ši-pa-an-tu-u-wa-an-zi /* UD-*at* UD-*at ki-iš-ša-an da-aš-kán-zi*

828. KBo VI 2+ I 26 f. (Laws, first tablet)
pí-e-di-iš-ši-ma an-tu-uh-ša-an pa-a-i[257] *nu* É-*ri-iš-ši / an-ni-eš-ki-iz-zi* ***ku-it-ma-na***-*aš* SIG$_5$-*at-ta-ri*

---

256 „Stray animals" should be added as object.
257 Subject to the first verb is a delinquent who hurt somebody, to the second a substitute worker, to the third the person hurt.

829. KUB XXIX 4 I 55 f. (Ritual for the transfer of the Black Goddess)
lu-uk-ta-ma I-NA UD.2.KAM ***ku-it-ma-an*** ^{D}UTU-*uš* ***na-a-ú-i*** *ar-ta-ri* / *nu a-pí-e-el IŠ-TU* É EN SÍSKUR *ki-i da-an-zi*

830. KUB XXII 70 obv. 15 f. (Oracle concerning the intrigues at the Hittite court)
nu-wa-ra-at ***ku-it-ma-an*** *A-NA* DINGIR^{LIM} ^{URU}*A-ru-uš-na* ***na-a-ú-i*** *up-pí-eš-ta* / *A-NA* MUNUS.LUGAL-*ma-wa me-mi-aš ú-wa-a-i ti-ya-at*

831. Bo 86/299 II 31 ff. (Bronze tablet, treaty of Tuthaliya IV)
ú-uk-ma ^{m}*Tu-ut-ha-li-ya-aš* LUGAL.GAL ***ku-it-ma-an***
LUGAL-*iz-zi-ah-ha-at-pát* ***na-ú-i*** / *ú-uk-ma* ^{mD}LAMMA-*an-na*
DINGIR^{LUM} *an-ni-ša-an-pát a-aš-šu-wa-an-ni an-da ar-nu-ut* /
nu-un-na-aš an-ni-ša-an-pát na-ak-ki-e-eš a-aš-ša-u-e-eš e-šu-u-en

832. KBo II 4 left edge 1 f. (Festival ritual)
A-NA DINGIR^{LIM} ***ku-wa-pí*** *ŠA* UD.KAM[258] *pár-ši-ya-an-zi nu* 1 NINDA.GUR$_4$.RA / *da-an-zi*

833. KBo X 34 IV 11' ff. (Ritual for an enthronement)
^{m}*Du-ut-ha-li-ya-aš-za-kán* DUMU ^{m}*Ar-nu-wa-an-da* / LUGAL.GAL ***ku-wa-pí*** *A-NA* ^{GIŠ}ŠÚ.A *A-BI-ŠU e-ša-at* / *nu ki-i* SÍSKUR *šar-ra-aš-ši-ya-aš* / *a-pí-ya i-e-ir*

834. KUB XXIV 8+ III 14 ff. (Story of Appu)
ku-u-wa-pí-*ši at-ta-aš-mi-iš* DINGIR^{MEŠ}-*aš* NÍG.SI.SÁ-*an* / KASKAL-*an Ú-UL e-ip-pir nu-za* ^{LÚ}HUL-*lu* KASKAL-*an har-ki-ir* / *nu-uš-ši-iš-ša-an* ^{LÚ}HUL-*lu ŠUM-an e-eš-du*

835. KUB XXI 5+ II 8 (Treaty with Alakšandu of Wiluša)
tu-uq-qa-aš ***ma-ah-ha-an*** ^{LÚ}KÚR-*aš A-NA* ^{D}UTU^{ŠI}-*ya-aš QA-TAM-MA-pát* ^{LÚ}KÚR-*aš*

836. KUB XIII 4 II 69 f. (Instructions for the priests and temple officials)
ma-ah-ha-an-*wa-mu-kán a-ši me-mi-aš pí-ra-an ar-ha ti-ya-zi* / *nu-wa* EZEN$_4$ *QA-TAM-MA i-ya-mi*

---

258 „Suspended genitive":„that of the day" = „the ration of the day".

837. KUB XLIII 50+ obv. 6 f. (Muršili's speech loss)
***ma-ah-ha-an**-ma ú-e-ir* MU$^{\text{HI.A}}$*-uš*[259] EGIR*-an-da pa-a-ir / nu-mu ú-it a-ši me-mi-aš te-eš-ha-ni-iš-ki-u-wa-an ti-ya-at*

838. Mşt. 75/112 obv. 4 ff. (Letter)
^{m}*Pí-hi-na-ak-ki-iš-za* ***ma-ah-ha-an*** */* ^{URU}*Li-ši-ip-ra-an e-eš-ki-it-ta-ri / nu-wa-za ka-ru-ú* 30 É^{TUM} *a-še-ša-an har-zi*

839. KBo VI 2+ I 27 f. (Laws, first tablet)
ma-a-na-aš SIG$_5$*-at-ta-ri-ma / nu-uš-ši* 6 GÍN KÙ.BABBAR *pa-a-i*

840. KBo III 1+ I 21 f. (Proclamation of Telipinu)
ma-a-an *ap-pí-iz-zi-ya-an-ma* ARAD^{MEŠ} DUMU^{MEŠ}.LUGAL *mar-še-eš-še-ir nu* É^{MEŠ}*-ŠU-NU / ka-ri-pu-u-wa-an da-a-ir*

841. KUB XXII 25 I 12 f. (Oracle questions of Muršili II)
nu IGI*-an-da* ***ma-a-an*** GUL*-ah-zi / nu* ***ma-a-an*** *Ú-UL-ma* GUL*-ah-zi na-at* GAM*-an ar-ha* GAR*-ru*

842. KBo V 9 I 16 f. (Treaty of Muršili II with Duppi-Tešub of Amurru)
nu-za ***ma-a-an*** *ir-ma-la-an-za-ša e-eš-ta* ^{D}UTU^{ŠI}*-ma-at-ta / A-NA A-ŠAR A-BI-KA ti-it-ta-nu-nu-un-pát*

843. KBo VI 2+ I 25 f. (Laws, first tablet)
ták-ku LÚ.U$_{19}$.LU*-an ku-iš-ki hu-u-ni-ik-zta-an iš-tar-ni-ik-zi nu a-pu-u-un / ša-a-ak-ta-a-iz-zi*

844. KUB XXIX 1 I 46 ff. (Foundation ritual)
ták-ku *i-la-aš kar-di-iš-mi na-aš-šu-ma* ^{D}UTU*-wa-aš / iš-tar-ni-in-ga-iš kar-di-iš-mi na-at-kán ša-ra-a / ša-a-ah-te-en*

845. KBo VI 25+ III 3' f. (Birth omen)
ták-ku MUNUS*-za ha-a-ši na-aš ta-aš-wa-an-za*[260] / EN É *A-NA* ZAG*-aš-ta Ú-UL a-ri*

---

259 Accusative for nominative.
260 Namely the child.

2.4.3.2. Relative clauses

Regularly, the pronoun follows its head in restrictive relative clauses while it precedes it in general relative clauses. However, there are occasional exceptions like the positioning of the relative pronoun between *regens* and attribute in genitival nominal phrases.

Lit.: Friedrich 1960: 167 ff.; Hahn 1949; Held 1957; Lehmann 1979; Garrett 1994; Lühr 2001a; Hoffner/Melchert 2008: 423 ff.

846. KUB XXX 28 rev. 1 f. (Ritual for Hamrišhara)
nam-ma-kán ^{LÚ}*pa-a-ti-li-iš* ***ku-iš*** *šu-uh-hi še-ir nu-kán* É-*ri kat-ta-an-da* / *hal-za-a-i*

847. KUB XXII 70 obv. 31 (Oracle concerning the intrigues at the Hittite court)
e-ni-ya ***ku-it*** ^{f}*Am-ma-tal-la-aš IQ-BI pu-nu-uš-šu-e-ni-ma na-a-ú-i*

848. KBo V 3+ III 69 f. (Treaty with Hukkanā of Hayaša)
ku-iš *ŠA* KUR ^{URU}*Ha-at-ti* NAM.RA$^{\text{HI.A}}$ *pa-ra-a Ú-UL pa-a-i na-at-kán* / *ša-an-na-a-i na-an zi-ik* ^{m}*Hu-uq-qa-na-a-aš e-ip*

849. KBo VI 2+ III 3 f. (Laws, first tablet)
ka-ru-ú ***ku-iš*** ^{URU}*A-ri-in-na* ^{LÚ}UŠ.BAR *ki-i-ša-at Ù* É-*ZU a-ra-a-u-wa-an* $^{\text{LÚ.MEŠ}}$HA.LA-*ŠU* / *Ù* LÚ^{MEŠ} *NI-ŠU-Ú-ŠU a-ra-u-e-eš*

850. KBo VI 2+ II 51 f. (Laws, first tablet)
ku-iš*-za* ^{LÚ}*hi-ip-pa-ri ha-a-ap-pár i-iz-zi na-aš-kán ha-a-ap-pa-ra-az* / *ša-me-en-zi*

851. KUB XXIII 1+ I 10 ff. (Treaty with Šaušgamuwa)
nu-ut-ta iš-hi-ú-la-aš ***ku-it*** *tup-pí* / *i-ya-nu-un nu-kán tup-pí-aš*[261] / *li-e wa-ah-nu-ši*

852. KUB I 1+ IV 55 f. (Apology of Hattušili III)
na-a-hu-u-wa-aš-ma-mu ***ku-iš*** LUGAL-*uš* / *e-eš-ta na-aš-mu-kán na-ah-ta*

853. KBo XXXII 14 II 26 f. (Epos of liberation)
a-li-ya-na-aš na-aš-ta ÍD-*an ta-pu-ša* ***ku-i-e-eš*** / *ú-e-še-eš nu a-pu-u-uš ú-e-ši-ya-at-ta-ri*

854. KUB I 1+ IV 75 f. (Apology of Hattušili III)
am-mu-uq-qa-za ***ku-it*** *ha-aš-ti-ya-aš* É-*ir* DÙ-*nu-un* / *na-at A-NA*

261 „Suspended genitive“:„that of the tablet“ = „the content of the tablet“.

DINGIR^{LIM} *pa-ra-a pí-ih-hu-un*

855. KUB I 1+ II 46 (Apology of Hattušili III)
^{GIŠ}TUKUL-*ma* ***ku-in*** *a-pí-ya har-ku-un na-an ha-li-iš-ši-ya-nu-un*

856. KBo XII 126+ I 9 f. (Malli's ritual)
nu UN-*aš* ***ku-iš*** UH_7-*an-za na-aš-za* ^{D}UTU-*i me-na-ah-ha-an-da / e-ša-ri*

857. KUB I 1+ IV 58 f. (Apology of Hattušili III)
A-NA PA-NI AB-BA$^{HI.A}$*-YA AB-BA AB-BA*$^{HI.A}$ / ***ku-i-e-eš*** *ku-u-ru-ur e-šir am-mu-uk-ma ták-šu-la-a-ir*

EXERCISES

858. KUB I 1+ IV 62 ff. (Apology of Hattušili III)
nu-za ŠEŠ-*YA* ^{m}NIR.GÁL-*iš / ku-it AŠ-RU* URU ^{D}U-*aš-ša-an pár-na-wa-iš-ki-it na-an a-pí-ya pí-di* / LUGAL-*iz-na-an-ni ti-it-ta-nu-nu-un*

859. KBo XVII 62+ I 18' ff. (Birth ritual)
ku-it-ma-an-ma-az MUNUS-*za nu-u-wa ú-i-ú-i-iš-ki-iz-zi / nu* UDU.SÍGxMUNUS *ku-iš ha-an-da-a-an-za ma-a-an ar-ma-u-wa-an-za / ma-a-an ša-an-na-pí-li-iš na-an-kán* É.ŠÀ-*ni / an-da-an u-un-ni-ya-an-zi*

860. KUB I 1+ III 60 f. (Apology of Hattušili III)
A-NA ^{D}U ^{URU}*Ne-ri-iq-qa-za ku-it* ^{LÚ}SANGA *e-šu-un / na-an-mu-kán a-pí-e-iz-za ar-ha Ú-UL da-a-aš*

861. KUB XXIII 1+ II 25 ff. (Treaty with Šaušgamuwa)
na-an da-at-ta ku-iš ^{m}NIR.GÁL-*iš* / ^{LÚ}*HA-DA-NU-ya-an ku-iš* DÙ-*at nu nam-ma a-pí-el* DUMU-*ŠU* / ^{m}*Úr-hi-*^{D}U-*up-an Ú-UL pa-ah-ha-aš-ta*

862. KUB XIX 6+ II 16 ff. (Treaty with Alakšandu of Wiluša)
ma-a-an-ma-at-ta / ARAD^{MEŠ}-*KA-ya wa-at-ku-nu-e-ir* ^{D}UTU^{ŠI}-*ma-at-ta* KUR-*KA* / EGIR-*pa AD-DIN*

863. KBo VI 2+ IV 6 f. (Laws, first tablet)
ták-ku $GU_4$$^{HI.A}$ A.ŠÀ-*ni pa-a-an-zi BE-EL* A.ŠÀ *ú-e-mi-ya-zi*[262] /

262 Object drop, add „them" to this and the following verb.

UD.1.KAM *tu-u-ri-ya-zi*

864. KUB XIII 35+ I 13 f. (Law court records)
MUNUS.LUGAL-*wa-mu ku-it* / EGIR-*pa pí-eš-ki-it nu-wa-kán ar-ha Ú-UL ku-it-ki pí-ni-nu-nu-un*

865. Mşt. 75/42 obv. 7 ff. (Letter)
am-me-el ku-it ^{LÚ}*TE-MU* / *a-pí-iz ú-it* ŠEŠ.DÙG.GA-*YA-ma-mu* / *aš-šu-ul ku-wa-at Ú-UL* / *ha-at-ra-a-eš*

2.4.4. Negation and interrogative clauses

2.4.4.1. Negation

For the negation of statements, there is the negation *natta*, often covered up by the akkadogram *UL*, and the composed negations *nāwi* „not yet" and *nūmān, nūwān* „not at all, not anymore". The prohibitive negation *lē* is regularly construed with the indicative.

As a rule, the negation precedes the negated word, if there is no general pronoun in the sentence that attracts the preponed negation, or a construction of preverb and verb where the negation regularly moves in between.

In interrogative clauses, *natta* moves to the head of the sentence. The occasional right-peripheral position at the end of a clause can be explained as a „stranding"-phenomenon in topicalisation processes. Sometimes double negation occurs which is probably of emphatic character.

Especially the phrases *natta memāi-* „to say no, refuse" and *mān natta* „otherwise" should be noted.

Lit.: Friedrich 1960: 145 f.; Morpurgo Davies 1975; Zeilfelder 2004; Hoffner/Melchert 2008: 341 ff.; Bauer forthcoming.

866. KBo VI 2+ III 65 f. (Laws, first tablet)
ma-a-na-an iš-ha-aš-ši-ša[263] *ú-e-mi-ya-zi* / *na-an-za ša-ku-wa-aš-ša-ra-an da-a-i* ^{LÚ}NÍ.ZU-*an* ***na-at-ta*** *e-ip-zi*

867. KBo XXII 2 obv. 18 (Tale of Zalpa, A)
ha-an-te-iz-zi DUMU^{MEŠ} *ni-ku-uš-mu-uš* ***na-at-ta*** *ga-ni-eš-šir*

263 Namely the owner of a stray animal.

868. KUB XXII 70 obv. 80 (Oracle concerning the intrigues at the Hittite court)
^{D}UTU$^{\textit{ŠI}}$*-ma-aš-ši kat-ta* ***Ú-UL*** *ar-ku-ut-ta*

869. KUB XXX 10 obv. 22 f. (Kantuzzili's prayer)
ma-a-am-ma-an[264] *da-an-du-ki-iš-na-ša* DUMU*-aš uk-tu-u-ri hu-iš-wa-an-za e-eš-ta ma-na-aš-ta ma-a-an / an-tu-wa-ah-ha-aš i-da-a-lu-wa i-na-an ar-ta ma-na-at-wa* ***na-at-ta*** *kat-ta-wa-tar*

870. KBo III 34 I 20 (Palace chronicle)
TÚG-*ZU-NU* ^{TÚG}*iš-hi-al-še-me-it-ta ku-it* ***na-at-ta*** *eš-ha-aš-kán-ta*

871. KUB XXIII 1+ I 13 f. (Treaty with Šaušgamuwa)
KUR ^{URU}*A-mur-ra* ***Ú-UL*** *IŠ-TU* ^{GIŠ}TUKUL / *ŠA* KUR ^{URU}*Ha-at-ti tar-ah-ha-an e-eš-ta*

872. KUB I 1+ II 37 (Apology of Hattušili III)
ÉRIN^{MEŠ}*-az-ma-mu* 1 LÚ*-ya kat-ta-an* ***Ú-UL*** *e-eš-ta*

873. KBo III 4+ I 8 f. (Annals of Muršili II)
ma-ah-ha-an-ma-za ^{m}*Ar-nu-an-da-aš* ŠEŠ-*YA* DINGIR$^{\textit{LIM}}$*-iš ki-ša-at*[265] *nu* KUR.KUR ^{LÚ}KÚR ***Ú-UL****-ya ku-i-e-eš ku-u-ru-ri-ya-ah-hi-eš-kir / nu a-pu-u-uš-ša* KUR.KUR^{MEŠ} ^{LÚ}KÚR *ku-u-ru-ri-ya-ah-hi-ir*

874. KUB XXXI 4+ obv. 12 f. (Chronicle of Puhanu)
KUR.KUR$^{\text{HI.A}}$*-ma hu-u-ma-an ku-iš har-zi* ***na-at-ta*** *ú-uk* ÍD^{MEŠ}*-uš* HUR.SAG^{MEŠ}*-uš a-ru-nu-uš-ša / a-ap-pa tar-ma-i-iš-ki-mi*

875. KUB I 16+ III 45 (Political testament of Hattušili I)
ŠA ^{LÚ}GAL.GAL$^{\textit{TIM}}$ É-*ŠU-NU ku-wa-pí* ***Ú-UL****-at kar-ki-e-ir*

876. KBo IV 10+ rev. 15 f. (Treaty with Ulmitešub)
ma-a-an ^{D}UTU$^{\textit{ŠI}}$ *A-NA* ^{m}*Ul-mi-*^{D}U*-up* 1 URU$^{\textit{LUM}}$ *na-aš-ma* 1 *AŠ-RU ku-it-ki ú-e-ik-zi na-at-ši* SILIM*-li pa-a-i* GÉŠPU*-ah-hu-aš* ***Ú-UL*** */ na-at A-NA NI-ÌŠ* DINGIR$^{\textit{LIM}}$ *kat-ta-an ar-ha* GAR*-ru*

877. KUB I 13+ II 1 ff. (Kikkuli's hippological texts)
na-aš 2 DANNA *pí-en-na-i*[266] *ma-ah-ha-an-ma-aš* / EGIR*-pa u-un-na-i*

264 = *mān=ma°*.
265 „Become a god" = „die".
266 Namely horses.

na-aš ar-ha la-a-an-zi / na-aš-kán aš-nu-an-zi ša-ak-ru-wa-an-zi-ia-aš ***Ú-UL***

878. KUB XXII 70 obv. 67 (Oracle concerning the intrigues at the Hittite court)
^{D}UTU^{ŠI}*-ma-aš-ši kat-ta-an* ***Ú-UL***[267]

879. KUB I 1+ IV 11 ff. (Apology of Hattušili III)
šal-la-nu-nu-un-wa-ra-an / ku-it am-mu-uk nu-wa-ra-an hu-wa-ap-pí DI-*eš-ni hu-wa-ap-pí* / DINGIR^{LIM}*-ni* ***Ú-UL*** *pa-ra-a* ***Ú-UL*** *ku-wa-pí-ik-ki tar-na-ah-hu-un*

880. KUB XIX 6+ I 66' ff. (Treaty with Alakšandu of Wiluša)
na-aš ma-a-an nu-u-wa-ya ma-ya-an-za / na-an-za-an KUR-*an-za* ***Ú-UL me-ma-a-i*** *nu kiš-an te-iz-zi* NUMUN-*wa-ra-aš* DUMU.LUGAL *e-eš-du* / ^{D}UTU^{ŠI}*-ma-za* ***Ú-UL me-ma-ah-hi***[268]

881. KBo V 4 II 1 (Treaty with Targašnalli of Hapalla)
nu KUR ^{URU}*Ha-pal-la ta-mi-e-ta-ni* ***Ú-UL ku-wa-at-qa*** *pí-ih-hi zi-ik-pát-ma-za iš-ha-a-aš e-eš*

882. Mşt. 75/45 lower edge 13 f. (Letter)
ma-a-an Ú-UL*-ma nu-za a-pí-e-el / wa-aš-túl zi-ik da-a-at-ti*

883. KBo III 40 rev. 12' (Chronicle of Puhanu)
hur-la-aš ***na-ú-i*** *ú-iz-zi nu pa-ra-a* MU.4.KAM *pa-a-an-zi*

884. KBo III 34 I 14 f. (Palace chronicle)
pí-di-iš-ši-ma ^{m}*Šar-ma-aš-šu-un ha-at-ra-a-it*[269] *pa-iz-zi-ma-aš* / ***na-a-ú-i***

885. KUB XV 17+ I 49 f. (Vow of Puduhepa)
3 UZ$_{6}$.GAL 2 UDU.NÍTA *A-NA* ^{DUG}BÁHAR *an-na-nu-ma-aš* / SANGA-*eš-na-za* ***na-a-ú-i*** EGIR-*pa*

886. KUB I 16+ II 47 (Political testament of Hattušili I)
ku-u-ru-ur ***nu-wa-an*** *e-eš-du*

887. KUB XVII 5 I 11 ff. (Myth of Illuyanka)
na-aš-ta ^{DUG}*pal-ha-an hu-u-ma-an-da-an e-ku-ir / ne-za ni-in-ki-e-ir / ne*

267 Nominal sentence, add „was" in the translation.
268 Here: „agree".
269 Here: „to appoint in writing".

nam-ma ha-at-te-eš-na-aš kat-ta-an-ta / ***nu-u-ma-a-an*** *pa-a-an-zi*[270]

888. KBo IV 10+ obv. 35' (Treaty with Ulmitešub)
A-NA MUN ^{URU}*Ša-ar-ma-na-kán ta-ma-iš* UN-*aš an-da* ***li-e*** *pa-id-du*

889. KUB XIII 4 II 58 (Instructions for the priests and temple officials)
nu-uš-ma-aš EGIR-*pa wa-ah-nu-mar* ***li-e****-pát e-eš-zi*

890. KUB VI 41 IV 13 (Treaty with Kupanta-^{D}KAL, D version)
i-da-la-wa-ah-ti-ma-an ***li-e*** *ku-it-ki*

891. KUB I 16+ II 55 (Political testament of Hattušili I)
a-pa-a-at-ta ku-uš-du-wa-a-ta ***li-e li-e*** *ha-an-da-a-an-pát e-eš-du*

892. KUB XIII 4 II 79 (Instructions for the priests and temple officials)
nu-za ÚŠ-*tar* ***li-e*** *uš-ni-ya-at-te-ni* ÚŠ-*tar-ma-za wa-a-ši-ya-at-te-ni* ***li-e***

2.4.4.2. Interrogative clauses

Beside word interrogatives with the *kuis-* pronouns, *kuwat* „why" or *mahhan* „how" there are yes-non-questions that are only marked by intonation. For the translation, one has to rely on contextual references if it is not a negated interrogative which, as described above, is marked by initial position of the negation.

Lit.: Friedrich 1960: 146 f.; Mascheroni 1980; Kowal 1983; Hoffner/ Melchert 2008: 348 ff.

893. KBo XXXII 15 II 26' f. (Epos of liberation: Ebla)
an-za-a-ša a-da-an-na / ***ku-iš*** *pí-iš-ki-iz-zi*

894. KBo III 34 I 19 (Palace chronicle)
ma-a-an lu-uk-ta-at nu A-BI LUGAL *hal-za-iš ku-u-uš ar-ha* ***ku-iš*** *pí-hu-te-it*

895. KUB XIV 3 II 37 (Tawagalawa letter)
na-at-za UL me-im-ma-aš ***ku-it*** *a-pa-a-at*

896. KUB XXXIII 102+ II 7 f. (Myth of Ullikummi)
ku-wa-at*-wa* / É-*ri* IGI-*an-da kar-tim-mi-ya-u-wa-an-za ú-it*

---

270 Modal: „could not go".

897. KUB XXXVI 35 I 8’ f. (El, Ašertum, and the stormgod)
^{D}*El-ku-ni-ir-ša-aš* ^{D}U-*an a-uš-ta na-an pu-u-nu-uš-ta* / ***ku-it***-*wa ú-wa-aš*

898. KUB XIX 5+ obv. 22 f. (Letter of Manapa-Datta)
tu-uk-wa ^{D}U-*tar pí-ya-na-it*[271] EGIR-*pa-wa-ra-at* ***ku-wa-at*** / *pí-eš-ti*

899. Mşt. 75/49 rev. 25 f. (Letter)
am-mu-ga-ma-an ***ma-ah-ha-an*** / *i-ya-nu-un*

900. KUB I 1+ I 50 f. (Apology of Hattušili III)
DINGIR^{LUM}-*mu-za-kán* GAŠAN-*YA hu-u-ma-an-da-za-pát da-aš-ki-ši* / ***Ú-UL*** *e-eš-ta*

901. KUB XXXIII 96 III 32’ f. (Myth of Ullikummi)
Ú-UL-*wa-ra-an ša-ak-ti* ^{D}*Ku-mar-bi-eš-wa ku-in nu-ut-ta-ri-ya-an* DINGIR^{LIM}-*in* / DINGIR^{MEŠ}-*aš* IGI-*an-da ša-am-na-it*

902. KUB XXIV 3+ II 3 f. (Muršili’s prayer to the sun goddess of Arinna)
ki-i DINGIR^{MEŠ} *ku-it i-ya-at-tin nu hi-in-kán tar-na-at-tin* / *nu* KUR ^{URU}KÙ.BABBAR-*ti hu-u-ma-an-pát* BA.ÚŠ

903. KUB XIV 11+ I 36’ f. (Plague prayer of Muršili II)
LÚ^{MEŠ} ^{URU}*Ha-at-ti-pát hu-u-da-a-ak šar-ri-i-e-ir* / *nu-wa-ra-aš* ***ma-a-an*** *A-NA* ^{D}IM ^{URU}*Ha-at-ti BE-LÍ-YA kar-tim-mi-ya-az ki-ša-at*

904. KUB XXII 25 I 19 ff. (Oracle questions of Muršili II)
pa-ra-a-ma-za-kán / ^{URU}*Ne-ri-iq-qa-az ar-ha a-ri-ya-mi* ***ma-a-an*** *ku-ru-ur*$^{\text{HI.A}}$ *hu-u-da-ak* RA-*mi* / *ma-a-an-za* EZEN$_4$ *wu*$_u$*-ru-li-ya-aš hu-u-da-ak* DÙ-*mi nu* DINGIR^{LUM} *ar-ha ú-da-ah-hi*

905. KUB I 16+ II 16 (Political testament of Hattušili I)
LUGAL-*ša-an i-da-a-lu ku-it-ki i-ya-nu-un Ú-UL-an* ^{LÚ}SANGA *i-ya-nu-un*

906. KUB XXXI 71 IV 16 f. (Protocol of a dream)
nu-wa a-ši DUMU.LUGAL *me-mi-iš-ki-iz-zi* / *e-ni-wa-kán ku-it* ŠÀ ÉSAG *e-ša-ri*

---

271 Object drop, add „it“ in the translation.

2.4.5. Irrealis and potentialis

As Hittite only shows morphological means of expression for the two *modi* indicative and imperative, irreal and potential conditions are expressed by the particle *man*.

Lit.: Friedrich 1960: 165 ff.; Lühr 2001; Hoffner/Melchert 2008: 314 ff.

907. KUB XXXIII 106+ II 7 ff. (Myth of Ullikummi)
nu ma-ah-ha-an ^{D}*Hé-pád-du-uš* ^{D}*Tàš-mi-šu-un a-uš-ta / nu-kán* ^{D}*Hé-pa-du-uš šu-uh-ha-az kat-ta ma-uš-šu-u-wa-an-zi wa-aq-qa-ri-eš* ***ma-an*** */ ti-ya-at* ***ma-na****-aš-kán šu-uh-ha-az kat-ta ma-uš-ta-at na-an* $^{MUNUS.MEŠ}$SUHUR.LA$_5$ */ e-ip-pir na-an Ú-UL tar-ni-ir*

908. KBo V 13+ I 21 f. (Treaty with Kupanta-^{D}KAL, C version)
A-NA KUR^{TIM}***-ma-an*** */ ta-me-a-in ku-in-ki* EN*-an i-ya-nu-un*

909. KUB XXIV 8+ II 16 ff. (Story of Appu)
KUR*-e-wa ni-ik-ku ku-wa-pí-ik-ki har-kán* ***ma-an****-wa* URU$^{DIDLI.HI.A}$ / *ni-ik-ku ku-u-wa-pí-ik-ki dan-na-ti-eš-ša-an-te-eš /* ***ma-a-an***[272]*-wa* ^{LÚ}ÉRIN^{MEŠ} *ni-ik-ku ku-wa-pí-ki hu-ul-la-an-te-eš*

910. KBo III 34 II 17 f. (Palace chronicle)
ma-na*-an-kán* ^{m}*A-aš-ka-li-ya-aš ku-i-en-zi ša-an A-NA* É.EN.NUN.UN *da-iš /* ^{m}*A-aš-ka-li-ma ud-da-a-ar a-ra-a-iš*

911. KUB VI 41 I 32 f. (Treaty with Kupanta-^{D}KAL, D version)
^{m}PÉŠ.TUR*-wa-aš-ma-mu-uš-ša-an šu-ul-li-it nu-mu* KUR ^{URU}*Pí-taš-ša* LÚ^{MEŠ} ^{URU}*Ha-at-ti-ya /* ARAD^{MEŠ}*-YA kat-ta-an har-nam-ni-ya-at* ***ma-an****-mu me-na-ah-ha-an-da ku-u-ru-ri-ya-ah-ta*

912. KUB XXI 27+ I 25 ff. (Puduhepa's prayer to the sun goddess of Arinna)
^{URU}*Ne-ri-iq-qa-aš-ši-kán* URU*-aš ap-pa-an-na / Ú-UL e-eš-ta* ^{URU}*Ne-ri-iq-qa-an-****ma-an*** URU*-an / Ú-UL tar-ah-ta*

913. Mşt. 75/66 lower edge 33 ff. (Letter)
ma-an*-kán ku-it / ma-ah-ha-an an-da* ***ma-an****-mu / hu-u-ma-an ha-at-ri-eš-ki-ši*

272 The plene-writing of the particle is somewhat strange, but the conjunction *mān* is impossible here.

914. KUB VI 41 IV 25 ff. (Treaty with Kupanta-^{D}KAL, D version)
^{m}*Maš-hu-i-lu-wa-aš ku-it* / *A-BU-KA IT-TI* ^{D}UTU^{ŠI} *wa-aš-ta-aš zi-ik-ma-za* ^{m}*Ku-pa-an-ta-*^{D}KAL-*aš* / *A-NA* ^{m}PÉŠ.TUR-*wa* DUMU-*la-aš e-eš-ta* ***ma-an***-*za zi-ik Ú-UL* ***ma-an***-*ga* / *wa-aš-du-la-aš e-eš-ta* ***ma-an***-*kán ma-a-an A-NA* ^{D}UTU^{ŠI} *ku-wa-pí* / HUL-*u-an-ni ki-it-ta-at* ***ma-an***-*ta* ^{D}UTU^{ŠI} *a-pí-ya-pát ar-ha pí-eš-ši-ya-nu-un*

915. Mşt. 75/113 rev. 15 ff. (Letter)
ma-an-*kán* ^{D}UTU^{ŠI} *BE-LÍ-YA BE-LU* / *ku-in-ki pa-ra-a na-it-ti* / ***ma-n****a* KUR-*i* ^{LÚ}KÚR *Ú-UL dam-mi-iš-ha-iz-zi*

916. Mşt. 75/111 obv. 4 ff. (Letter)
ma-an-*wa u-un-na-at-ti kat-ta-an* / LÚ^{MEŠ} ^{URU}*Ga-aš-ga-wa ki-iš-ša-an* / *me-mi-iš-kán-zi* ***ma-an***-*wa* GAL $^{LÚ.MEŠ}$KUŠ$_7$ / *u-un-na-i nu-wa ták-šu-la-u-e-ni*

EXERCISES

917. KUB XIII 35+ I 29 f. (Law court records)
ku-u-un-na-wa me-mi-an Ú-UL i-ya-mi ki-i-wa ku-it ka-ru-ú / *li-in-ku-un* EGIR-*zi-ma-an-wa-za da-ah-hi ku-it-ki*

918. KUB XXXI 4+ obv. 4 f. (Chronicle of Puhanu)
na-at-ta-aš-ta ku-it-ki ku-e-da-ni-ik-ka da-ah-hu-un GU$_4$-*na-aš-ta na-at-ta* / *ku-e-da-ni-ik-ka da-a-ah-hu-un* UDU-*na-aš-ta na-at-ta ku-e-da-ni-ik-ka da-a-ah-hu-un*

919. KBo VI 34+ I 36 (First military oath)
ki-i-wa ku-it Ú-UL-wa har-nam-mar

920. KUB I 1+ IV 33 ff. (Apology of Hattušili III)
ma-a-an-kán da-ma-a-in / *ku-pí-ya-ti-in ku-up-ta ma-an I-NA* KUR ^{URU}*Ka-ra-an-du-ni-ya* / *pí-en-ni-iš-ta*

921. KBo X 13 (+) I 20 f. (Treaty with Aziru of Amurru)
nu-za-kán ^{D}UTU^{ŠI} LUGAL.GAL *QA-TAM pa-ra-a me-ik-ki tu-uš-ku-un* / ^{D}UTU^{ŠI}-*za-kán* LUGAL.GAL *QA-TAM-MA pa-ra-a Ú-UL im-ma me-ik-ki tu-uš-ku-un*

922. Mşt. 75/9 obv. 6 ff. (Letter)
na-an-kán tu-uz-zi-ya / an-da ú-wa-te / ma-a-an Ú-UL-ma / ú-wa-ši har-ak-ši

923. KBo XXXII 14 III 13 f. (Epos of liberation)
Ú-UL UR.GI$_7$-*aš*[273] *nu*[274] *an-tu-wa-ah-ha-aš ma-ni-ya-ah-hi-aš iš-ha-a-an / ku-in BE-EL-ŠU i-e-zi*

924. KUB XXXIII 106+ I 32' f. (Myth of Ullikummi)
ku-en-ta[275]*-wa-ra-an-kán ku-wa-at-qa* / $^{\text{NA4}}$*ku-un-ku-nu-uz-zi-iš*[276] *am-me-el* LÚ-*an* ^{D}U-*an na-ak-ki-in* LUGAL-*un*

273 The quote is from an animal fable, and this is the explanation of the moral.
274 Here adversative: „but“.
275 Topicalized verb.
276 Here not the diorite as a stone, but a stone monster.

3. Translations of the Examples

1. Stench filled the windows, smoke filled the house.
2. The *panku* sentenced them to death.
3. The mighty weather god made a feast.
4. When I conveyed to him these words: „Come here!“, he fled from Maraššantiya.
5. Go down hastily in the evening!
6. This saying (is) important.
7. The goodwill of Ištar herself, my mistress, rested upon me.
8. The wing of the eagle brought (him) in.
9. Like this rock is eternal, so the master and his wife (and) his sons shall be eternal.
10. It shall be a great compensation for the gods.
11. He killed the family of Titti with all of his sons.
12. But these contract tablets had been made earlier.
13. They spin the years of the king.
14. When they reconcile the sun god of blood with the weather god, they take the following.
15. The weather god of heaven should strike that one!
16. It will happen that it turns out badly for this man.
17. So I, Telipinu, summoned the council in Hattuša.
18. My army was in Zizzilippa too, and there was a battle in Zizzilippa.
19. In their place I sowed weeds.
20. Inara built herself a house on a rock.
21. And send the army along a good way!
22. They brought grain (and) vine here.
23. He killed Zidanta, his father.
24. But I cannot overcome the pain inside of me, I cannot defeat the fear in my limbs anymore.
25. I set off and built the places Hawarkina and Delmuna.
26. I report the solicitous workings of the goddess Ishtar.
27. I always say: Those have done me harm, but I will not do them harm.
28. The deity gave us the love of husband (and) wife.
29. When people saw the favourable attitude of Ishtar, my mistress, and my brother's goodwill, they envied me.

30. If a free man sets fire to a house, he must rebuild that house.
31. He always plots evil against the weather god.
32. Now they wipe a lamb with the water.
33. He cast it, formed (it) and studded/trimmed it with applications.
34. Afterwards they bring livers roasted on the fire.
35. But Hūpašiya came and tied the dragon Illuyanka up with a rope.
36. She filled containers with faeces and put her sons inside.
37. The man seizes the well-being with his hand.
38. The King of Kuššara came down from the city with great power.
39. Then they draw the deity from Akkade, from Babylon, from Susa, from Elam, from Hursag-Kalamma, from the city that you love, from the mountains, from the river, from the sea, from the valley, from the meadows, from the well, from the sky, from earth on seven paths and seven side paths.
40. When Inara came back from the open country, he started to wail.
41. They shall be free from taxes and *luzzi*-services.
42. They mix the mentioned old fine oil of the flask with the water they wash the temple walls with.
43. This one brings back home whatever he finds.
44. So the divine hand struck me in my dream, and my mouth twisted sideways.
45. The Hurrite army comes into the land.
46. Let me (go) back home!
47. He shouted „Help!“
48. Don't you know (it), Ubelluri, didn't anybody tell you the message?
49. Come here, Telipinu!
50. Tarpattašši, take this (mouse) for you!
51. Therefore, I have come, my father.
52. My god, you have created me, you have raised me!
53. Oh place, feast yourself and und be always merciful!
54. Entrails overcome entrails.
55. Then the gods demanded retaliation for Muršili's blood.
56. The pregnant do not give birth there.
57. The entire land of Hatti, the land Hayaša and all the peoples, foreign (and) inland, have widely heard from you.
58. The gate keepers who got the stone house earlier shall be exempt from taxes and *luzzi*-services.
59. Then the pieces of meat remain lying before the deity.
60. All the countries revolted against me.

61. Many of the enemies mobilized behind his back from Gaška.
62. But as soon as the majesty, my lord, sets out hastily from this border, the *parzašša*- and *dāyalla*-times are here.
63. Aren't my words the words of the sun god and Kamrušepa?
64. The heads of barley (are) tied together, the heads of spelt (are) tied together.
65. Kumarbi is the father of the gods.
66. The chief of the palace servants walks in front of the carriage and carries a baton.
67. If you had protected the infantry in earlier times, (the deity) would have put the matter of the people in (your) hand already.
68. If (that) of the feet is done, they bring a rope here.
69. The will of the gods is strong.
70. He shall be Neša's foe and he shall be the foe of the whole population!
71. He held the country of the enemy defeated with strength wherever he marches into battle.
72. Behold, I took (away) the defamations of the population from you.
73. If somebody finds a cow, a horse, a mule, he must drive it to the gate of the kings.
74. But they shall bring property, silver, (and) gold to Hattuša (and) Arinna, to the cities of the gods!
75. They drove them into the bushes.
76. Zithariya bowed to all of the gods.
77. Then they offer a sheep to the divine fathers as a libation.
78. In earlier years Alalu was king in heaven.
79. He took care of him and brought him to (good) times.
80. Hhe has harmed all (people).
81. I increased the grain again.
82. You have spat out the evil curses, they fall to the ground.
83. I seized the leaders.
84. They roast the entrails of the sheep by the open fire.
85. I turned all the provinces in the land of Hatti, o Ištar, over to Hattušili.
86. He did not master the vassalages of his land's deity.
87. You lords, turn your ears to me and hear these, my prayers!
88. Antarawa has gone there and has delivered the offerings of atonement.
89. But keep my, the Labarna's, the great king's words!
90. The Hantašepa deities hold both human heads and lances.
91. In Neša I reinforced the town.

92. Where no cultivated land is near, (where) the plough does not get to, there the tent is made.
93. Do not bring here the water which (is) there above!
94. Afterwards I, Anitta, the Great king, brought the god Šiu from Zalpuwa back to Neša.
95. Ages ago Uhna, the King of Zalpuwa, took our god Šiu away from Neša to Zalpuwa.
96. They lured out the dragon Illuyanka up from his cave.
97. Illuyanka defeated the weather god.
98. Afterwards she washes herself with water.
99. The stench let go of the window, the smoke let go of the house.
100. Bewitchment, evil dreams shall be fastened, it shall not come up again, the dark earth shall keep hold of it!
101. A smith cast a goblet for his own glory.
102. Go and open the dark earth again!
103. In the future, nobody shall shatter this tablet!
104. When it gets light in the early morning, my servant comes down and brings up pure water with the aid of a can.
105. He put swift shoes on his feet and walked up to the top of an observation tower.
106. The chief of the bodyguards brings the silver *zau* of the pure priest of the town Zippalanda here.
107. On this day the dragging takes place: They drag it into the temple of the old deity.
108. When the king makes preparations at the ritual stone, the chief of the cupbearers takes a jar of wine and hands it to the king.
109. How often have you, Ištar, mistress, taken me and put me to kingship on an excellent place in the land of Hatti!
110. If the weather god thunders, the king descends from the carriage and bows down and libates and bows again.
111. The table setter takes two *tuninga* breads from the clean table.
112. The table setter takes a sweet bread from the clean table and hands it to the king.
113. He shall wake the weather god of Nerik from his sweet dream!
114. He goes to the palace either with a carriage or with a coach.
115. At first, I made you pregnant with the noble weather god, secondly, I made you pregnant with the Tigris of *ullazzuwa*, thirdly, I made you pregnant with the noble Tašmišu.

116. When the grain fields (are) ripe, harvest them and bring them to the threshing place!
117. In addition, those making the daily bread shall be pure.
118. However, if you keep these oaths and they (are) eternal for you, you yourselves will be eternal as well just like them!
119. The matters you have written to me, how the enemy has destroyed the grain fields, how he attacked (the property) of the queen's house in Kappušiya and how they took away a *happutri* cow of the queen's house and thirty heads of cattle from the poor and lead away ten men: I took note of all that.
120. In the beloved lap of the goddess Tešimi you dreamed sweet dreams.
121. But you, they say, have many sons.
122. Then they cut up the sheep and take ritually pure raw meat (from it).
123. Their hair and nails shall be removed, and they shall wear clean clothes.
124. You, Adadbēlī, know about the matters of the torches and the grass.
125. Who can see them still, the hard battles of the great gods?
126. They shall bring the seal of the old fathers here!
127. He also puts four *walla* on the four corner stones, on every single corner stone.
128. Ea started to speak to the old gods.
129. They lay it again on the clean tables of the king (and) queen.
130. And winds and rain shall not beat your eyes!
131. Oh Telipinu, you (are) a strong, mighty god!
132. I take the evil defamation of the whole mankind away from him.
133. But Šarmaššu and Nunnu took on the mountain Tahaya.
134. Behold, I brought a girl's property, but next year I will bring a boy's property!
135. Draw the evil rheumatism away from him!
136. The palace squire of the king (and) the palace squire of the queen come and take the king's and the queen's knee scarfs and footstools.
137. From this offerer of sacrifice draw away the evil impurity, the spell, the bewitchment, the wrath of the gods, the oath of the gods, the defamation of the public, the short year as well!
138. He went down to the shore of the nine seas.
139. If the moon dies, the army in its entirety will die in the battle.
140. When the seers draw near the gods from the eight ways, from the meadow, from the mountains, from the rivers, from the sea, from the wells, from the fire, from the sky, from the earth, then they take the following.
141. He gave me infantry and chariot fighters, but only in little number.

142. Son of Šulinkatte, come up from the four dark corners of the world, from the deep surge, turn towards Nerik again!
143. Look at the land of Hatti with benevolent eyes!
144. In this matter the weather god of the thunder, the sun goddess of Arinna, the weather god of Hatti, the weather god of Nerik, Ištar of Šamuha, Ištar of Lawazantiya (and) the thousand gods of Hatti shall be witnesses!
145. Like the spindle whorl turns, in the same way the bad entrails of this child shall be turned away and down!
146. Afterwards he drinks three times (the ritual cup) in honour of the thunder, the winds, the clouds, the downpours of the weather god while standing.
147. They poured out the evil tongues together with the vessel.
148. It shall be wiped off you, the evil words of the mouth, the tongue!
149. The palace squires lay down the knee scarves.
150. The kings that had been kings longer than me (and) which had good relations with me stayed in the same good relations with me.
151. But on open fields, cultivated soil, meadows, no plant shall grow for him, his cattle, his sheep shall not have calves or lambs!
152. I took the evil away from them and turned it towards a little mouse, and this little mouse shall carry it to high mountains, deep valleys, long roads!
153. If a woman gives birth and his (the child's) head is like a snake's head, (this is) the omen of Gilgameš.
154. Behold, (it is) a sin before the oaths and you violated the oaths.
155. He saw a fourth dream, where a heavy meteor fell down from the sky and killed the servants and a man of god.
156. I have never sworn on you, my god, and then violated the oath.
157. He says this incantation seven times.
158. A troublemaker could get drunk in the temple or in another ritual building and start an argument if he causes disturbance in the temple.
159. Afterwards she takes a *hupuwāi* vessel and fills it with wine, olive oil, honey.
160. Then they pour out a flask of fine oil.
161. Second tablet of the oath with Hukkanā.
162. The tablets of incantation (are) separate.
163. Afterwards I went into battle near Ulma.
164. In addition, when we slaughtered a sheep, we put down under oath the following.
165. But if you do not fight him then, behold, the oath god will crush you and the town Hattuša shall be free from the oath.
166. Be very careful with quarrels!

167. Behold, like it does not see the sky, like it does not see the piglets in the future, in the same way the evil curses shall not see these sacrifice offerers.
168. If somebody has not got a spear, then they are not lined up with the palace squires (bearing) the lituus because they only take sticks, but two other palace squires come forward.
169. The Wise woman brings clay of the river bank and clay of the well there, two clay figures, twelve clay tongues, bent back, two clay bulls, two clay hinges, a bit of blue wool, a bit of red wool and an intertwined skein of red wool, a wing of an eagle, bones in small quantity and some *walli*.
170. Like they grind this beer spice with the grind stone and mix it with water, cook it and crush it, in the same way those oaths shall grip him who violates these oaths and harms the king, the queen, the sons of the king, the land of Hatti, and grind his bones and roast him as well!
171. He tells the dreams that he sees whenever the deity appears before his eyes.
172. Whoever violates these oaths, the weather god shall break his plough completely!
173. When it dawns on the second day, the women go to the cremation place to pick up the bones.
174. Because Uhhaziti violated his oaths (he swore) to me, the oath gods gripped him.
175. He breaks the loaf of bread and lays it down by the windows.
176. They place three shekels of fine oil before the bones.
177. When she has finished, she pours water into five cups made from fired clay.
178. Whether one renews them in the ninth year or whenever one renews them - the point of time is irrelevant.
179. Behold, sun god of the blood and weather god, we want to reconcile you again.
180. The king comes up to the door of the gate building.
181. If somebody pushes a man into a fire and he dies, he gives again a lad.
182. And out of respect for my brother I did not do anything.
183. He also filled Šamuha, the town of the deity, with sorcery.
184. When they bring up the horn, they wipe it clean with water.
185. Afterwards she washes herself with water.
186. I defeated them and Hūhazalma through (divine) judgment.
187. He takes a piglet and slaughters it into the pit and lets its blood run down.
188. The king goes into the inner chamber and takes the robes.
189. And brothers and sisters passed heartless words on to him, and he always listended to their words!
190. These animals come from the upper *kašgaštipa* house down to the gate.

191. Like malt (and) beer spice are well-mixed, so your, Telipinu's, soul shall be well-fitted concerning the human matters!
192. They spread out a pillow between the stools on the ground.
193. She breaks a flatbread at the crossroads and puts it down on the left side of the road.
194. The herald runs ahead of the strangers into the inner chambers of the dignitaries and lets them sit down.
195. He went down to the banks of the venerable rivers.
196. If you are on the meadow, if you (are) in the valley, (or) somewhere else, come down amicably, come down to this man amicably!
197. In addition, be very careful with the matters of the fire.
198. The king goes to the clean bed.
199. She puts out the fire with water.
200. Search the deepest valleys, search the calm wave!
201. The good shall not perish with the bad!
202. When she comes to the river bank, she breaks a flatbread for the genius of the river bank.
203. But in the tenth year Anu fought a battle against Alalu and he defeated him, Alalu.
204. Still in the same year I went into battle against Šalatiwara.
205. Those few righteous men that are left, the men of the wine donation, those shall not die on me!
206. But none of the administrators, door keepers or ploughmen may open the granary of the king unauthorized.
207. There's a vessel rack in the courtyard, covered with a cloth.
208. When he drives them back again, they unharness them, he tends them and puts them on the bit and pulls them (sc. their heads) up the post.
209. Behold, I have dispatched the scouts, and they have spied out Malazziya and Taggašta.
210. But if you keep quiet about it and it comes out later, they will put you along with your wives, your children to an awful death.
211. This house is struck by a plague.
212. Then in the same way my, a human's, words shall stop the anger, resentment, rage of Telipinu!
213. The king takes the robes and walks out.
214. The height (is that of) a half-ell.
215. His (sc. Ullikummi's) width (was) 9000 miles.

216. You shall seize anyone who knows about sorcery among the clan members from the clan and bring him to the gate of the palace!
217. I experienced Ištar's care there in plenty.
218. In the same way the body of the king shall be clean from the sin of evil men, from horror, impurity, dirt!
219. The Wise woman takes it away from them and cuts the thread off them.
220. They started to dispatch envoys to me, they even started to send me presents.
221. The vow of the second year to the goddess Lelwani.
222. When the heat pesters him, bring him into the cold, when the cold plagues him, bring him into the warmth.
223. The mountain goddess Wašitta began to pant, and the god Kumarbi in the town heard the panting.
224. The gods of the land of Hatti have not taken anything from you, gods of the land Kašga, they have not done you any harm.
225. And as soon as they arrive there, they drive near another ox, adorned with jewellery and offer this other (ox). They burn these pieces of jewellery together with that substitute ox.
226. Sun god, you are the herdsman of all people!
227. Ištar, my mistress, placed enemies and envious people in my hand, and I finished them off completely.
228. Furthermore, guards shall be posted at night, they shall patrol all night. Outside of the temple, district temple guards shall keep watch.
229. Turn to the the land of Hatti amicably!
230. The sin of the father is visited upon the son, and thus the sin of my father was visited upon me.
231. Moreover, you, (being) water carriers, be very careful with the water and filter the water through a sieve!
232. The smiths make the idol from gold. Like their service for the goddess (is prescribed), they make an effort to execute it.
233. Send the plague, enmity, famine, the evil fever into the land Mittanni and into the land Arzawa!
234. After that he sets up the sacrificial altars at three places.
235. Then Kešši does not sacrifice bread and wine offering to the gods anymore.
236. But if a free man steals, then atonement (shall follow) for the theft.
237. If somebody abducts a woman and auxiliary troops are following her, (and) if (while doing so) two or three men die, then there will be no compensation.
238. Open them, the old, paternal and grandpaternal houses of the seal!

239. Only you, sun goddess of Arinna, (are) a gracious deity, and only you have mercy.
240. You are as stubborn as a mule.
241. But now I, the majesty, have fixed again the former border for him.
242. If a child (is) ill or its entrails (are) worm-eaten, then I will sacrifice to the sun deity of the plague for it as follows.
243. If a woman gives birth, and his (the child's) right ear clings tight to his cheeks, then in the house of the man an idiot will be born.
244. She gave them a forward pointing victorious spear.
245. You (are) a woman of woman kind and you do not understand anything!
246. I told it to the palace servant of Ušša.
247. If somebody abducts the dependant of a Luwian from Luwiya and brings him to Hatti, and his master recognises him, then he may only take his dependant, there is no compensation.
248. Be gracious, sun goddess of the sky, whose glow (is) sparkling, whose beams (are) full of light.
249. He lies down in the bed in boots to sleep.
250. She speaks as follows: „You have spat out (that) of the curse of this day".
251. A *partianza* has magically bound the eagle, the beardy snakes he has bound into a round.
252. Like the lock pushes back the bolt and the door always opens again, in the same way the sin, blasphemy, impurity, dirt of the wicked people shall also rise away from the king!
253. He was gripped with fear, he was seized with fright.
254. (It's shown) on a separate table how he speaks in Hurrite for this purpose.
255. Behold, I admitted to the sin before the weather god.
256. (There) above (is a) man, Appu is his name, the wealthiest within the land.
257. But if a woman has treated him – you, oh sun god, know it – then it shall be (like) a headscarf to her, and it shall weigh heavily on her head!
258. Now I take him up and appoint him for the priesthood of the sun goddess of Arinna.
259. I will examine it and I will replace it.
260. If I may sleep with you, then I will come and fulfil your wish.
261. I do not come to your house.
262. I will fight and destroy the land.
263. Or if you impose some additional atonement on me, then tell it to me in my dream and I will give it to you.

264. Also I, the majesty, protect you kindly.
265. But I take the mules of the palace for myself.
266. I, the king, dispatch it to a foreigner or give it to a servant.
267. On the first day I offered a sheep to the sun goddess of the plague.
268. Why do you always oppress us?
269. Why do you want to act now like Mašturi as well?
270. But now you do not write to me anything anymore.
271. You should not wish another rulership for you!
272. If you go into the house of your wife, ask her for (my) heart and (my) eyes!
273. You lay down an oven in front of them.
274. Do not kill any of his clan members, (that is) not good.
275. But if you were to tarry, the harm again (would be) like it once (was)!
276. But do not let his trader into your land.
277. But if you go there (and) betray it to them, then it shall be put under oath for you.
278. If he comes back from the campaign, then each of his sons will go into a land.
279. From now on nobody shall do evil to a son of the (royal) clan in Hattuša and (nobody) shall pull out a dagger against him.
280. Nanatalli still keeps back two young horses.
281. There shall be no sleep for you!
282. If an administrator or herdsman abducts a free woman (and) pays no bride price for her, then she becomes dependant in the third year.
283. Ištar, my mistress, for the first time on this campaign heralds my name for me.
284. If somebody bites off the nose of a free man, he gives one mine of silver.
285. He also pours fine oil on his head for him and binds red wool on his hand.
286. Nobody shall say anything!
287. But no one shall cause them harm.
288. We are dying of hunger.
289. The weather god says to Hannahanna: „What shall we do?“
290. When we are finished with it, then we will bring it back and lay it down completely.
291. Only we from the Hattiland have the habit to show our respect to you, to the gods.
292. Again and again we raise complaints before you.
293. We call the Gaškans and give them presents, then we swear them into service.
294. Why don’t you send me my messengers every time?
295. You eat (and) drink this again and again.
296. Only you know (it) because of your divine mind.

297. And if you do not hear the first time, then hear the second time, and if you do not hear the second time, then hear the third, fourth, fifth, sixth, seventh time!
298. You eat bread and drink water.
299. But other things you shall not tak e!
300. They offer a sheep to Zithariya.
301. They eat the fat (and) bread up.
302. Then they return to the army.
303. Additionally, they make a hut near there.
304. But house and land shall not be taken away from him, and they shall not give it to the descendants of someone else.
305. I do not say anything and I do not do anything.
306. If you always act well from now on and friendlily protect the majesty, then I, the majesty, will treat you and, accordingly, your sons well.
307. When I go to the field, do not look out of the window!
308. If somebody hits a free man or a free woman and he (she) dies, (if) his hand sins, then he shall do penance for the concerning person.
309. If somebody beats a trader from Hatti to death, he must give 100 mines of silver.
310. I fix the sea (in its place) and it does not flow back.
311. The majesty will not attack your land as long as we are not told about the judgement by the oracle.
312. But if you do not bring him, the people of the town must replace the granary.
313. Like a lame cripple I have given up walking and do not move on the dark ground as I did before.
314. I will become your king!
315. Will I now be protected?
316. I pull the string into a piece of reed.
317. When I, the majesty, come up from the land of Kummanni and sit down to royal power (= on the throne), then I will celebrate the feasts.
318. But now, wherever I turn on this field, you walk ahead of me.
319. You are pleased with your innermost, because you have swallowed my manhood.
320. You shall not become one of my men, not my brother-in-law.
321. Do not turn your eyes to someone else!
322. If you, Azira, do not mobilize infantry and chariot fighters with all your heart, […] behold, then you will violate the oath.
323. Whenever I go into the land of the enemy, you stand by me amicably.

324. You turn to the majesty amicably and you stand by me amicably.
325. There's an *eya* tree in front of Telipinu.
326. When it dawns on the twelfth day, (and) the idol (is) still in the house, then they offer one fattened ox and seven sheep to the statue.
327. The ninth day is over.
328. Oil is poured out, but those do not come out.
329. For the services he has a master baker at his disposal.
330. This matter will not be taken up.
331. But if he does not give it (back), then he becomes a thieve.
332. The king comes out of the *halentu*-building, he sits down in the carriage.
333. The cupbearer brings a vessel of vine, and on top of it lies a clay cup.
334. When he goes into the throne chamber, he may sit before me on the right side.
335. He takes the lamps as soon as it gets dark.
336. It is called, they prepare the cups.
337. We want to come (and) settle.
338. We especially take care of the feasts of the gods.
339. If we go to Nerik, then we want to settle there somewhere.
340. Where in the mountains of Kandurna shall we settle?
341. Like the gods live separately, so we want to settle separately.
342. But now come, let us fight!
343. If you do not keep them (sc. my words), your land will come under foreign rule!
344. If you keep those oaths, then the gods shall protect you as well.
345. But you must not become rebellious!
346. You shall not commit an outrage.
347. King and queen sit down.
348. Behold, they are lined up before you.
349. They are dressed in blood-red garments.
350. But when the king comes to the palace, the worshippers of the statues already stand in front of it.
351. The princes sit down, and the cooks put down the pots with the food.
352. When the feasts are over, they send out the two old shields as well.
353. The mighty Anu, the first of the gods, stands before him.
354. He is not lacking anything, he is only lacking one thing: He has neither son nor daughter.
355. Let us share (the inheritance) and settle separately.
356. When it dawns on the third day, the offerer of the sacrifice goes hurriedly to the temple early in the morning. The stars are still showing.

357. The offerer of the sacrifice follows.
358. And when the fat boils, he offers a libation with the boiled (sc. fat).
359. When he becomes a god, they do the following at the same day.
360. The Great king, the Labarna, says to Haštayar: „If you were only not to neglect me!"
361. After that I went into the town Zalpa and destroyed it.
362. Sun god of the blood, weather god and all you male gods, behold, I have broken the breadloaves of the well-being for you.
363. When I came back to Neša, I brought the man of Purušhanda with me.
364. When I had destroyed Aššuwa and had returned to Hattuša, I celebrated the feasts of the gods.
365. But I, the Great king, cut off his head.
366. I, the king, did not know it.
367. Then I made a vow and a curse.
368. I took their weapons from their shoulders and handed them shackles.
369. I conquered the land Haššuwa in the first year.
370. I seized his property and filled up my house with those goods.
371. But when I saw this, I was afraid because of it.
372. My god, since my mother gave birth to me, you, my god, have raised me.
373. Why did you appoint him king at that time?
374. You have never embraced me, did you embrace me now, then?
375. This (is), what you have done: behold, the troops are (still with) you outside.
376. You started quarrel against me.
377. Have you, oh god, demanded any *termaz*-garment?
378. You called for the rest of the gods and you called for the entire mankind.
379. Where have you sent these seeds to?
380. Why did you look at that (sc. woman)?
381. You devoured men like fresh leek.
382. In the land of Hatti, you, sun goddess of Arinna, have assumed your name; because you have made it to the land of cedar, you have assumed the name Hepat.
383. You have given a team of mules to Hellarizzi.
384. The tambourine and the lapislazuli, which you promised - why did you not give them to him?
385. The king came back to Hattuša (and) Arinna.
386. But the weather god complained to all the gods.
387. He broke three breadloaves for the weather god of the oath and his male gods.

388. He was loved by the weather god of the sky.
389. But he did not do harm to any of the inhabitants of Neša.
390. He killed his most noble servants.
391. All the uninhabited areas that I had populated again he also took away from me then.
392. But (it is) no roebuck but a man, a man who ran away from his town.
393. The queen of Kaneš gave birth to thirty sons in one year.
394. But she seated the ancient gods to the right of the weather god.
395. He told them: „The king has given this to me."
396. And the mountain cursed the roebuck after that.
397. We have found our mother.
398. We have, behold, summoned the thousand gods to the meeting for this matter.
399. We had (lit. made for us) sons and daughters.
400. We have not killed them violently.
401. We have taken care of him and treated the illness.
402. Why did you act on me like this?
403. But you, gods of the land of Gaška, have started quarrel.
404. You have warmed up the hall here.
405. Who did you bring to Arinna? That one, my adversary!
406. In the past you have made the price of three silver shekels for a *adupli*-garment.
407. Why did you not wait for the eagle?
408. But the gods picked up the children from the sea and raised them.
409. When they went to Neša, the gods put a different interior into them.
410. They did an evil deed and killed Muršili.
411. The Gaškans who were my enemies backed me.
412. Illuyanka and his sons came up and ate (and) drank.
413. In Hahha I harassed the enemy and put up a battle with him.
414. But behind me the Hurrite enemy came into the country.
415. I gave her what had been there from old times, and what I had (added) I gave to her, too.
416. I took away the Hittite population which he had with him and settled them as a whole again.
417. He went into the town Šanawitta, but he did not destroy it.
418. Why have you given me so little?
419. When they came and cut off heaven and earth with the sickle, I did not know that as well.

420. There I defeated these enemies, but the others made peace with me.
421. I became king of Hakpiš.
422. After I, Telipinu, had sat down on the throne of my father, I campaigned against Haššuwa.
423. When I then returned from Egypt, I went to Lawazantiya to make sacrifices to the deity.
424. I also stood there with a cup in my hand.
425. The more I grew up, the more I understood all the favour and wisdom of my god.
426. I already sat in his carriages.
427. Why did you join those?
428. But you were weak and ill.
429. As you flattered me so much, why did you not receive their messengers?
430. You have become a maid of Hepat.
431. The sun goddess girded herself and moved up and down before the weather god.
432. But when it blended together, when Kumarbi had swallowed the manhood of Anu, he was glad and laughed.
433. Appu woke up from sleep with a start.
434. He came from the gate of the land of Egypt and prostrated himself before the majesty.
435. Hantīli was afraid.
436. Behold, in Hattuša bloodshed has become numerous.
437. Now my house has become a house of misery because of illness.
438. When the mountain heard this, he was hurt inside.
439. For this reason, he was struck (with illness) by the deity.
440. Huzziya would have killed them, but then the matter came out and Telipinu chased them away.
441. But then this one sat down.
442. Also in Zikpara, Šarupšenna and I went to the *hurwaši*-stone.
443. Just now we, the Great king Arnuwanda and the Great queen Ašmunikal, have particularly cared for you, the gods.
444. You have grown under the sky.
445. You have become the mother of one of the fathers.
446. You have been praised again and again.
447. When you have sat yourselves on the basalt throne, and when the anointed ones have put down the lot, then the anointed one who has the god Zalinu will sit down where the basalt throne stands over the well.

448. What you ate your fill of on this day - behold, now the deity Āndaliya has cut off for you the tongues of these days with a knife.
449. She tips them (sc. the ashes) where the heads of the horses and the heads of the cattle were burned.
450. Uhhaziti died on the sea, but his sons could break free.
451. What (concerns) this: these bird oracles have been received as ominous.
452. But in the oven the logs suffocated, on the sacrificial altars the gods suffocated.
453. The sun and the moon prostrated themselves and bowed down before the silver.
454. Just like you have become, behold, exactly the same this shall become.
455. But Anu sat down on the throne.
456. I became Great king.
457. When Anu had finished speaking, he went up to the sky and hid.
458. But if I were to become healthy, would I not become healthy through your, the god's, word?
459. They obtained an oracle from the gods, and it was also established from the gods.
460. The oaths seized him, and he swelled up inside.
461. Kešši wandered about the mountains for three months.
462. Behold, now I have brought a boy's property, but next year I will bring a girl's property!
463. Now I will sincerely speak the following.
464. I will happily give him the sacrificial breads and wine rations which I give regularly to the weather god of the thunder, my lord.
465. I will perform the ritual for the river Mala, I want to set it up and I will do it.
466. Just like I cut off fire wood, in the same way I want to cut off from the weather god of Kuliwišna (his) rage, cut off (his) anger, cut off (his) sin, cut of (his) resentment, cut off (his) eyes of wrath, the furious!
467. In the hand of the majesty see good prospering!
468. Enough of it! That one is not my son anymore!
469. Now recognise, Hukkanā, only the majesty regarding the rule!
470. My son, you should not always do whatever (is) in your heart!
471. So protect the majesty in (his) rule, protect also the sons, grandsons, descendants of the majesty in (their) rule later.
472. Whoever breaks it (sc. the tablet), shall be Neša's enemy!
473. Now he may eat and drink!
474. But if he (the king) says: „He shall give compensation!", then he shall give compensation.

475. Only a descendant of Ulmitešub shall take (her as a wife).
476. Like the sheep lick up the salt, in the same way the sun god shall come and lick up the incantations.
477. And it shall end in disaster!
478. Come to eat and drink!
479. But the house that I gave to the deity - everybody shall work for the deity to the best of their ability in there!
480. Then the master of the vantage point shall write down the ritual utensils of the gods and send it (sc.the list) to the majesty.
481. Well, you gods, which sin you see, either a man of god shall come and say it, or the 'Wise women', the seers, the augurs shall find it out.
482. But you, people of the town, shall seize every person who opens it, and you shall bring him to the gate of the king!
483. Be very respectful towards the word of a deity!
484. Guard the temples very carefully!
485. Now come, eat and drink!
486. Go, you shall be the same as your companions.
487. They shall go (and) live (there), and they shall eat (and) drink.
488. Every month they shall read this tablet to you.
489. They shall put everybody who does it to an awful death.
490. Behold, for this affair the thousand gods (are) called to the meeting, and they shall see and hear, and they shall be witnesses!
491. They shall be exempt from everything.
492. They shall search for descendants of a daughter of Ulmitešub.
493. I want to stand on him, on his body!
494. I want to appear to you.
495. I want to withdraw from these oaths.
496. I want to face your enemy in battle.
497. Whenever a woman of the palace comes, jump far out of the way!
498. Grow old in the hand of the majesty!
499. Come to aid immediatetly!
500. But turn amicably to the Great princess again!
501. Also you shall be very cautious of a palace woman.
502. Only a son who (is) a royal prince of first rank shall become king.
503. Now this woman shall be located before the god, my master!
504. He shall melt like wax!
505. He shall be completely broken by the illness.

506. An *eya*-tree shall stand in front of them.
507. If there is no first-rank royal prince, then a son of second rank shall become prince.
508. Like I put out this one, in the same way the evil concerning the masters shall be put out!
509. One shall protect the other!
510. In the morning, at the mealtime of the gods, he shall be immediately present.
511. The tongues of these days shall be cut off, the words of these days shall be cut off!
512. You must keep my, the king's, words.
513. If there (is) any job to do, be it a construction work or whatever job (it might be), set about doing it!
514. Mobilize wit troops, with great power!
515. Now come, eat, drink and join me!
516. Did you sin, by any chance?
517. If you protect me in friendship, then you shall lay your heads on my head!
518. The rivers shall be bridged!
519. But the sparkling applications shall fall into the river.
520. The gods shall keep your life, they shall protect you amicably!
521. He (shall) not (be) my servant, they shall cut his throat and hang him on his gate.
522. But if he sells it, he shall not sell it in a secret place: Hittite lords shall be there and watch (it).
523. These may die, but I do not want to die!
524. Rise and come into my house!
525. Look, Hūpasiya, this I want to do, and you – help me!
526. Now you, Hukkanā, kindly protect only the majesty and stand (protecting) only behind the majesty.
527. When he says: „He shall die!", then he shall die.
528. Keep all leftovers of bread, beer (and) wine up in the temple!
529. I have spat on it and crushed it under my feet, now the ass shall piss on it and the cattle shall shit on it.
530. My old writing cane is broken, send me here, my dear brother, a writing cane!
531. I don't know if she still consults the 'Wise women' now.
532. Now I eat and drink.
533. If a refugee of the enemy (has been) caught, and he escapes from Hatti, but passes through your lands and you seize him and do not hand him over but give him back to the enemy - this shall be put under oath as well.

534. Because you, Ubelluri, are distant from the dark ground, that is why you do not know this swift god.
535. At first, he drinks for the sun goddess of Arinna, the Mezzula, three times.
536. But when he comes to the crossing of the ways he offers a kid to the male gods of the *šinapši*.
537. We do not know that.
538. We eat and drink, and the physicians are with me.
539. Only you gods know (it) through (your) divine sense.
540. You will eat bread and drink water.
541. As soon as they know the words of the exclamation, they start saying the same.
542. The dignitaries and the men with the bronze spear sit before them.
543. Then he passes them a cup with salt water and a cup with malt water, and they drink it.
544. This I do not eat yet.
545. He may be with her, but the woman does not eat with him.
546. When we come in front of the door of Ea's house, we prostrate ourselves at the doors.
547. If you keep the words of the father, you will eat bread and drink water.
548. But when they reach the gate of the *šinapši*-house, the offerer of the sacrifice sits down.
549. But afterwards he drinks the weather god of Zippalanda.
550. How can we do it? Shall we go to the mountains and die in the mountains?
551. I, the majesty, make them sit down wherever I like.
552. But the people whom the queen gives mules to (saying): „Go and give these to them!", for those I had them (sc. the mules) exchanged in each case. Either I take (animals) from my own or I take (them) from somebody else and give those.
553. I do not go yet, I do not see why yet!
554. You give them red furskin.
555. But if you look out, you will see your wife and children.
556. If someone throws a sheep to the wolf, then his owner takes the fat and the other one takes the hide of the sheep.
557. He calls the name of the offerer of sacrifice.
558. But the father of the majesty even looks out of the window.
559. We also see the contract with you, the gods.
560. Why do you give the utensils that (are) in the rock sanctuary of the protective deity to the deity of Arušna?
561. What you see, report!

562. They call for the old gods.
563. When they shoot before the king, they give wine to drink to the one who hits (the target).
564. But they see him when he steps forward.
565. I went to Hahha, and at the town gates of Hahha I put up the battle lines three times.
566. I found well-being in the hand of Ištar, my mistress.
567. He took me up again and put the army (and) the chariot fighters of Hattiland in my hand.
568. The cow shouted at the sky again and looked at the sun god angrily.
569. When he went there, he asked them for the heart, and they gave it to him. Later he asked them for the eyes, and they gave them to him, too.
570. The people of Ulma faced me twice in battle, and I defeated them twice.
571. Then they lifted up the sacrificial altar and put it in front of the statues.
572. But also I did not see any box for Ibri-Šarruma.
573. They did not give the wine which the king has seen!
574. They announce the main meal of the day.
575. I gave three *madnanu*-carriages to the sun goddess of Arinna.
576. They put the tables and the gods there, the eighteen tables of the king, the queen, the royal princes, the dignitaries they put there.
577. Within few days I conquered the river Puruna.
578. I gave 1 bull (made) of silver, 1 fist (made) of silver to the temple of the weather god.
579. Whether they renew it in the ninth year or whenever - the point of time does not matter.
580. Because the man concerned (is) wicked and harms me, hence, I, the majesty, will harm him, too.
581. All Gaška-lands became hostile.
582. But the king heard it, started marching and arrived at Harahšu.
583. The breadloaves that I break at dawn: during the day I break other bread-loaves, but in the evening I break others again. Also, I pour out different groats every time.
584. Our house made progress.
585. He had become fat and was looking for trouble.
586. The property of the Labarna, the king, shall increase more and more!
587. If you purify yourselves, it is the decision of your protective deity, if you remain impure, then it is a mortal sin for you.

588. Let infantry (and) chariot fighters precede and let them come to my help!
589. If the wife dies there and they burn the property of the husband, then the husband takes her dowry.
590. I made you, the sisters, your brothers and the land of Amurru swear to it.
591. Behold, he calls you, the *šuraššura*-bird, shall come to call!
592. Why does he give taxes and *luzzi*-services to the scribes?
593. In (my) dream, someone like a prince came in and said to me again and again: „Come, I will give to you what has turned inside your house“.
594. Telipinu came hurriedly, he thundered again and again with thunder, the dark earth below was in turmoil the whole time.
595. If somebody steals a ploughing bull, he had to give 15 heads of cattle every time in the past, and now he gives 10 heads of cattle.
596. For the lord with his wife, his sons speak well again and again!
597. Regularly bring the water for the daily breadloaf of the deity from the *gauriya*-forest, from the *dunnariya*-forest!
598. I defeated the enemy states one after the other.
599. Every time he sits down on the places where the kings used to sit.
600. On the first day he grows one ell, in the first month he grows 1 IKU.
601. They put each of them up there at every single (place) behind the ritual stone and fill up the pithos.
602. He passes the fat of the four sheep and the breads that he has broken at each time to the deity.
603. The sun god looked down from the sky and saw Ullikummi.
604. The woman went and lay down with Appu fully dressed.
605. They slaughter the sheep, they cut it up, they build an oven and burn it completely.
606. If the moon comes and gets dark, then the divine mistress will deal with the land badly.
607. In all future, whoever becomes king after me - seal the grain with your name!
608. The weather god, your father, (and) the sun goddess of Arinna, your mother, will not distort your word, they will hear you!
609. But Ištar, my mistress, appointed me step by step at a time.
610. Sons, daughters, grandchildren, greatgrandchildren shall become numerous!
611. He did not in each case seal which device he gave to whom on each occasion.
612. Only we in Hatti are used to giving you pure, big, tasty sacrifices.
613. Three times the tablet of forgiving from the deities of Nerik.
614. He shouts the word of calling in.

615. If somebody steals a draught horse, its legal position (is) the same.
616. The *šuraššura*-bird shall come here to call her an omen.
617. I have given a boy, Tatili, the brother of Titai, to Apallu to raise (him).
618. He did not go to hunt in the mountains anymore, he only listened to his wife.
619. Standing, the king gives the lords to drink in their hands.
620. Because he verbally calls for the distribution, they shall throw (him) out of the house.
621. Lead those down from that gate, from which they bring down men to kill (them).
622. But I brought Huzziya, the king of Zalpuwa, alive to Neša.
623. Because they have sat my young charioteers on the horses, Išputašinara must always look after them.
624. In Ankuwa, the partridges (are) lean.
625. The cedar-wood (is) already chopped for you and food (has been) cooked for you.
626. If a freak is born without ears, then the days of the king (will be) over.
627. The big towns were prospering.
628. Because Nerik had been destroyed since the days of Hantīli, I rebuilt it.
629. But they struck the towns of Hatti that had been encircled.
630. But the *subri*-people - those (belonging to) my father and grandfather, that had come back, that had come back to me - set off along with their property and came over into your land.
631. If your mother or your father in the end have let any offence happen, or you here let any offense happen - either in the divine work or by a dream message - and now the birthing seat has been damaged, the posts have been broken, oh deity, so she now has commanded double penance!
632. Whatever they held oppressed of Nerik and Hakpišša - I subjugated everyone.
633. He must give back everything he has taken twice over.
634. I have harnessed 3 mules of the palace, but they died.
635. Concerning the words that Muršili, the king, told you, oh sun goddess of Arinna: lend a willing ear and hear it!
636. When Hantīli had become an old man and was about to become a god, then Zidanta killed Pišeni, the son of Hantīli, along with his sons.
637. A dog took away a piece of *kugulla*-biscuits from in front of an oven. He dragged it out of the oven, dipped it into fat, dipped it into oil, sat down and started eating it.
638. They have already finished building the bridge from stone.
639. But when they stop walking around after the blood(-offering), they (start) cutting up the sheep and bulls.

640. If he builds a second temple of the black goddess elsewhere, apart from this temple of the black goddess and puts the idol there, then he must at first be completely finished with the construction.
641. When they are ready with the dragging of the deity, and tents (are) put up in front of the river, then they bring the *ulihi* into the tents.
642. He was very much looking for trouble and he does not look at the town anymore, and they could report him to his master.
643. In his town he goes to the gate and cannot open it.
644. But this one tried to destroy me at divine behest and on human command.
645. If somebody tries to kill you, Targašnalli, or your son, but then runs away and comes to Hattuša, then he (is) the enemy of the majesty just like he is your enemy.
646. He shall not let them be destroyed and lessened!
647. They give the king barley beer to drink.
648. The woman has got a prisoner of war.
649. The gods were angry with Kešši because of the wine libation and would hide all wild animals from him.
650. They give something to eat to all who (have) come to pick up the bones.
651. Then the offerer of the sacrifice takes a bath.
652. If a woman is struck with an illness by the goddess Išhara and gets the *išhara*-illness, so that she dies, and (if) her husband was instructed (to provide) bread and beer, then I would arrange for the dead as follows.
653. The enemy who did not notice me had left to harvest the grain fields.
654. Nobody had crossed the Māla river before, I, the Great king, the Tabarna, crossed it on foot.
655. I (have) sworn and do not say anything.
656. You, Alakšandu, shall know it!
657. You shall not come to my house.
658. The weather god said to Ašertum: „I killed 77 of your sons, I killed 88".
659. Now lead me there!
660. They shall read for you this tablet that I, Alakšandu, have written for you three times year after year.
661. They protect you at my behest.
662. At dawn, come to your feast, come from the Hahruwa-mountains, from your beloved, here to the place that (is) your self and your mind!
663. Wherever we have come, there a woman gives birth to one child only, she has given birth to us all at once.

664. If we settle on the mountain Kandurna, someone else will settle on the mountain Lalapaduwa.
665. Then you, the *panku*, grab him and devour him with (your) teeth.
666. But if a man causes you to tolerate it and you take up business for yourself, then the gods will pursue you in the future.
667. As long as the weather god of Halpa flees us, the weather god of Hatti will come to us, and he will start to help.
668. When the people of Ninašša saw me opposite, they opened the gates again.
669. This matter shall be put under divine oath for you!
670. Ištar of Šamuha and the weather god of Nerik will decide the trial for us!
671. The oaths shall not forgive you this matter.
672. Now I, the majesty, the Great king, took you, Šaušgamuwa, by the hand.
673. I gave you my sister as a wife.
674. I place you in the deity's hand, so do not be afraid!'
675. In the place where you, sun goddess of Arinna, my mistress, have put us, there (is) the place of your beloved son, the weather god of Nerik.
676. I defeat you with my word and I prick you with my spindle.
677. I am not dear to my father.
678. Now you (are) the Great king, but I (am) king of the only fortress you left (me).
679. You gods know through (your) divine mind: never before anybody cared as much for your temples as we did.
680. If a dependant flees and goes into the land Luwiya, then he (the owner) gives 6 shekels silver to the person who brings him back.
681. But when she dies in the house of her father and there are sons of hers, then the husband does not take the dowry.
682. Did not a palace maid come, and did he not look at her?
683. He takes a fat bread and breaks it and puts it down before the gods.
684. To any of my fathers or forefathers they did not send presents that (i.e. like the ones) they send me."
685. They give everything that has been established by oracle to the deity.
686. But this was the benevolence of Ištar, my mistress.
687. Whereever he went with the troops on the battle field, they usually did not come back well.
688. They oppressed them hard, and they died.
689. They slaughter the cattle and the cooks take it.
690. They have taken possession of your, the god's, servants (and) maids and they have made them slaves.

691. Whether I kill them, whether I deport them, if somebody runs away from me and goes into the same land, then you shall attack him from that side and I will attack him from this side.
692. Then I started to revolt against him.
693. But on this side Talmaliya was his border.
694. I took the cattle and sheep away from them.
695. Because they did not succeed in anything, they - (he) with his wife and his son - started to put witchcraft on me.
696. If a sin is inherent in him, then he shall treat him as the king of Hattiland wishes.
697. Behold, listen to the complaint we raise before you!
698. The deity, my mistress, made him inferior to me.
699. I made a special tablet about the countries which I defeated when I was young.
700. Ištar (is) my deity, and they will sacrifice to her as to the magnificent Ištar.
701. Whoever (owns) six cows, (will give) two cows, (whoever) owns four cows, (will give) one cow, and he will drive them here.
702. He seized him right after that.
703. But do not take anything (away) from him, until I write something (about it).
704. Was this enemy provided with witchcraft to such an extent that you did not notice him?
705. Muwatalli took up Mašturi, who was king of the Šēha-riverland.
706. But write this affair to the majesty immediately.
707. But do not accept anyone else further!
708. But when Muwatalli, the father-brother of the majesty, became king, the people of Amurru violated their loyalty and let pass to him as follows.
709. If somebody commits a bloodshed, then whatever the master of the blood says (will happened to him).
710. Also the big towns prospered in his hand.
711. I did not take away servants (or) maids from anybody.
712. He died because of that offence.
713. The mountain where I graze - may fire burn it completely!
714. But when a girl is born, they count from this month on.
715. On one side it is oppressed by the plague, on the other side it is oppressed by enmity.
716. I endowed (them) with the property that I brought home from the campaigns.
717. But those say: „This should be (like that)!“
718. Legitimate brothers of the majesty, and sons of concubines of the majesty‘s

father, and whoever else (is) of royal descendance (shall be) bastards for you, from those I do not wish anyone to rule!

719. We will defeat the scouts that (are) near to Marešta as well.
720. They take hoe and spade, also these (are) from wood.
721. Weather god, my master, hear my words, the words that I tell you!
722. They always pride themselves on their force (and) power.
723. But Parmanna was the capital for these kings.
724. The children I fought with before the gate tease me.
725. The oaths shall destroy whoever does something like that, along with your wives, your sons, your houses, your land.
726. We do not exchange anything.
727. In whatever town you come back, call out all the inhabitants there!
728. Then I led the infantry and the chariot fighters of those countries that I had colonized again down to my brother to the campaign against Egypt.
729. They shall bring forward the old saws, which they cut apart heaven and earth with.
730. He did not go to Durmitta (and) Kuruštama, but left me in these countries.
731. They give to the deity whatever lies next to the utensil of the deity, and they do not exchange it.
732. This (is) no wine, it (is) your blood.
733. (Are) you not my, the king's, friend?
734. But after Pithāna, my father, I put down a revolt in the same year.
735. I, the king, called him my son.
736. You shall not condemn my servant for me.
737. Hašša, also in your family everything (is) in order.
738. He went up to him and started asking him: „What (is) your sin?"
739. There is no son for the throne of your father.
740. Come back into your temple!
741. If one of your sons (or) your grandsons should sin, then the king of Hatti shall interrogate him.
742. His mother (is) a snake!
743. He did not accept the word of the king, but he accepted the word of his mother, the snake!
744. But if he appears making trouble or (if there is) any malevolence or any causing of disturbance, he must not come up and must stay in his house!
745. Nobody shall buy his child, his field, his vineyard.
746. Majesty! You, our master, (are) a man of war.

747. Whatever is in your heart, throw it out!
748. She has sucked out the blood of the sons of Hatti.
749. Give vitality and many years to your servant Hattušili, and this shall come from your mouth.
750. They have divided up your cattle and your sheep.
751. The sun god and the weather god shall make a treaty with the king, their word shall be in agreement!
752. Come to Zalpa, invade their land!
753. The two offerers of sacrifice pour the water on their heads and wash their hands and their eyes.
754. I have given my words to you.
755. A mountain drove away a roebuck from his body.
756. My brother gave him to me along with his whole house, his wife, his sons.
757. We brought the statues to their places.
758. Be good to your children!
759. Then they gathered their clan.
760. I have given a house to my son, the Labarna.
761. Then the sons said to themselves: „Who are we looking for?“
762. If their decision is passed then, he shall pay (for it) with (his) head (= life).
763. It will happen like that: He will start a carnage in the end.
764. Include me as well! Do not have pity on me!
765. Appu got up and went into his house.
766. But life (is) also connected to death, and death (is) connected to life.
767. I killed all Gaškans.
768. They shall examine the seal in the middle of the gate.
769. Look at the land of Hatti with benevolent eyes!
770. Nothing shall perish.
771. Just the town of Hattuša remained as the only town.
772. When my father gave them his son and they sent him there, they killed him; so my father became very angry and he went into the land of Egypt and defeated Egypt and killed the infantry and the riders of Egypt.
773. They shall purify whoever is sprinkled with water.
774. Then they stepped on the side of the king of Egypt.
775. Do not hide this matter from the majesty, tell it to the majesty!
776. I gave the pens that were there to the troops in garrison.
777. In the very same revolt he died.
778. In the very same night I went up to Zippašna.

779. The name of the wife (was) Šintalimeni, she was beautiful and endowed with everything. And Kešši only listened to his wife.
780. But now the king has abolished the tribute to the palace, and only the injured himself takes three shekels silver.
781. Shall I protect a bastard of all people?
782. But he shall not do this to his master and he shall not do this to his brother and his sister and his friend.
783. But if there is no legitimate royal prince, then they shall take a son-in-law for a princess of the first rank and he shall become king.
784. Now he writes us some bad news.
785. Now protect me in every regard!
786. There is no count of the prisoners of war that he brought with (him).
787. But do not say so: „I will clear up (the matter)". And you do not clear up anything, but you oppress even more.
788. To Āškaliya he himself says: „You (are) false!"
789. The cupbearer passes (it) to the king and asks the king: „Shall they pick up the Ištar-instruments?", and the king says: „They shall pick them up".
790. But when I write only to you: „Hurry here on your own!", then only you should hurry here.
791. Further, speak before the deity the word: „Whoever has taken from your, the deity's bread, shall be destroyed by the god, my master! And he shall make his house liable for this!"
792. But now (we are) not your vassals anymore!
793. Hantīli was a cupbearer, and he had Harapšeki, the sister of Muršili, as a wife.
794. But they are settled in the town Haštira.
795. He defeated the land Amurru completely with (his) arms and subjected it.
796. One gives the son bread and fat, and the other gives the son to drink, but Appu does not give bread to anyone.
797. The wailing women go behind that and wail.
798. If a dependant escapes and somebody brings him back, he (sc. the owner) gives him a pair of shoes, if he seized (him) nearby.
799. The people that were sat down around washed themselves.
800. A dog barks, but if he comes there, he is quiet.
801. Now when I heard this matter, I seized him.
802. But if you do not carry out the release in Ebla, the town of the thrones, and the 7th day (has come), then I will come to you personally.

803. But when it (sc. the town) suffered from hunger afterwards, my god Šiu handed it over to the throne goddess Halmašuitt.
804. She put her sons in (it) and sent them to the river, and the river brought them to the sea in the land Zalpuwa.
805. But the army of Zalpa came towards (him), and the king defeated it.
806. But they caught Damnaššu alive, and he brought him back to Hattuša.
807. There they oppressed them hard, and they died.
808. Now as the years went by the queen gave birth again to 30 daughters which she raised herself.
809. Indeed they found offences.
810. But now I, the king, have seen a lot of evil, and you shall not violate my, the king's, words!
811. If a heir cuts out for himself unused land, or the men of the village give land to him, he shall render the *luzzi*-services.
812. Then I let the eagle back to the sky.
813. I bury the clay troops and the cups in the ground and fix it and say the following.
814. We report to the king and the queen whatever omen happens.
815. If a man takes his wife and brings her into his house, then he may bring her dowry with him into it.
816. I will destroy the land with this arrow, you will also shoot it into their hearts.
817. In the night I captured it (sc. the town) with force.
818. Act only according to the will of the gods!
819. I went to Hattuša towards ruin, and the inhabitants of Zalpa (went) with me.
820. When you go to the meadow, you shall not tighten the rope!
821. Now they put there a basin and paint it with bird blood.
822. But when the day is favourable, they sweep and somebody shouts „to the *halentu*!".
823. It will not happen because the oracle sign concerning the curse has still not come to an end.
824. When your brother came, I did not report him in the palace.
825. Although my brother had made me superior against Armadatta through the judgement, I did not become hostile towards him again.
826. He must drive them back to their owner as soon as the stars come up.
827. While the seating figure remains (the same) for four days, they take for the sacrifice at each day the following.
828. As a substitute he gives a man, and (this one) works in his house until he becomes healthy again.

829. But before the sun comes up in the early morning of the second day, they take the following from the house of the offerer of the sacrifice.
830. Before they sent him to the deity of Arušna, the matter caused a lot of worry to the queen.
831. But even before I, Tuthaliya, the Great king, ruled as a king myself, the deity joined me and Kurunta in friendship even then, and we were each other dear even then.
832. When they break the daily ration for the deity, they take a breadloaf.
833. When Tuthaliya, son of Arnuwanda, the Great king, sat down on his father's throne, they performed this *šarrašši*-sacrifice there.
834. Because my paternal gods did not take the good path and trod the path of 'Evil', his name shall be 'Evil'!
835. Like he (is) an enemy to you, in the same way he (is) also the enemy of the majesty.
836. But when this matter is settled for me, I will duely celebrate the feast.
837. But when the years came (and) went again, this situation began to play a role in my dreams.
838. Because Pihinakki stays in Lišipra again and again, he has already settled thirty families (there).
839. But when he becomes healthy again, he gives 6 shekel silver.
840. But when the servants of the royal princes became unfaithful, they started to eat up their houses.
841. Whether she hits opposite or not, this shall be excluded from it.
842. Even though you were ill, I, the majesty, put you into your father's position.
843. If somebody has hurt a man or made him ill, then he must take care of the person concerned.
844. If (there is) weakness in your hearts or the illness of the sun god in your hearts, sweep it away!
845. If a woman gives birth and (the child) is blind, the owner of the house will not reach the border.
846. Additionally the *patili*-priest, who (is) on the roof above, calls down into the house.
847. We don't examine what Ammatalla said.
848. Hukkanā, seize every person who does not hand over or who keeps quiet about war prisoners from the land of Hatti!
849. Formerly the house of a man who became a weaver in Arinna was exempt, also his partners and relatives were exempt.

850. Whoever closes a deal with a 'locked up' must withdraw from the deal.
851. Do not change the tablet with the contract document that I have written for you!
852. Whoever was a king to show me respect, he actually showed me respect.
853. A roebuck grazes on pastures that are (situated) on the other side of the river.
854. I gave the 'Bone house', which I had put up, to the deity.
855. But I had plated the weapon that I carried there.
856. The man who (is) enchanted sits down opposite the sun god.
857. Those who had been enemies in the time of my fathers and forefathers made peace with me.
858. In the place which my brother Muwatalli had built in the town Tarhuntašša, there I appointed him to the royal rule.
859. But while the woman is still in labour, they drive the prepared female sheep, whether pregnant or not, into the inner chamber.
860. He did not take it (the town) away from me, because I was priest for the weather god of Nerik.
861. (Concerning) Muwatalli, who had taken him up and made him his brother-in-law: he didn't even protect his son Urhitešub.
862. But when your servants chased you away, I, the majesty, gave your land back to you.
863. When cattle go onto a field (and) the owner of the field finds (them), he can harness (them) for one day.
864. I had nothing removed from what the queen gave to me at each occasion.
865. But why, my dear brother, have you not sent greetings even though my messenger came from there?
866. But if its owner finds it, he can lawfully take it (and) he must not seize him as a thief.
867. At first, the sons did not recognise their sisters.
868. But the king did not apologize to her.
869. If the son of man lived eternally, it would not be awful if a man had a bad illness.
870. Why are her clothes and her scarf not bloody?
871. The land of Amurru had not been subjugated by Hatti's arms.
872. But there was not a single man from the infantry with me.
873. When my brother Arnuwanda died, those countries that had not been enemies before became enemies, too.
874. But who holds all the lands? Is it not me that keeps a firm hold on the rivers, mountains and seas again and again?

875. The houses of the great – where are they? Did they not disappear?
876. If the majesty asks Ulmitešub for a town or some area and he kindly gives it to him, (and there is) no violence, then this shall be exempted from the divine oath.
877. He makes them trot for two miles, and when they drive them back, they unharness them, look after them, but do not rub them down.
878. But the king (was) not with her.
879. Because I made him great, I have never handed him over to an evil court, to an evil deity.
880. If this one (is) also still under-age and the population rejects him and speaks the following: „A royal prince it shall be!", then I, the majesty, will not agree.
881. I will surely not give the land of Hapalla to anyone else, no one but you shall be the ruler.
882. Otherwise you must take over his guilt.
883. The Hurrite still does not come, four years pass by.
884. In his place he appointed Šarmaššu in writing, but this one does not go there yet.
885. Three billy goats, two rams for the training on the potter's wheel (are) not back yet from the temple service.
886. There must not be any quarrel anymore!
887. They drank up each barrel and drank their fill. Then they could not go down into the caves anymore.
888. No other man shall go up to the salt of Šarmana!
889. There is no compensation at all for that.
890. But do not harm him!
891. This kind of malevolence must not be inherent (in you) now or ever!
892. Do not sell death, but also do not buy death!
893. But who will give us food in each case?
894. When it started dawning, the father of the king shouted: „Who lead these two out?"
895. What he refused – what is that?
896. Why have you come angrily into my house?
897. Elkuniršа saw the weather god and asked him: „Why have you come?"
898. The deity has given (it) to you, why do you send it back?
899. How should I have done it, then?
900. You, the deity, my mistress, took me out of everything, didn't you?
901. Don't you know him, then, the terrible god, which Kumarbi raised against the gods?

902. What (is it), you gods, what you have done? A plague you allowed, the whole of Hatti has died.
903. The Hittites violated their word straightaway – did this cause the wrath of the weather god of Hatti, of my lord?
904. Additionally, I will consult the oracle about Nerik, whether I shall defeat the enemies first or whether I shall organize the *purulli*-feast first and take away the deity.
905. Did I, the king, do anything evil? Did I not make him a priest?
906. The mentioned prince says again and again: „What sits (there) in the granary?“
907. When Hepat saw Tašmišu, she, Hepat, almost fell off the roof. She was about to fall off but her maid servants grabbed her and did not let her fall.
908. I probably could have appointed somebody else as ruler of the land.
909. Should, by any chance, the land have perished somewhere, (have) towns become deserted somewhere, (have) soldiers been beaten somewhere?
910. Āškaliya probably wanted to kill him and sent him into prison, but then rumours started to spread against Āškaliya.
911. But Mašhuiluwa started quarrel with me and filled the land of Pitašša and the people of Hatti, my servants, with hatred for me, (and) probably would have revolted against me.
912. Nerik was for him no town to conquer, and he probably would not have defeated the town Nerik.
913. You could write to me everything everytime, about what (and) how it (is) there.
914. Because your father Mašhuiluwa sinned against the majesty, and you, Kupanta-KAL, were Mašhuiluwa's son, I, the majesty - although you were anything but guilty - could have expelled you, if it had ever been interpreted as evil by the majesty.
915. If you, majesty, my lord, were to send out any commander, then the enemy could not do any harm in the land.
916. If you were to go down, the Gašga-people would say the following: „If the marshal came here, we would sign a treaty!“
917. I would not do such a thing! What is this? At that time I have sworn; should I later take anything for myself?
918. I did not take anything from anybody. I took no cow from anybody, I took no sheep from anybody.
919. What is this? Is it not yeast?

920. If he had committed another attack, he would probably have escaped to the land Karduniya.
921. I, the majesty, the Great king, was very pleased about it – should I, the majesty, the Great king, not have been pleased about it?
922. Bring him here to the army, otherwise you must come (and) die.
923. (It is) no dog, but a man whom his lord makes master of administration.
924. Did the diorite(-man) defeat him, my husband, the weather god, the mighty king?

4. Glossaries

4.1. Hittite words

a, e, h, i,y, k/g, l, m, n, p/b, s, t/d, u, w, z

Homophones are distinguished by index numbers, references are only given when the second form is not given in the same or following lemma.

-a „and, but"

ak-/ek- „to die"; *ak-mi* 1.sg.pres.act.; *a-ki* 3.sg.pres.act.; *ak-ku-e-ni* 1.pl.pres. act.; *ak-kán-zi* 3.pl.pres.act.; *a-kir*, *e-kir*, *e-ki-ir* 3.pl.pret.act.; *a-ku (=war=aš)* 3.sg.imp. act.; *ak-kán-du* 3.pl.imp.act.; *ak-kán-ti* part. dat.sg.c.

akueni*, *akuwanzi*, *akuwanna see ***eku-/aku-*** „to drink"

akkušk°- see ***eku-/aku-*** 'to drink'

allapahh- „to spit, spit upon; *para a.* to spit out"; *al-la-pa-ah-hu-un* 1.sg.pret.act.; *al-la-pa-ah-tin* 2.pl.pret.act.

aliyana- c. „roebuck, deer"; *a-li-ya-na-aš* nom.sg.; *a-li-ya-na-an(=za)* acc.sg.

alpa- c. „cloud"; *al-pu-ú-uš* acc.pl.

alpant- „bewitched, entchanted"; *al-pa-an-za* nom.sg.c.

alwanzahh- „to bewitch, enchant"; *al-wa-an-za-ah-hu-u-wa-an-zi* inf. I

alwanzahhant- „supplied with magic powers"; *al-wa-an-za-ah-ha-an-za* nom.sg.c.

alwanzata(r) n. „witchcraft, sorcery, magic"; *al-wa-an-za-ta*, *al-wa-an-za-tar*, *al-wa-za-tar* nom.-acc.sg.

alwanzeššar n. „witchcraft, sorcery, magic"; *al-wa-an-zi-eš-na-za* abl.

ammiyant- „little, small, young"; *a-am-mi-ya-an-tu-uš(=muš)* acc.pl.c.

ammuk „I, me"; a*m-mu-uk(=ma/=ma=az/=ma=wa/=ma=war=aš=kán/ =ma =wa=kán/=wa=za)*, *am-mu-uq-q(=a/=a=za)*, *am-mu-ug-g(=a/ =a=za=apa)*, *am-mu-g(=a=man)* nom.; *am-me-el* gen.;

am-me-e-da-za, *am-mi-ta-az*, *am-mi-e-da-za(=ma=wa =ta)* abl.

1. ***-an*** „him, her“ (acc.sg.c. of *-aš* ‘he“)

2. ***-an*** enclitic particle

anna- c. „mother“; *an-na-aš(=šiš)* nom.sg.; *an-na-aš(=šaš)* gen.sg.

annalla- „ maternal; old“; *an-na-al-la-an* acc.sg.n.; *an-na-al-la* acc.pl.n.

annalli- „old“; *an-na-al-li-in* acc.sg.c.

annanu- „to educate, teach“; *an-na-nu-ma-aš* verbal noun gen.sg.

aniya- „to make, produce; to sow“; *a-ni-e-nu-un* 1.sg.pret.act.; *a-ni-ya-u-e-en* 1.pl.pret.act.; *a-ni-ya-u-wa-an-zi* inf. I; *a-ni-ya-an* part. nom.sg.n.; *an-ni-eš-ki-iz-zi* iter. 3.sg.pres.act.

aniyatt- c. „regalia, official robes“; *a-ni-ya-at-ta* acc.pl.n.

aniur n. „work, task“; *a-ni-u-ur(=šet)* nom.sg.

annišan „earlier, at that time“: *an-ni-ša-an(=pát/=war=an)*

anš- „to wipe, spread“; *a-an-ša-an-zi* 3.pl.pres.act.

anda „into“; *an-da(=ma=kán/=ma=šmaš/=ma=za)*

andan „inside“; *an-da-an*

antara- „blue“; *an-da-ra-aš* nom.sg.c.

LÚ***antiyant-*** c. „son in law“; LÚ*an-ti-ya-an-ta-an* acc.sg.

antu- n. „property“; *an-tu-u(=šmet)* nom.sg.

antuhša- c. „man, human being“; a*n-tu-uh-ša-an* acc.sg.; *an-tu-uh-ši* dat.-loc.sg.; *an-tu-uh-ša-aš*, *an-du-uh-ša-aš*, *an-tu-uh-ša-š(=a=kán)* gen.pl.; *an-tu-uh-šu-uš* acc.pl.

antūriya- „located, situated inside, domestic, inland“; *an-tu-u-ri-e-eš* nom.pl.c.

antuwahha- c. „man, human being“; *an-tu-wa-ah-ha-aš* nom.sg.

anzaš „us“ (dat. and acc. of *weš* „we“); *an-za-aš*, *an-za-a-aš*, *an-za-a-š(=a)*

anzel „our“ (gen. of *weš* ‘we“); *an-zi-el*

anzidaz „from us“ (abl. of *weš* ‘we“); *an-zi-ta-az*

-apa enclitic particle

apā- „that one“; see also *apez*, *apizza*, *apada; a-pa-aš*, *a-pa-aš-š(=a)*, *a-pa-a-aš(=ma=kán/=ma=mu/=pát*, *a-pa-a-š(=a/ =an=kán/=az)*, *a-pa-a-aš-š(=a)* nom.sg.c.; *a-pu-u-un(=wa)* acc.sg.c.; *a-pa-a-at*, *a-pa-a-at (=ta/=ši)* nom.-acc.n.; *a-pí-el(=kán/ =ma=kán)*, *a-pí-e-el*, *a-pí-e-el-l(=a)* gen.sg.; *a-pí-e-da-ni*, *a-pí-da-ni(=wa=šmaš=kán)* dat.sg.; *a-pí-e-iz*[1], *a-pí-e-iz-z(=a)*, *a-pí-iz* abl. (also adv., see there); *a-pí-e-da-an-da* instr.; *a-pí-e(=ya/=ma/ =pát/=wa=mu)* nom.pl.c.; *a-pád-da*[1]*(=ya)* nom.pl.n. (also adv., see there); *a-pu-uš(=ma=kán)*, *a-pu-u-uš*, *a-pu-u-uš-š(=a)*, *a-pu-u-š(=a=kán)* acc.pl.c.; *a-pí-en-za-an* gen.pl.; *a-pí-da-aš*, *a-pí-e-da-aš(=za)* dat.-loc.pl.

āppa „back, again"; *a-ap-pa(=ma/=wa=mu)*

āppan „behind, after"; *a-ap-pa-an*

appantat, ***appandu***, ***appanza***, ***appanzi*** see ***ep-*** „to pack"

apata „therefore, because of that"; *a-pád-da*[2]

apašila- „personally"; *a-pa-ši-la*

apeniššan „so"; *a-pí-ni-eš-ša-an*, *a-pí-e-ni-iš-ša-an*

apēz „except"; *a-pí-e-iz*[2]

apiya- „there"; *a-pí-ya(=ya/=ma=aš/=ma=at/=pát)*, *a-pí-i-a*, *a-pí-e-ya*

appišziaz „in the end, at last"; *ap-pí-iš-zi-az*

appizza „therefore, because of that"; *a-pí-iz-za*

appizzi- „last, humblest"; *ap-pí-iz-zi-ya-n(=a)*, *ap-pí-iz-zi-ya-an(=a=šmaš/ =ma/ma=at)* acc.sg.n.

1. ***ar-*** „to get somewhere, reach something"; *a-ar-hi* 1.sg.pres.act.; *a-ar-ti* 2.sg.pres.act.; *a-ri* 3.sg.pres.act.; *e-ru-u-e-ni* 1.pl. pres.act.; *a-ra-an-zi* 3.pl.pres.act.; *a-ru-me-en* 1.sg.pret.act.; *a-ar-aš*, *a-ra-aš* 3.sg. pret.act.; *a-ru* 3.sg.imp.act.; *a-ra-an-za* part. nom.sg.c.; *a-ra-an-te-eš* part. nom.pl.c.

2. ***ar-*** „to stand, stand up; to care for somebody"; *ar-ta*, *ar-ta-ri*, *ar-ta-ri-i* 3.sg.pres.med.; *ar-wa-aš-ta* 1.pl.pres.med.; *a-ra-an-ta*, *a-ra-an-da*, *a-ra-an-ta-ri* 3.pl.pres.med.; *ar-ha-ti* 1.sg.pret.med.; *ar-wa-aš-ta-at* 1.pl. pret.med.; *ar-ha-ha-ru* 1.sg.imp.med.; *ar-hu-ut* 2.sg.imp.med.; *ar-ta-ru* 3.sg.imp.med.; *ar-du-ma-at* 2.pl.imp.med.; *a-ra-an-ta-ru* 3.pl.imp.med.

$^{\text{(LÚ)}}$***ara-*** c. „friend, follower"; *a-ra-aš(=miš)* nom.sg.; ^{LÚ}*a-ri(=ši=ya)* dat.sg.; *a-ri-eš(=šmeš)* nom.pl.

ārra- „to wash"; *a-ar-ri* 3.sg.pres.act.; *ar-ra-an-zi* 3.pl.pres.act.

arahza „outside"; *a-ra-ah-za*

arahzena- „living in the surroundings, foreign"; *a-ra-ah-zé-ni-eš* nom.pl.c.

^{LÚ}***arahzena-*** c. „foreigner"; ^{LÚ}*a-ra-a-ah-ze-e-ni(=ma)* dat.sg.

arāi- „to rise, revolt; to halt"; *a-ra-a-iš*, *a-ra-i-š(=apa)* 3.sg.pret.act.; *a-ra-id-du* 3.sg.imp.act.; *a-ra-an-du* 3.pl.imp.act.

arāwa- „free"; *a-ra-a-u-wa-an* nom.sg.n.; *a-ra-u-e-eš* nom.pl.c.

arha „away"; *ar-ha(=ma/=ši=kán/=wa/=wa=šmaš=kán)*

arhayan „separate, isolated"; *ar-ha-ya-an(=ma)*

ariya- „to consult the oracle"; *a-ri-ya-mi* 1.sg.pres.act.; *a-ri-ya-u-e-ni* 1.pl.pres.act.; *a-ri-ya-ir* 3.pl.pret.act.

ārk- „to cut up, split up"; *a-ar-ki* 3.sg.pres.act.; *ar-kán-zi* 3.pl.pres.act.

arkuwāi- „to apologise"; *ar-ku-ut-ta* 3.sg.pret.act.

arkuwar n. „prayer"; *ar-ku-wa-ar-ri*$^{\text{HI.A}}$ nom.-acc.pl.

armahh- „to impregnate"; *ar-ma-ah-hu-un* 1.sg.pret.act

arma(u)want- „pregnant"; *ar-ma-u-wa-an-za* nom.sg.c.; *ar-ma-u-wa-an-te-š(=a)* nom.pl.c.

^{GIŠ}***armizzi-*** n. „bridge"; ^{GIŠ}*ar-mi-iz-zi(=wa)* acc.sg.

armizziya- „to bridge"; *ar-mi-iz-zi-ya-an-da-ru* 3.pl.imp.act.

arnu- „to transport, carry somewhere; to do penance; to make (complaints)"; *ar-nu-mi* 1.sg.pres.act.; *ar-nu-zi* 3.sg.pres.act.; *ar-nu-um-me-ni* 1.pl. pres.act.; *ar-nu-ut*[1] 3.sg.pret.act.; *ar-nu-ut*[2] 2.sg.imp.act.; *ar-nu-ud-du* 3.sg.imp.act.; *ar-nu-ut-tin* 2.pl. imp.act.; *ar-nu-uš-ki-u-wa-ni* iter. 1.pl. pres.act.

^{LÚ}***aršanatalla-*** c. „envious person, rival"; $^{\text{LÚ.MEŠ}}$*ar-ša-na-tal-lu-uš* acc.pl.

aršaniya- „to envy, be jealous"; *ar-ša-ni-i-e-ir* 3.pl.pret.act.

^{URUDU}***ardāla-*** „saw"; ^{URUDU}*ar-da-a-la* nom.-acc.n.

aruna- c. „sea"; *a-ru-na-an* acc.sg.; *a-ru-ni* loc.sg.; *a-ru-na-az* abl.; *a-ru-na-aš-š(=aš)* gen.pl.; *a-ru-nu-uš-š(=a)* acc.pl.

aruwāi- „to prostrate oneself, bow, worship"; *a-ru-wa-a-iz-zi* 3.sg.pres.act.; *ar-ú-i-iš-ki-iz-zi* iter. 3.sg.pres.act.

-aš „he, she"

āš- „to stay, remain"; *a-aš-zi* 3.sg.pres.act.; *a-aš-ta* 3.sg.pret.act.; *a-aš-ša-an* part. nom.sg.n.; *a-aš-ša-an-te-eš* part. nom.pl.c.

ašandu, ***ašanzi*** see ***eš-*** ‘to be’

ašandula- c. „garrison"; *a-ša-an-du-li* dat.-loc.sg.

ašš(a)nu- „to set, bring in order, supply"; *aš-nu-zi* 3.sg.pres.act.; *aš-nu-an-zi*, *aš-ša-nu-wa-an-zi* 3.pl.pres.act.; *aš-ša-nu-nu-un*

1.sg.pret.act.; *a-aš-ša-nu-ul-lu* 1.sg.imp. act.; *aš-ša-nu-ut* 3.sg.pret.act.; *aš-ša-nu-wa-an-za* part. nom.sg.c.

ašauwar n. „fold, pen, reserve“; *a-ša-u-wa-ar* nom.pl.

ašeš- „to set, settle, populate; to let someone sit“; *a-ša-ši*, *a-ša-a-ši* 3.sg. pres.act.; *a-ša-aš-ta* 3.sg.pret.act.; *e-še-šir* 3.pl.pret.act.; *a-še-ša-an* part. nom.sg.n.; *a-še-eš-kat-ta-ri* iter. 3.sg.pres.med.

ašešanu- „to let someone settle, colonize“; *a-še-ša-nu-un*, *a-še-ša-nu-nu-un* 1.sg.pret.act.

aši- „this, the relevant“ (indeclinable); *a-ši(=wa)*

āššiya- „to love“; *a-aš-ši-ya-an-ta-aš* part.gen.sg.; *a-aš-ši-ya-an-ti* part.loc. sg.c.; *a-aš-ši-ya-an-ta-za* part.abl.

āššiyātar n. „love“; *a-aš-ši-ya-tar* nom.-acc.

āška- c. „gate“; *a-aš-ka* dir.; *a-aš-ki(=ši/=za)* loc.sg.

āšma „first, at first“; *a-aš-ma-a(=ta)*

-ašta enclitic particle

aštayarātar n. „sin“; *a-aš-ta-ya-ra-tar* nom.-acc.

āššu- „good, dear; noun: property; the good“; *a-aš-šu-uš* nom.sg.c.; *a-aš-šu (=ma/=ma=ši/=šet)*, *a-aš-šu-u* nom.-acc.sg.n.; *aš-ša-u-it*, *a-aš-ša-u-i-it*, *a-aš-ša-a-u-it* instr.; *a-aš-ša-u-e-eš* nom.pl.c.; *a-aš-ša-u-wa-aš(=pát)* dat.-loc.pl.

aššul n. „wellbeing, good; greeting“; *aš-šu-ul* nom.-acc.sg.; *aš-šu-la-aš* gen.sg.; *aš-šu-li* loc.sg., also adverb

āššula- c. „favour, goodwill“; *a-aš-šu-la-an* acc.sg.c.

āššuwātar n. „goodness, kindness, friendship“; *a-aš-šu-wa-an-ni* dat.-loc.sg.

-at „it“

atta- c. „father“; *ad-da-aš*[1] nom.sg.; *ad-da-aš-ša-an = attan=šan* acc.sg. + *-šan*; *at-ta-aš(=maš/ =šaš=a/=taš=wa* gen.sg.; *at-ti(=mi)* dat.sg.; *at-ta-aš(=miš)* voc.sg.; *at-ta-aš(=meš)* nom.pl.; *ad-da-aš*[2] gen.pl.; *ad-da-aš*[3] dat.pl.

attalla- „paternal“; *at-ta-al-la* nom.-acc.pl.n.

adanna, ***adanzi***, ***adanteš***, ***atueni*** see ***ed-/ad-*** „to eat“

^{TÚG}***adupli-*** n. a kind of garment, dress; ^{TÚG}*a-tu-up-li* uninflected

au(wa)ri- c. „tower, watch tower, lookout, observation point“; *a-ú-ri-ya-aš*, *a-ú-wa-ri-ya-aš* gen.sg.

auš- „to see“; *u-uh-hi* 1.sg.pres.act.; *a-ut-ti* 2.sg.pres.act.; *a-uš-zi* 3.sg.pres. act.; *a-ú-um-me-ni* 1.pl. pres.act.; *a-ut-te-ni* 2.pl.pres.act.; *ú-wa-an-zi*[1] 3.pl.pres.act. (cf. also *uwa-* „to come“); *u-wa-it-ta-ri* 3.sg.pres.med.; *u-uh-hu-un* 1.sg.pret.act.; *a-uš-ta* 3.sg. pret.act.; *a-ú-ir*, *a-ú-e-ir* 3.pl.pret. act.; *a-ú* 2.sg.imp.act.; *a-uš-te-en* 2.pl.imp.act.; *ú-wa-an-du* 3.pl.imp. act.; *uš-ki-iz-zi* iter. 3.sg.pres.act.; *uš-ka-at-te-ni* iter. 2.pl. pres.act.; *uš-kán-du* iter. 3.pl.imp.act.; *uš-ga-ah-hu-ut* iter. 2.sg.imp.med.

awan only in ***awan arha*** „completely gone“; *a-wa-an*

-***az*** see -***za/-az*** enclitic particle

azzik- „to feast; (iter. to *ed-*)“; *az-zi-ik-ki-ta-ni* 2.pl.pres.act.; *az-zi-ik-ki-id-du* 3.sg.imp.act.; *az-zi-ik-kán-du* 3.pl. imp.act.

-***e*** „they“ (nom.pl.c.)

ehu „come!, up!“; *e-hu(=wa/=wa=ta)*

^{GIŠ}***eya(n)-*** n. a type of tree, symbol of tax exemptiont; ^{GIŠ}*e-ya*, ^{GIŠ}*e-ya-an* nom.-acc.sg.

eku-/aku- „to drink“; *e-ku-mi* 1.sg.pres.act.; *e-ku-uš-ši* 2.sg.pres.act.; *e-ku-zi* 3.sg.pres.act.; *a-ku-e-ni* 1.pl. pres.act.; *e-ku-ut-te-ni* 2.pl.pres.act.; *a-ku-wa-an-zi* 3.pl.pres.act.; *e-ku -ut-ta* 3.sg. pret.act.; *e-ku-ir* 3.pl.pret.act.; *e-ku-ut-te-en*, *e-ku-ut-tin* 2.pl.imp.act.; *a-ku-wa-an-na* inf. II; *ak-ku-uš-ki-it-ta-ni* iter. 2.pl.pres.act.; *ak-ku-uš-ki-id-du* iter. 3.sg.imp.act.; *ak-ku-uš-kán-du* iter. 3.pl.imp.act.

ekuna- „cold, heartless“; *e-ku-na* nom.-acc.pl.n.

ekunima- c. „cold“; *e-ku-ni-ma-aš* nom.sg.; *e-ku-ni-mi* loc.sg.

eni- „this“ (uninflected); *e-ni(=ya/=wa=kán)*

ep- „to grab, seize; arrest, apprehend“; *e-ip-ti* 2.sg.pres.act.; *e-ip-zi* 3.sg. pres.act.; *ap-pa-an-zi* 3.pl.pres.act.; *e-ip-pu-un*, *e-ip-pu-u-un* 1.sg.pret. act.; *e-ip-ta(=an)* 3.sg.pret.act.; *e-ip-pir* 3.pl.pret.act.; *ap-pa-an-ta-at* 3.pl.pret.med.; *e-ip* 2.sg.imp.act.; *e-ip-du* 3.sg.imp.act.; *e-ip-tin* 2.pl. imp.act.; *ap-pa-an-du*, *ap-pa-a-an-du* 3.pl.imp.act.; *ap-pa-an-za* part. nom.sg.c.; *ap-pa-an-na* inf. II

erueni see ***ar***- „to arrive“

1. ***eš***- act. „to be, exist“; *e-eš-zi* 3.sg.pres.act.; *e-eš-te-ni* 2.pl.pres.act.; *a-ša-an-zi* 3.pl.pres.act.; *e-šu-un* 1.sg. pret.act.; *e-šu-u-en* 1.pl.pret.act.;

e-eš-ta 3.sg.pret.act.; *e-šir*, *e-še-ir* 3.pl.pret.act.; *e-eš* 2.sg.imp.act.; *e-eš-du*, *e-eš-tu* 3.sg.imp.act.; *e-eš-tin*, *e-eš-te-en* 2.pl.imp.act.; *a-ša-an-du* 3.pl. imp.act.

2. *eš*- med. „to sit, sit down; to stay"; *e-eš-ha-ha-ri* 1.sg.pres.med.; *e-ša*, *e-ša-a-ri*, *e-ša-ri(=ma=at=za)* 3.sg.pres.med.; *e-šu-wa-aš-ta*, *e-šu-wa-aš-ta-ti* 1.pl.pres.med.; *e-ša-an-da*, *e-ša-an-da-ri* 3.pl.pres.med.; *e-eš-ha-at*, *e-eš-ha-ti* 1.sg.pret.med.; *e-ša-at*, *e-ša-ti* 3.sg.pret.med.; *e-eš-tum-ma-at* 2.pl. pret.med.; *e-eš-ki-it-ta-ri* iter. 3.sg.pres.med.

ēšhar n. „blood, bloody deed, bloodshed"; *e-eš-har*, *e-eš-har(=šet/=šmet)* nom.-acc.sg.; *iš-ha-na-a-aš*, *iš-ha-na-aš*, *e-eš-ha-na-aš (=pát)* gen.sg.; *e-eš-ha-ni-i* dat.-loc.sg.; *e-eš-har*$^{\text{HI.A}}$ nom.-acc.pl.

***ešharnumāi*-** „to make bloody, to paint with blood"; *iš-har-nu-ma-an-zi* 3.pl. pres.act.

***ešharwant*-** „bloody"; *iš-har-wa-an-tu-uš* acc.pl.c.

***ešhaškant*-** „bloody"; *eš-ha-aš-kán-ta* nom.pl.n.

***ešša*-** „to do, achieve, act"; *iš-ša-at-ti* 2.sg.pres.act.; *iš-ša-i* 3.sg.pres.act.; *e-eš-ša-an-zi* 3.pl.pres.act.; *e-iš-ši* 2.sg.imp.act.; *e-eš-ša-ú* 3.sg.imp.act.; *i-iš-šu-wa-an* supinum

ešešir see ***ašeš*-** 'to let sit'

***ed-/ad*-** „to eat"; *e-it-mi* 1.sg.pres.act.; *e-iz-za-aš-ši* 2.sg.pres.act.; *e-iz-za-zi* 3.sg.pres.act.; *a-tu-e-ni* 1.pl.pres.act.; *e-iz-za-at-te-ni*, *az-za-aš-te-ni* 2.pl.pres.act.; *a-da-an-zi* 3.pl.pres.act.; *e-te-ir* 3.pl.pret.act.; *e-it(=za)* 2.sg.imp.act.; *iz-za-at-te-en*, *iz-za-at-tin* 2.pl.imp.act.; *a-da-an-te-eš* part.nom.pl.c.; *a-da-an-na*, *a-da-a-an-na* inf. II; *a-da-an-na-aš* inf. II gen.sg.

***hahhal*-** n. „bushes"; *ha-ah-hal-la-aš* dat.-loc.pl.

***hahharš*-** „to laugh"; *ha-ah-har-aš-ta* 3.sg.pret.med.

$^{(\text{É})}$***halentu*-** n. a building in the temple district; ^{É}*ha-li-in-tu-wa-az* abl.; *ha-la-an-tu-wa* dir.

***halhaldumari*-** n./c. „corner stone; corner"; *hal-hal-du-um-ma-ri* loc.sg.; *hal-hal-tu-ma-ra-za* abl.; *hal-hal-du-um-ma-ri-ya-aš-š (=a)* dat.-loc.pl.

***hāli*-** n. „district"; *ha-a-li* nom.-acc.sg.

***haliya*-** „to bow, prostrate oneself"; *ha-li-ya-at-ta-at* 3.sg.pret.med.

^{LÚ}***haliyatalla***- c. „temple guard"; $^{\text{LÚ.MEŠ}}$*ha-li-ya-at-tal-li-iš* nom.pl.

hališšiyanu- „to mount, set, frame, plate; to equip"; *ha-liš-ši-ya-nu-un*, *ha-li-iš-ši-ya-nu-un* 1.sg.pret.act.

halki- c. „grain, wheat; grain field"; *hal-ki-in* acc.sg.; *hal-ki-aš* gen.sg.; *hal-ki-e-eš* nom.pl.; *hal-ki-uš* acc.pl.

hallu- „deep"; *hal-lu-u-wa-za* abl.; *hal-lu-wa-mu-uš* acc.pl.c.; *hal-lu-u-wa-aš* dat.-loc.pl.

halupant- „bend"; *ha-lu-pa-an-te-eš* nom.pl.c.

halluwāi- c. „quarrel, row"; *hal-lu-u-wa-a-in* acc.sg.; *hal-lu-wa-ya-za* abl.

halzāi- „to call, name"; *hal-za-a-i* 3.sg.pres.act.; *hal-zi-wa-ni* 1.pl.pres.act.; *hal-zi-an-zi*, *hal-zi-ya-an-zi* 3.pl. pres.act.; *hal-zi-ih-hu-un* 1.sg.pret.act.; *hal-za-a-iš*[1] 2.sg. pret.act.; *hal-za-iš*, *hal-za-a-iš*[2] 3.sg.pret.act.; *hal-zi-ú-en* 1.pl.pret.act.; *hal-zi-ya*, *hal-zi-ya-ri* 3.sg.pres.med.; *hal-zi-ya-an-te-eš* part. nom.pl.c.; *hal-zi-ya-u-wa-an-zi* inf. I

halzeš- „to call"; *hal-zi-eš-ša-i* 3.sg.pres.act.; *hal-zi-eš-ša-an-du* 3.pl.imp.act

halziyauwar n. „the calling"; *hal-zi-ya-aš* gen.sg.

hamink-/hamank- „to (magically) bind"; *ha-ma-an-ki* 3.sg.pres.act.; *ha-mi-ik-ta* 3.sg.pret.act.; *ha-mi-in-kán* part. nom.-acc.sg.n.

hanna- „to judge, decide"; *ha-an-na-at-te-ni* 2.pl.pres.act.; *ha-an-na-an-zi* 3.pl.pres.act.

hanneššar n. „judgement, decision, trial, case"; *ha-an-ne-eš-šar*, *ha-an-ni-eš-šar* nom.-acc.sg.; *ha-an-ne-eš-ni-it* instr.

handāi- „to arrange, prepare"; *ha-an-ta-iz-zi* 3.sg.pres.act.; *ha-an-da-a-an-ta-ri* 3.sg.pres.med.; *ha-an-da-it-ta-at*, *ha-an-da-a-it-ta-at* 3.sg.pret. med.; *ha-an-da-a-an-za* part. nom.sg.c.; *ha-an-da-a-an (=pát)* part. nom.sg.n.

handaiš- n. „heat"; *ha-an-da-iš* nom.sg.; *ha-an-da-ši* loc.sg.

parā handandātar n. „care, benevolence"; *pa-ra-a ha-an-da-an-da-tar* nom.-acc.sg.

handaš „according, in accordance with; sincere, honest"; *ha-an-da-aš* nom.sg.c.; *ha-an-da-an* acc.sg.n. adv.; *ha-an-ta* nom.pl.n.

parā handātar n. „wisdom; care"; *pa-ra-a ha-an-da-an-ni* dat.-loc.sg.

hanteššar n. „cave, pit"; *ha-an-te-eš-na-az* abl.

hantezzi- „first, front(most)"; *ha-an-te-iz-zi-iš*, *ha-an-te-iz-zi-ya-aš(=pát/ =šmiš)* nom.sg.c.; *ha-an-te-iz-zi* nom.sg.n. adv.; *ha-an-te-iz-zi(=kán)* dat.-loc.sg.; *ha-an-te-iz-zi-uš-š(=a)* acc.pl.c.

hantezziaz „before"; *ha-an-te-iz-zi-az(=ma)*

hantī „separate, extra"; *ha-an-ti*, *ha-an-ti-i*

hanzaššeš see ***hašša hanzašša*** „descendants"

hap- „to succeed"; *ha-ap-ta-at* 3.sg.pret.med.

happar n. „trade"; *ha-a-ap-pár* nom.-acc.sg.; *ha-a-ap-pa-ra-az* abl.; *ha-ap-pár-ra-a(=šmaš)* nom.-acc.pl.

happarnuwašha- c. „beam of light"; *ha-ap-pár-nu-wa-aš-hi-eš* nom.pl.

happešnāi- „to take to pieces, cut up"; *ha-ap-pí-eš-na-an-zi* 3.pl.pres.act.

hapina- c. „open flame"; *ha-ap-pí-ni-it* instr.

happinant- „rich"; *ha-ap-pí-na-an-za* nom.sg.c.

happutri- a kind of cattle; *ha-ap-pu-ut-ri* nom.-acc.sg.n.

har(k)- „to have, hold; to preserve, keep hold of"; *har-zi* 3.sg.pres.act.; *har-kán-zi*[1]*(=ma=an)* 3.pl.pres.act.; *har-ku-un* 1.sg.pret.act.; *har-ta*[1] 2.sg.pret. act.; *har-ta*[2] 3.sg.pret.act.; *har-kir*, *har-ki-ir* 3.pl.pret.act.; *har-ak* 2.sg.imp. act.; *har-du* 3.sg.imp.act.; *har-tin* 2.pl.imp.act.; *har-kán-du* 3.pl.imp.act.

harranu- „to crumble, crush"; *har-ra-nu-uš-kán-zi* iter. 3.pl.pres.act.

hara(na)-$^{\text{(MUŠEN)}}$ c. „eagle"; *ha-a-ra-aš*^{MUŠEN} nom.sg.; *ha-ra-na-aš*^{MUŠEN} gen.sg.; ^{MUŠEN}*ha-a-ra-na-an* acc.sg.

hāri- c. „valley"; *ha-a-ri-ya* dat.-loc.sg.; *ha-a-ri-ya-az* abl.; *ha-a-ri-i-uš (=kán)* acc.pl.; *ha-a-ri-ya-aš* dat.-loc.pl.

hariya- „to bury"; *ha-ri-e-mi* 1.sg.pres.act.

hark- „to perish"; *har-ak-ši* 2.sg.pres.act.; *har-ak-zi* 3.sg.pres.act.; *har-ku-e-ni* 1.pl.pres.act.; *har-kán-zi*[2] 3.pl.pres.act.; *har-ak-ta* 3.sg.pret.act.; *har-ga-an-za* part. nom.sg.c.; *har-kán* part. nom.sg.n.; *har-kán-na*, *har-ga-an-na* inf. II

harganu- „to destroy, ruin, conquer, defeat, overcome"; *har-ga-nu-ut* 3.sg. pret.act.

harnau- c. „birthing seat, birth-stool"; *har-na-a-uš* nom.sg.

harnamma(r) n. „yeast; rebellion, turmoil, fermentation"; *har-nam-ma*, *har-nam-mar* nom.-acc.sg.

harnamniya- „to bring into turmoil, bring into fermentation; to incite, stir up“; *har-nam-ni-ya-at* 3.sg.pret.act.

harni(n)k- „to destroy“; *har-ni-ik-mi* 1.sg.pres.act.; *har-ni-in-ku-un* 1.sg.pret.act.; *har-ni-ik-ta* 3.sg.pret.act.; *har-ni-ik-du* 3.sg.imp.act.; *har-ni-in-kán-du* 3.pl.imp.act.

harpiya- „to join someone; to help“; *har-ap-du-ma-ti* 2.pl.imp.med.; *har-ap-hu-ut* 2.sg.imp.med.

haršar n. „head“; *har-ša-a-ar* nom.-acc.sg.; *har-ša-a-ar-ra* nom.-acc.pl.

haršauwar n. „agriculture, farming“; *har-ša-u-wa-ar* nom.-acc.sg.; *har-ša-ú-na-aš* gen.sg.

^{NINDA}***harši-*** c. „breadloaf (thick bread as opposed to flatbread)“; ^{NINDA}*har-ši-in* acc.sg.; ^{NINDA}*har-ši-it* instr.; ^{NINDA}*har-ši-ya-az* abl.; ^{NINDA}*har-ša-uš* acc.pl.

^{DUG}***haršiyali-*** n. „storage receptacle, pithos“; ^{DUG}*har-ši-ya-li(=ya=kán)* nom.-acc.sg.

1. ***hašš-*** „to beget, bear, give birth“; *ha-a-ši*^{1} 3.sg.pres.act.; *ha-aš-ša-an-zi*^{1} 3.pl.pres.act.; *ha-a-aš-ta* 3.sg.pret.act.

2. ***hašš-/hešš-*** „to open“; *ha-a-ši*^{2} 3.sg.pres.act.; *ha-aš-ša-an-zi*^{2} 3.pl.pres. act.; *hi-eš-šir* 3.pl.pret.act.; *ha-a-aš* 2.sg.imp.act.; *hi-e-eš-tin* 2.pl.imp. act.; *hi-eš-ki-iz-zi* iter. 3.sg. pres.act.

hašša hanzašša- c. „children and grandchildren, descendants“; *ha-aš-še-eš ha-an-za-aš-še-eš* nom.pl.

haššannaša- c. „family, clan“; *ha-aš-ša-an-na-ša-an(=za=kán)* acc.sg.

haššātar n. „begetting; family, clan“; *ha-aš-ša-tar(=šet)* nom.-acc.sg.; *ha-aš-ša-an-na-aš* gen.sg.; *ha-aš-ša-an-na-an-za* abl.; *ha-aš-ša-an-na-an* gen.pl.

haššik- „to eat one's fill“; *ha-aš-ši-ik-du-ma-at* 2.pl.pret.med.

haštāi- n. „bone; strength, powers“; *ha-aš-ta-i*^{1} nom.-acc.sg.; *ha-aš-ta-i*^{2} *(=šet)* nom.-acc.pl.; *ha-aš-ti-aš* gen.pl.; *ha-aš-ti-ya-aš* dat.pl.

hattāi- „to slaughter; to cut off“; *ha-at-ta-an-zi*, *ha-ad-da-an-zi* 3.pl.pres. act.; *ha-at-ta-ri* 3.sg.pres.med.; *ha-at-ta-an-ta-ru* 3.pl.imp.med.

^{LÚ}***hattalwala-*** „gate keeper, door guard“; $^{\text{LÚ.MEŠ}}$*ha-at-tal-wa-la-aš* gen.pl.

^{GIŠ}***hattalwant-*** c. „bolt“; ^{GIŠ}*ha-at-tal-wa-an-za*

hattarai- „to prick“; *ha-at-ta-ra-a-mi* 1.sg.pres.act.

hattareššar see ***hattreššar*** „crossroads“

hattata(r) n. „wisdom“; *ha-at-ta-ta* nom.-acc.sg.

hatteššar n. „pit“; *ha-at-te-eš-na* dir.; *ha-at-te-eš-na-aš* dat.-loc.pl.

hatkišnu- „to attack, plague, press“; *ha-at-ki-iš-nu-ši* 2.sg.pres.act.

hatrāi- „to write“; *ha-at-ra-a-mi* 1.sg.pres.act.; *ha-at-ra-a-ši* 2.sg.pres.act.; *ha-at-ra-a-iz-zi* 3.sg.pres.act.; *ha-at-ra-a-eš* 2.sg.pret.act.; *ha-at-ra-a-it* 3.sg.pret.act.; *ha-at-ri-eš-ki-ši* iter. 2.sg.pres.act.

hatt(a)reššar n. „crossroads“; *ha-at-ta-ri-eš-na-aš, ha-at-ri-eš-na-aš* dat.-loc.pl.

hazz- „to push, stab, strike“; *ha-az-zi-iz-zi* 3.sg.pres.act.; *ha-az-zi-e-it-tu* 3.sg.imp.act.

hazziknu- „to beat, hit, strike; to fight someone“; *ha-az-zi-ik-ki-nu-un* 1.sg. pret.act.

$^{\text{NA4}}$***hekur*** n. „rock sanctuary“; $^{\text{NA4}}$*hé-kur* uninflected

henkan n. „death, ruin“; *hi-in-kán, hi-in-ga-n(=a=ma=apa)* nom.-acc.sg.; *hi-in-ga-ni* dat.-loc.sg.; *hi-in-ga-na-za, hi-in-ga-na-an-za* abl.

hēu- c. „rain“; *hé-e-u-uš* nom.sg.; *hé-e-uš* acc.pl.

^{É}***hīla-*** c. „courtyard“; ^{É}*hi-i-li(=ma=kán)* dat.-loc.sg.

^{LÚ}***hilamma-*** c. „gate keeper, door guard“; $^{\text{LÚ.MEŠ}}$*hi-lam-mi-e-eš-š(=a)* nom.pl.

^{É}***hilammar*** n. „gate building“; ^{É}*hi-lam-na-aš* gen.sg.

1. ***hink-*** „to offer, hand over“; *hi-in-ga-zi* 3.sg.pres.act.

2. ***hink-*** „to bow, prostrate“; *hi-in-ku-e-ni* 1.pl.pres.act.; *hi-in-kán-ta-ti* 3.pl. pret.med.

hinkan° see ***henkan*** „death, ruin“

^{LÚ}***hippara-*** „locked up man“; ^{LÚ}*hi-ip-pa-ri* dat.-loc.sg.

huek-/huk- „to conjure up, raise“; *hu-u-uk-zi* 3.sg.pres.act.

huelpi- „fresh, young, green; noun: young animal“; *hu-el-pí* nom.-acc.sg.n.

hūhatalla- „grandpaternal, of one's grandfather“; *hu-u-ha-da-al-la* nom.-acc.pl.n.

huya° see ***hūwāi-*** „to walk“

^{GIŠ}***huhupāl-*** n. „tambourine“; ^{GIŠ}*hu-hu-pa-a-la* nom.-acc.pl.

^{LÚ}***piran huiyatalla-*** c. „military leader“; $^{\text{LÚ.MEŠ}}$*pí-ra-an hu-u-i-ya-tal-lu-uš (=ma)* acc.pl.

huinu- „to let walk, move, start moving"; *hu-u-i-nu-ut* 2.sg.imp.act.

huiš- „to live"; *hu-iš-wa-an-za* part. nom.sg.c.; *hu-i-iš-wa-an-da-an*, *hu-šu-wa-an-ta-an* part. acc. sg.c.

$^{\text{(GIŠ)}}$***huiša-*** c. „spindle"; *hu-i-ša-aš(=wa)* gen.sg.

^{UZU}***huišu-*** n. „raw meat"; ^{UZU}*hu-i-šu* nom.-acc.sg.

huišwātar n. „life"; *hu-iš-wa-tar(=ma=apa)* nom.-acc.sg.; *hu-iš-wa-an-ni (=ya)* dat.-loc.sg.

huittar n. „wild animal, game"; *hu-u-i-tar* nom.-acc.sg.; *hu-u-i-ta-a-ar* nom.-acc.pl.

huiteššar n. „rheumatism"; *hu-it-ti-eš-šar* nom.-acc.sg.

huittiya- „to pull"; *hu-it-ti-ya-ši* 2.sg.pres.act.; *hu-it-ti-ya-zi* 3.sg.pres.act.; *hu-it-ti-ya-an-zi* 3.pl.pres.act.; *hu-it-ti-at* 3.sg.pret.act.; *hu-it-tah-ha-ri* 1.sg.pres.med.; *hu-it-ti-ya* 2.sg.imp.act.; *hu-it-ti-ya-u-wa-an-zi* inf. I

huk° see ***huek-*** „to conjure up, raise"

hukmāi- c. „conjuration, incantation, raising"; *hu-u-uk-ma-in* acc.sg.; *hu-uk-mi-ya-aš* gen.sg.; *hu-u-uk-ma-uš* acc.pl.

hullāi- „to beat, fight"; *hu-ul-li-e-iz-zi*, *hu-ul-li-iz-zi* 3.sg.pres.act.; *hu-ul-li-iš* 3.sg.pret.act.; *hu-ul-la-an-te-eš* part. nom.pl.c.

hullanu- „to fight"; *hu-ul-la-nu-un*, *hu-ul-li-ya-nu-un* 1.sg.pret.act.

hulaleššar n. „wrapping, winding"; *hu-u-la-liš-ni* dat.-loc.sg.

hullanza- c. „fight, battle"; *hu-ul-la-an-za-an* acc.sg.; *hu-ul-la-an-za-an-ni(=pát)* dat.-loc.sg.

hullanzai- c. „fight, battle"; *hu-ul-la-an-za-iš* nom.sg.

^{GIŠ}***huluganni-*** „carriage, wagon, coach"; ^{GIŠ}*hu-u-lu-ga-an-ni*, ^{GIŠ}*hu-lu-ga-an-ni(=ya)* dat.-loc.sg.; ^{GIŠ}*hu-lu-ga-an-ni-az* abl.; ^{GIŠ}*hu-lu-ga-an-ni-it* instr.

hūmant- „every, all, entire"; *hu-u-ma-an-za* nom.sg.c.; *hu-u-ma-an-da-an*[1] acc.sg.c.; *hu-u-ma-an(=pát)* nom.-acc.sg.n.; *hu-u-ma-an-ti* dat.-loc.sg.; *hu-u-ma-an-ti(=ya=pát)* dat.-loc.sg.; *hu-u-ma-an-da-az(=za)*, *hu-u-ma-an-ta-za(=pát)* abl.; *hu-u-ma-an-te-eš* nom.pl.c.; *hu-u-ma-an-du-uš* acc. pl.c.; *hu-u-ma-an-da*, *hu-u-ma-an-ta* nom.-acc.pl.n.; *hu-u-ma-an-da-aš*, *hu-u-ma-an-da-an*[2] gen.pl.; *hu-u-ma-an-ta-aš* dat.-loc.pl.

hūmantaziya „utterly, completely, entirely"; *hu-u-ma-an-ta-az-zi-ya*

huni(n)k- „to smash (to pieces), damage“; *hu-u-ni-ik-zi* 3.sg.pres.act.; *hu-u-ni-ik-ta-at* 3.sg.pret.med.; *hu-u-ni-in-kán-za(=pát)* part. nom.sg.c.

^{DUG}***hupuwāi-*** n. a vessel; ^{DUG}*hu-pu-wa-i* nom.-acc.sg.

hurkel- n. „heinous deed, horror“; *hur-ki-il* nom.-acc.sg.; *hur-ki-la-za* abl.

hurlili- „in Hurrite“; *hur-li-li(=ma=kán)*

hurla- c. „Hurrite, hurrite“; *hur-la-aš* nom.sg.

hurna- „to hunt“; *hu-ur-nu-wa-an-zi* inf. I

hurtāi- c. „curse, malediction“; *hur-ti-ya-aš* gen.sg.; *hur-da-a-e-eš* nom.pl.; *hur-da-a-uš* acc.pl.

hurtallima- c. „adversary, antagonist“; *hu-ur-ta-li-im-ma-an* acc.sg.

hurwaša- „secret, clandestine“; *hur-wa-ši* dat.-loc.

$^{\mathrm{NA4}}$***hurwaši-*** n. „ritual stone“; $^{\mathrm{NA4}}$*hur-wa-ši* dat.-loc.sg.

hušk- „to wait, bide“; *hu-u-uš-ki-it-tin* 2.pl.pret.act.

hušuwant- see ***huiš-*** „to live“

hūdāk „quick, fast, immediately, at once“; *hu-u-da-a-ak, hu-u-da-ak*

hūwāi- „to walk, flee, escape“; *hu-u-i-ya-ši* 2.sg.pres.act.; *hu-wa-a-i, hu-u-wa-i, hu-u-wa-a-i* 3.sg.pres.act.; *hu-wa-iš* 3.sg.pret.act.; *hu-ya-an-za* part.nom.sg.c.; *hu-wa-a-i-iš-ki-wa-an* iter. supinum

hu(wa)nhueššar n. „wave, surge, flood“; *hu-wa-an-hu-eš-šar(=kán)* nom.-acc.sg.; *hu-u-un-hu-e-eš-na-za* abl.

hūwant- c. „wind“; *hu-u-wa-an-te-eš*$_{17}$ nom.pl.; *hu-wa-an-te-mu-uš* acc.pl.

huwappi- „bad, evil“; *hu-wa-ap-pí* dat.-loc.sg.

hūwart- „to swear, curse“; *hu-u-wa-ar-tah-hu-un* 1.sg.pret.act.; *hu-wa-ar-za-aš-ta* iter. 3.pl.pret.act.

$^{\mathrm{NA4}}$***huwaši-*** n. „ritual stone“; $^{\mathrm{NA4}}$*hu-u-wa-ši-ya* dat.-loc.sg.

-i „they“ (nom.pl.c.)

1. ***iya-*** act. „to make, do; to treat“; *i-ya-mi(=ya=at=za/=ya=wa)* 1.sg.pres. act.; *i-ya-ši* 2.sg.pres.act.; *i-ya-zi, i-ya-az-zi, i-e-zi, i-e-iz-zi, i-iz-zi* 3.sg. pres.act.; *i-ya-u-e-ni* 1.pl.pres.act.; *i-ya-at-te-ni* 2.pl.pres.act.; *i-ya-an-zi, i-en-zi* 3.pl.pres.act.; *i-ya-nu-un* 1.sg. pret.act.; *i-ya-aš, i-ya-at* 2.sg.pret. act.; *i-e-it* 3.sg.pret.act.; *i-ya-u-en* 1.pl.pret.act.; *i-ya-at-te-en, i-ya-at-tin*[1] 2.pl.pret.act.; *i-e-ir* 3.pl.pret.act.; *i-ya-al-lu* 1.sg.imp.act.; *i-ya-ad-du* 3.sg.imp.act.; *i-ya-at-tin*[2] 2.pl.imp.act.; *i-ya-an-za* part. nom.sg.c.; *i-ya-an* part. nom.sg.n.

2. ***iya***- med. „to go“; *i-ya-at-ta-ri*[1] 3.sg.pres.med.; *i-ya-at-ta-ri*[2] 3.pl.pres. med.; *i-ya-ah-ha-ha-at* 1.sg. pret.med.; *i-ya-at-ta-at* 3.sg.pret.med.; *i-it (=wa=šmaš)* 2.sg.imp.act.; *i-it-te-en* 2.pl. imp.act.

iyannāi- „to go, march; to act, proceed, deal“; *i-ya-an-na-i* 3.sg.pres.act.; *i-ya-an-ni-iš*, *i-ya-an-ni-eš* 3.sg.pret.act.

^{UDU}***iyant***- c. „sheep“; ^{UDU}*i-ya-an-ta-an* acc.sg.

ila- c. „weakness (?)“; *i-la-aš* nom.sg.

ilaliya- „to desire, wish“; *i-la-li-ya-ši* 2.sg.pres.act.

ilan- c. „step, grade, rank“; *i-la-ni* dat.-loc.sg.

imma „even, rather; so much“; *im-ma*

immiya- „to mix“; *i-mi-ya-an-zi* 3.pl.pres.act.

inan- n. „illness”; *i-na-an* nom.-acc.sg.; *i-na-na-aš* gen.sg.; *i-na-ni* dat.-loc.sg.

innarahh- „to make healthy“ (impersonal); *in-na-ra-ah-ha-at(=ma)* 3.sg.pret.med.

inu- „to heat, make hot“; *i-nu-ut-te-en* 2.pl.pret.act.; *i-nu-uš-ki-du* iter. 3.sg. imp.act.

irhāi- „to go the rounds, to deal with one after the other“; *ir-ha-u-wa-an-zi* inf. I

irmalant- „ill, sick“; *ir-ma-la-an-za-š(=a)* nom.sg.c.

irmaliya- „to fall ill“; *ir-ma-al-li-ya-at-ta-at* 2.sg.pret.med.

iššati see ***ešš***- „to act“

išhā(n)- c. „master, lord; owner“; *iš-ha-a-aš*, *iš-ha-aš(=šiš/=šiš=a/=šiš=an)* nom.sg.; *iš-ha-a-an* acc.sg.; *iš-hi-i(=ši)* dat.-loc.sg.

išhanaš see ***ēšhar*** „blood“

išhaltuhmeyant- c. „troublemaker“; *iš-hal-túh-me-ya-an-za* nom.sg.

išhariš̆h- „to fall ill with the *Išhara* sickness“; *iš-ha-ri-iš-ha-ri* 3.sg. pres.med.

išharnumanzi see ***ešharnumāi***- „to make bloody“

išharwant- see ***ešharwant***- „bloody“

išhiya- „to bind; to impose“; *iš-hi-ya-at-te-e-ni* 2.pl.pres.act.; *iš-hi-ya-an-da* part.nom.-acc.pl.n.

^{TÚG}***išhial***- n. „bandage“; ^{TÚG}*iš-hi-al(=šmet=a)* nom.-acc.sg.

išheni- c. „hair“; *iš-hi-e-ni-uš(=šmaš=kán)* acc.pl.

išhiman- c. „rope, cord“; *iš-hi-ma-an-ta* instr.

išhiul- n. „bond, obligation; contract“; *iš-hi-ú-ul* nom.-acc.sg.; *iš-hi-ú-la-aš*, *iš-hi-ú-ul-la-aš* gen.sg.

išhuwāi- „to pour out, tip, empty, fill up“; *iš-hu-u-wa-i* 3.sg.pres.act.; *iš-hu-iš-kán-zi* iter. 3.pl.pres.act.

išhuwannāi- „to pour out“; *iš-hu-u-wa-an-na-ah-hi* 1.sg.pres.act.

išhuzziya- „to gird oneself; to constrict“; *iš-hu-zi-ya-it* 3.sg.pret.act.

išiyahh- „to track down, pursue, chase, report“; *i-ši-ya-ah-hu-u-an-zi* inf. I

išpand- c. „night“; *iš-pa-an-di* dat.-loc.sg.

išpanduzzi- n. „vine allowance; vine donation“; *iš-pa-an-du-uz-zi(=ya)* nom.-acc.sg.

DUG***išpanduzzi***- n. „vine vessel, barrel, keg“; DUG*iš-pa-an-du-uz-zi-az* abl.

LÚ***išpanduziyala***- c. „man of the vine donation“; LÚ.MEŠ*iš-pa-an-tu-uz-zi-ya-li-e-eš* nom.pl.

išpar- „to spread out; to crush, tread on“; *iš-pa-ra-an-zi* 3.pl.pres.act.; *iš-pár-ra-ah-hu-un* 1.sg.pret.act.

išpart- „to flee, escape“; *iš-pár-za-zi* iter. 3.sg.pres.act.

ištamaš- „to hear“; *iš-ta-ma-aš-ta-ni* 2.pl.pres.act.; *iš-ta-ma-aš-ša-an-zi(=ta)* 3.pl.pres.act.; *iš-ta-ma-aš-ta* 3.sg.pret.act.; *iš-ta-ma-aš-šir* 3.pl.pret.act.; *iš-ta-ma-aš* 2.sg.imp.act.; *iš-ta-ma-aš-tin*, *iš-ta-ma-aš-te-en* 2.pl.imp. act.; *iš-ta-ma-aš-ki-it* iter. 3.pl.pret.act.; *iš-ta-ma-aš-kán-du (=ya)* iter. 3.pl.imp.act.

ištanana- c. „sacrificial table“; *iš-ta-na-na-aš* dat.-loc.pl.

ištanza- c. „soul, will, sense“; *iš-ta-an-za-ni-it* instr.

ištapp- „to block up, close“; *iš-tap-pa-an-te-eš* part. nom.pl.c.

ištark- „to fall ill, make ill“; *iš-tar-ak-ki-it* 2.sg.pret.med.; *iš-tar-ak-ki-at* 3.sg.pret.med.

ištarnink- „to make ill; to insult“; *iš-tar-ni-ik-zi* 3.sg.pres.act.

ištarningāi- c. „illness“; *iš-tar-ni-in-ga-iš* nom.sg.

ištarna „in between, in the middle“; *iš-tar-na*

īt, ***ītten*** see ***iya***- „to go“

išduwā- „to become known, come out“; *iš-tu-wa-a-ri* 3.sg.pres.med.; *iš-du-wa-a-ti* 3.sg.pret.med.

iššuwan dāi- see ***ešša***- „to make“

idālu- „wicked, evil, bad“; *i-da-a-lu-uš* nom.sg.c.; *i-da-lu-un*, *i-da-a-lu-un* acc.sg.c.; *i-da-lu*, *i-da-a-lu(=ya=kán/ =ma=šmaš=kán/=man)* nom.-acc.sg.n.; *i-da-la-u-e-eš(=wa=kán)*, *i-da-a-la-u-eš*, *i-da-a-la-u-e-eš* nom.pl.c.; *i-da-a-la-mu-uš* acc.pl.c.; *i-da-a-lu-wa*, *i-da-a-la-u-wa* nom.-acc.pl.; *i-da-a-la-u-wa-aš* dat.-loc.pl.

idalawātar n. „badness, wickedness, depravity“; *i-da-la-wa-tar* nom.-acc.sg.; *i-da-la-a-wa-an-ni* at.-loc.sg.

idala(u)wah- „to run down, treat bad“; *i-da-la-u-wa-ah-mi* 1.sg.pres.act.; *i-da-la-wa-ah-ti(=ma=an)* 2.sg.pres.act.; *i-da-la-u-wa-ah-zi(=ya=mu)* 3.sg.pres.act.

idala(u)wēš- „to become bad, wicked, evil“; *i-da-la-u-e-eš-zi* 3.sg.pres.act.

iwar c.gen. „like, as“; *i-wa-ar*

izzaten see ***ed/ad***- „to eat“

iwaru- n. „dowry“; *i-wa-ru-u(=šet/=šet=za)* nom.-acc.sg.

iwaruwa- c. „heir“; *i-wa-ru-wa-aš* nom.sg.

-***ya*** „and, but“

kā „here“; *ka-a*

kā- „this“; *ka-a-aš*^{1}*(=ma/=ta)* nom.sg.c. (also interjection, see there); *ku-u-un(=a=wa/=za)* acc.sg.c.; *ki-i(=ma/=mu/=ya/=wa)* nom.-acc.sg.n.; *ki-e-el* gen.sg.; *ki-e-da-ni (=ya=kán/=ma/=za=kán)* dat.-loc.sg.; *ki-e-iz-z (=a=ma=ši/=at/=za)* abl.; *ki-i-da-an-da* instr.; *ki-e(=ma)* nom.pl.c.; *ku-u-uš*, *ki-e-uš* acc.pl.c.; *ki-e-da-aš* dat.-loc.pl.

^{LÚ}***gaena***- c. „relative, relative by marriage“; *ga-a-i-na-aš(=miš)* nom.sg.

kakkapi- c. „partridge“; *ka-aq-qa-pí-iš* nom.pl.c.

kallarātar n. „disaster, harm“; *kal-la-ra-an-ni* dat.-loc.sg.

kaleliya- „to tie up, bind“; *ka-li-e-li-e-it* 3.sg.pret.act.

kalleš- „to call, lure“; *kal-li-iš-ta* 3.sg.pret.act.

kalmišana- c. „piece of wood; thunderbolt“; *kal-mi-i-ša-ni-iš* nom.pl.c.

^{GIŠ}***kalmuš***- n. „lituus“; ^{GIŠ}*kal-mu-ša-aš* gen.sg.

kammara- c. „stench“; ~~*kam-ma-ra-aš*~~ nom.sg.

kammaršk- „to shit“; *kam-mar-ši-eš-ki-id-du* 3.sg.imp.act.

-***kan*** enclitic particle

ganešš- „to find out, realise; to acknowledge, accept“; *ga-ni-eš-zi* 3.sg. pres.act.; *ga-ni-eš-šir* 3.pl.pret.act.

kāni „here“; *ka-a-ni(=wa)*

kaniniya- „to prostrate, bow down“; *ka-ni-ni-e-ir* 3.pl.pret.act.

kaniššuwar n. „favour, goodwill“; *ka-ni-iš-šu-u-wa-ar(=ma=at/=ma=mu)* nom.-acc.sg.

kank- „to hang up“; *kán-kán-du* 3.pl.imp.act.

kangur- n. „wine barrel, wine keg“; *ka-an-gur* nom.-acc.sg.

kard° see ***kēr*** „heart“

kappilazza- „to become angry“; *kap-pí-la-az-za-at-ta* 3.sg.pret.med.

kapru- n. „throat“; *kap-ru-u(=šet)* nom.-acc.sg.

kappuwāi- „to count, calculate; to look after; to provide with“; *kap-pu-iz-zi* 3.sg.pres.act.; *kap-pu-u-wa-an* part. nom.-acc.sg.n.; *kap-pu-uš-kán-zi* iter. 3.pl.pres.act.

kappuwant- „numbered, little, few“; *kap-pu-wa-an-da-aš* dat.-loc.pl.c.

kappūwar n. „count“; *kap-pu-u-wa-u-wa-ar* nom.-acc.sg.

karāt- c. „inner body, interior, entrails“; *ka-ra-a-ta-an* acc.sg.; *ka-ra-a-ti-iš*, *ka-ra-a-te-eš*, *ga-ra-a-ti-eš* nom.pl.; *ka-ra-a-du-uš (=wa=za)* acc.pl.

^{É}***karim(n)i-*** „ritual building, temple“; ^{É}*ka-ri-im-me*, ^{É}*ka-ri-im-ni-i(=ti)* dat.-loc.sg.

karip- „to eat, devour“; *ka-ri-ip-ta* 2.sg.pret.act.; *ka-ri-ip-tin* 2.pl.imp.act.; *ka-ri-pu-u-wa-an* supinum

karnan marnan „to the best of one's ability“; *kar-na-an ma-ar-na-an*

kark- „to disappear“; *kar-ki-e-ir* 3.pl.pret.act.

karp- „to lift; to achieve, accomplish something; med. to finish, complete, end“; *kar-ap-mi* 1.sg.pres.act.; *kar-pí-iz-zi* 3.sg.pres.act.; *kar-pa-an-ti* 3.pl.pres.act.; *kar-ap-ta-ri* 3.sg.pres.med.; *kar-pa-an-ta-ri* 3.pl.pres. med.; *kar-pa-an-du* 3.pl.imp.act.

karpi- c. „rage, anger, fury, wrath“; *kar-pí-in* acc.sg.

karpiwala- „angry, furious“; *kar-pí-wa-a-la* nom.-acc.pl.n.

karš- „to cut off, take off, remove“; *kar-aš-mi* 1.sg.pres.act.; *kar-aš-ta* 3.sg. pret.act.; *kar-ša-al-lu* 1.sg.imp.act.

kardiyaš(-) „that of the heart, wish, desire“; *kar-di-aš(=taš)* gen.sg.

kartimmiyauwant- „angry, furious“; *kar-tim-mi-ya-u-wa-an-za* nom.sg.c.; *kar-tim-mi-ya-u-wa-an-te-eš* nom.pl.c.

kartimmiyatt- c. „anger, fury, resentment, grudge“; *kar-tim-mi-ya-az* nom.sg.; *kar-di-mi-ya-at-ta-an* acc.sg.; *kar-di-mi-at-ta-aš* gen.sg.

karū „earlier; already"; *ka-ru-ú(=za)*

karūili- „old"; *ka-ru-ú-i-li-iš* nom.sg.c.; *ka-ru-ú-i-li* nom.-acc.n.; *ka-ru-ú-i-li-aš* gen.sg.; *ka-ru-ú-li-uš (=ma=za)* acc.pl.c.; *ka-ru-ú-i-li-ya* nom.-acc. pl.n.; *ka-ru-ú-i-li-ya-aš*[1] gen.pl.; *ka-ru-ú-i-li-ya-aš*[2] dat.-loc.pl.

karūiliyatta „in the usual way, like in the past"; *ka-ru-ú-i-li-ya-at-ta*

karuššiya- „to be silent"; *ka-ru-uš-ši-ya-zi* 3.sg.pres.act.

karūwariwar „at dawn"; *ka-ru-ú-wa-ri-wa-ar*, *ka-ru-ú-a-ri-wa-ar*

kāš(a) „behold! see!"; *ka-a-aš*[2], *ka-a-š(=a/=a=wa/a=wa=ta/=a=wa=za)*, *qa-a-š(=a/=a=šmaš)*

kāšata „behold! see! "; *ka-a-ša-ta-a(=šmaš=kán)*

^É^***kaškaštipa-*** c. a building; ^É^*ka-aš-ga-aš-ti-pa-az* abl.

kašt- c. „hunger, famine"; *ga-aš-ta-an* acc.sg.

katta „down"; *kat-ta(=war=aš=šmaš=kán)*

kattaya „accordingly, in the same way"; *kat-ta-ya*

kattan „below"; *kat-ta-an*

kattanda „down"; *kat-ta-an-ta*, *kat-ta-an-da*

kattawātar n. „revenge, retribution, retaliation, compensation"; *kat-ta-wa-tar* nom.-acc.sg.

katterahh- „to cause to lose, make inferior"; *kat-te-ir-ra-ah-ta* 3.sg.pret.act.

katti „at, by, with"; *kat-ti(=mi/=ši=ya=aš/=ši=ma/=ti)*, *kat-te(=mi)*

gauri- a kind of forest; *ga-ú-ri-ya-az* abl.

kē, ***kēl***, ***kedani***, ***kēz*** see ***kā-*** „this"

genu- n. „knee, lap"; *gi-nu-wa* dat.-loc.sg.; *gi-nu-wa-aš* gen.pl.

genzu- n. „lap, genitals; affection, pity"; *gi-in-zu* nom.-acc.sg.

genzuwāi- „to have pity"; *gi-en-zu-wa-i-ši* 2.sg.pres.act.

genzuwala- „kind, gracious"; *gi-in-zu-wa-la-aš* nom.sg.c.

kēr n. „heart"; *kar-di(=šmi)*, *kar-di-e(=šmi)*, *kar-ti-i(=šmi)* dat.-loc.sg.; *kar-da-a(=šma)* dir.

keššar c./n. „hand"; *ki-eš-šar(=šiš)* nom.sg.c.; *ki-iš-ša-ri-i*, *ki-iš-ši-ri(=mi)* dat.-loc.sg.; *ki-iš-šar-ta* instr.

kī see ***kā-*** „this"

kī- „to lie, be laid; to lay, put out"; *ki-it-ta*, *ki-it-ta-ri* 3.sg.pres.med.;

ki-it-ta-at 3.sg.pret.med.; *ki-it-ta-ru* 3.sg.imp.med.; *ki-id-du-ma-ti* 2.pl. imp.med.

gimra- c. „field“; *gi-im-ra* dir.; *gi-im-ra-az* abl.

ginu° see ***genu-*** „knee, lap“

kikkiš- „to become“; *ki-ik-ki-iš-ta-ru* 3.sg.imp.med.; *ki-ik-ki-iš-šu-u-wa-an* supinum

kinu- „to open“; *ki-nu-uz-zi(=ma)* 3.sg.pres.act.

kinun „now“; *ki-nu-un(=ma=wa=tu=za/=pát/=wa=za/=za)*, *ki-nu-n(=a/ =a=ya/=a=ya/=war=an/ =a=mu/ =a=ši/=a=wa/=a=wa=šmaš=kán*

^{É}kipa- c. „hut“; *^{É}kip-pa-an* acc.sg.

kiš- „to become, occur, happen“; *ki-iš-ha* 1.sg.pres.med.; *ki-iš-ta* 2.sg.pres. med.; *ki-ša*, *ki-i-ša*, *ki-ša-ri*, *ki-i-ša-ri* 3.sg. pres.med.; *ki-iš-ha-ha-at* 1.sg.pret.med.; *ki-iš-ta-at* 2.sg.pret.med.; *ki-ša-at*, *ki-i-ša-at* 3.sg.pret. med.; *kiš-du-um-ma-at* 2.pl.pret.med.; *ki-ša-an-ta-at* 3.pl.pret.med.; *ki-ša-ru* 3.sg.imp.med.

kiššan „so, as follows“; *ki-iš-ša-an*, *ki-iš-ša-an-n(=a)*, *kiš-an*

kišt- „to go out, extinguish“; *ki-iš-ta-ru* 3.sg.imp.act.

kištant- c. „hunger“; *ki-iš-ta-an-ti-it* instr.

kištanu- „to put out“; *ki-iš-ta-nu-zi* 3.sg.pres.act.; *ki-iš-ta-nu-nu-un* 1.sg. pret.act.

kištanziya- „suffer from hunger“; *ki-iš-ta-an-zi-at-ta-at* 3.sg.pret.med.

kit pa(n)dalaz „from now on“; *ki-it pa-da-la-az*

kuen-/kun- „to kill“; *ku-e-mi* 1.sg.pres.act.; *ku-en-ti* 2.sg.pres.act.; *ku-en-zi*, *ku-i-en-zi* 3.sg.pres.act.; *ku-e-nu-un* 1.sg.pret.act.; *ku-en-ta(=wa =an =kán)* 3.sg.pret.act.; *ku-e-u-e-en*, *ku-in-nu-um-mi-en* 1.pl.pret.act.; *ku-en-nir*, *ku-e-en-ni-ir* 3.pl.pret.act.; *ku-na-an-na* inf. II

kuer(š)- „to cut off“; *ku-e-ir-šu-un* 1.sg.pret.act.; *ku-e-ri-ir* 3.pl.pret.act.

kui- „who, which“ (*kuit* also conjunction, see below); *ku-iš(=ma=za/=wa=kán/=war=an/=za)*, *ku-iš-š(=a)*[1], *ku-i-š(=an/=at)*, *ku-i-iš (=wa=kán)* nom.sg.c.; *ku-in (=wa)* acc.sg.c.; *ku-it*[1] *(=šmaš=kán/=wa/=wa=ši)* nom.-acc.sg.n. (also conjunction, see there); *ku-e-el* gen.sg.; *ku-e-da-ni (=ma=šan)* dat.-loc.sg.; *ku-e-iz(=za)* abl.; *ku-i-eš*, *ku-e-eš*, *ku-e-iš*, *ku-i-e-eš(=ma=mu)* nom.pl.c.; *ku-i-uš* acc.pl.c.; *ku-e* nom.-acc.pl.n.; *ku-e-da-aš* dat.-loc.pl.

kuiša „whoever“; *ku-iš-ša*^{2}, *ku-i-ša(=kán)* nom.sg.c. (also *kuiš* + *-a*)

kuiška „every, each, whoever“; *ku-el-ka* gen.sg.; *ku-e-da-ni-ik-ka* dat.-loc.sg.; *ku-e-iz-qa* abl.

kuiški „anybody, any“; *ku-iš-ki* nom.sg.c.; *ku-in-ki* acc.sg.c.; *ku-it-ki* nom.-acc.sg.n.; *ku-e-da-ni-ik-ki*, *ku-i-ta-ni-ik-ki* dat.-loc.sg.c.

kuit „because, as, when, although“; *ku-it(=mu=za/=wa)*, *ku-i-t(=a/=aš=a)*, *ku-i-d(=a)*

kuitanikki see ***kuiški*** „anybody, any“

kuitman „while, as long as“; *ku-it-ma-an(=ma=za/=wa)*, *ku-it-ma-n (=aš/=ašta)*

kuitman nāwi „before“

kuinummen see ***kuen-/kun-*** „to kill“

^{NINDA}***kugulla-*** c. a kind of lard biscuits; ^{NINDA}*ku-gul-la-an* acc.sg.

kuli- n. „unused“; *ku-li-i* nom.-acc.pl.

kūn see ***kā-*** „this“

$^{\text{NA4}}$***kunkunuzzi-*** c. „diorite; meteorite“; $^{\text{NA4}}$*ku-un-ku-nu-uz-zi-iš* nom.sg.

kunnaz „right“; *ku-un-na-az*

^{GIŠ}***kuppeššar*** n. „stool“; ^{GIŠ}*ku-up-pí-iš-na-aš* dat.-loc.pl.

kup- „to plan“; *ku-up-ta* 3.sg.pret.act.

kupiyati c. „plan, attack“; *ku-pí-ya-ti-in* acc.sg.

^{TÚG}***kureššar*** n. „headscarf, bonnet, kerchief; length of cloth“; ^{TÚG}*ku-ri-eš-šar* nom.-acc.sg.

^{KUŠ}***kurša-*** c. „fur, hide, shield“; ^{KUŠ}*kur-šu-uš* acc.pl.

kurtali- n. „container, vessel“; *ku-úr-da-a-li* uninflected

kūrur n. „enemy; hostile, adversary“; *ku-ru-ur*, *ku-u-ru-ur* nom.sg.n.; *ku-ru-ur*$^{\text{HI.A}}$, *ku-u-ru-ri*$^{\text{HI.A}}$ nom.pl.n.

kururant- c. „enmity“; *ku-ru-ra-an-za* nom.sg.

kururiyahh- „to revolt, become hostile“; *ku-ru-ri-ya-ah-hu-un* 1.sg.pret.act.; *ku-u-ru-ri-ya-ah-ta* 3.sg.pret.act.; *ku-ru-ri-ah-hi-ir*, *ku-ru-ri-ya-ah-hi-ir*, *ku-u-ru-ri-ya-ah-hi-ir* 3.pl.pret.act.; *ku-u-ru-ri-ya-ah-hi-eš-kir* iter. 3.pl. pret.act.

^{URUDU}***kuruzzi-*** „sickle (?)“; ^{URUDU}*ku-ru-uz-zi-it* instr.

kūš see ***kā-*** „this“

kuššanka „anytime, sometime, ever“; *ku-uš-ša-an-ka*, *ku-uš-ša-an-qa*

kūšata- n. „bride price"; *ku-u-ša-ta-a(=ši)* acc.sg.
kušduwāta(r) n. „evilness, wickedness"; *ku-uš-du-wa-a-ta* nom.-acc.sg.
kutt- c. „wall"; *ku-ut-ta-an* acc.sg.
kuttan- c. „shoulder, forearm; power, might, strength"; *ku-ut-ta-ni-it* instr.
kutru- c. „witness"; *ku-ut-ru-e-eš* nom.pl.
kuwāliu- „calm, silent"; *ku-wa-a-li-ú* acc.sg.n.
kuwapi „where; as, when, because, although"; *ku-wa-pí(=ya/=kán)*, *ku-wa-a-pí(=ši)*
kuwapit „where"; *ku-wa-pí-it(=za)*
kuwapikki „anywhere, somewhere"; *ku-wa-pí-ki*, *ku-wa-pí-ik-ki*, *ku-u-wa-pí-ik-ki*
kuwaš- „to press, push, suppress"; *ku-wa-aš-ki-ši* 2.sg.pres.act.
kuwat „why; because"; *ku-wa-at(=mu/=wa/=war=at=ši)*
kuwatta „where"; *ku-wa-at-ta(=aš)*
kuwatten „where"; *ku-wa-tin*
kuwatka „somehow, about"; *ku-wa-at-qa*, *ku-at-qa*
lā- „to loosen, unbind"; *la-a-an-zi* 3.pl.pres.act.
lahha- „(war) campaign"; *la-ah-hi* dat.-loc.sg.; *la-ah-ha-az(=ma)* abl.; *la-ah-ha(=ma)* dir.
^{LÚ}***lahhiyala-*** c. „man of war, soldier"; ^{LÚ}*la-ah-hi-ya-la-aš* nom.sg.
lahlahima- c. „grief, affliction"; *la-ah-la-ah-hi-ma-an* acc.sg.
lahuwāi- „to pour, tip, pout out; to flow"; *la-hu-i*, *la-a-hu-i*, *la-a-hu-wa-i* 3.sg.pres.act.; *la-a-hu-uš*, *la-a-hu-š(=an)* 3.sg.pret.act.; *la-ah-hu-wa-an-zi*, *la-a-hu-u-wa-an-zi* 3.pl.pres.act.; *la-hu-wa-ta-ri* 3.sg.pres.med.
lahhurnuzzi- n. „sacrificial altar"; *la-ah-hu-ur-nu-zi* nom.-acc.sg.
lak- „to bend, incline, make lop-sided"; *la-ga-a-an* part. nom.-acc.n.
lāla- c. „tongue"; *la-a-lu-uš* acc.pl.
lalukkiuwant- „light, splendid"; *la-lu-uk-ki-u-wa-an-te-eš* nom.pl.c.
lammar n. „hour; adv. immediately"; *lam-mar* nom.-acc.sg.
labarna- c. „Labarna" (royal title); *la-ba-ar-na-aš*^{1} nom.sg.; *la-ba-ar-na-aš*^{2} gen.sg.; *la-ba-ar-ni* dat.-loc.sg.
lē „(prohibitive) not"; *li-e(=ma/=ma=mu=šan/=mu/=pát)*
lengāi- c. „oath"; *li-in-ga-in-n(=ašta)* acc.sg.; *li-in-ki-ya-aš*, *li-in-ki-aš* gen.

sg.; *li-in-ki-ya* dat.-loc.sg.; *li-in-ki-ya-az* abl.; *li-in-ga-uš*, *li-in-ga-a-uš* acc.pl.

lelaniya- „to hurry“; *li-e-la-ni-ya-an-za* part. nom.sg.c.

leššāi- „to pick up“; *li-eš-šu-u-wa-an-zi* inf. I

lilā(r)- „to reconcile“; *li-la-a-an-zi* 3.pl.pres.act.; *li-la-a-ri-iš-ki-wa-ni* iter. 1.pl.pres.act.

lilipāi- „to lick up, lap up“; *li-li-pa-an-ti* 3.pl.pres.act.; *li-li-pa-iš-ki-id-du* iter. 3.sg.imp.act.

liliwant- „hurried, quick, agile“; *li-li-wa-an-du-uš* acc.pl.c.

link- „to swear, vow“; *li-in-ku-un* 1.sg.pret.act.

lingāi- see ***lengāi-*** „oath“

linganu- „to swear someone in“; *li-in-ga-nu-ma-ni* 1.pl.pres.act.; *li-in-ga-nu-nu-un* 1.sg.pret.act.; *li-in-ga-nu-wa-an-za* part. nom.sg.c.

lingant- c. „oath“; *li-in-ka-an-te-eš* nom.pl.

1. ***lukk-*** „to light, light up, set fire to“; *lu-uk-ki-iz-zi* 3.sg.pres.act.

2. ***lukk-*** „to become light, dawn“; *lu-uk-ta-at*, *lu-uk-kat-ta(=ma)* 3.sg. pret.med.

lukkatti „the next morning“; *lu-uk-kat-ti*

lukta „the next morning, at dawn“; *lu-uk-ta(=ma)*

lūlu- n. „prospering, well-being“; *lu-ú-lu* nom.-acc.sg.

$^{\text{(GIŠ)}}$***luttāi-*** c./n. „window“; ^{GIŠ}*lu-ut-ta-i* nom.-acc.sg.n.; *lu-ut-ti-ya-aš* dat.-loc.pl.; ^{GIŠ}*lu-ut-ta-a-uš* acc.pl.

^{GIŠ}***luttant-*** c. „window“; ^{GIŠ}*lu-ut-ta-an-za* abl.

luzzi- n. „socage, forced labour“; *lu-uz-zi*^{1} nom.-acc.sg.; *lu-uz-zi*^{2} dat.-loc.sg.; *lu-zi-ya-za* abl.

-ma „but, and“

mahhan „how, as, when, because“; *ma-ah-ha-an(=kán/=ma/=ma=aš/=ma =at/ =ma=kán/=ma=za/=wa=mu=kán)*, *ma-a-ah-ha-an*

māi- „to grow, prosper“; *mi-i-ya-ri* 3.sg.pres.med.

mayant- „adult, grown-up“; *ma-ya-an-za* nom.sg.c.

maišzašti- c. „glow, shine“; *ma-iš-za-aš-ti-iš* nom.sg.

makkeš- „to become much, to become many, to multiply“; *ma-ak-ki-iš-kat-ta-ru* iter. 3.sg.imp.med.; *ma-ak-ki-eš-ki-an-du* iter. 3.pl.imp.act.

maklant- „lean, thin, meager"; *ma-ak-la-an-te-eš* nom.pl.c.
maknu- „to multiply, increase, pile up"; *ma-ak-nu-nu-un* 1.sg.pret.act.
malla- „to grind, mill"; *mal-la-an-zi* 3.pl.pres.act.; *ma-al-la-an-du* 3.pl. imp.act.
malk- „to spin"; *ma-al-ki-ya-an-zi* 3.pl.pres.act.
mald- „to vow, swear"; *ma-a-al-tah-hu-un* 1.sg.pret.act.
malteššar n. „vow"; *ma-al-te-eš-šar* nom.-acc.sg.
māmman see ***mān*** + ***man***
man irrealis particle; *ma-an(=kán/=mu/=ta/=wa/=za)*; *ma-n(=a/=an=kán/ =aš=kán/=ašta/=at=wa)*; *ma-a- (=wa/=war=ašta/=wa=šan)*
mān „when, as; if, whether"; *ma-a-an(=kán/=ma=aš/=ma=ta/=mu=kán/ =šan/=ši/=wa/=wa=kán/=war=at/=za)*; *ma-a-an-n(=a)*; *ma-a-n(=an/ =apa/=aš/=uš/ =uš=kán)*; *ma-a-am (=man)*
maniyahh- „to hand over; to administer"; *ma-ni-ya-ah-mi* 1.sg.pres.ind.; *ma-ni-ya-ah-zi* 3.sg.pres.ind.; *ma-ni-ya-ah-hi-eš-ki-iz-zi* iter. 3.sg.pres.act.
maniyahhāi- c. „administration"; *ma-ni-ya-ah-hi-aš* gen.sg.
maninkuwa- „near"; *ma-an-ni-in-ku-wa-a-e-eš* nom.pl.c.
maninkuwant- „near"; *ma-ni-in-ku-u-wa-an-da-an* acc.sg.c.; *ma-ni-in-ku-wa-an*, *ma-an-ni-in-ku-wa-an*, *ma-an-ni-in-ku-an* nom.-acc.sg.n.
manga(n) „somehow"; *ma-an-qa*, *ma-an-ga*, *ma-a-an-ga-an*
marri „very, quite"; *mar-ri*
marnan siehe ***karnan marnan***
marlant- „stupid, foolish"; *mar-la-an-da-an* acc.sg.c.
marnu- c. a kind of beer; *mar-nu-an* acc.sg.
marša- „wrong, spoilt, off"; *mar-ša-an-za(=wa)* nom.sg.c.
maršeš- „to go bad, go off, become spoilt"; *mar-še-eš-še-ir* 3.pl.pret.act.
mašiwant- „as much as"; *ma-ši-wa-an* nom.-acc.sg.n.
mašdu- c. „chain, rope, shackles"; *maš-du-uš* acc.pl.
mauš- „to fall"; *ma-uš-zi* 3.sg.pres.act.; *ma-uš-ha-ha-at* 1.sg.pret.med.; *ma-uš-ta-at* 3.sg.pret.med.; *mu-wa-an-ta-ru* 3.pl.imp.med.; *ma-uš-šu-u-wa-an-zi* inf. I
māwa° see ***mān*** + ***-wa***

mehur n. „time, point of time“; *me-hur* nom.-acc.sg.; *me-e-hu-u-ni* dat.-loc.sg.; *me-hur-ra*, *me-hur-ri*$^{\text{HI.A}}$ nom.-acc.pl.; *me-e-hu-na-aš* dat.-loc.pl.

mekki- „much, many; adv. very“; *me-ik-ki* nom.-acc.sg.n.; *me-ig-ga-uš* acc.pl.c.

memāi- „to say, tell, speak“; *me-ma-ah-hi* 1.sg.pres.act.; *me-ma-at-ti* 2.sg. pres.act.; *me-ma-i*, *me-ma-a-i* 3.sg.pres.act.; *me-ma-an-zi* 3.pl.pres.act.; *me-mah-hu-un* 1.sg.pret.act.; *me-mi-iš-ta*^{1} 2.sg.pret.act.; *me-mi-iš-ta*^{2} 3.sg.pret.act.; *me-e-mi-ir* 3.pl.pret.act.; *me-ma-al-lu* 1.sg.imp.act.; *me-mi* 2.sg.imp.act.; *me-mi-eš-tin* 2.pl.imp.act.; *me-e-ma-a-ú* 3.sg.imp.act.; *me-mi-ya-u-wa-an-zi* inf. I; *me-mi-iš-ki-mi* iter. 1.sg.pres.act.; *me-mi-iš-ki-iz-zi*, *me-mi-eš-ki-iz-zi* iter. 3.sg.pres.act.; *me-mi-iš-kán-zi* iter. 3.pl. pres.act.; *me-mi-iš-ki-te-en* iter. 2.pl.imp.; *me-mi-iš-ki-u-an* iter. supinum

memal- n. „groats, porridge“; *me-ma-al-la-aš-š(=a)* gen.sg.

memiya(n)- c. „word, matter, thing, affair, reason“; *me-mi-aš*, *me-mi-ya-aš* nom.sg.; *me-mi-an*, *me-mi-ya-an*, *me-mi-ya-an-n(=a=wa=ta)* acc.sg.; *me-mi-ni* dat.-loc.sg.; *me-mi-ya-na-az* abl.; *me-mi-ya-na-aš* dat.-loc.pl.

memma- see ***mimma-*** „to refuse“

menahhanda „opposite, contrary to“; *me-na-ah-ha-an-da*, *me-e-na-ah-ha-an-da*

meš- „to grow, prosper“; *mi-eš-ha-ti* 1.sg.pret.med.

-mi- „my“; *-miš* nom.sg.c.; *-man* acc.sg.c.; *-mit*, *-met* nom.-acc.sg.n.; *-maš* gen.sg.; *-mi*^{1} dat.-loc.sg.; *-mi*^{2} voc.sg.; *-meš* nom.pl.c.; *-muš* acc.pl.c.

miyahhuwanta- „to become old“; *mi-ya-hu-wa-an-ta-ah-hu-ut* 2.sg. imp.med.

mimma- „to say no, refuse“; *me-im-ma-aš* 3.sg.pret.act.

mišriwant- „sparkling, glittering“; *mi-iš-ri-wa-an-za* nom.sg.c.

mīti- „red“; *mi-i-ti-iš*, *mi-i-ti-iš-š(=a)* nom.sg.c.

-mu „to me, me“

mūgāi- „to wail“; *mu-ú-ga-it* 3.sg.pret.act.

mulātar n. „dirt“; *mu-la-a-tar* nom.-acc.sg.; *mu-la-at-na-za* abl.

munnāi- „to hide“; *mu-un-na-a-ir* 3.pl.pret.act.; *mu-un-na-it-ta-at* 3.sg. pret.med.

-muš see ***-mi-*** „my“

muwantaru see ***mauš-*** „to fall“

nah- „to be afraid, be scared; to show one's respect, honour“; *na-ah-ti* 2.sg. pres.act.; *na-a-hu-un* 1.sg.pret.act.; *na-ah-ta* 3.sg.pret.act.; *na-ah-ha-an-te-eš* part. nom.pl.c.; *na-a-hu-u-wa-aš(=ma=mu)* verbal noun gen.sg.

nahšaratt- c. „fear, awe, respect“; *na-ah-ša-ra-az* nom.sg.; *na-ah-ša-ra-at-ta-an* acc.sg.

nahšariya- „to be scared, be afraid, fear“; *na-ah-ša-ri-ya-ta-ti* 3.sg.pret.med.

nāi- „to steer, send, turn“; *na-it-ti*, *ne-ya-ti* 2.sg.pres.act.; *ne-an-zi* 3.pl.pres. act.; *ne-ya-ah-ha-ri* 1.sg.pres.med. *na-iš-ta-ri*, *ne-ya-at-ta-ti* 2.sg.pres. med.; *ne-ih-hu-un* 1.sg.pret.act.; *na-a-iš* 3.sg.pret.act.; *ne-ya-at-ta-at* 3.sg.pret.med.; *ne-i-ya* 2.sg.imp.act.; *ne-iš-hu-ut*, *ne-eš-hu-ut* 2.sg.imp. med.; *ne-ya-an-ta-an* part. acc.sg.c.

nakki- „mighty, powerful, important, strong“; *na-ak-ki-iš* nom.sg.c.; *na-ak-ki-in* acc.sg.c.; *na-ak-ki-i* nom.-acc.sg.n.; *na-ak-ki-it* instr.; *na-ak-ki-ya-š(=aš)* gen.pl.; *na-ak-ki-e-eš* nom.pl.c.

nakkiyātar n. „importance; respect“; *na-ak-ki-ya-an-ni* dat.-loc.sg.

namma „further“; *nam-ma(=an/=an=za=an/=aš/=ya/=kán/=ma/ =ma=kán =ma=za/=šan/=šmaš/=za)*

nanna- „to drive, shove, push“; *na-an-na-i*, *na-an-na-a-i* 3.sg.pres.act.; *na-an-na-an-zi* 3.pl.pret.act.

nanakuššiyant- „dark“; *na-na-ku-uš-ši-ya-an-ta-za* abl.

-naš „us“; *na-aš*

našma „or, either … or“; *na-aš-ma(=at/=kán/=ši=kán/=wa)*

naššu „either … or“; *na-aš-šu(=ma)*

natī- c. „reed, arrow“; *na-ti-i-da* instr.n

natta „not“; *na-at-ta(=ašta)*

nāwi „not yet“; *na-a-ú-i*, *na-a-wi$_4$*, *na-ú-i*

nega- c. „sister“; *ni-ku-uš(=muš)* acc.pl.

nekut- c. „evening“; *ne-ku-uz(=(z)a)* gen.sg.

nepiš- n. „sky, heaven“; *ne-pí-iš* nom.-acc.sg.; *ne-pí-ša-aš*, *ne-pí-iš-za (=ašta)* gen.sg.; *ne-pí-ši* dat.-loc.sg.; *ne-pí-ša-az(=kán)* abl.; *ne-e-pí-ša* dir.

netta see ***nu***

newahh- „to renew“; *ne-wa-ah-ha-an-zi* 3.pl.pres.act.

nikku „by any chance, surely not“; *ni-ik-ku*

nink- „to mobilize, muster; to cause trouble“; *ne-ni-ik-ta-ti* 2.sg.pres.med.; *ni-ni-ik-ta-ri* 3.sg.pres.med.; *ni-ni-ik-ta-at* 3.sg.pret.med.; *ni-ni-ik-tum-ma-at* 2.pl.imp.med.

nink- „to drink one's fill, get drunk“; *ni-ik-zi* 3.sg.pres.act.; *ni-in-ki-e-ir* 3.pl. pret.act.

nu „and, also“; *nu(=kán/=mu/=mu=kán/=mu=šan/=mu=za/=naš=naš =šan/=še/=ši/=ši=apa/=ši=kán/ši=šan/=šmaš/=šmaš=(š)an/=šmaš= at/=šmaš=at=kán/=šmaš=kán/=ta/=ta=kán/=uš/=uš=apa/=uš=kán/ =uš=šan/=uš=za/=za/=za=an/=za=kán/=za=ta/=wa/=wa(r)=an/=wa r=an=kán/=war=aš/=war=at/=war=at=kán/=war=at=mu=kán/ =war=at=ši/=wa=kán/=wa=mu/=wa=naš/=wa=naš=kán/=wa=šan/ =wa=ši/=wa=šmaš/=wa=šmaš=ta/=ta=kán/ =wa=za/=wa=za=kan)*; *nu-u(=kán/=za), na-an(=kán/=mu/=mu=kán/ =ši/=wa/=za/=za=an) = nu + -an; na-pa = nu + -apa; na-aš(=ašta/kán/=šan/=ši/=ši=apa/ =za) = nu + -aš; na-at(=kán/=mu/=šan/=ši/=šmaš =kán/=za/=za =kán) = nu + -at; ne(=at=ta/=ta=kán/=za) = nu + -e* „they“

nūmān, ***nūwan*** „not yet“; *nu-u-ma-a-an*, *nu-wa-an*

nuntara- „fast, quick, hurriedly“; *nu-un-tar-aš* nom.sg.c.

nuttariya- „hurriedly, fast, quick“; *nu-ut-ta-ri-ya-an* nom.-acc.sg.n.

nūwa „still, yet“; *nu-u-wa(=ya/=za=kán)*, *nu-u-a*

nūwān see ***nūmān*** „not yet“

pahš- „to guard, protect, observe“; *pa-ah-ha-aš-hi* 1.sg.pres.act.; *pa-ah-ha-aš-ti* 2.sg.pres.act.; *pa-ah-ha-aš-te-ni* 2.pl. pres.act.; *pa-ah-ha-aš-ha* 1.sg.pres.med.; *pa-ah-ha-aš-ta*[1] 2.sg.pres.med.; *pa-ah-ha-aš-du-ma* 2.pl.pres.med.; *pa-ah-ha-aš-ta*[2] 3.sg.pret.med.; *pa-ah-ši* 2.sg. imp.act.; *pa-ah-ha-aš-tin* 2.pl.imp.act.; *pa-ah-ša-an-da-ru* 3.pl.imp.act.; *pa-ah-ša-ru* 3.sg.imp.med.; *pa-ah-ha-aš-du-ma-at* 2.pl.imp.med.

pahšnu- „to offer protection, protect“; *pa-ah-ha-aš-nu-ut* 2.sg.pret.act.; *pa-ah-ha-ša-nu-ir* 3.pl.pret.act.; *pa-ah-ha-aš-nu-ut-te-en* 2.pl.imp.act.

pahhuenant- c. „fire“; *pa-ah-hu-e-na-an-za* nom.sg.

pahhur n. „fire“; *pa-ah-hur* nom.-acc.sg.; *pa-ah-hu-u-e-na-aš-š(=a)* gen.sg.; *pa-ah-hu-e-ni* dat.-loc.sg.; *pa-ah-hu-e-na-az* abl.

^{LÚ}***pahhurši-*** c. „bastard, illegal child“; ^{LÚ}*pa-ah-hur-ši-in(=pát)* acc.sg.; $^{\text{LÚ.MEŠ}}$*pa-ah-hur-ši-iš(=ta)* nom.pl.

pāi- „to go, walk“; *pa-i-mi* 1.sg.pres.act.; *pa-a-i-ši*, *pa-it-ti*[1] 2.sg.pres.act.; *pa-iz-zi(=ma=aš)* 3.sg.pres.act.; *pa-i-u-wa-ni*, *pa-i-u-e-ni*, *pa-i-wa-ni (=wa)* 1.pl.pres.act.; *pa-a-an-zi* 3.pl.pres.act.; *pa-a-un* 1.sg.pret.act.; *pa-it*, *pa-a-it*, *pa-a-i-t(=a/=aš)* 3.sg. pret.act.; *pa-a-ir* 3.pl.pret.act.; *pa-id-du* 3.sg.imp.act.; *pa-it-tin* 2.pl.imp.act.; *pa-a-an-du (=wa=za)* 3.pl. imp.act.

pāi-/pe- „to give“; *pí-ih-hi* 1.sg.pres.act.; *pa-it-ti*[2], *pí-eš-ti* 2.sg.pres.act.; *pa-a-i* 3.sg.pres.act.; *pí-ú-e-ni* 1.pl.pres.act.; *pí-eš-te-ni* 2.pl.pres.act.; *pí-an-zi*, *pí-ya-an-zi(=pát)* 3.pl.pres.act.; *pí-ih-hu-un* 1.sg.pret.act.; *pa-it-ta*, *pí-eš-ta*[1] 2.sg.pret.act.; *pa-iš*, *pa-iš-ta*, *pí-eš-ta*[1], *pí-e-eš-ta* 3.sg.pret.act.; *pí-i-e-ir* 3.pl.pret.act.; *pí-an-du* 3.pl.imp.act.; *pí-ya-an-te-eš* part. nom. pl.c.; *pí-eš-ki-mi* iter. 1.sg.pres.act.; *pí-eš-ki-iz-zi*, *pí-iš-ki-iz-zi* iter. 3.sg. pres.act.; *pí-iš-ga-u-e-ni* iter. 1.pl.pres.act.; *pí-eš-ki-it* iter. 3.sg.pret.act.; *pí-eš-kir* iter. 3.pl.pret.act.; *pí-iš-ki-el-lu* iter. 1.sg.imp.act.

^{DUG}***palha-*** c. „cauldron“; ^{DUG}*pal-ha-an* acc.sg.

palhašti- c. „width“; *pal-ha-aš-ti-iš(=ma=ši)* nom.sg.

palša- c. „times, (multiplied) by“; *pal-ši* dat.-loc.sg.

pangarit „with great force, with great power, with great number“; *pa-an-ga-ri-it*

pangariya- „to get out of hand, increase uncontrollably“; *pa-an-ga-ri-ya-at-ta-ti* 3.sg.pret.med.

panku- „all, whole; the entirety, the whole; *panku*“; *pa-an-ku-uš* nom.sg.c.; *pa-an-ga-u-wa-aš* gen.sg.; *pa-an-ga-u-i* dat.-loc.sg.

pa(n)dalaz see ***kit pa(n)dalaz*** „from now on“

panzakiti- c. „whorl“; *pa-an-za-ki-it-ti-iš* nom.sg.

paprātar n. „impurity, stain“; *pa-ap-ra-tar* nom.-acc.sg.; *pa-ap-ra-an-na-za* abl.

papreš- „to be/become impure“; *pa-ap-ri-iš-te-ni(=ma)* 2.pl.pres.act.

parā „forward, in front“; *pa-ra-a(=an=kán/=ma=wa/=ma=za=kán/=wa/*

=war=an=kán)

parranda „over, across; beyond it, past it, in addition"; *pár-ra-an-ta*

parn° see ***pir-/parna-*** „house"

parh- „to rush, chase, chase away; to attack"; *pár-ah-zi* 3.sg.pres.act.; *pár-ah-ta* 3.sg.pret.act.; *pár-hi-ir* 3.pl.pret.act.

parkiya- „to raise, grow; to remove; to flatter"; *pár-ki-ya-at-ta-at* 2.sg.pret. med.; *pár-ki-i-ya-ta-at* 3.sg.pret.med.; *pár-ki-iš-kat-ta-ri* iter. 3.sg.pret. med.

pargašti- c. „height"; *pár-qa-aš-ti* uninflected

parku- „high; noun: top, peak"; *pár-ga-u-wa-aš* dat.-loc.pl.

parkueš- „to become clean, clean oneself"; *pár-ku-eš-te-ni* 2.pl.pres.act.; *pár-ku-eš-du* 3.sg.imp.act.

parkui- „pure, clean"; *pár-ku-iš* nom.sg.c.; *pár-ku-i*[1] nom.-acc.sg.n.; *pár-ku-wa-iš* nom.pl.c.; *pár-ku-wa-ya*, *pár-ku-i*[2] nom.-acc.pl.n.

parkunu- „to clean, clean up, settle"; *pár-ku-nu-um-mi* 1.sg.pres.act.; *pár-ku-nu-ši(=ma=za)* 2.sg.pres.act.

parnawāi- „to extend"; *pár-na-wa-iš-ki-it* 3.sg.pret.act.

1. ***parš-*** „to flee, escape"; *pár-aš-ta* 3.sg.pret.act.

2. ***parš-*** „to crumble, break (bread) "; *pár-ši-ya* 3.sg.pres.act.; *pár-ši-ya-an-zi* 3.pl.pres.act.; *pár-ši-ya-nu-un* 1.sg.pret.act.; *pár-ši-at* 3.sg.pret.act.; *pár-ši-ya-ad-da-ru* 3.pl.imp.med.

paršiyannāi- „to crumble"; *pár-ši-ya-an-na-ah-hi* 1.sg.pret.act.; *pár-ši-ya-an-ni-iš-ki-it* iter. 3.sg.pret.act.

paršina- c. „cheek"; *pár-še-nu-š(=uš)* acc.pl.

partauwar n. „wing"; *pár-ta-u-wa-ar* nom.-acc.sg.

partianza- noun of unknown meaning; *pár-ti-an-za*

parzašša- adjective of unknown meaning; *pár-za-aš-ša*

paš- „to swallow"; *pa-aš-ta* 2.sg.pret.act.

paškuwāi- „to neglect, ignore, forget"; *pa-aš-ku-i-it-ta* 2.sg.pres.med.

-pat enclitic particle to emphasize words

pata- c. „foot"; *pa-ta-a-an-n(=a)* gen.pl.

pattar n. „wing"; *pát-tar* nom.-acc.sg.

LÚ***patili-*** c. a priest; LÚ*pa-a-ti-li-iš* nom.sg.

pe prefix „here, up, along, on"; *pí-e*

pehute- „to take there"; *pí-e-hu-te-iz-zi* 3.sg.pres.act.; *pí-e-hu-da-an-zi* 3.pl. pres.act.; *pí-e-hu-te-nu-un* 1.sg. pret.act.; *pí-e-hu-te-it*, *pí-hu-te-it* 3.sg. pret.act.; *pí-e-hu-te-it-te-en*[1] 2.pl.pret.act.; *pí-hu-te-ir*, *pí-e-hu-te-ir* 3.pl. pret.act.; *pí-e-hu-te-it-te-en*[2] 2.pl. imp.act.

penna- „to drive, go (by); to make trot"; *pí-en-na-i* 3.sg.pres.act.; *pí-en-ni-iš-ta* 3.sg.pret.act.

^{NA4}***peru(n)-*** n./c. „rock"; ^{NA4}*pí-e-ru* nom.-acc.sg.n.; ^{NA4}*pí-ru-ni* dat.-loc.

peššiya- „to throw; to dismiss, reject, abolish"; *pí-eš-ši-iz-zi* 3.sg.pres.act.; *pí-eš-ši-ya-nu-un* 1.sg.pret.act.; *pí-eš-ši-it* 3.sg.pret.act.; *pí-eš-ši-ya-an-du* 3.pl.imp.act.

peda- „to take there, carry over"; *pí-da-at-ti* 2.sg.pres.act.; *pí-e-da-i*, *pí-e-da-a-i*, *pí-it-ta-iz-zi*, *píd-da-a-iz-zi* 3.sg.pres.act.; *pí-e-da-an-zi*, *pí-e-tah-hu-un* 1.sg.pret.act.; *pí-e-da-aš*[1] 3.sg.pret.act.; *pí-e-du-me-en* 1.pl. pret.act.; *pí-e-da-ú*, *pí-e-da-a-ú* 3.sg.imp.act.; *píd-da-a-an-du* 3.pl. imp.act.; *pí-e-da-eš-kir* iter. 3.pl.pret.act.; *píd-da-iš-ki-it-tin* iter. 2.pl. imp.act.

peda(n)- n. „place"; *pí-e-da-aš*[2] gen.sg.; *pí-e-da-an* loc.sg.; *pí-di*, *pí-di-i(=ši=ma/=šmi=pát)*, *pí-e-di (=ši=ma)* dat.-loc.sg.

pedant- c. „place"; *pí-e-ta-an-ti* voc.sg.

pian see ***piran*** „in front, before"

pihašašši- „belonging to the thunderstorm, thunder"; *pí-ha-aš-ša-aš-ši* dat.-loc.sg.c.

piyannāi- „to give someone present"; *pí-ya-na-it* 3.sg.pret.act.

pininu- „to make remove, make get rid of"; *pí-ni-nu-nu-un* 1.sg.pret.act.

pir-/parna- n. „house"; *pár-na*, *pár-na-a(=ša)* dir.

pirammit, ***pirašmit*** see ***piran*** „in front" + ***-mit***, ***-šmit***

piran „in front, before"; *pí-ra-an(=šet/=ti/=tit)*; *pí-e-ra-am-mi-it = piran + -mit*; *pí-ra-aš-mi-it = piran + -šmit*; *pí-an*

piddai- „to run"; *píd-da-an-zi* 3.pl.pres.act.

pidi see ***peda(n)-*** „place"

pittenu- „to take away, remove; to abduct"; *pít-te-nu-zi*, *pít-te-nu-uz-zi* 3.sg. pres.act.; *pít-te-nu-ut* 3.sg.pret.act.

pitteyauwar n. „the going"; *pít-te-ya-u-wa-ar* nom.-acc.sg.

pittuliya- c. „worry, misery"; *pít-tu-li-ya-an* acc.sg.; *pít-tu-li-ya-aš* gen.sg.

(GU4) ***puhugari***- c. „substitute ox, expiatory sacrifice of a bull or ox"; *pu-u-hu-ga-ri-in* acc.sg.; *pu-u-hu-ga-ri* dat.-loc.sg.

puggant- „hated, destested; causing a nuisance"; *pu-ug-ga-an-za* nom.sg.c.

pūl- n. „lot"; *pu-u-ul* nom.-acc.sg.

puntarriyalli- „stubborn, obstinate, headstrong"; *pu-un-tar-ri-ya-li-iš* nom. sg.c.

punuš- „to ask, question, examine, discover, determine"; *pu-nu-uš-mi* 1.sg. pres.act.; *pu-nu-uš-šu-e-ni(=ma)* 1.pl.pres.act.; *pu-u-nu-uš-ta* 3.sg. pret. act.; *pu-nu-uš-du* 3.sg.imp.act.; *pu-nu-uš-ki-iz-zi* iter. 3.sg.pres.act.; *pu-nu-uš-ki-wa-an* iter. supinum

puriyalli- n. „bit, muzzle"; *pu-ri-ya-al-li* nom.-acc.sg.

šah- „to pollute, make dirty; to sprinkle"; *ša-ha-a-ri* 3.sg.pres.med.

šahhan- n. „fief; fief service, tribute, tax"; *ša-ah-ha-an*, *ša-ah-ha-n(=a)* nom.-acc.sg.; *ša-ah-ha-na-za* abl.

šāi-/šiya- „to press; iter. to shoot, seal; med. to run, flow"; *ši-ya-an* part. nom.-acc.sg.n.; *ši-i-e-eš-ki* iter. 2.sg.imp.act.; *ši-eš-kán-zi* iter. 3.pl. pres.act.; *ši-ya-eš-ki-it* iter. 3.sg.pret.act.

šak- „to know; to discover, find out, notice"; *ša-ag-ga-ah-hi* 1.sg.pres.act.; *ša-ak-ti*, *ša-a-ak-ti* 2.sg.pres.act.; *ša-ak-ki* 3.sg.pres.act.; *še-ik-ku-e-ni* 1.pl.pres.act.; *še-ik-te-ni* 2.pl.pres.act.; *še-ik-kán-zi* 3.pl.pres.act.; *ša-qa-ah-hu-u-un*, *ša-aq-qa-ah-hu-un* 1.sg.pret.act.; *ša-a-ak-ta* 2.sg.pret.act.; *ša-ak-ta* 3.sg.pret.act.; *ša-a-ak*, *ša-ki* 2.sg.imp.act.

šagāi- c. „omen"; *ša-ga-iš*, *ša-ga-i-iš* nom.sg.

šakkar n. „excrement, faeces"; *ša-kán-da* instr.

šakinu- „to understand (?)"; *ša-ki-nu-un* 1.sg.pret.act.

šakni- c. „oil, fat"; *ša-ak-ni-ya(=an=kán)* dat.-loc.sg.

šakruwāi- „to rub off"; *ša-ak-ru-wa-an-zi-i(=aš)* 3.pl.pres.act.

šaktāi- „to nurse back to health"; *ša-a-ak-ta-a-iz-zi* 3.sg.pres.act.

šakunni- c. „well"; *ša-ku-ni-ya-aš-š(=a)* gen.sg.

šakuwa- n. „eye"; *ša-a-ku-wa*, *ša-ku-wa(=ya)* nom.-acc.pl.n.

šakuwāi- „to see"; *ša-ku-wa-it* 3.sg.pret.act.; *ša-ku-iš-ki-iz-zi* iter. 3.sg. pres.act.

šakuwaššar- „right, sincere"; *ša-ku-wa-aš-ša-ra-an* acc.sg.c.; *ša-ku-wa-aš-ša-ri-it* instr.; *ša-ku-wa-šar-ru-uš* acc.pl.c.

šallanu- „to raise, bring up"; *šal-la-nu-nu-un(=war=an)* 1.sg.pret.act.; *ša-al-la-nu-uš* 2.sg.pret.act.; *šal-la-nu-ma-an-zi* inf. I; *ša-al-la-nu-uš-kat* iter. 3.sg.pret.act.; *ša-al-la-nu-uš-kir* iter. 3.pl.pret.act.

LÚ***šālašha-*** c. „palace servant"; LÚ*ša-la-aš-hi* dat.-loc.sg.; LÚ.MEŠ*ša-a-la-aš-ha-aš* gen.pl.

šalli- „big, great"; *šal-la-i* dat.-loc.sg.; *šal-li* nom.-acc.pl.n.; *šal-la-ya-aš* gen.pl.

šalliya- „to melt (away), dissolve"; *šal-li-it-ta-ru* 3.sg.imp.med.

šalik- „to come near; to commit an outrage; to shoot"; *ša-li-ik-ti* 2.sg. pres.med.; *ša-li-ik-tu-ma-ri* 2.pl.pres.med.

šamankurwant- „bearded"; *ša-ma-an-ku-úr-wa-du-uš(=kán)* acc.pl.c.

šamen- „to step back, withdraw, resign, renounce, refrain"; *ša-me-en-zi* 3.sg. pres.act.

šamnāi- „to create, bring up, raise"; *ša-am-na-a-eš* 2.sg.pret.act.; *ša-am-na-it* 3.sg.pret.act.

-šan enclitic particle

šanna- „to hide, withhold, keep (secret) "; *ša-an-na-at-ti* 2.sg.pres.act.; *ša-an-na-a-i* 3.sg.pres.act.; *ša-a-na-at-te-e-ni(=ma)* 2.pl. pres.act.

šannapili- „empty; not pregnant"; *ša-an-na-pí-li-iš* nom.sg.c.

šanezzi- „sweet, pleasant"; *ša-ni-iz-zi-ya-az* abl.; *ša-ni-iz-zi-uš* acc.pl.c.; *ša-ne-iz-zi* nom.-acc.pl.n.

1\. ***šanh-*** „to search, look for; to demand; to try"; *ša-an-ha-an-zi*[1] 3.pl.pres. act.; *ša-an-ah-ta*[1] 2.sg.pret.act.; *ša-an-ah-ta*[2] 3.sg.pret.act.; *ša-an-hi-ir* 3.pl.pret.act.; *ša-a-ah* 2.sg.imp.act.; *ša-an-ha-an-du*[1] 3.pl.imp.act.; *ša-an-hi-iš-ki-iz-zi* iter. 3.sg.pres.act.; *ša-an-hi-iš-ki-u-e-ni* iter. 1.pl.pres. act.; *ša-an-hi-eš-kán-zi* iter. 3.pl.pres.act.

2\. ***šanh-*** „to wipe, sweep"; *ša-an-ha-an-zi*[2] 3.pl.pres.act.; *ša-a-ah-te-en* 2.pl. imp.act.; *ša-an-ha-an-du*[2] 3.pl. imp.act.

šani- „one and the same"; *ša-ni-ya* dat.-loc.sg.

LÚ***šapašalli-*** „scout, spy"; LÚ.MEŠ*ša-pa-ša-al-li-e-eš* nom.pl.

šarā „up, upwards"; *ša-ra-a(=kán/=mu)*

šarra- „to divide, split up, break; to exceed, overstep; to violate, break (an oath, a commandment)"; *šar-ra-at-ti* 2.sg.pres.act.; *šar-ri-iz-zi* 3.sg.

pres.act.; *šar-ra-u-e-ni* 1.pl.pres.act.; *šar-ri-it* 3.sg.pret.act.; *šar-ri-i-e-ir*, *šar-ri-ir* 3.pl.pret.act.; *šar-ra-ah-ha-at* 1.sg.pret.med.; *šar-ra-at-ta*, *šar-ra-ad-da* 3.sg.pret.med.; *šar-ra-an-da-at* 3.pl. pret.med.; *šar-ra-at-tu-ma* 2.pl.imp.med.; *šar-ra-an-na* inf. II

šarašši- adjective of unknown meaning; *šar-ra-aš-ši-ya-aš* gen.sg.c.(?)

šarazzi- „the upper, higher, superior"; *ša-ra-az-zi-ya-az* abl.

šarazziya- „to make someone superior, let someone win"; *ša-ra-a-az-zi-ya-ah-ta* 3.sg.pret.act.

šarkaliya- „to be arrogant, feel superior"; *šar-ka-li-ya-tu-ma-ri* 2.pl. imp.med.

šarku- „mighty, powerful"; *šar-ku-uš* nom.sg.c.

šarkuwāi- „to put on shoes"; *šar-ku-it* 3.sg.pret.act.

šarkuwant- „in boots"; *šar-ku-wa-an-za* nom.sg.c.

šarlaimmi- „elevated, sublime, superior"; *šar-la-im-mi-in* acc.sg.c.

šarnikzēl n. „penance, atonement"; *šar-ni-ik-zi-el*, *šar-ni-ik-zi-il* nom.-acc.sg.n.

šarni(n)k- „to atone, do penance"; *šar-ni-ik-mi* 1.sg.pres.act.; *šar-ni-in-kán-zi* 3.pl.pres.act.; *šar-ni-ik-ta* 3.sg.pret.act.; *šar-ni-ik-du(=wa)* 3.sg. imp.act.

^{KUŠ}***šarpašši-*** c. „pillow"; ^{KUŠ}*šar-pa-aš-ši-š(=a=kán)* nom.-acc.sg.

šardiya- c. „helper, supporter"; *šar-di-ya-aš* nom.sg.

šašanna- c. „lamp"; *ša-ša-an-na-aš* acc.pl.(!)

šašta- c. „bed"; *ša-aš-ta-aš-š(=an)* dat.-loc.pl.

šaušiyar n. „anger, rage"; *ša-ú-ši-ya-ar* nom.-acc.sg.

šāuwar n. „resentment, anger"; *ša-a-u-ar*, *ša-a-u-wa-ar* nom.-acc.sg.

šawātar n. „horn (musical instrument) "; *ša-wa-tar* nom.-acc.sg.

šehurešk- „to piss"; *še-hur-ri-eš-ki-id-du* iter. 3.sg.imp.act.

šena- c. „figure, model"; *še-na-aš* nom.pl.

šēr „at the top; because of"; *še-ir*, *še-e-r(=a=šan)*

šeš- „to sleep"; *še-eš-mi* 1.sg.pres.act.; *še-eš-zi* 3.sg.pres.act.; *še-eš-ki-it* 3.sg.pret.act.

šešariya- „to filter"; *še-ša-ri-iš-ki-tin* iter. 2.pl.imp.act.

^{GIŠ}***šešarul-*** n. „sieve"; ^{GIŠ}*še-ša-ru-li-it* instr.

1. ***-ši*** „him, her"

2. ***-ši-*** „his“; *-šiš* nom.sg.c.; *-šit*, *-šet* nom.-acc.sg.n.; *-šaš* gen.sg.; *-ši* dat.-loc.sg.; *-ša* dir.

$^{\text{(É)}}$***šinapši-*** n. a ritual building; ^{É}*ši-na-ap-ši* uninflected; *ši-na-ap-ši-ya-aš* gen.sg.

šipand- „to offer, libate“; *ši-pa-an-ta-ah-hi* 1.sg.pres.act.; *ši-pa-an-ti* 3.sg.pres.act.; *ši-pa-an-da-an-zi*, *ši-ip-pa-an-da-an-zi* 3.pl.pres.act.; *ši-pa-an-tu-u-wa-an-zi* inf. I; *ši-pa-an-za-kán-zi* iter. 3.pl.pres.act.

šišdu see ***māu šišdu*** „may prosper“

šiuna- c. „god“; *ši-ú-na-aš* gen.sg.; *ši-i-ú-ni(=mi)* voc.sg.; *ši-ú-na-an* gen.pl.

šiuniyahh- „to be smitten with illness by god“; *ši-ú-ni-ya-ah-ha-ti* 3.sg.pret.med.

1. ***-šmaš*** „her“

2. ***-šmaš*** „you (2.p.pl.) “

3. ***-šmaš*** „their“

1. ***-šmi-*** „your (2.p.pl.) “; *-šmet*^{1} nom.-acc.sg.n.; *-šmi*^{1} dat.-loc.sg.; *-šmiš*^{1} nom.pl.c.

2. ***-šmi-*** „you, their“; *-šmet*^{2}, *-šmit* nom.-acc.sg.n.; *-šmi*^{2} dat.-loc.sg.; *-šma* dir.; *-šmiš*^{2} nom.pl.c.

šu „and; sentence introductory particle“; *šu(=uš/=wa)*; *ša-an = šu + -an*; *ša-aš = šu + -aš*; *še(=a) = šu + -e*

šuēl- n. „thread“; *šu-ú-il* nom.-acc.sg.

šuhha- c. „roof“; *šu-uh-hi* dat.-loc.sg.; *šu-uh-ha-az* abl.

šuhha- „to pour, tip“; *šu-uh-ha-ir* 3.pl.pret.act.

šullāi-/šulliya- „to quarrel, look for quarrel“; *šu-ul-li-ya-at(=wa=mu=kán)* 2.sg.pret.act.; *šu-ul-li-it*, *šu-u-ul-li-it*, *šu-u-ul-li-e-it* 3.sg.pret.act.; *šu-ul-li-it-te-en* 2.pl.pret.act.

šummanza(n)- c. „rope, cord“; *šu-um-ma-an-za* nom.sg.; *šum-ma-an-za-na-an* acc.sg.

šumēl, ***šumenzan*** see ***šumēš*** „you“

šumēš „you (pl.) “; *šu-me-š(=a/=an)*, *šu-me-eš-š(=a=wa=za/=an/=ma/=pát)* nom.; *šu-ma-aš*, *šu-ma-aš-š(=a)*, *šu-ma-a-aš*, *šu-ma-a-š(=a)* dat./acc.; *šu-me-el* poss. gen.sg.; *šu-me-en-za-an(=wa)* poss. gen.pl.

šunna- „to fill“; *šu-un-na-i* 3.sg.pres.act.; *šu-un-na-ah-hu-un* 1.sg.pret.act.; *šu-un-na-aš*, *šu-un-ni-iš-ta* 3.sg.pret.act.

šuniya- „to dip into“; *šu-ú-ni-at* 3.sg.pret.act.

šuppariya- „to sleep“; *šu-up-pa-ri-ya-an-za* part. nom.sg.c.

šuppi- „(ritually) clean, pure; noun n. sacrificial meat“; *šu-up-pa* nom.-acc.sg.n.; *šu-up-pa-ya-aš* gen.sg.; *šu-up-pa-az*, *šu-up-pa-ya-az* abl.

šuppišduwara- c. „application, decoration, ornament“; *šu-up-pí-iš-du-wa-ri-it* instr.; *šu-up-pí-iš-du-wa-ri-i-e-eš(=ma=kán)* nom.pl.c.

^{MUŠEN}***šuraššura***- c. an oracle bird; ^{MUŠEN}*šu-ra-aš-šu-ra-aš* nom.sg.

šūwa- „to swell up“; *šu-ut-ta-ti* 3.sg.pret.med.

šūwāi- „to push; to drive out, edge out“; *šu-ú-e-it* 3.sg.pret.act.

-ta „you, to you (sg.) “

ta „and (sentence introductory particle)“; *ta(=an/=ašta)*, *ta-a*; *tu-uš* = *ta* + *-uš*

dā- „to take“; *da-ah-hi* 1.sg.pres.act.; *da-a-at-ti* 2.sg.pres.act.; *da-a-i*[1] 3.sg. pres.act.; *da-at-te-ni* 2.pl. pres.act.; *da-an-zi*, *da-a-an-zi*, *ta-an-zi* 3.pl. pres.act.; *da-at-ta-ri* 3.sg.pres.med.; *da-ah-hu-un*, *da-a-ah-hu-un* 1.sg. pret.act.; *da-at-ta*[1] 2.sg.pret.act.; *da-at-ta*[2], *da-a-aš* 3.sg.pret.act.; *da-a-ir*[1] 3.pl.pret.act.; *da-at-tin(=ma=ši=kán)* 2.pl.imp.act.; *da-a* 2.sg. imp. act.; *da-ad-du* 3.sg.imp.act.; *da-an-du* 3.pl.imp.act.; *da-a-an* part. nom.-acc.sg.n.; *da-an-te-eš* part. nom.pl.c.; *da-aš-ki-mi* iter. 1.sg.pres. act.; *da-aš-ki-ši* iter. 2.sg. pres.act.; *da-aš-kán-zi* iter. 3.pl.pres.act.; *da-aš-ki-ir-r(=a)* iter. 3.pl.pret.act.

dāi-/tiya- „to set, put, lay“; *te-ih-hi* 1.sg.pres.act.; *da-it-ti* 2.sg.pres.act.; *da-a-i*[2] 3.sg.pres.act.; *ti-ya-u-e-ni* 1.pl. pres.act.; *ti-an-zi*, *ti-ya-an-zi* 3.pl. pres.act.; *te-ih-hu-un* 1.sg.pret.act.; *da-iš-ta* 2.sg. pret.act.; *da-iš*, *da-a-iš*, *da-i-iš(=šan)* 3.sg.pret.act.; *da-i-ú-en* 1.pl.pret.act.; *da-a-ir*[2], *da-i-ir* 3.pl.pret.act.; *da-i* 2.sg.imp.act.; *ti-ya-an-du* 3.pl.imp.act.; *ti-iš-ki-it* iter. 3.sg.pret.act.

dāya- „to steal, abduct“; *da-a-i-iz-zi*, *ta-a-i-iz-zi*, *da-i-ya-zi* 3.sg.pres.act.

dayazil- n. „theft“; *da-i-ya-zi-la-aš* gen.sg.

dāyalla- adjective of unknown meaning; *da-a-ya-al-la* nom.-acc.pl.n.

daganzipa- c. „earth, genius of earth“; *da-ga-an-zi-pa-aš* nom.sg.; *ta-ga-an-zi-pa-an* acc.sg.; *ta-ka-an-zi-pí* dat.-loc.sg.

takš- „to join together; to cause someone something“; *tág-ga-aš-ši*, *ták-ki-iz-zi, ták-ki-eš-zi* 3.sg.pres.act.; *ták-ki-iš-ta* 3.sg.pret.act.; *ták-ša-an-za* part. nom.sg.c.; *ták-ša-an-ta* part. nom.-acc.pl.n.

takšan- n. „half; half part"; *ták-ša-an* nom.-acc.sg.

takšul- n. „contract, treaty, peace, peace treaty"; *ták-šu-li(=šit)* dat.-loc.sg.

takšulāi- „to make a contract, sign a treaty, make peace"; *ták-šu-la-u-e-ni* 1.sg.pres.act.; *ták-šu-la-a-ir* 3.pl.pret.act.

takku „if"; *ták-ku(=an/=aš/=wa=kán)*

dāla- „to let, let be, let down"; *da-li-ya-at* 2.sg.pret.act.; *da-a-li-ya-at* 3.sg. pret.act.; *da-a-la* 2.sg.imp.act.

^{GIŠ}***tallāi-*** n. „flask, small bottle"; ^{GIŠ}*tal-la-i* nom.-acc.sg.; ^{GIŠ}*tal-la-ya-aš* gen.sg.

talliya- „to call, implore"; *tal-li-ya-zi* 3.sg.pres.act.; *tal-li-ya-u-wa-aš* verbal noun gen.sg.

daluki- „long"; *da-a-lu-ga-u-wa-aš* dat.-loc.pl.

damāi- „another, second"; *ta-ma-iš(=ma=wa=kán)* nom.sg.c.; *da-ma-a-in, ta-ma-in, ta-ma-i-in, ta-me-a-in* acc.sg.c.; *da-ma-a-i, ta-ma-i(=za), ta-ma-a-i(=ma)* nom.-acc.sg.n.; *da-me-e-el, ta-me-el* gen.sg.; *da-me-e-da-ni, ta-me-e-da-ni, ta-mi-e-ta-ni* dat.-loc.sg.; *da-ma-a-e-eš* nom.pl.c.; *da-ma-uš* acc.pl.c.

damaš- „to attack, pester, force"; *ta-ma-aš-mi* 1.sg.pres.act.; *ta-ma-aš-ta*[1], *ta-ma-a-aš-ta* 3.sg.pres.med.; *da-ma-aš-šu-un* 1.sg.pret.act.; *ta-ma-aš-ta*[2] 3.sg.pret.act.; *dam-mi-iš-šar, ta-me-eš-šir* 3.pl.pret.act.; *da-ma-aš-ša-an, ta-ma-aš-ša-an* part. nom.-acc.sg.n.

damešha- c. „damage, destruction"; *dam-mi-iš-ha-an-n(=a=šmaš)* acc.sg.

damešha adv. „forcibly, by force"; *dam-mi-eš-ha*

damešhāi- „to damage, do harm, oppress forcibly"; *dam-mi-iš-ha-iz-zi* 3.sg. pres.act.; *dam-me-iš-hi-iš-ki-iz-zi* Iter. 3.sg.pres.act.

tameuman- n. „foreign rule (?)"; *ta-me-u-ma-an* nom.-acc.sg.

dān „second, twice, double, for the second time"; *ta-a-an*; *da-an(=ma=ta)*

dannatta- „empty, uninhabited"; *dan-na-at-ta* nom.-acc.pl.n.

dannateššant- „empty, cleared, vacated"; *dan-na-ti-eš-ša-an-te-eš* nom.pl.c.

dankui- „dark"; *da-an-ku-i-iš* nom.sg.c.; *da-an-ku-in-n(=apa)* acc.sg.c.; *da-an-ku-i* nom.-acc.sg.n.; *da-an-ku-wa-i* dat.-loc.sg.

dandukeššar n. „mankind"; *da-an-du-ki-iš-na-š(=a)* gen.sg.

Tabarna- c. „Tabarna" (royal title); *Ta-ba-ar-na-aš* nom.sg.

tapašša- c. „fever"; *ta-pa-aš-ša-an* acc.sg.

dapiya- „entire, whole, all"; *da-pí-uš* acc.pl.c.

^{MUNUS}***taptara***- c. „wailing woman"; $^{\text{MUNUS.MEŠ}}$*tap-da-ra-aš* nom.pl.

tapuš- n. „side"; *ta-pu-ša*, *ta-pu-ú-ša* dir.

tar-/te- „to say"; *te-e-mi* 1.sg.pres.act.; *te-e-ši* 2.sg.pres.act.; *te-iz-zi(=ma)* 3.sg.pres.act.; *ta-ru-e-ni* 1.pl. pres.act.; *da-ra-an-zi* 3.pl.pres.act.; *te-e-it*, *ti-e-it* 3.sg.pret.act.; *te-it-te-en* 2.pl.imp.act.; *tar-ši-ki-mi* iter. 1.sg. pres.act.

tarh- „to defeat, overcome; to cope with, be able to"; *tar-ah-mi* 1.sg.pres. act.; *tar-hu-uz-zi* 3.sg.pres.act.; *tar-ru-uh-ha-an-zi* 3.pl.pres.act.; *tar-ah-hu-un*, *ta-ru-uh-hu-un* 1.sg.pret.act.; *tar-ah-ta(=an=za=an)* 3.sg.pret. act.; *tar-hu-ir* 3.pl.pret.act.; *tar-ah-ha-an* part. nom.-acc.sg.n.; *tar-ah-hi-iš-ki-nu-un* iter. 1.sg.pret.act.

tarhuili- „strong, mighty, powerful"; *tar-hu-i-li-in* acc.sg.c.

tarriya- „to try hard, endeavour"; *da-a-ri-ya-u-en* 1.sg.pret.act.

tarkummāi- „to announce, report"; *tar-kum-mi-ya-nu-un* 1.sg.pret.act.

tarkuwa- „angry"; *tar-ku-wa* nom.-acc.sg.n.

tarkuwalāi- „to give someone a black look"; *tar-ku-wa-al-li-iš-ki-nu-un* iter. 1.sg.pret.act.

tarmāi- „to attach, fix"; *tar-ma-a-mi*, *tar-ma-e-mi* 1.sg.pres.act.; *tar-ma-a-an-te-eš* part. nom.pl.c.; *tar-ma-i-iš-ki-mi* iter. 1.sg.pres.act.

tarna- „to send, dispatch; to leave; to remit, forgive"; *tar-na-ah-hi* 1.sg. pres.act.; *tar-na-at-ti* 2.sg.pres.act.; *tar-na-i* 3.sg.pres.act.; *tar-na-an-zi* 3.pl.pres.act.; *tar-na-ah-hu-un* 1.sg.pret.act.; *tar-na-aš* 3.sg.pret.act.; *tar-na-at-tin*[1] 2.pl.pret.act.; *tar-ni-ir* 3.pl.pret.act.; *tar-na* 2.sg.imp.act.; *tar-na-at-tin*[2] 2.pl.imp.act.; *tar-na-an-za* part. nom.sg. c.; *tar-na-an* part.nom.-acc.sg.n.; *tar-nu-wa-aš* verbal noun gen.; *tar-nu-mar* verbal noun

tarupp- „to gather, combine, unite"; *ta-ru-up-pí-ir* 3.pl.pret.act.; *ta-ru-up-pa-an-za* part. nom.sg.c.

daššu- „heavy"; *da-aš-šu-uš*, *da-aš-šu-š(=a=ši)* nom.sg.c.; *da-aš-ša-u-uš* acc.pl.c.

dašwant- „blind"; *ta-aš-wa-an-za* nom.sg.c.

tekan n. „earth, ground“; *te-kán*^{1}, *te-e-kán*, *te-kán-n(=a)* nom.-acc.sg.; *ták-na-a-aš* gen.sg.; *te-kán*^{2}, *ta-ga-a-an* loc.sg.; *ták-na-az*, *ták-na-a-az* abl.; *ta-ak-na-a* dir.

tekuššāi- „to appear, show“; *te-ik-ku-uš-ki-iz-zi* iter. 3.sg.pres.act.

tēpu- „little, few, small“; *te-pu* nom.-acc.sg.n.; *te-pa-u-wa-az* abl. adv.; *te-e-pa-u-e-eš* nom.pl.c.

tepnu- „to reduce, lessen, diminish“; *te-ip-nu-um-ma-an-zi(=ya)* inf. I

terišk- „to irritate, tease (?)“; *te-ri-iš-kán-zi* 3.pl.pres.act.

^{TÚG}***termaz-*** n. a kind of garment, dress; ^{TÚG}*te-ir-ma-az* nom.-acc.sg.

tešha- c. „dream, sleep“; *te-eš-ha-aš* nom.sg.; *te-eš-ha-az* abl.; *te-eš-hu-uš*, *ti-eš-hu-uš* acc.pl.

tešhanešk- „to appear in a dream“; *te-eš-ha-ni-iš-ki-u-wa-an* supinum

teššummi- c. „cup, goblet“; *te-eš-šum-mi-in* acc.sg.; *te-eš-šu-um-mi-uš-š(=a)* acc.pl.

tethāi- „to thunder“; *ti-it-ha* 3.sg.pres.; *ti-it-hi-iš-ki-it-ta* Iter. 3.sg.pret.act.

tethima- c. „thunderstorm“; *te-it-hi-im-mu-uš* acc.pl.

-ti- „your (sg.)“; *-tan* acc.sg.c.; *-tit* nom.-acc.n.; *-taš* gen.sg.; *-ti* dat.-loc.sg.

tiya- „to step, come here, stand“; *ti-ya-zi*, *ti-ya-az-zi*, *ti-i-e-iz-zi* 3.sg.pres. act.; *ti-en-zi* 3.pl.pres.act.; *ti-ya-at* 3.sg.pret.act.; *ti-i-e-ir* 3.pl. pret.act.; *ti-i-ya* 2.sg.imp.act.

tiššāi- „to form“; *ti-iš-ša-a-it* 3.sg.pret.act.

tittanu- „to put up, erect“; *ti-it-ta-nu-mi* 1.sg.pres.act.; *ti-it-ta-nu-nu-un (=pát)* 1.sg.pret.act.; *ti-it-ta-nu-ut*^{1} 2.sg. pret.act.; *ti-it-ta-nu-ut*^{2} 3.sg. pret.act.; *ti-it-ta-nu-uš-kán-zi* iter. 3.pl.pres.act.

tittiyant- „well-supplied“; *ti-it-ti-ya-an-te-eš* nom.pl.c.

-tu „you“

tuekka- c. „body; personally“; *tu-e-ig-ga-š(=šmaš)* nom.sg.; *tu-e-ig-ga-az (=šet)* abl.

tuēl „your“ (gen. of *zik* „you“ sg.); *tu-el*, *tu-e-el(=wa=kán)*

tuēdaz „from you“ (abl. of *zik* „you“ sg.); *tu-e-da-az*

tuhhāi- „to pant, gasp“; *túh-ha-a-it* 3.sg.pret.act.

tuhhima- c. „panting, gasping“; *túh-hi-ma-an(=ma)* acc.sg.

tuhhui- c. „smoke“; *túh-hu-iš* nom.sg.

tuhš- „to cut off; to finish, stop“; *túh-ša-ri*, *túh-hu-uš-ta* 3.sg.pres.med.;

túh-ša-ru 3.sg.imp.med.

tuk „you (sg.)"; *tu-uk(=ma/=ma=wa/=pát/=wa), tu-uq-q(=aš)*

dugg- „to be important, play a part, matter"; *du-uq-qa-a-ri* 3.sg.pres.med.

tuliya- c. „council meeting"; *tu-li-ya-an* acc.sg.; *tu-li-ya* dir.

tunnakeššar n. „inner chamber"; *tu-un-na-ak-ki-iš-šar* nom.-acc.sg.; *tu-un-na-ki-iš-na (=ma)* dir.; *tu-un-na-ak-ki-eš-na-aš* dat.-loc.pl.

dunnariya- c. a kind of forest; *du-un-na-ri-ya-za* abl.

tuninga- c. a kind of bread; *tu-ni-in-ga-aš* gen.sg.

tuppa- c. „vessel, container"; *tup-pu-uš* acc.

tuppi- n. „clay tablet"; *tup-pí*^{1} nom.-acc.sg.; *tup-pí-aš* gen.sg.; *tup-pí*^{2} loc.sg.

turiya- „to harness"; *tu-u-ri-ya-zi* 3.sg.pres.act.; *tu-u-ri-ya-an* part. nom.-acc.n.; *tu-u-ri-ya-u-wa-aš* verbal noun gen.sg.

dušk- „to be glad"; *tu-uš-ku-un* 1.sg.pret.act.; *du-uš-kat-ta* 3.sg.pret.med.; *du-uš-ki-iš-ki-it-ta* iter. 2.sg. pres.med.; *du-uš-ki-iš-ki* iter. 2.sg.imp.act.

dušgarauwant- „joyful,happy, glad"; *du-uš-ga-ra-u-wa-an-za* nom.sg.c.

duddumar n. „mercy, favour"; *du-ud-du-mar* nom.-acc.sg.

dudduwarant- „paralyzed, stiff"; *du-ud-du-wa-ra-an-za(=kán)* nom.sg.c.

tuwadd- „to have mercy, have pity"; *tu-wa-ad-du* 2.sg.imp.act.

duwarnāi- „to break"; *du-wa-ar-na-ad-da-at* 3.sg.pret.med.; *du-wa-ar-na-a-ú* 3.sg.imp.act.; *du-wa-ar-na-an* part. nom.-acc.sg.n.

tuzzi- c. „army, troops"; *tu-uz-zi-in* acc.sg.; *tu-uz-zi-ya* dat.-loc.sg.

ug(a) „I"; *ú-uk(=ma/=wa), ú-ga(=an/=a=war=uš), ú-uq-qa*

uktūri- „eternal, lasting; (noun) cremation place"; *uk-tu-u-ri* nom.-acc.sg.n.; *uk-tu-u-ri-ya* dat.-loc.sg.; *uk-tu-u-ri-eš* nom.pl.c.

ullazzuwa- noun (?) of unknown meaning; *ú-ul-la-az-zu-wa-aš*

$^{(\text{SÍG})}$***ulihi-*** c. an object from wool; *ú-li-hi-in* acc.sg.

uliliya- „to grow, blossom"; *ú-li-li-iš-ki-id-du-ma-at* 2.pl.pret.med.

ulāi- „to unite, blend"; *ú-li-iš-ta-ma-a-an*

ūnna- „to drive here, travel here"; *u-un-na-at-ti* 2.sg.pres.act.; *u-un-na-i* 3.sg.pres.act.; *u-un-ni-ya-an-zi* 3.pl.pres.act.; *u-un-ni* 2.sg.imp.act.

uni- „that one"; *u-ni* uninflected

unuwāi- „to adorn, decorate oneself"; *ú-nu-wa-an-da-an* part. acc.sg.c.

unuwašha- c. „adornment, decoration, ornamentation"; *ú-nu-wa-aš-ha-za* abl.; *ú-nu-wa-aš-hu-uš* acc.pl.

uppa- „to send here“; *up-pa-ah-hi* 1.sg.pres.act.; *up-pí-eš-ta* 3.sg.pret.act.; *up-pí-ir* 3.pl.pret.act.; *up-pí* 2.sg. imp.act.; *up-pa-ú* 3.sg.imp.act.; *up-pí-iš-kán-zi* iter. 3.pl.pres.act.; *up-pí-iš-ki-u-wa-an* iter. supinum

uppeššar n. „sending, present“; *up-pí-eš-šar*$^{\text{HI.A}}$*(=ma=mu)* nom.-acc.sg.

-uš „them“ (acc.pl.c. to *-aš* „he, she“)

ušš(a)niya- „to sell“; *uš-ša-ni-ya-zi(=ma=at=za)* 3.sg.pres.act.; *uš-ni-ya-at-te-ni* 2.pl.pres.act.

uššarunta- c. „well (?)”; *uš-ša-ru-un-ta-az* abl.

uššiya- „to throw out“; *uš-ši-it-tin* 2.pl.imp.act.

uda- „to bring here“; *ú-da-ah-hi* 1.sg.pres.act.; *ú-da-i*, *ú-da-a-i* 3.sg.pres. act.; *ú-du-um-me-e-ni* 1.pl.pres.act.; *ú-da-an-zi* 3.pl.pres.act.; *ú-da-ah-hu-un*, *ú-tah-hu-un* 1.sg.pret.act.; *ú-da-aš* 3.sg.pret.act.; *ú-da-al-lu* 1.sg. imp.act.; *ú-da-at-tin* 2.pl.imp.act.; *ú-da-an-du* 3.pl.imp.act.; *ú-te-eš-kir* iter. 3.pl.pret.act.

uttar n. „word; matter, affair“; *ut-tar(=šet/=šmet)* nom.-acc.sg.; *ud-da-ni-i* dat.-loc.sg.; *ud-da-an-ta* instr.; *ud-da-a-ar (=met/=met=a/=mu/=ta)*, *ud-da-a-ar-r(=a=met)* nom.-acc.pl.; *ud-da-na-a-aš* gen.pl.

utnant- c. „word“; *ut-ta-na-an-te-eš* nom.pl.

utnē- n. „land“; *ut-ne-e*, *ut-ni-i(=šmet)* nom.-acc.sg.; *ut-ni-ya* dir.

utniyant- c. „population“; *ut-ni-an-da-an*, *ut-ni-ya-an-da-an* gen.pl.

uwa- „to come“; *ú-wa-mi*, *ú-wa-a-mi* 1.sg.pres.act.; *ú-wa-ši* 2.sg.pres.act.; *ú-iz-zi* 3.sg.pres.act.; *ú-wa-an-zi*^{2} 3.sg.pres.act. (see also *auš-* „to see“); *ú-wa-nu-un* 1.sg.pret.act.; *ú-wa-aš* 2.sg.pret.act.; *ú-it*, *ú-wa-it* 3.sg.pret. act.; *ú-e-ir(=ma)* 3.pl.pret.act.; *ú-id-du(=aš)* 3.sg. imp.act.; *ú-wa-at-te-en*, *ú-wa-at-tin*, *ú-it-te-en* 2.pl.imp.act.; *ú-wa-ah-ha-ru* 1.sg. imp.med.; *ú-wa-an-te-eš* part. nom.pl.c.; *ú-iš-ki-it-ta* iter. 3.sg.pres. med.; *ú-e-eš-kán-ta* iter. 3.pl.pret.med.

uwāi- n. „worry“; *ú-wa-a-i* nom.-acc.sg.

uwantiwant(a)- c. „lightning (?)“; *ú-wa-an-ti-wa-an-ta-az* abl.

uwarra see ***warra-*** „help“

uwate- „to bring here“; *ú-wa-te-iz-zi* 3.sg.pres.act.; *ú-wa-te-nu-un* 1.sg.pret. act.; *ú-wa-da-te-e-ni* 2.pl.pres.act.; *ú-wa-te-it* 3.sg.pret.act.; *ú-wa-te* 2.sg.imp.act.; *ú-wa-te-it-tin* 2.pl.imp.act.

uwitar see ***wātar*** „water“

-wa, ***-war*** enclitic particle of direct speech
wahnu- „to turn; to exchange; to distort"; *wa-ah-nu-um-me-e-ni(=wa=kán)* 1.pl.pres.act.; *wa-ah-nu-wa-an-zi* 3.pl.pres.act.; *wa-ah-nu-ši* 2.sg. imp.act.; *wa-ah-nu-uš-ki-nu-un* iter. 1.sg.pret.act.
wahnumar n. „compensation"; *wa-ah-nu-mar* nom.-acc.sg.
wāk- „to bite, bite off"; *wa-a-ki* 3.sg.pres.act.
waggar- „to miss; to almost do something"; *wa-aq-qa-ri* 3.sg.pres.act.; *wa-aq-qa-ri-eš* 3.sg.pret.act.
walla- „to pride oneself on something"; *wa-al-li-iš-kán-zi* iter. 3.pl.pres.act.
walh- „to hit, beat; to attack, invade"; *wa-al-ah-zi*, *wa-la-ah-zi* 3.sg.pres. act.; *wa-al-hu-u-wa-ni* 1.pl.pres.act.; *wa-al-ah-ta* 3.sg.pret.act.; *wa-al-ah-te-en* 2.pl.imp.act.
walhannāi- „to hit, beat"; *wa-al-ha-an-ni-ya-an-zi* 3.pl.pres.act.
walli- c. noun of unknown meaning; *wa-al-li-in* acc.sg.; *wa-al-lu-uš* acc.pl.
walliyātar n. „praise, fame"; *wa-al-li-ya-an-ni* dat.-loc.sg.
wallu- „to praise"; *wa-al-lu-uš-ki-id-du-ma-at(=wa=za)* 2.pl.pret.med.
wappiya- „to bark"; *wa-ap-pí-ya-zi* 3.sg.pres.act.
wappu- c. „river shore"; *wa-ap-pu-wa-aš*[1] gen.sg.; *wa-ap-pu-i*, *wa-ap-pu-ú-i* dat.-loc.sg.; *wa-ap-pu-wa-aš*[2] dat.-loc.pl.
-war see ***-wa***, ***-war*** particle of direct speech
war- „to burn"; *wa-ra-an-da-at* 3.pl.pret.med.
warra- c. „help, aid"; *wa-ar-ri* dat.-loc.sg.; *ú-wa-a-ar-ra* dir.
^{GIŠ}***warašma-*** c. „fire wood"; ^{GIŠ}*wa-ar-aš-ma-an* acc.sg.
warkeš- „to become fat"; *wa-ar-ki-eš-ta* 3.sg.pret.act.
warnu- „to burn, scorch"; *wa-ar-nu-zi* 3.sg.pres.act.; *wa-ar-nu-an-zi*, *wa-ar-nu-wa-an-zi* 3.pl.pres.act.
warp- „to bathe"; *wa-ar-pu-wa-an-zi* inf. I
warš- „to wipe off, slip off; to pluck, harvest"; *wa-ar-aš-tin* 2.pl.imp.act.; *wa-ar-ša-an* part. nom.-acc.sg.n.; *wa-ar-šu-u-wa-an-zi* inf. I
waš- „to buy"; *wa-a-ši* 3.sg.pres.act.; *wa-a-ši-ya-at-te-ni* 2.pl.pres.act.
waš-/weš- „to dress, put on"; *wa-aš-ša-an-za* part. nom.sg.c.; *wa-aš-ša-an* part. nom.-acc.sg.n.; *wa-aš-ša-an-ta* part. instr.; *ú-e-eš-ša-an-da(=ma)* part. nom.-acc.pl.n.
wašta- „to sin, violate"; *wa-aš-ta-i* 3.sg.pres.act.; *wa-aš-ta-aš* 2.sg.pret.act.;

wa-aš-te-ir 3.pl.pret.act.; *wa-aš-du-ma-ti* 2.pl.pret.med.

waštāi- c. „sin, violation, offence“; *wa-aš-ta-i-iš* nom.sg.; *wa-aš-ta-uš* acc.pl.

waštanu- „to let a sin happen“; *wa-aš-ta-nu-wa-an* part. nom.-acc.sg.n.

waštul- n. „sin, violation, offence“; *wa-aš-túl(=tit)*, *wa-aš-du-ul* nom.-acc.sg.; *wa-aš-du-la-aš* gen.sg.

wātar n. „water“; *wa-a-tar(=ma)*, *wa-a-tar-r(=a)*, *ú-wi-ta-ar* nom.-acc.sg.; *ú-wi-te-na-aš* gen.sg.; *ú-e-te-ni-it* instr.; *ú-e-te-na-az*, *ú-e-te-na-za*, *ú-i-te-na-za* abl.

watarnahh- „to inform, let someone know“; *wa-tar-na-ah-hu-un* 1.sg.pret. act.; *wa-a-tar-na-ah-hi-ir* 3.pl.pret.act.

wattaru- n. „well“; *wa-tar-wa* dir.

watku- „to jump“; *wa-at-ku-uz-zi* 3.sg.pres.act.; *wa-at-ka-ah-hu-ut* 2.sg. imp.med.

watkunu- „to chase away“; *wa-at-ku-nu-e-ir* 3.pl.pret.act.

wawarkima- c. „door hinge“; *wa-wa-ar-ki-ma-aš* nom.pl.

weh/wah- „to turn, move around; to roam, wander around“; *ú-e-ha-ah-ha* 1.sg.pres.med.; *ú-e-ha-at-ta*^{1} 3.sg.pres.med.; *ú-e-ha-at-ta*^{2} 3.sg.pret. med.; *wa-ha-an-du* 3.pl.imp.act.; *ú-e-ha-at-ta-ru* 3.sg.imp.med.; *ú-e-hi-eš-kán-du* iter. 3.pl. imp.act.

^{LÚ}***weheškattalla-*** c. „guard“; $^{\text{LÚ.MEŠ}}$*ú-e-hi-eš-kat-tal-li-iš* nom.pl.

wek- „to wish, beg, implore“; *ú-e-ik-zi* 3.sg.pres.act.; *ú-e-ik-ta* 3.sg.pret.act.; *ú-e-ik* 2.sg.imp.act.

wellu- c. „meadow“; *ú-e-el-lu-ú-i* dat.-loc.sg.; *ú-el-lu-u-wa-az*, *ú-e-el-lu-wa-az* abl.; *ú-el-lu-wa-aš* dat.-loc.pl.

welkuwan- n. „grass, plant“; *ú-el-ku-wa-an* nom.-acc.sg.

wemiya- „to find; to receive; to reach, arrive“; *ú-e-mi-ya-zi*, *ú-e-mi-iz-zi* 3.sg.pres.act.; *ú-e-mi-ya-at* 2.sg.pret.act.; *ú-e-mi-ya-u-en* 1.pl. pret.act.; *ú-e-mi-ir* 3.pl.pret.act.

wen- „to harm“; *ú-e-en-ta* 3.sg.pret.act.

weriya- „to call; to instruct“; *ú-e-ri-iz-zi* 3.sg.pres.act.; *ú-e-ri-ya-an-za* part. nom.sg.c.

weritema- c. „fear, fright“; *ú-e-ri-te-ma-aš* nom.sg.

wēš „we“; *ú-e-eš*, *ú-e-š(=a/=a=wa=za/=a=za)*

weši- c. „pasture"; *ú-e-še-eš* nom.pl.

wešiya- „to graze"; *ú-e-ši-ya-ah-ha-ri* 1.sg.pres.med.; *ú-e-ši-ya-at-ta-ri* 3.sg. pret.med.

wešk- „to wail"; *ú-e-eš-kán-zi* 3.pl.pres.act.; *ú-e-eš-ga-un* supinum

weštara- c. „herdsman"; *ú-e-eš-ta-ra-aš* nom.sg.

wešuriya- „to suffocate"; *ú-i-šu-u-ri-ya-an-ta-ti* 3.pl.pret.med.

wete- „to build"; *ú-e-te-iz-zi* 3.sg.pres.act.; *ú-e-da-ah-hu-un* 1.sg.pret.act.; *ú-e-te-it* 3.sg.pret.act.; *ú-e-tum-ma-an-zi*, *ú-e-du-ma-an-zi* inf. I

wetummar n. „construction, building; construction work"; *ú-e-tum-mar* nom.-acc.sg.

wetenu- „to have something built, reinforced, fortified"; *ú-e-te-nu-un* 1.sg. pret.act.

wiya- „to send, dispatch"; *u-i-eš-ki-it-ta-ni* iter. 2.pl.pres.act.; *u-i-iš-ki-u-wa-an* iter. supinum

wilan- c. „clay, loam"; *ú-i-il-na-aš* gen.sg.

wet- c. „year"; *ú-it-ti* dat.-loc.sg.

wetantātar n. „course of a year"; *ú-e-it-ta-an-da-an-ni-e(=ši=ma)* dat.-loc.sg.

wida- „to send, dispatch"; *ú-i-da-at-tin* 2.pl.imp.act.

wiwišk- „to be in labour"; *ú-i-ú-i-iš-ki-iz-zi* 3.sg.pres.act.

wurulli- a Hittite ritual feast, *purulli*-feast; *wu$_u$-ru-li-ya-aš* gen.sg.

-za/az enclitic particle

zahhāi- c. „fight, battle"; *za-ah-ha-in* acc.sg.; *za-ah-hi-ya(=kán)* dat.-loc.sg.; *za-ah-ha-a-uš* acc.pl.

zahhiya- „to beat, fight, battle"; *za-ah-hi-ya-mi* 1.sg.pres.act.; *za-ah-hi-ya-ši* 2.sg.pres.act.; *za-ah-hi-ya-u-wa-aš-ta-ti* 1.pl.pres.med.; *za-ah-hi-ya-nu-un* 1.sg.pret.act.; *za-ah-hi-ya-ah-ha-ru* 1.sg.imp.med.; *za-ah-hi-ya-ah-hu-ut* 2.sg.imp.med.; *za-ah-hi-iš-ki-mi* iter. 1.sg. pres.act.; *za-ah-hi-iš-ki-iz-zi* iter. 3.sg.pres.act.

^{GIŠ}***zahurti***- c. a device; ^{GIŠ}*za-hur-ti-aš* gen.sg.

zāi- „to cross"; *zi-ih-hu-un* 1.sg.pret.act.; *za-a-iš* 3.sg.pret.act.

zankilātar n. „expiatory offering, penance, atonement"; *za-an-ki-la-tar-ri*$^{\text{HI.A}}$ nom.-acc.pl.

zanu- „to cook, roast, fry, bake"; *za-nu-an-zi* 3.pl.pres.act.; *za-nu-wa-an* part. nom.-acc.sg.n.; *za-nu-an-da* part. nom.-acc.pl.n.; *za-nu-uš-kán-zi* Iter. 3.pl.pres.act.

zašhāi-, ***zazhāi-*** c. „dream“; *za-aš-ha-in* acc.sg.; *za-az-hi-i*, *za-aš-hi-ya* dat.-loc.sg.; *za-aš-hi-it* instr.; *za-aš-hi-mu-uš* acc.pl.

zāu- n. a ritual object; *za-a-u* nom.-acc.sg.

zeya- „to cook, boil“; *zé-e-a-ri* 3.sg.pres.med.; *zé-e-ya-an-te-it* part. instr.

zeriyalli- n. „vessel stand“; *zé-ri-ya-al-li* nom.-acc.sg.

zik „you (sg.)“; *zi-ik(=ma/=ma=za/=mu/=pát/=pát=ma=za/=pát=za/=wa/ =wa=kán/=wa=za)*, *zi-g(=a/ =a=šmaš=at/a=war=ašta/=an/)*, *zi-iq-q (=a)*

zikk- „to set, put, lay“ (iter. of *dāi-*); *zi-ik-ki-u-wa-ni* 1.pl.pres.act.; *zi-ki-e-it*, *zi-ke-e-it* 3.sg.pret.act.

zila- c. „oracle, oracle reply“; *zi-la-aš(=wa)* nom.sg.

zinna- „to finish; to stop, be finished“; *zi-in-na-i*, *zi-in-ni-iz-zi* 3.sg.pres.act.; *zi-in-nu-um-me-e-ni* 1.pl.pres.act.; *zi-in-na-an-zi* 3.pl.pres.act.; *zi-in-na-at-ta-ri* 3.sg. pres.med.; *zi-en-na-ah-hu-un* 1.sg.pret.act.; *zi-in-ni-it* 3.sg. pret.act.; *zi-in-na-an-da* 3.pl. pret.med.; *zi-in-na-an-te-eš* part. nom.pl.c.

^{GIŠ}***zuppari-*** n. „torch“; ^{GIŠ}*zu-up-pa-ri-ya-aš* gen.pl.

4.2. Sumerographic words

A.AB.BA „sea“ (Hitt. *aruna-*); A.AB.BA-*az* abl.

^{LÚ}**A.ÍL.LÁ** „water carrier“

A.ŠÀ „field“; A.ŠÀ-*ni* loc.sg.; A.ŠÀ$^{\text{HI.A}}$-*an* acc.pl.

^{LÚ}**A.ZU** „physician“; $^{\text{LÚ.MEŠ}}$A.ZU-*š(=a)* nom.sg.

Á^{MUŠEN} „eagle“ (Hitt. *hara(na)-*); Á^{MUŠEN}-*aš* gen.sg.

^{GIŠ}**AB** „window“ (Hitt. $^{\text{(GIŠ)}}$*luttāi-*); ^{GIŠ}AB-*az* abl.

^{DUG}**ÁBxA** „water basin“

^{LÚ}**AGRIG** „administrator“ (Hitt. *maniyahhatalla-*); ^{LÚ}AGRIG-*ma*

^{GIŠ}**AL** „hoe, pick“

AL.GAZ „crushed, pounded“

ALAM „statue, idol“; ALAM-*kán*

^{LÚ}**ALAM.ZU$_9$** „worshipper of a statue, worshipper of idols“

AMA „mother“ (Hitt. *anna-*)

AMAR „calf“

AN „sky, heaven“ (Hitt. *nepiš-*); AN-*iš* acc.sg.; AN-*ši* loc.sg.

ANŠE „ass, donkey“; ANŠE-*aš(=ma=za)* nom.sg.

ANŠE.GÌR.NUN.NA „mule“; ANŠE.GÌR.NUN.NA-*an* acc.sg.; ANŠE.GÌR.NUN. NA$^{\text{HI.A}}$*(=wa)*

ANŠE.KUR.RA „horse; charioteer, chariot fighter“; ANŠE.KUR.RA-*aš* loc.pl.

^{GIŠ}**APIN** „plough“

^{LÚ}**APIN.LÁ** „ploughman, countryman“; ^{LÚ}APIN.LÁ-*aš* gen.pl.

$^{\text{NA4}}$**ARA$_5$** „grinder, grindstone“

ARAD „servant, dependant“; ARAD-*iš*, ARAD-*aš* nom.sg.; ARAD*(=miš)*, ARAD^{MEŠ}-*n(=ašta)*; ARAD-*YA (=wa=mu)*, ARAD-*ZU(=pát)*, ARAD^{MEŠ}-*KA(=ya)*

ARAD-*nahh-* „to subject, make subservient“; ARAD-*ah-hu-un* 1.sg. pret.act.; ARAD-*na-ah-ta* 3.sg.pret.act.; ARAD-*na-ah-hi-iš-kir* iter. 3.pl.pret.act.

^{LÚ}**AZU** „seer, prophet“

BA.ÚŠ „died“ (Hitt. *aki*)

^{DUG}**BÁHAR** „potter's wheel“

BAL „to sacrifice, offer“ (Hitt. *šipand-*); BAL-*u-wa-an-zi* inf. I

^{GIŠ}**BAL.TUR** „small spindle“; ^{GIŠ}BAL.TUR-*az* abl.

^{GIŠ}**BANŠUR** „table“ (Hitt. *ištanana-* „sacrificial altar“?); ^{GIŠ}BANŠUR-*az* abl.; ^{GIŠ}BANŠUR$^{\text{HI.A}}$-*aš* loc.pl.; ^{GIŠ}BANŠUR*(=kán)*

BAPPIR „beer spice“

DAM „wife“; DAM-*ŠU(=pát)*

DAM-*ātar* n. „marriage“; DAM-*an-ni* dat.-loc.sg.

DAM-*ŪTTU* „marriage“; DAM-*UT-TIM* (gen.)

^{LÚ}**DAM.GÀR** „trader“ (Hitt. *unatalla-*)

DANNA „mile“

DI „case, court, trial“ (Hitt. *hanneššar*); DI-*eš-ni* dat.sg.; DI-*eš-na-az* abl.

DIM$_4$ „malt“

DINGIR „god“ (Hitt. *šiuna-*); DINGIR-*aš-š(=a)* gen.sg.; DINGIR^{LIM}-*aš (=mu)* (gen.) nom.sg.; DINGIR^{LIM}-*iš (=ma=aš)* (gen.) nom.sg.;

DINGIR^{LIM}-*in* (gen.) acc.sg.; DINGIR^{LIM}-*ni(=wa=ta)* (gen.) dat.-loc.sg.; DINGIR^{LIM}-*az* (gen.) abl.; DINGIR^{LUM}*(=mu =za=kán)* (nom.); DINGIR^{LIM}*(=ma/=wa)* (gen.); DINGIR^{LAM} (acc.); DINGIR^{DIDLI}-*eš*, DINGIR^{DIDLI}-*š(=a)* nom.pl.; DINGIR^{MEŠ}-*iš*, DINGIR^{MEŠ}-*eš(=kán)* nom.pl.; DINGIR^{MEŠ}-*aš*^{1} nom.pl.; DINGIR^{MEŠ}-*aš*^{2}*(=ma/=pát)* gen.pl.; DINGIR^{MEŠ}-*na-aš* dat.pl.; DINGIR^{MEŠ}-*aš*^{3} dat.pl.; DINGIR^{MEŠ}-*uš* acc.pl.; DINGIR^{MEŠ}-*az(=ya)* abl.; DINGIR^{MEŠ} *(=ma=kán/ =ya/=pát)*

DINGIR^{MEŠ}-*niyant*- c. „man of god" (Hitt. **šiunant*-); DINGIR^{MEŠ}-*ni-ya-an-za* nom.sg.

DINGIR.LÚ „male deity"; DINGIR.LÚ^{MEŠ}*(=ya)*

DÙ „to make" (Hitt. *iya*-); DÙ-*mi* 1.sg.pres.act.; DÙ-*nu-un* 1.sg.pret.act.; DÙ-*at* 3.sg.pret.act.

DUB „clay tablet" (Hitt. *tuppi*-)

DUB.2.KAM „second tablet"

^{LÚ}**DUB.SAR** „tablet scribe"

DUG „vessel, container", also determinative

^{LÚ}**DUGUD** „dignitary"

DUH.LÀL „wax"; DUH.LÀL-*aš* gen.sg.

DUMU „son, child"; DUMU-*aš*^{1}, DUMU-*la-aš* nom.sg.; DUMU-*an* acc.sg.; DUMU-*la-ma-an* = °*lan-man* acc.sg. + -*man* „my son"; DUMU-*aš*^{2} gen.sg.; DUMU-*li (=ya)* dat.sg.; DUMU-*la (=ma=šan)* voc.sg.; DUMU^{MEŠ}-*uš* acc.pl.; DUMU*(=mi)*; DUMU^{MEŠ}-*ŠU-NU(=ma=za)*

DUMU.DUMU „grandchild"

DUMU.É.GAL „palace squire, page"; DUMU^{MEŠ}.É.GAL*(=kán)*

DUMU.LÚ.U$_{19}$.LU „man, human being" (Hitt. *antuhša*-); DUMU.LÚ.U$_{19}$.LU-*an* acc.sg.; DUMU.LÚ.U$_{19}$.LU*(=ma=ši=kán)*

DUMU.LUGAL „son of a king, royal prince"; DUMU.LUGAL*(=ma)*

DUMU.MUNUS „daughter, girl"; DUMU.MUNUS-*iš* nom.sg.; DUMU.MUNUS*(=ma)*

DUMU.MUNUS.GAL „Great princess"; DUMU.MUNUS.GAL*(=ma=kán)*

DUMU.NITA „son, boy"; DUMU.NITA-*an* acc.sg.; DUMU.NITA-*li* dat.sg.; DUMU.NITA*(=ši)*

^{KUŠ}**E.SIR** „shoe"; ^{KUŠ}E.SIR-*uš*, ^{KUŠ}E.SIR$^{\text{HI.A}}$-*uš* acc.pl.

É „house" (Hitt. *pir-/parna*-), also determinative; É-*ir(=ma/=mit/=za)* nom.-acc.sg.; É-*na* dir.; É-*ri(=ši)* loc.sg.; É*(=ti=ya=kán)*; É^{TI}-*KA* *(=wa=ta=kán)*; É^{TUM} *(=ma=ši=kán)*

É.EN.NUN.UN „prison, jail“

É.GAL „palace“; É.GAL^{LIM}*(=ya=za/=ma=wa=za/=wa)* (gen.)

É.^{NA4}KIŠIB „house of the seal, storehouse“

É.NA$_4$ „stone house“

É.ŠÀ „inner chamber“ (Hitt. *tunnakeššar*); É.ŠÀ-*ni* loc.sg.

EGIR „again, back, behind“ (Hitt. *āppa*); EGIR-*pa(=at/=ma/=ma=wa=za =kán/=war=at/=wa=za)*

EGIR-*an* „behind, after that, then“ (Hitt. *āppan*); EGIR-*an(=ma)*; EGIR-*pa-an-n(=a)*

EGIR-*anda* „after that, then, afterwards“ (Hitt. *appanda*); EGIR-*an-da* *(=ma/=ma =šmaš/=pát)*, EGIR-*pa-an-da*

EGIR-*az* „afterwards, behind; around the back, secretly“ (Hitt. *āppaz*); EGIR-*az(=ya=za=ma=mu=kán/=ma)*

EGIR-*pa-an-na* see **EGIR-*an***

EGIR-*pa-an-da* see **EGIR-*anda***

EGIR-*zi* „rear, back, last“ (Hitt. *appezzi-*); EGIR-*zi(=man=wa=za)*

EGIR-*ŠU* „after that, then, afterwards“ (Hitt. *appanda*); EGIR-*ŠU(=ma/ =ma=za=kán)*

EGIR.UD^{MI} „future“

EME „tongue; talk, rumours“ (Hitt. *lāla-*); EME-*an* acc.sg.; EME-*un* acc.sg.; EME-*aš* gen.sg.

EN „master, lord; owner“ (Hitt. *išhā-*); EN-*aš* nom.sg.; EN-*an* acc.sg.

EN-*ŪTU* „rule“; EN-*UT-TI* (gen.); EN-*UT-TA* (acc.)

^{GIŠ}ERIN „cedar, cedar-wood“; ^{GIŠ}ERIN-*pí* nom.sg.; ^{GIŠ}ERIN-*aš* gen.sg.

ÉRIN^{MEŠ} „soldiers, infantry“ (Hitt. *tuzzi-*, *tuzziyant-*); ÉRIN^{MEŠ}-*za(=miš=a)* nom.sg.; ÉRIN^{MEŠ}-*an* acc.sg.; ÉRIN^{MEŠ}-*az(=ma=mu)* abl.; ÉRIN^{MEŠ}-*it(=ma)* instr.; ÉRIN^{MEŠ}-*uš* acc.pl.; ÉRIN^{MEŠ}*(=ya=kán/=ma=mu/ =wa=za)*

^{LÚ}ÉRIN „soldier“

ÉSAG „granary, silo“; ÉSAG-*an* acc.sg.

EZEN$_4$ „ritual feast“

GA.RAŠ^{SAR} „leek“

GADA „cloth“; GADA-*it* instr.

^{GIŠ}**GAG** „post, stake“; ^{GIŠ}GAG$^{HI.A}$*(=ma=wa)*

1. **GAL** „big, great; chief, , leader“ (Hitt. *šalli-*); GAL-*iš(=za)* nom.sg.

2. $^{(DUG)}$**GAL** „cup, goblet“ (Hitt. *teššumi-*, *zeri-*); GAL-*ri(=ya)* nom.sg.; GAL$^{HI.A}$*(=kán)*

^{LÚ}**GAL** „leader, powerful person“

GAL.GIR$_4$ „cup from fired clay“

GAM „below, down; at, by , beside“ (Hitt. *katta*)

GAM-*an* „below, down; down, away“ (Hitt. *kattan*)

GAM-*anda* „down“ (Hitt. *kattanda*); GAM-*an-ta*

GAM-*andan* „down“ (Hitt. *kattandan*); GAM-*an-ta-an*

GAR „to set, put, lay; Med. to be laid, lie“ (Hitt. *kī-*); GAR-*ri* 3.sg.pres. med.; GAR-*ru* 3.sg.imp.pres.med.

GAŠAN „mistress“; GAŠAN*(=ma)*

1. **GE$_6$** „dark“ (Hitt. *dankui-*); GE$_6$-*ya-aš* gen.sg.

2. **GE$_6$** „night“ (Hitt. *išpand-*); GE$_6$-*an* acc.sg.; GE$_6$-*az(=pát)* abl.

GE$_6$-*eš*- „to get dark“ (Hitt. *dankueš-*); GE$_6$-*iš-zi* 3.sg.pres.act.

GÉME „maid, maid servant, female dependant“; GÉME*(=šan)*

GÉME-*ahh*- „to make someone a dependant“; GÉME-*ah-hi-iš-kir* iter. 3.pl. pret.act.

GÉME-*aššareš*- „to become a dependant“; GÉME-*aš-ša-ri-eš-zi* 3.sg. pres.act.

GÉŠPU „fist; violence“

GÉŠPU-*ahh*- „to use force“; GÉŠPU-*ah-hu-aš* verbal noun. gen.sg.

GEŠTIN „wine“ (Hitt. *wiyana-*); GEŠTIN-*an* acc.sg.; GEŠTIN-*it* instr.

GEŠTU „ear“ (Hitt. *ištamana-*); GEŠTU-*an* acc.sg.

GI „cane“

GI.É.DUB.BA „writing cane, stylus“; GI.É.DUB.BA*(=mu=kán)*

GÍD.DA „long“ (Hitt. *daluki-*); GÍD.DA*(=ya)*

^{GIŠ}**GIDRU** „baton, sceptre“; ^{GIŠ}GIDRU*(=ya)*

GIG „to fall ill“ (Hitt. *irmaliya-*, *ištark-*); GIG-*zi* 3.sg.pres.ind.

^{GIŠ}**GIGIR** „carriage, coach“; ^{GIŠ}GIGIR-*it* instr.

GIM-*an* „like, as, when, if, because“ (Hitt. *mahhan*, *mān*); GIM-*an(=ma/ =ma= war=at)*

GÍN „shekel“

GÍR „dagger, knife“; GÍR-*an* acc.sg.

GÌR „foot“ (Hitt. *pata-*); GÌR-*it* instr.; GÌR^{MEŠ}-*aš* gen.pl.; GÌR^{MEŠ}-*it* instr.pl.; GÌR^{MEŠ}-*ŠÚ(=ma=za)*

^{GIŠ}**GÌR.GUB** „stool, footstool“

GISKIM „omen“ (Hitt. *šagāi-*); GISKIM*(=ši)*

GIŠ „wood“ (Hitt. *taru-*), also determinative

GIŠ ^{D}INANNA$^{\text{HI.A}}$ „harp“

^{GIŠ}**GU.ZA** „throne“ (Hitt. *halmašuitt-*)

GU$_4$ „bull, cow, cattle“; GU$_4$-*uš(=za=kán)* nom.sg.; GU$_4$-*un*, GU$_4$^{MEŠ}-*un*, GU$_4$-*n(=ašta)* acc.sg.; GU$_4$$^{\text{HI.A}}$*(=ma)*, GU$_4$$^{\text{HI.A}}$*(=KUNU=ya)*

GU$_4$.APIN.LÁ „ploughing ox“

GU$_4$.MAH „bull“; GU$_4$.MAH$^{\text{HI.A}}$*(=ya)*

GU$_4$.NIGA „fattened ox“

GUB „to stand“; GUB-*aš* part. nom.sg.c.

GÙB „left; unfavourable, wrong“; GÙB-*za* abl. adv.

^{LÚ}**GUDU$_{12}$** „anointed, priest“

1. **GUL** „to beat, hit; to strike“ (Hitt. *walh-*); GUL-*ah-zi* 3.sg.pres.act.; GUL-*hi-eš-ki-ir* Iter. 3.pl.pret.act.

2. **GUL** „to carve, scratch into, write down“; GUL-*aš-du* 3.sg.imp.pres.act.

GUNNI „stove, oven, fireplace“ (Hitt. *hašša-*); GUNNI*(=ma)*

GUŠKIN „gold“

^{LÚ}**HA.LA** „heir“

HI.HI „belonging to thunderstorm, thunder“ (Hitt. *pihašašši-*); HI.HI-*aš-ši-iš* nom.sg.c.

HUL-*lu*- „bad, evil ‚wicked“ (Hitt. *idālu-*); HUL-*lu* nom.sg.n.; HUL-*u-wa-aš*, HUL-*u-wa-aš-š(=a)* gen.pl.c.

^{LÚ}**HUL-*lu*** „Bad, Evil (as personal name)“; ^{LÚ}HUL-*lu* uninflected

HUL-*ātar* „malice, , wickedness“ (Hitt. *idalauwātar*); HUL-*u-an-ni* dat.-loc.sg.

HUR.SAG „hill, mountain, moutains“; HUR.SAG-*aš*, HUR.SAG-*aš-š(=a)* nom.sg.; HUR.SAG-*i* dat.-loc.sg.; HUR.SAG-*az* abl.; HUR.SAG$^{\text{HI.A}}$-*aš*, HUR.SAG^{MEŠ}-*aš*, HUR.SAG^{MEŠ}-*ša-aš* dat.-loc.pl.; HUR.SAG^{MEŠ}-*uš* acc.pl.

$^{(UZU)}$**Ì** „oil, fat, grease"; Ì-*an(=ma=kán)* acc.sg.; Ì-*i* dat.-loc.sg.; ^{UZU}Ì*(=ya)*
Ì.DÙG.GA „fine oil"; Ì.DÙG.GA*(=ya=aš=ši=šan)*
Ì.GIŠ „tree oil"
ÍD „river" (Hitt. *hāpa-*); ÍD-*š(=a)* nom.sg.; ÍD-*an* acc.sg.; ÍD-*i* loc.sg.; ÍD-*az* abl.; ÍD-*a* dir.; ÍD-*aš* gen.pl.; ÍD^{MEŠ}-*uš* acc.sg.; ÍD$^{HI.A}$*(=wa)*
^{GIŠ}**IG** „door"; ^{GIŠ}IG-*aš* dat.pl.; ^{GIŠ}IG*(=ya)*
IGI „eye" (Hitt. *šakuwa-*); IGI$^{HI.A}$-*wa* nom.-acc.pl.; IGI$^{HI.A}$-*it* instr.pl.
IGI-*anda* „opposite" (Hitt. *menahhanda*); IGI-*an-da*
IGI-*zi* „front, first" (Hitt. *hantezzi-*); IGI-*zi* loc.sg.c.
IKU a measure of length; IKU-*an* acc.sg.
IM „loam, clay" (Hitt. *wila(n)-* c.); IM-*an* acc.sg.
IM.ŠU.NÍG.RIN.NA „oven"
INIM „word, thing, matter, affair" (Hitt. *memiya-*); INIM-*an* acc.sg.
ITU „month"; ITU-*mi* dat.-loc.sg.; ITU-*az* abl.
ITU.x.KAM „x. month"; ITU.3.KAM-*aš* loc.pl.; ITU.1.KAM*(=ma=aš)*
IZI „fire" (Hitt. *pahhur*); IZI-*it* instr.
KA.GÌR „side road"; KA.GÌR*(=ya)*
KAxU „mouth" (Hitt. *aiš-* n.); KAxU-*iš-š(=a=mu=kán)* nom.sg.; KAxU-*aš* gen.sg.; KAxU-*az* abl.
$^{(UZU)}$**KAxZU$_9$** „tooth"; ^{UZU}KAxZU$_9$-*it* instr.
KÁ „door"; KÁ-*aš* dat.pl.
KÁ.GAL „gate" (Hitt. *āška-*); KÁ.GAL-*az* abl.; KÁ.GAL$^{HI.A}$-*aš* dat.-loc.pl.; KÁ.GAL$^{HI.A}$-*za* abl.pl.
KARAŠ „army" (Hitt. *tuzzi-*?)
KASKAL „road, way" (Hitt. *palša-*); KASKAL-*an* acc.sg.; KASKAL-*ši* loc.sg.; KASKAL-*az*, KASKAL-*za* abl.; KASKAL-*aš*, KASKAL-*ša-aš* gen.pl.; KASKAL$^{HI.A}$-*aš* dat.-loc.pl.
KAŠ „beer" (Hitt. *šeššar*)
KI „earth; place" (Hitt. *tekan*; *peda(n)-*); KI-*aš* gen.sg.
KI.BAD „distant"; KI.BAD-*aš* nom.sg.c.
KIN „work, achievement; oracle by lot" (Hitt. *aniur*); KIN-*az* abl.; KIN *(=ma)*
KIN-*ta* „robes" (Hitt. *aniyatta*); KIN$^{HI.A}$-*ta* nom.-acc.pl.
$^{(UZU)}$**KIR$_4$** „nose"; KIR$_4$*(=šet)*

^{GIŠ}**KIRI$_{6}$.GEŠTIN** „vineyard“

KISLAH „threshing floor“

$^{\text{NA4}}$**KIŠIB** „seal“

KÙ.BABBAR „silver“; KÙ.BABBAR-*i* dat.-loc.sg.

KU$_{7}$ „sweet“ (Hitt. *šanezzi-*)

KUR „land, country“ (Hitt. *utnē-*, *utniyant-*); KUR-*e(=kán/=šmet/=wa)* nom.-acc.sg.; KUR-*i*, KUR-*ya* loc.sg.; KUR.KUR-*KA (=ma=aš=kán)*; KUR.KUR$^{\text{HI.A}}$*(=ma)*; KUR.KUR^{MEŠ}*(=ya)*; KUR^{TUM}*(=ya)* (nom.); KUR^{TI}*(=man)* (gen.)

KUR-*ant-* „population“ (Hitt. *utniyant-*); KUR-*an-za* nom.sg.

^{LÚ}**KÚR** „enemy“ (Hitt. *kurur-*); ^{LÚ}KÚR-*aš* nom.sg.; ^{LÚ}KÚR-*an* gen.pl.; ^{LÚ}KÚR*(=ya)*; ^{LÚ}KÚR^{MEŠ}*(=mu=kán)*

KUŠ „leather“, also determinative

^{LÚ}**KUŠ$_{7}$** „charioteer, steerer of a carriage“

LÀL „honey“ (Hitt. *militt-*); LÀL-*it* instr.

LÍL „field, open fields, steppe“ (Hitt. *gimra-*); LÍL-*ri* loc.sg.; LÍL*(=ma=ši)*

LÚ „man“ (Hitt. *pešna-*), also determinative; LÚ-*aš* nom.sg.; LÚ-*an* acc.sg.; LÚ*(=ya/=kán)*; LÚ^{MEŠ}*(=ya)*; LÚ^{MEŠ}-*a(=šmiš)*

LÚ-*nātar* „manhood“; LÚ-*na-tar(=mit=wa)* nom.-acc.sg.

LÚ.U$_{19}$.LU „man, human being“ (Hitt. *antuhša-*); LÚ.U$_{19}$.LU-*an* acc.sg.

LUGAL „king“ (Hitt. *haššu-*); LUGAL-*uš(=miš/=za)*, LUGAL-*uš-š(=a/ =šan)*, nom.sg.; LUGAL-*š(=an/ =an=za/=at)*; LUGAL-*un* acc.sg.; LUGAL-*wa-aš*, LUGAL-*aš* gen.sg.; LUGAL-*i(=ya)* dat.sg.; LUGAL-*an* gen.pl.

LUGAL-*izziya-* „to become king; to make someone king“; LUGAL-*iz-zi-at* 3.sg.pret.med.; LUGAL-*iz-zi-ah-ha-at(=pát)* 1.sg.pret.med.

LUGAL-*iznātar* „kingdom, monarchy“; LUGAL-*iz-na-ni*, LUGAL-*iz-na-an-ni* dat.-loc.sg.

LUGAL-*ŪTU-* „kingdom“; LUGAL-*UT-TI* (gen.)

LUGAL.GAL „Great king“; LUGAL.GAL*(=ma=an=kán)*

MA.NA „mine“

^{GIŠ}**MAR** „spade“

^{LÚ}**MÁŠDA** „poor“; $^{\text{LÚ.MEŠ}}$MÁŠDA*(=ya)*

MÈ „battle, battle formation“ (Hitt. *zahhāi-*); MÈ-*in* acc.sg.; MÈ-*ya* loc.sg.

MU „year" (Hitt. *wet-*); MU-*an* acc.sg.; MU$^{\text{HI.A}}$-*uš* acc.pl.; MU$^{\text{HI.A}}$-*aš* dat.-loc.pl.

MU-*ant-* „year" (Hitt. *wetant-*); MU-*ti*, MU-*an-ti* loc.sg.

MU-*ātar* „course of a year" (Hitt. *wetantātar*); MU-*an-ni* loc.sg.

MU.KAM „year" (Hitt. *wet-*); MU.KAM-*ti* loc.sg.; MU.KAM$^{\text{HI.A}}$-*uš* acc.pl.

MU.x.KAM „x. year"

^{LÚ}**MUHALDIM** „cook"

MUL „star" (Hitt. *hašter-*)

MUN „salt"

MUNUS „woman" (Hitt. *gwen(ant)-*), also determinative; MUNUS-*an-za (=wa=za)*, MUNUS-*za*, MUNUS-*aš*^{1} nom.sg.; MUNUS-*an* acc.sg.; MUNUS-*aš*^{2} gen.sg.; MUNUS*(=ma)*; MUNUS^{TI}*(=kán)* (gen.)

MUNUS-*nili-* „female, of womankind"; MUNUS-*ni-li-ya-az* abl. adv.

MUNUS.LUGAL „queen" (Hitt. *haššušara-*); MUNUS.LUGAL-*aš* nom.sg.; MUNUS.LUGAL-*aš-š(=a)* gen.sg.; MUNUS.LUGAL *(=ya/ =ya=wa/=ma=wa/=wa=mu)*

MUNUS.LUGAL.GAL „Great queen"

MUŠ „snake"; MUŠ-*aš*^{1} nom. Sg.; MUŠ-*aš*^{2} gen. Sg.; MUŠ$^{\text{HI.A}}$-*uš* acc.pl.

MUŠEN „bird", also determinative

^{LÚ}**MUŠEN.DÙ** „augur"

^{GIŠ}**NÁ** „bed" (Hitt. *šašta-*); ^{GIŠ}NÁ-*aš* loc.pl.

NA$_4$ „stone", also determinative

$^{\text{(LÚ)}}$**NAM.RA** „prisoner of war"

NÍ.TE „body, person" (Hitt. *tuekka-*); NÍ.TE-*i(=ši)* dat.-loc.sg.; NÍ.TE-*az (=ma=za)* abl.

^{LÚ}**NÍ.ZU** „thieve; spy, scout" (Hitt. *tayazila-*); ^{LÚ}NÍ.ZU-*aš* nom.sg.; ^{LÚ}NÍ.ZU-*an* acc.sg.; NÍ.ZU$^{\text{HI.A}}$*(=ya=wa)*

NÍG.BA „present"

NÍG.GA „property" (Hitt. *āššu-*)

^{UZU}**NÍG.GIG** „liver" (Hitt. *lišši-*)

NÍG.SI.SÁ „just, fair"; NÍG.SI.SÁ-*an* acc.sg.c.

NIN „sister" (Hitt. *nega-*); NIN-*uš* acc.pl.; NIN^{MEŠ}-*uš* acc.pl.

NINDA „bread", also determinative; NINDA-*an* acc.sg.; NINDA$^{\text{HI.A}}$*(=ya)*

^{LÚ}**NINDA.DÙ.DÙ** „baker"

NINDA.GUR$_4$.RA „breadloaf, thick bread"; NINDA.GUR$_4$.RA$^{\text{HI.A}}$*(=ya)*
NINDA.Ì „fatbread"
NINDA.SIG „flatbread"
NU.GÁL „there is not"
NUMUN „semen, descendants, family"; NUMUN-*aš*^{1} nom.sg.; NUMUN-*aš*^{2} dat.pl.; NUMUN*(=war=aš)*
PÉŠ.TUR „little mouse"
^{GIŠ}**PISAN** „box, chest"; ^{GIŠ}PISAN*(=ya=wa=kán)*
PÚ „well" (Hitt. *wattaru-*); PÚ^{MEŠ}-*az* abl.pl.
RA „to hit, beat" (Hitt. *walh-*); RA-*mi* 1.sg.pres.act.
^{UZU}**SA** „string"
SA$_5$ „red" (Hitt. *mīti-*)
SAG.DU „head" (Hitt. *haršar-*); SAG.DU-*aš* gen.sg.; SAG.DU-*na-az* abl.
SAG.GÉME.ARAD^{MEŠ} „servants"
^{GIŠ}**SAG.KUL** „bolt" (Hitt. *hattalu-*)
^{LÚ}**SAGI(.A)** „cupbearer"; ^{LÚ}SAGI-*aš*, ^{LÚ}SAGI.A-*aš* nom.sg.
^{LÚ}**SANGA** „priest" (Hitt. *šankunni-*)
^{LÚ}**SANGA-*ŪTU*** „priesthood"; ^{LÚ}SANGA-*UT-TIM* (gen.)
SANGA-*eššar* „temple service"; SANGA-*eš-na-za* abl.
SAR „plant", also determinative
SixSÁ „to find out by oracle, establish" (Hitt. *ariya-*); SIxSÁ-*ta-ri* 3.sg. pres.med.; SIxSÁ-*an-du* 3.pl.imp.act.
SIG.KÙŠ „half ell, span"
SÍG „wool" (Hitt. *hulana-*), also determinative
1. **SIG$_5$** „good" (Hitt. *āššu-*); SIG$_5$-*an* acc.sg.c.; SIG$_5$-*in* acc.sg.n.
2. **SIG$_5$-** „to become favourable; to become healthy"; SIG$_5$-*ri*, SIG$_5$-*at-ta-ri (=ma)* 3.sg.pres.med.

SILA$_4$ „lamb"
SILIM-*li* „kind, benevolent, friendly" (Hitt. *aššuli*)
SILIM.BI „good"
^{LÚ}**SIMUG** „smith"; $^{\text{LÚ.MEŠ}}$SIMUG*(=ma)*
^{LÚ}**SIPA** „herdsman" (Hitt. *weštara-*)
SISKUR „sacrifice, offer, ritual"
SÍSKUR „sacrifice, offer, ritual"; SÍSKUR*(=ya=kán)*; SÍSKUR$^{\text{HI.A}}$

(=a=šmaš)

^{MUNUS}**SUHUR.LÁ** „palace maid, maid servant"

^{MUNUS}**SUHUR.LA$_5$** „palace maid, maid servant"

SUM „to give" (Hitt. *pāi-*); SUM-*an-zi* 3.sg.pres.act.; SUM-*eš-ta* 3.sg. pret.act.

SUMUN „old" (Hitt. *karūili-*); SUMUN^{TIM} (gen.)

$^{(UZU)}$**ŠÀ** „inside; heart; in the middel, in, inside"; ŠÀ-*az* abl.; ŠÀ-*KA* *(=wa=az)*

ŠAH.TUR „piglet"

ŠExNAGA „to wash" (Hitt. *ārra-*); ŠExNAGA-*an-zi* 3.pl.pres.act.

ŠEŠ „brother" (Hitt. *negna-*); ŠEŠ^{MEŠ}-*uš* acc.pl.; ŠEŠ*(=ya=at=za=an)*; ŠEŠ-*YA(=an=mu/=ya)*

ŠEŠ.DÙG.GA „dear brother"; ŠEŠ.DÙG.GA-*YA(=ma=mu)*

ŠU „hand" (Hitt. *keššar*); ŠU-*i* loc.sg.; ŠU-*ta* instr.

^{LÚ}**ŠU.DAB** „prisoner of war"

^{LÚ}**ŠU.GI** „old man"

^{MUNUS}**ŠU.GI** „old woman, Wise woman"; $^{MUNUS.MEŠ}$ŠU.GI-*uš* acc.pl.

^{NA4}**ŠU.U** „basalt"

$^{(GIŠ)}$**ŠÚ.A** „chair, throne" (Hitt. *halmašuitt-*); ^{GIŠ}ŠÚ.A-*aš* gen.sg.; ^{GIŠ}ŠÚ.A-*ši*, ^{GIŠ}ŠÚ.A-*ki(=ma=šan)* dat.-loc.sg.

^{GIŠ}**ŠUKUR** „spear, lance"; ^{GIŠ}ŠUKUR$^{HI.A}$*(=ya)*

^{LÚ}**ŠUKUR.ZABAR** „man wit the bronze spear (a dignitary)"

1. **TI** „life" (Hitt. *huišwātar* n.); TI-*tar* nom.-acc.sg.

2. **TI** „to live" (Hitt. *huiš-*); TI-*an* part. acc.sg.n.

^{GIŠ}**TIR** „forest" (Hitt. *tieššar* ?)

TÚG „garment, dress, cloth", also determinative; TÚG$^{HI.A}$-*uš* acc.pl.

^{GIŠ}**TUKUL** „tool, weapon; craft services"; ^{GIŠ}TUKUL$^{HI.A}$-*uš-š(=ašta)* acc.pl.; ^{GIŠ}TUKUL*(=ma/=ma=ši)*

TUR „little, small, young"; TUR-*aš* nom.sg.c.

Ú „plant, grass, weed, leaves"; Ú$^{HI.A}$*(=ya)*

Ú.SAL „meadow" (Hitt. *wellu-*); Ú.SAL-*wa* dir.

Ù „sleep, dream" (Hitt. *tešha-*, *zašhāi-*); Ù-*az* abl.

UD „day" (Hitt. *šiwatt-*); UD-*ti* loc.sg.; UD-*aš* gen./dat.pl.; UD^{MI} (gen.)

UD-*at* UD-*at* „daily, every day"

UD.KAM „day" (Hitt. *šiwatt-*); UD.KAM-*az* nom.sg.; UD.KAM-*aš* gen.sg.; UD.KAM-*ti(=ma)* dat.-loc.sg.; UD.KAM$^{HI.A}$-*aš* dat.-loc.pl.

UD.x.KAM „x. day"; UD.7.KAM-*az* nom.sg.; UD.1.KAM*(=ya=aš)*; UD.3.KAM*(=ma)*

UDU „sheep", also determinative; UDU-*un*, UDU-*n(=ašta)*, UDU$^{HI.A}$-*un* acc.sg.; UDU*(=ma=kán)*; UDU$^{HI.A}$*(=ya)*; UDU$^{HI.A}$*(=KUNU)*

UDU.NÍTA „ram"

UDU.SÍGxMUNUS „female sheep"

UDUN „oven"; UDUN-*ni-ya* loc.sg.; UDUN-*ni-ya-az* abl.

UGU „at the top, up, upper"

UH$_7$-*ant-* „enchanted, bewitched" (Hitt. *alwanzenant-* ?); UH$_7$-*an-za* nom.sg.c.

UMBIN „fingernail" (Hitt. *šankuwāi-*); UMBIN^{MEŠ}*(=ya)*

UN „man, human being" (Hitt. *antuhša-*); UN-*aš* nom.sg.; UN-*an* acc.sg.; UN-*ši(=pát)* dat.sg.; UN^{MEŠ}-*aš*^{1} gen.pl.; UN^{MEŠ}-*aš*^{2} dat.pl.

UN^{MEŠ}*annant-* „people" (Hitt. *antuhšannant-*); UN^{MEŠ}-*an-na-an-za* nom.sg.

UR.BAR.RA „wolf"

UR.GI$_7$ „dog"; UR.GI$_7$-*aš* nom.sg.

UR.MAH „lion"

URU „town" (Hitt. *happiriya-*); URU-*aš*^{1}, URU-*ri-aš* nom.sg.; URU-*an* acc.sg.; URU-*ri* dat.-loc.sg.; URU-*az* abl.; URU-*aš*^{2} loc.pl.; URU$^{DIDLI.HI.A}$*(=ma)*; URU^{LUM} (nom.); URU^{LIM} (gen.)

URUDU „copper", also determinative

^{LÚ}UŠ.BAR „weaver"

ÚŠ „death, ruin" (Hitt. *aggātar* n.?); ÚŠ-*tar(=ma=za)* nom.-acc.sg.

^{D}UTU^{ŠI} „'my sun', majesty"; ^{D}UTU^{ŠI}-*an* acc.sg.; ^{D}UTU^{ŠI}*(=ya/=ya=aš/ =kán/=ma/=ma=kán/=ma=ši/=ma=ta/ =ma=za/ =pát/=wa/=za=kán*

ÚTUL „pot, container; pot with food, food"; ÚTUL$^{HI.A}$*(=ya=ta)*

UZ$_6$.GAL „billy goat"

UZ$_6$.TUR „kid (goat) "

UZU „meat", also determinative

^{NA4}ZA.GÌN „lapislazuli"; ^{NA4}ZA.GÌN*(=ya)*

^{GIŠ}ZA.LAM.GAR „tent"; ^{GIŠ}ZA.LAM.GAR-*aš* loc.pl.

ZÀ.AH.LI „cress; weed"; ZÀ.AH.LI-*an* acc.sg.

1. ZAG „border“ (Hitt. *irha-*); ZAG-*aš* nom.sg.; ZAG-*za* abl.; ZAG*(=ašta)*
2. ZAG „right“ (Hitt. *kunna-*); ZAG-*an* nom.-acc.sg.n.; ZAG-*az* abl. adv.
ZAG.UDU „shoulder“; ZAG.UDU-*za* abl.
ZI „soul, will, life, person“ (Hitt. *ištanza-* c.); ZI-*an-za* nom.sg.; ZI-*ni* dat.sg.; ZI-*it*, ZI-*ni-it* instr.; ZI-*KA(=ya)*
$^{\text{NA4}}$**ZI.KIN** „ritual monument, ritual stone“ (Hitt: *huwaši-*)
ZÍZ „spelt“; ZÍZ$^{\text{HI.A}}$-*aš-š(=a)* gen.pl.

4.3. Akkadographic words

abu „father“ (Hitt. *atta-*); *A-BU* (nom.); *A-BU-YA(=ma)*; *A-BU-ŠU(=kán)*; *AB-BA* (acc.); *A-BI* (gen.)
AD-DIN see ***nadānu*** „to give“
ammatu „ell“; *AM-MA-DU* (nom.)
ana preposition of the dative; *A-NA*
ana minuti „complete“; *A-NA MI-NU-TI*
anzellu „impurity“; *AN-ZI-EL-LU* (nom.)
AŠ-ME see ***šemū*** „to hear“
AŠ-PUR see ***šapāru*** „to write“
ašru „place“ (Hitt. *pedan-*); *AŠ-RU* (nom.); *AŠ-RI*$^{\text{HI.A}}$ (gen.); *A-ŠAR* (stat. constr.)
aššum „because of, for“; *AŠ-ŠUM*
AṢ-BAT see ***1abatu*** „to seize“
bēlu „master, lord“ (Hitt. *išhā-*); *BE-LU* (nom.); *BE-LÍ(=ma=at=šan)* (gen.); *BE-EL* (stat. constr.)
bēlūtu „rule“; *BE-LU-TIM* (gen.pl.); $^{\text{LÚ.MEŠ}}$*BE-LU-TIM* (gen.pl.)
dīnu „case, trial“ (Hitt. *hanneššar*); *DI-NAM* acc.sg.
ellu „free“ (Hitt. *arawa-*); *EL-LUM* (nom.); *EL-LAM(=ma)* (acc.)
^{LÚ}***hatanu*** „brother-in-law“; ^{LÚ}*HA-DA-NU(=ya=an)* (nom.)
hal1u „fortress“; *HAL-ṢÌ* (gen.)
MUŠEN ***HUR-RI*** „partridge“
ina preposition of the locative; *I-NA*
IQ-BI see ***qabū*** „to say“
^{MUNUS}***išertu*** „concubine“; $^{\text{MUNUS.MEŠ}}$*I-ŠAR-TI(=ya)* (gen.)

IŠ-ME see ***šemû*** „to hear“

ištu preposition of ablative and instrumental; *IŠ-TU*

IṢ-BAT, ***IṢ-BA-TU*** see ***ṣabātu*** „to seize“

itti „together with“; *IT-TI*

izbu „freak“; *IZ-BU* nom.sg.

-***ya*** „my“

-***ka*** „your (sg.) “

-***kunu*** „your (pl.) “

^{DUG}***kukūbu*** „jug, pot, can, rhyton“; ^{DUG}*KU-KU-BI* (gen.); ^{DUG}*KU-KU-UB* (stat. constr.)

līmu „thousand“; *LI-IM*

madnanu a kind of carriage; *MA-AD-NA-NU* (nom.)

mahar „before, in front of, opposite“; *MA-HAR*

mahrû „first“ (Hitt. *hantezzi-*); *MAH-RU(=YA)* nom.sg.

māmētu „oath“ (Hitt. *lengāi-*); *MA-ME-TUM* (nom.); *MA-MIT* (stat. constr.)

1. ***mê*** „hundred“; *ME*

2. ***mê*** „water“ (Hitt. *wātar*); *ME-E*

mešedi „body guard“; *ME-ŠE-DI*

^{LÚ}***mutu*** „husband“; ^{LÚ}*MU-DU* (nom.); ^{LÚ}*MU-ZA(=ŠU=ma=ši)* (sic!) acc.sg.

^{LÚ}***munnabtu*** „refugee“; ^{LÚ}*MU-NAB-TUM* (nom.)

^{LÚ}***MU-ZA-ŠU-ma-aš-ši*** see ***mutu*** „husband“

nadānu „to give“ (Hitt. *pāi-*); *AD-DIN* 1.sg.pret.act.

naptānu „meal“; *NAP-TA-NU* (nom.)

-***ni*** „our“

nišû „people (fem.pl.) “; *NI-ŠU-Ú(=ŠU)* (nom.)

nīšu „oath“ (Hitt. *lengāi-*); *NI-IŠ*, *NI-ÌŠ*, *NI-EŠ* (stat. constr.)

pani „before, in front of“; *PA-NI*

qabû „to say, speak“; *IQ-BI* 3.sg.pret.act

qadu „together with“; *QA-DU*

qātu „hand“ (Hitt. *keššar*); *QA-TI(=ŠU=ya=aš=ši=šan)* (gen.); *QA-TI-TE*^{MEŠ}*(=ŠUNU=ya=za=kán)* (gen.pl.); *QA-TAM* (acc.)

qatamma „just as, in the same way“ (Hitt. *apeniššan*); *QA-TAM-MA (=pát)*

sirdu „olive tree“; *SE_{20}-IR-TUM*

^{LÚ}***subru*** indicates a certain person; $^{\mathrm{LÚ.MEŠ}}$*SÚ-UB-RI-E(=ma=ta)*

ṣabātu „to seize“ (Hitt. *ep-*); *AṢ-BAT* 1.sg.pret.act.; *IṢ-BAT* 3.sg.pret.act.; *IṢ-BA-TU* 3.pl.pret.act.
ša preposition of the genitive
šapal „under“ (Hitt. *kattan*); *ŠA-PAL*
šapāru „to write“ (Hitt. *hatrāi-*); *AŠ-PUR* 1.sg.pret.act.; *ŠU-PUR* 2.sg.imp.act.
šemû „to hear“ (Hitt. *ištamaš-*); *AŠ-ME* 1.sg.pret.act.; *IŠ-ME* 3.sg.pret.act.
šīmu „price“; *ŠI-IM(=ŠU)* (stat. constr.)
-šu „his, her“; *-ŠU, -ŠÚ, -ZU*
-šunu „their“; *-ŠU-NU, -ZU-NU*
šumu „name“ (Hitt. *lāman-* n.); *ŠUM-an(=šet), ŠUM(=šet)* nom.-acc.sg.; *ŠUM-aš-mi-it = laman + -šmit* instr.; *ŠUM*^{UM} (nom.)
ŠU-PUR see ***šapāru*** „to write“
tarammi „beloved“; *TA-RA-AM-MI*
temu „messenger, envoy“; ^{LÚ}*TE-MU* (nom.); $^{\text{LÚ.MEŠ}}$*TE-MI(=YA=mu/ =ŠUNU)* (gen.); $^{\text{LÚ.MEŠ}}$*TE-ME(=ya=mu)*
tuppu, ṭuppu „clay tablet“; *ṬUP-PU, TUP-PU* (nom.); *T UP-PA*$^{\text{HI.A}}$ (acc.)
u „and“; *Ù*
^{LÚ}***ubaru*** „stranger, foreigner, guest“; $^{\text{LÚ.MEŠ}}$*Ú-BA-RUM* (nom.)
ul „not“ (Hitt. *natta*); *Ú-UL(=an/=at/=ya/=ma/=wa/=war=an/=war=at), UL*
umma „so, as follows“ (Hitt. *kiššan*); *UM-MA*
ummu „mother“ (Hitt. *anna-* c.); *UM-MA(=NI=šan)* (acc.sg.)
ūmu „day“ (Hitt. *šiwatt-* c.); U_4*-UM*
unūtu „device, object“; *Ú-NU-TUM* (nom.); *Ú-NU-UT* (stat. constr.); *Ú-NU-TE*^{MEŠ}*(=wa=kán)* (nom.pl.)
urram šēram „in the future“; *UR-RA-AM ŠE-RA-AM*
-ZU, -ZUNU see ***-ŠU, -ŠUNU*** „his, her; their“

4.4. Determinatives

D for DINGIR „god“, preceding divine names
DIDLI placed after nouns to indicate the plural
DUG „vessel, container“, preceding terms of vessels or containers

É „house“, preceding building terms
f preceding female personal names
GIŠ „wood“, preceding terms for objects made from wood or parts of wood
HI.A placed after nouns to indicate the plural, originally only with inanimate nouns
ÍD „river“, preceding river names
HUR.SAG „hill, mountain“, preceding hills and mountains
KI „place“, placed after place names
KUŠ „leather“, preceding terms for objects from leather or with parts of leather
LÚ „man“, preceding terms for men
m preceding male personal names
MEŠ placed after nouns to indicate the plural, originally only with animate nouns
MUNUS „women“, preceding terms for women
MUŠEN „bird“, preceding terms for birds (preceding and postpositioned)
NA$_4$ „stone“, preceding terms for objects from stone or with parts of stone
NINDA „bread“, preceding terms for bread, cakes and pastries
SAR „plant“, placed after terms for plants
SÍG „wool“, preceding terms for objects from wool or with parts of wool
TÚG „cloth“, preceding terms for clothes
UDU „sheep“, for elucidation of *iyant-* „sheep“
URU „town“, preceding place names
URUDU „copper“, preceding terms for objects of copper or with parts of copper
UZU „meat“, preceding terms for meat or body parts

4.5. Personal names

^{m}***Alakšandu-*** *A-la-ak-ša-an-du-uš* nom.
^{f}***Ammatalla-*** ^{f}*Am-ma-tal-la-aš* nom.
^{m}***Anitta-*** ^{m}*A-ni-it-ta-aš* nom.
^{m}***Anatarawa-*** ^{m}*An-ta-ra-wa-aš* nom.
^{m}***Apallū-*** ^{m}*A-pal-lu-ú* nom.

^{m}***Appu-*** ^{m}*Ap-pu*; ^{m}*Ap-pu-uš(=ma)* nom.
^{m}***Armadatta-*** ^{m}*Ar-ma-*^{D}IM-*an* acc.
^{m}***Arnuwanda-*** ^{m}*Ar-nu-wa-an-da*, ^{m}*Ar-nu-wa-an-ta*; ^{m}*Ar-nu-an-da-aš* nom.
^{m}***Āškali(ya)-*** ^{m}*A-aš-ka-li-ya-aš* nom.; ^{m}*A-aš-ki-li(=pát)*, ^{m}*A-aš-ka-li(=ma)* dat.
^{f}***Ašmunikal-*** ^{f}*Aš-mu-ni-kal*
^{m}***Adadbēlī-*** ^{mD}IM-*BE-LÍ-iš* nom.
^{m}***Azira-*** ^{m}*A-zi-ra-aš* nom.
^{m}***Hantīli-*** ^{m}*Ha-an-ti-li*, ^{m}*Ha-an-ti-i-li*; ^{m}*Ha-an-ti-li-iš*, ^{m}*Ha-an-ti-li-iš-š(=a)*, ^{m}*Ha-an-ti-i-li-iš-š(=a)* nom.
^{f}***Harapšeki-*** ^{f}*Ha-ra-ap-še-ki-in* acc.
^{m}***Hašša-*** ^{m}*Ha-aš-ša*
^{f}***Haštayar-*** ^{f}*Ha-aš-ta-ya-ar*
^{m}***Hattušili-*** ^{m}*Ha-at-tu-ši-li*
^{m}***Hellarizzi-*** ^{m}*Hi-el-la-ri-iz-zi*
^{m}***Hūhazalma-*** ^{m}*Hu-u-ha-za-al-ma-n(=a)* acc.
^{m}***Hukkanā-*** ^{m}*Hu-uq-qa-na-a*; ^{m}*Hu-uq-qa-na-a-aš* nom./voc.
^{m}***Hūpašiya-*** ^{m}*Hu-u-pa-ši-ya-aš-š(=a)* nom.; ^{m}*Hu-u-pa-ši-ya* voc.
^{m}***Huzziya-*** ^{m}*Hu-uz-zi-ya-aš* nom.; ^{m}*Hu-uz-zi-ya-n(=a)* acc.
^{m}***Ibrišarruma-*** ^{m}*Ib-ri-*LUGAL-*ma*
^{mD}IM-***BE-LÍ-iš*** see ***Adadbēlī***
^{m}***Išputašinara-*** ^{m}*Iš-pu-ta-aš-i-na-ar-aš* nom.
^{m}***Kešši-*** ^{m}*Ki-eš-ši-iš* nom.; ^{m}*Ki-eš-ši-ya* dat.
^{m}***Kupanta-***^{D}**KAL**-***a-*** ^{m}*Ku-pa-an-ta-*^{D}KAL-*aš* nom./voc.
^{m}***Kurunta-*** ^{mD}LAMMA-*an-n(=a)* acc.
^{m}***Mašhuiluwa-*** ^{m}PÉŠ.TUR-*wa*; ^{m}*Maš-hu-i-lu-wa-aš*, ^{m}PÉŠ.TUR-*wa-aš (=ma=mu=uš=šan)* nom.
^{m}***Mašturi-*** ^{m}*Ma-aš-tu-ri*; ^{m}*Ma-aš-tu-ri-iš* nom.
^{m}***Muršīli-*** ^{m}*Mur-ši-i-li*; ^{m}*Mur-ši-*DINGIR^{LIM}-*iš* nom.; ^{m}*Mur-ši-i-li-ya-aš* gen.; ^{m}*Mur-ši-li-in* acc.
^{m}***Muwatalli-*** ^{m}NIR.GÁL-*iš* nom.
^{m}***Nanatalli-*** ^{m}*Na-na-ta-al-li*
^{m}***Nunnu-*** ^{m}*Nu-un-nu-un-n(=a)* acc.
^{m}**PÉŠ.TUR-*wa*** see ***Mašhuiluwa***

^{m}***Pihinakki-*** ^{m}*Pí-hi-na-ak-ki-iš(=za)* nom.
^{m}***Pišeni-*** ^{m}*Pí-še-ni-in* acc.
^{m}***Pithāna-*** ^{m}*Pí-it-ha-a-na-aš* nom.
^{m}***Šarmaššu-*** ^{m}*Šar-ma-aš-šu-un* acc.
^{m}***Šarupšenna-*** ^{m}*Šar-ru-up-še-en-na-aš* nom.
^{f}***Šintalimeni-*** ^{f}*Ši-in-ta-li-me-ni*
^{m}***Damnaššu-*** ^{m}*Dam-na-aš-šu-un-n(=a)* acc.
^{m}***Targašnalli-*** ^{m}*Tar-ga-aš-na-al-li-in* acc.
^{m}***Tatili-*** ^{m}*Ta-ti-li-iš* nom.
^{m}***Telipinu-*** ^{m}*Te-li-pí-nu-uš* nom.
^{f}***Titai-*** ^{f}*Ti-ta-i*
^{m}***Tittiya-*** ^{m}*Ti-it-ti-ya-aš* gen.
^{m}***Tuthaliya-*** ^{m}*Tu-ut-ha-li-ya-aš*, ^{m}*Du-ut-ha-li-ya-aš(=za=kán)* nom.
^{m}***Ūhna-*** ^{m}*U-uh-na-aš* nom.
^{m}***Ūhhaziti-*** ^{m}*Uh-ha*-LÚ-*iš*, ^{m}*U-uh-ha*-LÚ-*iš* nom.
^{m}***Ulmitešup-*** ^{m}*Ul-mi-*^{D}U-*up(=pát)*
^{m}***Urhitešup(a)*** ^{m}*Úr-hi-*^{D}U-*up-an* acc.
^{m}***Zidanta-*** ^{m}*Zi-dan-ta-aš* nom.; ^{m}*Zi-dan-ta-an* acc.

4.6. Divine names

^{D}***Alalu-*** ^{D}*A-la-lu-uš* nom.; ^{D}*A-la-lu-un* acc.; ^{D}*A-la-lu-u-i* dat.
^{D}***Āndaliya-*** ^{D}*A-an-da-a-li-ya-aš* nom.
^{D}***Anu-*** ^{D}*A-nu*; ^{D}*A-nu-uš* nom.
^{D}***Ašertum*** ^{D}*A-še-ir-tum*
^{D}***É-A*** ^{D}*É-A-aš* nom.
^{D}***Elkuniirša-*** ^{D}*El-ku-ni-ir-ša-aš* nom.
^{D}GAŠAN „divine mistress“ = *Ištar*
^{D}GIŠ.“GIM“.MAŠ „Gilgameš“
^{D}***Halmašuitt-*** ^{D}*Hal-ma-šu-it-ti* dat.
^{D}***Hannahanna-*** ^{D}NIN.TU-*ni* dat.
^{D}***Hantašepa-*** ^{D}*Ha-an-ta-še-pí-eš* nom.pl.
^{D}***Hepat-*** ^{D}*Hé-pát*; ^{D}*Hé-pát-du-uš*, ^{D}*Hé-pa-du-uš* nom.
^{MUŠ}***Illuyanka-*** ^{MUŠ}*Il-lu-ya-an-ka-aš* nom.; ^{MUŠ}*Il-lu-ya-an-ka-an* acc.

^{D}**IM** „weather god“ see ***Tarhu(nt)-***
^{D}***Inara-*** ^{D}*I-na-ra-aš*, ^{D}*I-na-ra-aš-š(=a)* nom.
^{D}***Išhara-*** ^{D}*Iš-ha-ra-az* abl.
^{D}***IŠTAR*** ^{D}*IŠTAR(=ma=mu=kán/=mu=kán/=pát)*
^{D}***IŠTAR*-A.A-*an*** see ***Šaušgamuwa***
^{D}***Ištanu-*** ^{D}UTU-*uš* nom./voc.; ^{D}UTU-*aš*, ^{D}UTU-*wa-aš* gen.; ^{D}UTU-*an*, ^{D}UTU-*un* acc.; ^{D}UTU-*i*, ^{D}UTU-*u-i*^{1} dat.; ^{D}UTU-*u-i*^{2} voc.
^{D}***Kamrušepa-*** ^{D}*Kam-ru-ši-pa-aš-š(=a)* gen.
^{D}***Kumarbi-*** ^{D}*Ku-mar-bi-iš*, ^{D}*Ku-mar-bi-eš(=wa)* nom.
^{D}**LAMMA** „protective god“
^{D}***Lelwani-*** ^{D}*Li-el-wa-ni*
^{D}**MAH** „mother goddess, genius“
^{D}***Mezzula-*** ^{D}*Mi-iz-zu-la-an* acc.
^{D}**NIN.TU-*ni*** see ***Hannahanna***
^{D}***Šaušgamuwa-*** ^{D}*IŠTAR*-A.A-*an* acc.
^{D}***SÎN*** „moon god“; ^{D}*SÎN-aš-š(=a)* nom.
^{D}***Šiušmi-*** ^{D}*Ši-i-uš-mi-iš* nom.; ^{D}*Ši-ú-šum-mi-in*, ^{D}*Ši-u-šum-mi-in* acc.
^{D}***Šuli(n)katte-*** ^{D}*Šu-li-kat-ti*
^{D}***Tarhu(nt)-*** „weather god“; ^{D}IM-*aš*^{1}, ^{D}IM-*aš-š(=a)*, ^{D}IM-*aš(=taš=ša)* nom./voc.; ^{D}IM-*aš*^{2} gen.; ^{D}IM-*an*, ^{D}IM-*an-n(=a)*, ^{D}IM-*n(=a)* acc.; ^{D}IM-*un-ni* dat.; ^{D}IM-*ni-it* instr.
^{D}***Tarpattašši-*** ^{D}*Tar-pa-at-ta-aš-ši-iš* voc.
^{D}***Tašmišu-*** ^{D}*Tàš-mi-šu-un* acc.; ^{D}*Ta-aš-mi-šu-ut* instr.
^{D}***Telipinu-*** ^{D}*Te-li-pí-nu*^{1}; ^{D}*Te-li-pí-nu-uš* nom.; ^{D}*Te-li-pí-nu-wa-aš* gen.; ^{D}*Te-li-pí-nu-i* dat.; ^{D}*Te-li-pí-nu*^{2} voc.
^{D}***Tešimi-*** ^{D}*Te-ši-mi(=wa=kán)*
^{D}**U** „weather god“; ^{D}U-*aš* nom.; ^{D}U-*an* acc.; ^{D}U-*ni* dat.
^{D}***Ullikummi-*** ^{D}*Ul-lu-kum-mi-in* acc.
^{D}***Ubelluri-*** ^{D}*Ú-pí-el-lu-ri-iš* nom.; ^{D}*Ú-pí-el-lu-ri* voc.
^{D}**U-*tar*** „deity (?)“
^{D}**UTU** see ^{D}***Ištanu-***
^{D}**XXX** „moon god“; ^{D}XXX-*aš* nom.
^{D}***Zalinu-*** ^{D}*Za-li-nu-un* acc.
^{D}***Zithariya-*** ^{D}*Zi-it-ha-ri-ya*; ^{D}*Zi-it-ha-ri-ya-aš* nom.

4.7. Place and country names

^{URU}***Akada-*** „Akkade"; ^{URU}*A-ag-ga-ta-az* abl.
^{URU}***Amurra-*** ^{URU}*A-mur-ra*; ^{URU}*A-mur-ri-ya*
^{URU}***Ānkuwa-*** ^{URU}*A-an-ku-wa*
^{URU}***Arinna-*** ^{URU}*A-ri-in-na*, ^{URU}*A-ri-in-na*^{KI}; ^{URU}PÚ-*na*
^{ÍD}***Aranzahi-*** „Tigris"; ^{ÍD}*A-ra-an-za-hi-it* instr.
^{URU}***Arušna-*** ^{URU}*A-ru-uš-na*
^{URU}***Arzawa-*** ^{URU}*Ar-za-u-wa*
^{URU}***Āššuwa-*** ^{URU}*A-aš-šu-wa*
^{URU}***Ēbla-*** „Ebla"; ^{URU}*E-eb-la-i* loc.
^{URU}***Elamta-*** „Elam"; ^{URU}*E-lam-ta-az* abl.
$^{\text{HUR.SAG}}$***Hahruwa-*** $^{\text{HUR.SAG}}$*Ha-ah-ru-wa*
^{URU}***Hahha-*** ^{URU}*Ha-ah-ha*; ^{URU}*Ha-ah-ha-an(=ma=za=kán)* acc.
^{URU}***Hayaša-*** ^{URU}*Ha-ya-ša*
^{URU}***Hakpiš-*** ^{URU}*Ha-ak-piš*, ^{URU}*Ha-ak-piš-š(=a)* nom.
^{URU}***Hapalla-*** ^{URU}*Ha-pal-la*
^{URU}***Halpa-*** ^{URU}*Hal-pa-aš*
^{URU}***Harahšuwa-*** ^{URU}*Ha-ra-ah-šu-wa-aš* nom.
^{URU}***Haštira-*** ^{URU}MUL-*ra*
^{URU}***Haššuwa-*** ^{URU}*Ha-aš-šu-wa*
^{URU}***Hatti-*** ^{URU}*Ha-at-ti*, ^{URU}*Hat-ti(=kán/=ma=ašta/=ma=wa=kán/=pát)*; ^{URU}*Ha-at-ti-ya*
^{URU}***Hattuša-*** ^{URU}*Ha-at-tu-ša*; ^{URU}*Ha-at-tu-ša-an(=ma)*; ^{URU}*Ha-at-tu-ša-š(=a /=pát)*; ^{URU}*Ha-at-tu-ši* loc.; ^{URU}KÙ.BABBAR-*ti*
^{URU}***Hawarkina-*** ^{URU}*Ha-wa-ar-ki-na-an* acc.
$^{\text{(URU)}}$***Hurri-*** „Hurrite"; ^{URU}*Hur-ri*; *Hur-ri*
^{URU}**HUR.SAG.KALAM.MÁ** ^{URU}HUR.SAG.KALAM.MÁ-*az* abl.
^{URU}**KÁ.DINGIR.RA** „Babylon"; ^{URU}KÁ.DINGIR.RA-*az* abl.
^{URU}***Kaneš-*** ^{URU}*Ka-ni-iš*
$^{\text{HUR.SAG}}$***Kandurna-*** $^{\text{HUR.SAG}}$*Kán-dur-na*
^{URU}***Kappušiya-*** ^{URU}*Kap-pu-ši-ya*
^{URU}***Karanduniya-*** ^{URU}*Ka-ra-an-du-ni-ya*
$^{\text{(LÚ/URU)}}$***Gašga*** „Gaškan"; $^{\text{(LÚ)}}$*Ga-aš-ga*; ^{URU}*Ga-aš-ga(=ma/=wa)*;

^{URU}*Ga-aš-ga-az* abl.

^{URU}**KÙ.BABBAR-*ti*** see ***Hatti***

^{URU}***Kuliwišna-*** ^{URU}*Ku-li-ú-iš-na-ya*

^{URU}***Kummanni-*** ^{URU}*Kum-ma-an-ni*

^{URU}***Kuruštama-*** ^{URU}*Ku-ru-uš-ta-ma*

^{URU}***Kuššara*** ^{URU}*Ku-uš-ša-ra*

$^{\mathrm{HUR.SAG}}$***Lalapaduwa-*** $^{\mathrm{HUR.SAG}}$*La-la-pa-du-wa*

^{URU}***Lawazantiya*** ^{URU}*La-wa-za-an-ti-ya*

^{URU}***Lišipra-*** ^{URU}*Li-ši-ip-ra-an* acc.

LÚ ^{URU}***Luiumna-*** „Luwian“; ^{URU}*Lu-i-um-na-aš* gen.

^{URU}***Luwiya-*** „Luwia“; ^{URU}*Lu-ú-i-ya*; ^{URU}*Lu-ú-i-ya-az* abl.

^{ÍD}***Māla-*** ^{ÍD}*Ma-a-la*; ^{ÍD}*Ma-a-la-an-n(=a)* acc.

^{URU}***Malazziya-*** ^{URU}*Ma-la-az-zi-an* acc.

^{URU}***Maraššantiya-*** ^{URU}*Ma-ra-aš-ša-an-ti-ya-za* abl.

^{URU}***Marešta-*** ^{URU}*Ma-ri-eš-ta*

^{URU}***Mittanni-*** ^{URU}*Mi-it-ta-an-ni*

^{URU}***Miz(a)ri*** „Egypt“; ^{URU}*Mi-iz-ri*, ^{URU}*Mi-iz-za-ri-i*; *Mi-iz-ri*, *Mi-iz-ri-i*

^{URU}**MUL-*ra*** see ^{URU}***Haštira-***

^{URU}***Nerik(a)-*** ^{URU}*Ne-ri-ik*; ^{URU}*Ne-ri-iq-q(=a/=ši=kán)*; ^{URU}*Ne-ri-iq-qa(=ya/=za)*; ^{URU}*Ne-ri-iq-qa-aš* nom.; ^{URU}*Ne-ri-iq-qa-an(=man)* acc.; ^{URU}*Ne-ri-iq-qa-az* abl.; ^{URU}*Ne-ri-ik-ki* loc.

^{URU}***Neša-*** ^{URU}*Ne-e-ša*; ^{URU}*Ne-e-ša-aš* gen.; ^{URU}*Ne-e-ša-az* abl.; ^{URU}*Ne-e-ši* loc.

^{URU}***Ninašša-*** ^{URU}*Ni-na-aš-ša*

^{URU}***Parmanna-*** ^{URU}*Pár-ma-an-na-aš(=ma=kán)* nom.

^{URU}***Pitašša-*** ^{URU}*Pí-taš-ša*

^{URU}**PÚ-*na*** see ^{URU}***Arinna-***

^{ÍD}***Pūruna-*** ^{ÍD}*Pu-u-ru-na-an* acc.

^{URU}***Purušhanda-*** ^{URU}*Pu-ru-uš-ha-an-da*

^{URU}***Šalatiwara-*** ^{URU}*Ša-la-ti-wa-ra*

^{URU}***Šamuha-*** ^{URU}*Ša-mu-ha*; ^{URU}*Ša-mu-ha-an-n(=a)* acc.

^{URU}***Šanawitta-*** ^{URU}*Ša-na-u-i-it-ta*

^{URU}***Šarmana-*** ^{URU}*Ša-ar-ma-na(=kán)*

^{ÍD}***Šēha-*** ^{ÍD}*Še-e-ha*

^{URU}***Šūša-*** „Susa“; ^{URU}*Šu-u-ša-az*
$^{\text{HUR.SAG}}$***Tahaya-*** $^{\text{HUR.SAG}}$*Ta-ha-ya-i* loc.
^{URU}***Taggaštanna-*** ^{URU}*Tág-ga-aš-ta-an-n(=a)* acc.
^{URU}***Talmaliya-*** ^{URU}*Tal-ma-li-ya-aš*
^{URU}***Tarhuntašša-*** URU ^{D}U-*aš-ša-an* acc.
^{URU}***Dilmunana-*** ^{URU}*Di-el-mu-na-an-n(=a)* acc.
^{URU}***Durmitta-*** ^{URU}*Dur-mi-it-ta(=ma=aš)*
URU ^{D}U-*aš-š(=an)* see ***Tarhuntašša***
^{URU}***Ulma-*** ^{URU}*Ul-ma*
(LÚ) ^{URU}***Uššumna-*** „inhabitant of Ušša“; ^{URU}*Uš-šu-um-na-aš* nom.
$^{\text{HUR.SAG}}$***Wāšitta-*** $^{\text{HUR.SAG}}$*Wa$_{a}$-a-ši-it-ta-aš* nom.
^{URU}***Zalp(uw)a-*** ^{URU}*Za-al-pa*, ^{URU}*Za-al-pu-wa*, ^{URU}*Za-a-al-pu-wa*; ^{URU}*Za-a-al-pu-wa-az* abl.
^{URU}***Zikparayašša-*** ^{URU}*Zi-ik-pa-ra-ya-aš-ša-an* acc.
^{URU}***Zippalanda-*** ^{URU}*Zi-ip-pa-la-an-da*
^{URU}***Zippašna-*** ^{URU}*Zi-ip-pa-aš-na-an* acc.
^{URU}***Zizzilippa-*** ^{URU}*Zi-iz-zi-li-ip-pí* loc.

4.8. Numbers

1-*aš* „one, alone“; 1-*an* acc.; 1-*e-da-ni* dat.; 1^{EN} = Akkad. *ištēn* „one“
1-*NU-TUM* = Akkad. ***ištēnūtum*** „set“
1-*ŠU* etc. „once“; 2-*ŠU(=ma/=pát)*
2-*dān* „secondly“; 2-*ta-a-an*
3-*anna* „third“; 3-*an-na-a(=ta)*
4-*anna* „fourth“; 4-*an-n(=a=za=kán)* acc.
9-*aš* „nine“
10-*ta* „tenth“; 10-*ti(=ma)* loc.

5. Literature

5.1. Used text editions

Alp, Sedat, 1991: Hethitische Briefe aus Maşat-Höyük, Ankara

Archi, Alfonso, 1979: „L"humanité des Hittites", in: Florilegium Anatolicum, Mélanges offerts à E. Laroche, Paris, 37-48

–, 1988: „Eine Anrufung der Sonnengöttin von Arinna", in: Documentum Asiae minoris antiquae. Festschrift für H. Otten zum 75. Geburtstag, ed. by Erich Neu, Wiesbaden, 5-31

Badalì, Enrico, 1985: „Una festa in onore di Zababa (CTH 612)", in: Studi epigrafici e linguistici sul Vicino Oriente antico 2, 53-80

–, / Zinko, Christian, 1989: Der 16. Tag des AN.TAH.ŠUM-Festes; Text, Übersetzung, Kommentar, Glossar (Scientia 20), Innsbruck

Beckman, Gary, 1983: Hittite birth rituals (Studien zu den Boğazköy-Texten 29), Wiesbaden

Boysan-Dietrich, Nilüfer, 1987: Das hethitische Lehmhaus (Texte der Hethiter 12), Heidelberg

Carruba, Onofrio, 1966: Das Beschwörungsritual für die Göttin Wišurijanza (Studien zu den Boğazköy-Texten 2), Wiesbaden

Houwink ten Cate, Philo H.J., 1967: „Muwatallis' prayer to the stormgod of Kummanni (KBo XI 1)", in: Revue hittite et asianique 25/81, 101-140

–, 1983/84: „Sidelights on the Ahhiyawa Question. From Hittite vassals and royal correspondence", in: Jaarbericht Ex Oriente Lux 28, 33-79

Friedrich, Johannes, 1926/30: Staatsverträge des Hatti-Reiches in hethitischer Sprache, Leipzig

–, 1950: „Churritische Märchen und Sagen in hethitischer Sprache", in: Zeitschrift für Assyriologie 49 (N.F.15), 213-255

–, 1959: Die hethitischen Gesetze, Leiden

García Trabazo, José Virgilio, 2002: Textos religiosos hititas, Madrid

Glocker, Jürgen, 1997: Das Ritual für den Wettergott von Kuliwišna. Textzeugnisse eines lokalen Kultfestes im Anatolien der Hethiterzeit, Firenze

Götze, Albrecht, 1933: Die Annalen des Muršiliš, Leipzig

–, 1938: The Hittite ritual of Tunnawi, New Haven

–, / Pedersen, Holger, 1934: Muršilis Sprachlähmung, Kopenhagen
Gurney, Oliver R., 1940: „Hittite prayers of Mursili II“, in: Annals of Archaeology and Anthropology 27, 3-119
Güterbock, Hans Gustav, 1951: „The song of Ullikummi. Revised text of the Hittite version of a Hurrian myth“, in: Journal of cuneiform studies 5, 135-161
–, 1983: „A hurro-hittite hymn to Ishtar“, in: Journal of the American Oriental Society 103, 155-164 [= Perspectives on Hittite civilization: Selected writings of H.G. Güterbock, ed. by H.A. Hoffner, Chicago 1997, 65-74]
–, / van den Hout, Theo, 1990: The Hittite instruction for the royal bodyguard, Chicago
Haas, Volkert, 1970: Der Kult von Nerik, Roma
Hagenbuchner, Albertine, 1989: Die Korrespondenz der Hethiter, 2. Teil: Die Briefe mit Transkription, Übersetzung und Kommentar (Texte der Hethiter 16), Heidelberg
Hoffmann, Inge, 1984: Der Erlaß Telipinus (Texte der Hethiter 11), Heidelberg
Hoffner, Harry A., 1981: „The Hurrian story of the Sungod, the Cow and the Fisherman“, in: Fs. for Ernest R. Lacheman, Winona Lake, 189-194
–, 1988: „The song of the Silver – A member of the Kumarbi cycle of ‘songs’, in: Documentum Asiae minoris antiquae. Festschrift für H. Otten zum 75. Geburtstag, hrsg. von E. Neu, Wiesbaden, 143-166
–, 1997: The laws of the Hittites, Leiden
Hölscher, Monika: Das Reinigungsritual der Ambazzi, Marburg o.J.
van den Hout, Theo, 1995: Der Ulmitešub-Vertrag (Studien zu den Boğazköy-Texten 38), Wiesbaden
Hutter, Manfred, 1988: Behexung, Entsühnung und Heilung, Freiburg/ Schweiz
Imparati, Fiorella / Saporetti, Claudio, 1965: „L’autobiografia di Hattusili I.“, in: Studi Classici e Orientali 14, 40-85
Jakob-Rost, Liane, 1961: „Zu den hethitischen Bildbeschreibungen“, in: Mitteilungen des Instituts für Orientforschung 8, 161-217
–, 1972: Das Ritual der Malli aus Arzawa gegen Behexung (Texte der Hethiter 2), Heidelberg
Kammenhuber, Annelies, 1961: Hippologia hethitica, Wiesbaden
Kronasser, Heinz, 1961: „Fünf hethitische Rituale“, in: Die Sprache 7, 140-167
–, 1963: Die Umsiedelung der schwarzen Gottheit, Wien
Kühne, Cord / Otten, Heinrich, 1971: Der Šaušgamuwa-Vertrag (Studien zu den Boğazköy-Texten 16), Wiesbaden
Kümmel, Hans Martin, 1967: Ersatzrituale für den hethitischen König (Studien zu

den Boğazköy-Texten 3), Wiesbaden

Laroche, Emmanuel, 1975: „Textes mythologiques hittites en transliteration I.“, in: Revue hittite et asianique 77, 65 ff.

Lebrun, René, 1980: Hymnes et prières hittites, Louvain

de Martino, Stefano, 1996: L'Anatolia occidentale nel medio regno ittita, Firenze

McMahon, John Gregory, 1988: The Hittite state cult of the tutelary deities, Chicago

del Monte, Giuseppe, 1986: Il trattato fra Muršili II di Hattuša e Niqmepa' di Ugarit, Roma

Neu, Erich, 1970: Ein althethitisches Gewitterritual (Studien zu den Boğazköy-Texten 12), Wiesbaden

–, 1974: Der Anitta-Text (Studien zu den Boğazköy-Texten 18), Wiesbaden

–, 1980: Althethitische Ritualtexte in Umschrift (Studien zu den Boğazköy-Texten 25), Wiesbaden

–, 1996: Das hurritische Epos der Freilassung I. Untersuchungen zu einem hurritisch-hethitischen Textensemble aus Hattuša (Studien zu den Boğazköy-Texten 32), Wiesbaden

Oettinger, Norbert, 1976: Die Militärischen Eide der Hethiter (Studien zu den Boğazköy-Texten 22), Wiesbaden

Otten, Heinrich, 1958: Hethitische Totenrituale, Berlin

–, 1959/60: „Ein Brief aus Hattuša an Bâbu-ahu-iddina“, in: Archiv für Orientforschung 19, 39-46

–, 1967: „Ein hethitischer Vertrag aus dem 15./14. Jahrhundert v.Chr. (KBo XVI 47)“, in: Istanbuler Mitteilungen 17, 55-62

–, 1969: Ein althethitisches Ritual für das Königspaar (Studien zu den Boğazköy-Texten 8), Wiesbaden

–, 1971: Ein hethitisches Festritual (Studien zu den Boğazköy-Texten 13), Wiesbaden

–, 1973: Eine althethitische Erzählung um die Stadt Zalpa (Studien zu den Boğazköy-Texten 17), Wiesbaden

–, 1981: Die Apologie Hattusilis III. Das Bild der Überlieferung (Studien zu den Boğazköy-Texten 24), Wiesbaden

–, 1988: Die Bronzetafel aus Boğazköy. Ein Staatsvertrag Tuthalijas IV. (Studien zu den Boğazköy-Texten Beiheft 1), Wiesbaden

–, / Souček, Vladimir, 1965: Das Gelübde der Königin Puduhepa an die Göttin Lelwani (Studien zu den Bočazköy-Texten 1), Wiesbaden

Riemschneider, Kaspar Klaus, 1970: Babylonische Geburtsomina in hethitischer

Übersetzung (Studien zu den Boğazköy-Texten 9), Wiesbaden
–, : Die hethitischen und akkadischen Omentexte aus Boğazköy, Dresden 2004
von Schuler, Einar, 1957: Hethitische Dienstanweisungen für höhere Hof- und Staatsbeamte, Graz
–, 1959: „Hethitische Königserlässe als Quellen der Rechtsfindung und ihr Verhältnis zum kodifizierten Recht“, in: Festschrift Johannes Friedrich zum 65. Geburtstag, hrsg. von R. v. Kienle u.a., Heidelberg, 435-472
–, 1965: Die Kaškäer, Berlin
Schwartz, Benjamin, 1947: „A Hittite ritual text (KUB 29.1 = 1780/c)“, in: Orientalia 16, 23-55
Siegelová, Jana, 1971: Appu-Märchen und Hedammu-Mythus (Studien zu den Boğazköy-Texten 14), Wiesbaden
Singer, Itamar, 1984: The Hittite KI.LAM-festival (Studien zu den Boğazköy-Texten 28), Wiesbaden
–, 1996: Muwatalli's prayer to the assembly of gods through the storm-god of lightning, Atlanta
Sommer, Ferdinand, 1932: Die Ahhiyava-Urkunden, München
–, / Ehelolf, Hans, 1924: Das hethitische Ritual des Papanikri von Komana (KBo V 1 = Bo 2001), Leipzig
–, / Falkenstein, Adam, 1938: Die hethitisch-akkadische Bilingue des Hattušili I., München
Soysal, Oğuz, 1987: „KUB XXXI 4 + KBo III 41 und 40 (Die Puhanu-Chronik). Zum Thronstreit Hattusilis I.“, in: Hethitica 7, 173-253
–, 1989: Muršili I., Würzburg
Sturtevant, Edgar H., 1934: „A Hittite text on the duties of priests and temple servants“, in: Journal of the American Oriental Society 54, 363-406
Szabó, Gabriella, 1971: Ein hethitisches Entsühnungsritual für das Königspaar Tuthaliya und Nikalmati (Texte der Hethiter 1), Heidelberg
Tischler, Johann, 1981: Das hethitische Gebet der Gaššulijawija, Innsbruck
Ünal, Ahmet, 1974: Hattušili III., Teil I: Hattušili bis zu seiner Thronbesteigung, Band 2: Quellen und Indices (Texte der Hethiter 4), Heidelberg
–, 1978: Ein Orakeltext über die Intrigen am hethitischen Hof (Texte der Hethiter 6), Heidelberg
–, 1996: The Hittite ritual of Hantitaššu from the city of Hurma against troublesome years, Ankara
Werner, Rudolf, 1967: Hethitische Gerichtsprotokolle (Studien zu den Boğazköy-Texten 4), Wiesbaden

5.2. Secondary literature

Bauer, Anna (forthcoming): „Verberstsätze im Hethitischen“, in: Krisch, T. et al. (eds.), Proceedings of the Indo-European Conference held in Salzburg, September 2008

Boley, Jacqueline, 1979: „The 'local' sentence particles in Hittite“, in: Per una grammatica ittita/Towards a Hittite grammar, hrsg. von O. Carruba, Pavia, 1-31

–, 1984: The Hittite *hark*-construction, Innsbruck

–, 1989: The sentence particles and the place words in Old and Middle Hittite, Innsbruck

–, 1992: „The Hittite periphrastic construction“, in: Per una grammatica ittita/Towards a Hittite grammar, hrsg. von O. Carruba, Pavia, 33-59

–, 1993: The Hittite particle *-z/-za*, Innsbruck

Carruba, Onofrio, 1969: Die satzeinleitenden Partikeln in den indogermanischen Sprachen Anatoliens, Roma

Cowgill, Warren, 1979: „Anatolian *hi*-conjugation and Indo-European perfect: instalment II“, in: Hethitisch und Indogermanisch. Vergleichende Studien zur historischen Grammatik und zur dialektgeographischen Stellung der indogermanischen Sprachgruppe Altkleinasiens, hrsg. von E. Neu und W. Meid, Innsbruck, 25-39

Disterheft, Dorothy, 1984: „Non-final verbs in Hittite“, in: Zeitschrift für vergleichende Sprachforschung 97, 221-227

Dressler, Wolfgang U. 1968: Studien zur verbalen Pluralität, Wien

Eichner, Heiner, 1975: „Die Vorgeschichte des hethitischen Verbalsystems“, in: Flexion und Wortbildung. Akten der V. Fachtagung der Indogermanischen Gesellschaft, Regensburg 1973, hrsg. von H. Rix, Wiesbaden, 71-103

–, 1985: Das Problem des Ansatzes eines urindogermanischen Numerus „Kollektiv“ („Komprehensiv“), in: Grammatische Kategorien. Funktion und Geschichte. Akten der VII. Fachtagung der Indogermanischen Gesellschaft, Berlin 1983, hg. von B. Schlerath, Berlin, 134-169

Friedrich, Johannes, 1960: Hethitisches Elementarbuch, 2. Auflage, Heidelberg

Garrett, Andrew, 1994: „Relative Clause Syntax in Lycian and Hittite“, in: Die Sprache 36, 29-69

Güterbock, Hans Gustav, 1978: „Hethitische Literatur“, in: Neues Handbuch der Literaturwissenschaft, Bd. 1: Altorientalische Literaturen, hg. von W. Röllig, Wiesbaden, 211-253

–, 1983: „Hittite historiography: a survey“, in: History, Historiography and interpretation, ed. by H. Tadmor and M. Weinfeld, Jerusalem, 21-35

Hahn, Adelaide, 1949: „The non-restrictive relative in Hittite“, in: Language 25, 346-374

Harðarson, Jón Axel, 1994: „Der Verlust zweier wichtiger Flexionskategorien im Uranatolischen“, in: Historische Sprachforschung 107, 30-41

Held, Warren, 1957: „The Hittite relative sentence“, in: Language 33, 1-52

Hoffmann, Karl, 1970: „Das Kategoriensystem des indogermanischen Verbums“, in: Münchener Studien zur Sprachwissenschaft 28, 19-41

Hoffner, Harry, 1975: „Hittite mythological texts: a survey“, in: Unity and diversity, ed. by H. Goedicke and J.J.M. Roberts, Baltimore, 136-145

–, 1979: „Studies in the Hittite particles, II: on some uses of *-kan*“, in: Per una grammatica ittita/Towards a Hittite grammar, hrsg. von O. Carruba, Pavia, 137-151

Josephsson, Folke, 1972: The function of the sentence particles in Old and Middle Hittite, Uppsala

Kammenhuber, Annelies, 1954: „Studien zum hethitischen Infinitivsystem II: Zur Syntax der Infinitive auf *-anna (-ātar)* und *-uwanzi (-uwar)*“, in: Mitteilungen des Instituts für Orientforschung 2, 44-77, 245-265, 403-444

–, 1969: „Hethitisch, Palaisch, Luwisch und Hieroglyphenluwisch“, in: Handbuch der Orientalistik, 1.Abt., II. Bd., 1. und 2. Abschn., Lf. 2, Leiden, 119-357

Katz, Joshua T., 1998: „Archaische keltische Personalpronomina aus indogermanischer Sicht“, in: Sprache und Kultur der Indogermanen. Akten der X. Fachtagung der Indogermanischen Gesellschaft Innsbruck 1996, hg. von W. Meid, Innsbruck, 265-291

Kowal, Bela, 1983: „Das Problem des Fragesatzes in den hethitischen mythologischen Texten des hurrischen Kreises“, in: Philologie und Sprachwissenschaft, Akten der 10. Österreichischen Linguisten-Tagung, Innsbruck 1982, hrsg. von W. Meid und H. Schmeja, Innsbruck, 119-136

Lehmann, Christian, 1979: „Der Relativsatz vom Indogermanischen bis zum Italienischen“, in: Die Sprache 25, 1-25

Lühr, Rosemarie, 1998: „Einräumung und Zugeständnis. Skalare und universale konzessive Konditionalsätze im Hethitischen“, in: Intellectual life of the Ancient Near East. Papers presented at the 43rd Rencontre Assyriologique Internationale Prag 1996, ed. by Jiří Prosecký, Prag, 221-230

–, 2001: „Zum Modalfeld im Hethitischen“, in: Anatolisch und Indogermanisch. Akten des Kolloquiums der Indogermanischen Gesellschaft Pavia 1998, hrsg. von O. Carruba, Innsbruck, 239-262

–, 2001a: „Relativsätze im Hethitischen“, in: Akten des IV. Internationalen Kongresses für Hethitologie Würzburg 1999, hrsg. von G. Wilhelm, Wiesbaden, 333-346

Luraghi, Silvia, 1979: „I verbi derivati in *-nu* e il loro valore causativo“, in: Per una grammatica ittita/Towards a Hittite grammar, hrsg. von O. Carruba, Pavia, 153-180

Mascheroni, Lorenza, 1980: „Il modulo interrogativo in eteo – I: note sintattiche“, in: Studi micenei ed eteo-anatolici 22, 53-62

Morpurgo Davies, Anna, 1975: „Negation and disjunction in Anatolian - and elsewhere“, in: Anatolian Studies 25, 157-168

Neu, Erich 1968a: Das hethitische Mediopassiv und seine indogermanischen Grundlagen (Studien zu den Boğazköy-Texten 6), Wiesbaden

–, 1968b: Interpretation der hethitischen mediopassiven Verbalformen (Studien zu den Boğazköy-Texten 5), Wiesbaden

–, 1979: „Zum Kollektivum im Hethitischen“, in: Per una grammatica ittita/Towards a Hittite grammar, hrsg. von O. Carruba, Pavia, 197-212

–, 1985: „Zur Stammabstufung bei *i-* und *u*-stämmigen Substantiven des Hethitischen“, in: Sprachwissenschaftliche Forschungen. Festschrift für J. Knobloch, hrsg. von H.M. Ölberg u.a., Innsbruck, 259-264

Oettinger, Norbert, 1976: „Der indogermanische Stativ“, in: Münchener Studien zur Sprachwissenschaft 34, 109-149

–, 1986: „Indo-Hittite“-Hypothese und Wortbildung, Innsbruck

–, 1987: „Anatolische Wortbildung und indogermanische Chronologie“, in: Studien zum indogermanischen Wortschatz. Akten der Tagung der Indogermanischen Gesellschaft in Innsbruck 1985, hrsg. von W. Meid, Innsbruck, 189-192

–, 1992: „Die hethitischen Verbalstämme“, in: Per una grammatica ittita/Towards a Hittite grammar, hrsg. von O. Carruba, Pavia, 215-252

–, 2002: Die Stammbildung des hethitischen Verbums, Dresden [Reprint of the edition Nürnberg 1979]

Ose, Fritz, 1944: Supinum und Infinitiv im Hethitischen, Leipzig

Rieken, Elisabeth, 1994: „Der Wechsel *-a-/-i-* in der Stammbildung des hethitischen Nomens“, in: Historische Sprachforschung 107, 42-53

–, 1999: Untersuchungen zur nominalen Stammbildung des Hethitischen (Studien zu den Boğazköy-Texten 44), Wiesbaden

–, 2004: „Die hethitische „Ortsbezugspartikel *-apa*“, in: Die Indogermanistik und ihre Anrainer. Dritte Tagung der Vergleichenden Sprachwissenschaftler der Neuen Länder, Greifswald 19.-20.5.2000, Innsbruck, 243-258.

–, 200: „Zur Wiedergabe von hethitisch /o/“, in: Sprachkontakt und Sprachwandel. Akten der XI. Fachtagung der Indogermanischen Gesellschaft, 17.-23.9.2000, Halle an der Saale, hg. von Gerhard Meiser und Olav Hackstein, Wiesbaden 2005.

Starke, Frank, 1977: Die Funktionen der dimensionalen Kasus und Adverbien im Althethitischen (Studien zu den Boğazköy-Texten 23), Wiesbaden

–, 1995: Ausbildung und Training von Streitwagenpferden. Eine hippologisch orientierte Interpretation des Kikkuli-Textes (Studien zu den Boğazköy-Texten 41), Wiesbaden

Sternemann, Reinhard, 1967: „Temporale und konditionale Nebensätze des Hethitischen“, in: Mitteilungen des Instituts für Orientforschung 12, 377-415

Streck, Michael (ed.), 2007: Sprachen des Alten Orients, Darmstadt, 3.Aufl.

Weitenberg, J.J.S., 1984: Die hethitischen *u*-Stämme, Amsterdam

–, 1992: „The use of asyndesis and particles in Old Hittite simple sentences“, in: Per una grammatica ittita/Towards a Hittite grammar, hrsg. von O. Carruba, Pavia, 305-353

Yoshida, Kazuhiko, 1990: The Hittite mediopassive endings in *-ri*, Berlin/New York

Zeilfelder, Susanne, 2001: Archaismus und Ausgliederung. Studien zur sprachlichen Stellung des Hethitischen, Heidelberg

–, 2001a: „Zum Ausdruck der Finalität im Hethitischen“, in: Anatolisch und Indogermanisch. Akten des Kolloquiums der Indogermanischen Gesellschaft Pavia 1998, hrsg. von O. Carruba, Innsbruck, 395-410

–, 2001b: „Zur Indikativität hethitischer Abstrakta“, in: Akten des IV. Internationalen Kongresses für Hethitologie Würzburg 1999, hg. von G. Wilhelm, Wiesbaden, 730-738

–, 2002: „Komplexe Hypotaxe im Hethitischen“, in: Novalis Indogermanica. Festschrift für Günter Neumann, hg. von M. Fritz und S. Zeilfelder, Graz, 527-536

–, 2004: „Topik, Fokus und rechter Satzrand im Hethitischen“, in: *šarnikzel.* Hethitologische Studien zum Gedenken an Emil Orgetorix Forrer, hg. von D. Groddek und S. Rößle, Dresden 2004 (Dresdner Beiträge zur Hethitologie Band 10)